PEARL

PEARL

An Edition with Verse Translation

Translated by

WILLIAM VANTUONO

University of Notre Dame Press
Notre Dame, Indiana

Published in the United States of America

Reprinted in 2007

Cover: Woodcut of "Pearl" by F. Kredel
from *The Complete Works of the Gawain Poet*, published by
the University of Chicago Press © 1965 by the University of Chicago.

Library of Congress Cataloging-in-Publication Data
Pearl (Middle English poem). English & English (Middle English)
 Pearl : and edition with verse translation / translated by William
Vantuono.
     p.   cm.
 Includes bibliographical references (p.).
 ISBN 13: 978-0-268-03811-3 (pbk. : alk. paper)
 ISBN 10: 0-268-03811-2 (pbk. : alk. paper)
 1. Christian poetry, English (Middle)—Modernized versions.
I. Vantuono, William, 1927– .   II. Title.
PR2111.A28   1995
821'.—dc20   95-16890

TO ORNELLA

"When one finds a worthy wife,
her value is far beyond pearls."
Proverbs 31.10

ACKNOWLEDGMENTS

When I had difficulty with technical matters involving the use of software in my computer, my son, Bill, was ready to help me. My thanks go to him.

I also wish to thank the many professors and editors with whom I corresponded in order to secure books and articles related to my work. All of them gave their time generously to grant my requests. Their names follow: Malcolm Andrew, Lorraine Attreed, Richard W. Barber, Robert J. Blanch, Margaret Bridges, Michael D. Cherniss, Denise Despres, Eugenie Freed, Thomas J. Garbáty, Warren Ginsberg, Arthur F. Marotti, Kevin Marti, Susan J. Rastetter, W.T. Ross, Geoffrey R. Russom, Anne Howland Schotter, Julian N. Wasserman, Douglas J. Wurtele.

CONTENTS

PREFACE

The purpose of this work on *Pearl* is to offer a Middle English text, a Modern English verse translation, and extensive scholarly apparatus. The best edition of *Pearl* is E.V. Gordon's (London: Oxford University Press, 1953), but it has no translation. Marie Borroff's verse translation (New York: Norton, 1977) is arguably the best to date, but her book has no Middle English text or commentary.

The heart of the present work is the text, with translation on facing pages and notes at the bottom of the pages. The translation keeps as close to the original as possible without sacrificing the poem's essential meaning and mood, and the notes reveal the literal sense of the Middle English vocabulary wherever changes were made, for a translator , to achieve poetic effect, must frequently employ words with denotations different from the original vocabulary. Thus, by comparing the Middle English original, the translation, and these notes, scholars can learn about the old language, the content of the poem, the poet's artistry, and the process of translation.

The introduction, in dealing with the manuscript, the poet and his audience, his purpose, and *Pearl*'s theme and structure, examines the main controversies surrounding the poem since it came into prominence with Richard Morris' edition for the *Early English Text Society* in 1864. The variorum-type commentary covers scholarship on *Pearl* through the early 1990s. Appendices discuss versification, dialect and language, and sources and analogues. A Glossary, followed by An Index of Names, is provided at the end of the book. This Glossary lists every form of every word, with literal meanings, line numbers, grammatical elements, and etymological derivatives.

References in this book are brief: name of author, year of publication, and, if needed, page number(s). For full listings, the reader is directed to Bibliography I, a section containing approximately 420 items. Bibliography II, of about 90 items, contains primarily listings of bibles, dictionaries, grammars, other texts and translations, and other bibliographies.

Since the best verse translations of *Pearl* appear in books that offer little more than the translation itself, and the best editions, though they contain adequate scholarly apparatus, do not include verse translations, the present work makes available, for the first time, all of these components combined in one volume. It is hoped that *Pearl: An Edition with Verse Translation* will attract not only scholars confronted with the tasks of studying and teaching medieval literature but also any reader who finds enjoyment in the perusal of literary masterpieces.

xi

INTRODUCTION

The Manuscript

Pearl, followed by *Cleanness*, *Patience*, and *Sir Gawain and the Green Knight*, appears in the unique Cotton MS. Nero A.x. Article 3, dated not later than A.D. 1400 by Wright (1960) 15. Mathew (1968) 117 would date it early fifteenth century. The writing, in a quarto volume of vellum measuring about 7 x 5 inches, is by one hand—small, sharp, and irregular—resembling printing rather than penmanship.

The dialect is Northwest Midlands, as Menner (1922) established with solid evidence, but it is difficult to determine a precise location within this area. McIntosh (1963) 5 stated that *Gawain*, as it stands in the manuscript, "can only *fit* with reasonable propriety in a very small area either in SE Cheshire or just over the border in NE Staffordshire," but other scholars have hesitated to pinpoint so specific a locale.

Osgood (1906) xii noted that the requirements of meter and the "poet's familiarity with the speech and literature of other regions than his own" make his literary language "not purely that of any spoken dialect." Davis (1967) xxvii also observed that the language "is not a simple and self-consistent local dialect." It "is to some extent eclectic; yet the basis of it is no doubt, as most scholars have long believed, a dialect of the north-west midlands."

A non-dialectal piece of evidence pointing to Cheshire is the naming of the *wyldrenesse of Wyrale* in *Gawain* 701. The poet writes as though he knew the area well, telling how Gawain had to pass through that dangerous forest in search of the Green Knight. "Wonde þer bot lyte/Þat auþer God oþer gome wyth goud hert louied" (701–2). Savage (1931) noted that the Wirral was used as a place of shelter by outlaws and marauders in the late fourteenth century.

There are twelve illustrations in the manuscript, four for *Pearl*, two each for *Cleanness* and *Patience*, and four for *Gawain*. Gollancz (1923) 9 called their workmanship "crude." Greg (1924) 227 also expressed a negative opinion regarding their quality.

However, Lee (1977), observing that Cotton Nero A.x. is one of the earliest literary manuscripts to be illustrated, gave more credit to the artist by suggesting that the painting was done by a second hand, that of an amateur who spoiled the draftsman's work (18–19). She maintained that the illustrator, in depicting main characters in situations showing their spiritual progress, "represented well the primary 'instruction' of each poem." Though not exceptionally skilled as an illuminator or literary critic, he, nevertheless, offers the modern scholar the "rare opportunity of seeing the first critical judgment of these poems, a medieval mind reacting to a medieval work" (43–44).

Horrall (1986) 191–92, noting that "the presence of pictures is an extremely rare phenomenom in a fourteenth-century Middle English manuscript," cited Doyle (1982) 92 who suggested that it was copied in two stages, the script in the last quarter of the fourteenth century and the pictures later, perhaps early fifteenth century. In support of Doyle, Horrall pointed out that whereas the first folio of the text of *Pearl* looks dark and rubbed, "as if it had lain for a time as an unprotected outer quire," the four *Pearl* pictures appear on a separate bifolium inserted before the text of the poem, and the "outer leaf of this bifolium shows no such wear" (193).

Like Lee (1977), Horrall, pp. 195–98, refuted the views of critics who said that all the illustrations are crude and not well adapted to the poems in the manuscript. In her conclusion, p. 198, she also argued against the suggestion of Mathew (1948) 356 and (1968) 117 that both the text and the pictures were copied from a repertory book commissioned by a magnate of wealth, and that the pictures are clumsy copies of larger illuminations in a contemporary manuscript de luxe.

There is no record of the manuscript for a long time after 1400, but *Gawain* must have been known in the following century, for, as Newstead (1967) 57 observed, *The Grene Knight*, composed in the South Midland dialect about 1500, "appears to be a condensed version of *Sir Gawain and the Green Knight* with none of the literary distinction that marks its model." Robbins (1943) showed that gentleman author Humfrey Newton (1466–1536), who lived in the Hundred of Macclesfield in Cheshire, may well have had an intimate acquaintance with *Gawain*. (See also Robbins [1950] and Cutler [1952] on this connection.) Wrenn (1943) 48 suggested that "Spenser may have known something of the work of the *Gawain*-poet."

The earliest record of the manuscript is an entry in the catalogue of the library of Henry Savile (1568–1617) of Banke in Yorkshire. Savile collected manuscripts from the Northern monasteries. His cataloguer described the one containing the *Pearl* poems as "an owld boke in English verse beginning 'Perle pleasants to princes pay' in 4° limned." Gilson (1908) 135 and 209, in noting this information, erred in printing *Paper* instead of *pay*, and this prompted him to say that he had not been able to track down this "copy of the *Pearl* described as written on paper." Gollancz (1924) 3-4 pointed out the error, recalling there is only one known manuscript, and it is on vellum. As Salter (1983) 199 noted, the monograph of Watson (1969), *The Manuscripts of Henry Savile of Banke*, has superseded Gilson's work.

The noted bibliophile Sir Robert Cotton (1571–1631) probably acquired the manuscript from Savile. Richard James, Cotton's librarian, described it as "Vetus Poema Anglicanum, in quo, sub insomnii figmento, multa ad religionem et mores spectantia explicantur." James, apparently not having read the whole manuscript, did not distinguish *Pearl* from the other poems. He bound the manuscript between two unrelated Latin works. Madden (1839) xlvii-l, in giving this information, noted that the preceding portion of 36 folios consisted of a panegyrical oration by Justus de Justis, on John Chedworth, archdeacon of Lincoln, dated at Verona, 16 July 1468; the concluding portion, extending from f. 127 to f. 140b, consisted of theological excerpts written in a hand at the end of the thirteenth century, and at the end is added *Epitaphium de Ranulfo, abbate Ramesiensi*, who was abbot from 1231 to 1253. In 1964 the manuscript with the *Pearl* poems was rebound separately in the British Museum.

Williams (1967) 6 noted, "In Cotton's library, books were catalogued according to their places in one or other of fourteen presses, surmounted by busts of Cleopatra, Faustina, and twelve Roman Emperors. The Pearl-Poet's book became Cotton Nero A.X." Cotton's collection, enlarged by his son Thomas, was given to the British nation in 1700. The 958 volumes were transferred to Ashburnham House. A fire there in 1731 destroyed 114 books and damaged 98, but fortunately the *Pearl* group was not ruined.

In 1753 the Cotton collection was taken to the British Museum. That Warton (1774-1790) had access to it is known by his citation of lines from *Pearl* and *Cleanness* on pp. 107-8 in Volume 3 of his *The History of English Poetry*. Madden (1839) 299 thought it singular that Warton should not have noticed *Gawain*, "which he seems to have confounded with a preceding one, on a totally different subject." With his edition of *Gawain*, Madden preceded the long line of scholars who have brought the four poems of the manuscript into deserved prominence.

The whole of *Pearl* became known with the edition of Morris (1864). Though it appears first in the manuscript, it apparently was not composed before the other three poems, for scholars generally agree that this Middle English gem and *Gawain*, another acknowledged masterpiece, came after the two homilies, *Cleanness* and *Patience*. Gordon (1953) xliv, after setting the limits for the whole group of poems as c. 1360-1395, concluded that the "maturity of *Pearl* would put it late rather than early in this period."

The Poet, His Audience, and *Pearl*

That one man, called by some the *Pearl*-poet, by others the *Gawain*-poet, wrote all four poems in the manuscript is generally accepted today by most scholars. The following edited the four poems together: Cawley & Anderson (1976), Moorman (1977), Andrew & Waldron (1978), and

Vantuono (1984); the following translated the four poems together and included *Saint Erkenwald*: Gardner (1965), Williams (1967), and Finch (1993); book-length studies bringing *Pearl, Cleanness, Patience*, and *Gawain* together are by Moorman (1968), Spearing (1970), Wilson (1976), Davenport (1978), Johnson (1984), and Stanbury (1991); among writers of articles or parts of books favoring common authorship for the four poems in Cotton MS. Nero A.x. Article 3 are Brewer (1966 and 1967), Spearing (1966), Burrow (1971), Vantuono (1971), Muscatine (1972), Hieatt (1976), and Clark & Wasserman (1978).

Nevertheless, as Finch (1993) 2 observed, the "idea of common authorship, more or less originated by Carl Horstmann in his 1881 *Altenglische Legenden* (265-75), has been disputed." Fuhrmann (1886), among early scholars, favored Horstmann's theory. Clark (1949, 1950a, 1950b, and 1951) argued against it, but, as Loomis-HZ (1959) 5 stated, his reasons are "more ingenious than convincing." Attempts by Kjellmer (1975) and Tajima (1978) to disprove common authorship by comparing language and syntax are also open to question. Derolez (1981) refuted Kjellmer, as did Cooper & Pearsall (1988) 371-72.

Lawton (1982) 9 stated that the debate on common authorship "arrives not at a conclusion but at a series of cruces, of style, language and treatment of theme, which sum up the whole problem of the nature of Middle English alliterative poetry." For Lawton, "the debate should be kept open," but his views have been submerged in the light of later scholarship.

Computer studies have come into play. Joyce (1984) dealt only with *Pearl* among the four poems; McColly & Weier (1983) included *Saint Erkenwald* with the four but reached no definite conclusion. However, Cooper & Pearsall (1988), in a computer-assisted study, measured stylistic features of alliteration, syntax, and word-frequency in *Cleanness, Patience*, and *Gawain* against *Morte Arthure, The Parliament of the Three Ages*, and *The Siege of Jerusalem*, concluding, pp. 384-85, that none of the three *Gawain* poems is by the author of any of the other three poems, the three *Gawain* poems clearly distinguish themselves as a group from the other three, and the clustering and overlapping of so many metrical and stylistic features in *Cleanness, Patience*, and *Gawain* cannot be explained, except in terms of common authorship. Cooper & Pearsall, since they were dealing only with the unrhymed alliterative line, did not include *Pearl* in their study, but their refutation, pp. 371-72, of Kjellmer (1975) indicates their belief that it should not be removed from the canon.

Whether or not *Saint Erkenwald* should be included remains more controversial. Benson (1965) questioned the attribution, and not all of the editors of that poem are in agreement. For example, Savage (1926) liii-lxv upheld the theory that it was written by the *Pearl*-poet, Morse (1975) 45-48 agreed with Benson, but Peterson (1977b) 15-23 argued that one man wrote all five poems.

Schmidt (1984) also attributed the five to one man and favored the theory that he was a Massey who had read *Piers Plowman*. According to Schmidt, the poet, in writing about the salvation of the just pagan in *Saint Erkenwald*, was influenced by Langland's discussion of Trajan at the end of the B-Text, Passus XII. "The 'London' setting of *St Erkenwald* is consonant with the poet's knowledge of the 'London' author Langland" (155).

Attempting to identify the *Pearl*-poet remains a challenge, though recent scholars have repeatedly pointed to a John de Mascy. Earlier scholars made other attributions, none of which have been accepted. Guest (1838 [revised 1882]) 459-62 and Madden (1839) 302-4 first pointed to the Scottish poet Huchown, to be followed by McNeil (1888), Neilson (1900-01 and 1902b), and Mackenzie (1933) 29-38 who stated that the *Pearl*-poet was "far more than Chaucer, the forerunner of the fifteenth century Scots poets" (30). However, Morris, in his second edition of *Early English Alliterative Poems* (1869), pp. v-ix, and MacCracken (1910) argued strongly against the Huchown theory.

Gollancz, in the introduction to his 1891 edition of *Pearl*, first put forward the name of Ralph Strode as the author, but Brown (1904) 146-48 dispelled that theory. Gollancz had based his argument on the naming of a *philosophical Strode* by Chaucer in the next to last stanza of *Troylus and Criseyde*. Gosse (1923) 182 called Gollancz' identification "pleasing" but "pure guesswork." Nevertheless, Medcalf (1973) 673-74 advocated the theory.

Cargill & Schlauch (1928), viewing *Pearl* as an elegy written in 1369 on the death of Margaret, granddaughter of King Edward III, and daughter of John Hastings, Earl of Pembroke, suggested John Donne or John Prat, two of Hastings' clerks. Reisner (1973), noting that *powdered* in line 44 of *Pearl* was also a heraldic term and that families named Prat "had arms with fields either powdered or charged with a variety of floral devices," revived the theory about John Prat.

Chapman (1932) suggested John de Erghome, an Augustinian friar of York, but Everett (1932) 104-5 counteracted his supposition. Savage (1938) surmised *Gawain* was written either for the marriage of Enguerrand de Coucy and Isabella, eldest daughter of Edward III, in 1365, or around the time of Coucy's return to France in 1376. In his book, *The Gawain-Poet: Studies in his Personality and Background* (1956a), Savage, pp. 213-17, mentioned the possibility of the poet's being a Hornby (especially William or Robert), member of a Lancashire family connected with John of Gaunt and Coucy.

Pearsall (1982) 52-53 and 135-36 briefly reviewed theories about the poet's identity, expressed his skepticism, and noted the "ingenious case" put forward by Bennett (1979) who theorized that *Gawain* was written for the Cheshire retainers of King Richard II. For Pearsall, the weakest part of the argument is the "attempt at an individual attribution—to one Richard Newton, whose family documents show him to be the author of some doggerel which Bennett unfortunately asserts (p. 69) to have 'definite stylistic affinities' with *Gawain*." Bennett noted that this Richard Newton was an ancestor of the Cheshire author Humfrey Newton (1466–1536) who was apparently influenced by *Gawain*. (See Robbins [1943] and [1950], and Cutler [1952].)

Bond (1991) 99–121 argued that the poet, whom he does not try to name, told the story of real people of an earlier period in the history of England when he wrote *Pearl*. The maiden is identified as Eleana Margareta, born, supposedly illegitimate, on May 6, 1306, to Queen Margaret, wife of King Edward I. The narrator is identified as the queen's lover, Henry, a son of Edmund Crouchback, first Earl of Lancaster. Eleana was placed in the convent of Amesbury before she was two years old, died in 1311 before her fifth birthday, and was buried within the grounds of Beaulieu Abbey, Hampshire.

Attention has turned in recent decades to the identification of a Mascy as the *Pearl*-poet. Greenwood (1956) 3–16 argued for Hugh Mascy, noting the 'Hugo de' written in a fifteenth-century hand atop f. 95 of *Gawain*, the name 'Thomas Masse' found in the British Museum MS. Harleian 2250 containing *Saint Erkenwald*, numerology in *Pearl*, and play on the word *mascelleʒ* in Stanza-Group XIII.

Nolan (1971) 297–300, supporting Greenwood's thesis on numerology, identified John de Mascy, rector of Stockport in Cheshire, who died in 1376. She noted that Section XV of *Pearl*, with six stanzas instead of five, ends at line 912: "Let my bone vayl, neuerþelese." Since in the medieval alphabet the initials for *Iohan Mascy* ($I = 9$ and $M = 12$) merge into 912, she asked, "Does the numerical signature *I M* combined with the prayer conceal a plea for favour by the poet addressing a patron" (298). In the same article, Farley-Hills (1971) 301–2 pointed to the 'maister Massy' Hoccleve praises in a short poem, written between 1411–1414, in MS. Huntington 111.

Peterson (1974a) first noted what he considered to be an anagram in *Saint Erkenwald* for *I. d. Masse* and then associated Hoccleve's 'maister Massy' with a John Massey of Cotton in Cheshire (1974b). Turville-Petre (1975) 129–33 argued that Hoccleve's 'maister Massy' was a William Massy, John of Lancaster's General Attorney, not a poet. In the same article, Wilson (1975) 133–43 argued against the studies of Nolan and Peterson. Farley-Hills (1975) answered Turville-Petre's argument.

Vantuono (1975), noting the name 'J. Macy' among the ornamental designs beneath the illuminated *N* on f. 62b of *Cleanness* and 'Macy' at the bottom of f. 114 of *Gawain*, identified John de Mascy of Sale, rector of Ashton-on-Mersey in Cheshire between 1364 and 1401. Adam (1976) argued for an acrostic signature of *I Masi*, to be found in the anomalous stanza 76 of *Pearl* (lines 901–12). Peterson (1977a) again wrote in favor of John Massey of Cotton, arguing against Turville-Petre and Wilson along the way. Wilson

(1977) 55–56, in defense of his position, added a note to Peterson's article. Peterson (1977b) 21–23 restated his argument.

Vantuono (1981) 81–87, after reviewing past scholarship on the subject, presented more evidence in favor of John de Mascy of Sale, who was rector of Ashton-on-Mersey between 1364 and 1401. This man relates well to the time, the place, and the *Pearl*-poet's career. He is named in documents as both priest and civil servant between 1377 and 1389, and the poet was well versed in law, as well as in matters of religion. In regard to locale, Sale and Ashton-on-Mersey in Northern Cheshire are very close to the Dunham-Massy estate, which must have been a center for cultural activity in the fourteenth century, as it was in the fifteenth under the Booths. The *wyldrenesse of Wyrale*, mentioned in *Gawain* 701, is a place the poet knew, a forest one passed through to reach the Delamere Forest on the way eastward to Dunham-Massy.

Kooper (1982) 161–62 examined *Gawain* and found that by discounting the bob (which is always written in the margin and never given a line of its own in the manuscript), line 101 in stanza five (line 106 in the editions) contains the word *mas*. This word combined with *CI*, the Roman numeral for 101, produces the name *Masci*. The number 101 is significant in both *Pearl* and *Gawain*, for each poem contains 101 stanzas, and the poet, to reach that total in *Pearl*, apparently added stanza 76 in Group XV deliberately. Group XV is the only one of the twenty groups to have six stanzas instead of five.

Kooper, p. 166, recalled Greenwood (1956) who had also noted the 101 (*CI*) relationship to the last two letters of *Masci*. Greenwood, p. 11, unwittingly gave additional support for John de Mascy of Sale when he bolstered his theory about a pun on *mascelleȝ* in *Pearl* by relating it to the coat of arms of the family of Sale: "ARGENT A CHEVRON BETWEEN THREE MASCLES SABLE (to be seen in the Derby Chapel of Manchester Cathedral, and the Brereton Chapel, Cheadle)."

The opening of Stanza-Group XIII is about the innocent child who enters heaven and the jeweler who sold all his wealth, "To bye hym a perle watȝ mascelleȝ" (732). Greenwood interpreted: "To buy him a Margery that was a Mascy." The poet's use of *mascelleȝ* may reveal a pun in two other ways. A *Mascé* is *les* his pearl, and the pearl is separated from *Mascé*. Perhaps it is not a coincidence that *mascelleȝ* (732) is the only *c* spelling for that word in Stanza-Group XIII; all the others are spelled with *k* that could not be pronounced as a sibilant.

While many scholars have attempted to identify the poet, others, in considering his audience, have provided significant insights. Gerould (1936), seeing the influence of Dante, maintained that he was a learned man who wrote in his own Northwest Midlands dialect to do for it what Dante had done for Tuscan in *Il Convivio*, defend his native speech. With reference to the "alliterative school," Gerould asked, "Is it not probable that he and the vastly different and even more enigmatic author of *Piers Plowman*, between them, brought back into effective use what had been a medium for rural versifiers" (32–33)?

Richardson (1962) stated that the theme of *Pearl* is salvation, and because "a subject so large has more than academic interest. . . . there is no need to suppose a limited audience: a lay or mixed one is equally possible." The poet may have been a monk or priest, addressing his audience "not merely as a writer with an experience to share, not merely as a teacher with a doctrine to impart, but also as a pastor with a message for them to put into practice" (315).

According to Salter (1983), though alliterative poetry was especially fostered in the West and Northwest, it was "certainly not an alien or despised form of composition in East Anglia or in London" (81). Both the *Pearl*-poet and Chaucer "were consciously enlarging and enriching the English poetic language: they responded to the same sort of stimuli, exerted, we may be sure, by books, patrons, and a growing sense of national achievement and identity" (82).

Hendrix (1985), like Salter, argued in favor of a wide audience for all four poems in the manuscript. With reference to Turville-Petre (1977) 44–47, he stated, "Only very recently has the 'plausible audience' for these works been expanded to include readers ['listeners' could be added here] other than the higher nobility and high clergy" (459). Hendrix, p. 466, concluded that *Pearl* appealed to both spiritually-oriented and materialistically-oriented members of the audience. The use of courtly words for spiritual purposes, and the use of dream-vision, a form with secular popularity and biblical precedent, "point up all the more the multidimensionality of the text and the audience for which it was written."

Thorpe (1991) 32–33 studied four viewpoint levels—journeyman, narrator, poet, and reader—in *Pearl* in comparison to *The Divine Comedy* and *Piers Plowman*. Just as Dante the pilgrim journeys, and Dante the narrator tells of this journey, and behind them stands Dante the poet who wants his readers to share in his conversion—and just as the naive Will the dreamer journeys, and behind him stands Will the narrator who has already journeyed, and behind both stands the poet William Langland who wants his audience to move from journey to conversion—so is there in *Pearl* the obtuse dreamer who journeys in his vision, the narrator who has already learned the lesson of the vision, and the poet who expects in his audience a "turning around that amounts to a new way of seeing," a way to arrive at true spirituality.

Though the many studies centering on the identity of the poet and his audience have increased our knowledge of the man and the period in which he wrote, unanswered questions remain about the circumstances surrounding his writing of *Pearl*. Was he a layman or a priest? Is *Pearl* primarily elegy or allegory? Was the pearl-maiden his daughter, and if she were, can that fact be reconciled with the possibility that the poet was a clergyman?

From his survey of biblical material in *Patience, Cleanness,* and *Pearl,* Brown (1904) 126–27 found it difficult to understand on what ground Gollancz, in his edition of *Pearl* (1891c, p. xlvii), denied the author's ecclesiastical character. Osgood (1906) l–li argued, in his edition, that the poet was a layman. Both he and Gollancz believed the pearl-maiden was his daughter, named Margaret or Margery. Before them, *Pearl*'s first editor, Morris (1864) xi, had stated that the poet "evidently gives expression to his own sorrow for the loss of his infant child."

Early translators did not question this view. For example, Coulton (1906) 8 wrote about "the sincere cry of a father's heart at the grave of his infant girl," Mead (1908) xi called *Pearl* the lament of a father for his infant daughter, and Kirtlan (1918) 5 stated, as though it were a fact, that the poet "had lost his 'pearl,' his little two-year-old daughter."

Greene (1925), who interpreted *Pearl* as a "literary fiction" with a purpose "probably no less homiletic than *Cleanness* and *Patience*" (815), observed that the placement of these poems before *Gawain* and *Pearl* in order of composition "suggests that the poet was an orthodox ecclesiastic in his earlier years" (820). Gordon (1953) favored the concept of layman father writing from grief over the death of his daughter. "He may have been a chaplain in an aristocratic household: that he once had a daughter is no decisive argument against this, for he may, for instance, have been ordained later in life" (xlii).

Andrew (1981) concluded that the poet's use of *faunt* 'child' in line 161 of *Pearl* "provides a small but significant piece of evidence in support of the literal interpretation of the Maiden" (5). Attreed (1983), in studying the history of medieval childhood, cited *Pearl* to refute the idea that medieval family relations in regard to children lacked the emotions and affections now taken for granted. *Pearl*, "a highly detailed and formally structured account of a man's grief at the loss of a loved one, . . . presents a father who so grieves over the death of his two-year-old daughter that he forgets, as did Boethius, what man is and how the world is ordered" (48).

The question of genre is closely related to the mystery of the poet's station in life. Scholars who see *Pearl* as an elegy view the maiden as a historical figure; many of them maintain that she was the poet's daughter, and, therefore, the poet must have been a layman. Those who believe that *Pearl* is pure allegory need not deal with such questions. Nevertheless, one such scholar, Schofield (1909), suggested an approach for those who pursue the elegiac theory.

Referring to lines with personal touches, such as: "Ho watʒ me nerre þen aunte or nece" (233); "We meten so selden by stok oþer ston" (380); and "Þou lyfed not two ʒer in oure þede" and could never pray, "Ne neuer nawþer Pater ne Crede" (483–85), he wrote, " 'Perhaps' we have here the secret of the whole story: it was not the loss of his own child that the poet had in mind, but only that of a little girl whom he had been accustomed to meet 'by stock or stone' (i.e. by the wayside), and had become devotedly attached to." Schofield concluded with the picture of a lonely priest who had taught the Pater Noster and the Crede to "this little child who had become nearer and dearer to him than aunt or niece" (664).

Madeleva (1925) and Hamilton-B (1955), like Schofield (1904), interpreted *Pearl* as purely a dream-vision allegory. Whereas Schofield had called the pearl-maiden a symbol of virginity, Madeleva maintained she represented the dreamer's own soul, seeking peace, and Hamilton, p. 39, called the pearl "the maiden soul, who through baptismal regeneration and incorporation into the Mystical Body of Christ, the Church, has become 'a perle of prys.' " Among others who favored allegory over elegy, Hillmann, in her edition of 1961 (pp. xix–xxi), took a unique stand which started on an extremely literal level. She first saw the dreamer and the pearl as a real jeweler and a real gem in the opening stanza, and then argued that when the maiden appears to him in his dream, she represents the dreamer's material pearl now transformed into his soul.

In the midst of such debates, however, other writers began to see that the opposing theories of genre—elegy vs allegory—can be reconciled. Fletcher (1921) was the first scholar to demonstrate a multi-level approach, Wellek-B (1933), in his review of scholarship on *Pearl*, leaned toward elegy but called Fletcher's study "the sanest and most convincing solution of the main questions" (18), and Allen (1971) noted that the letter and the spiritual allegory need not be in opposition, since "biblical and historical people may be understood as figures without denying their existence" (138). Eldredge (1975), in his review of scholarship from Wellek's time to his, perceived modern approaches to the poem, for *Pearl* is more than just an elegy combined with dream-vision allegory. It contains a strong homiletic base, set in the long central portion, and its thematic development leads to the *consolatio*.

Conley-C (1955), Watts (1963), and Means (1972) studied the movement from despair to consolation in the dreamer's mind. Heiserman (1965), after noting that the adventure concludes when the dreamer accepts his fate, stated, "Reason and 'ideas' play their roles in this resolution, but it is in fact accomplished by a dialectal structure of joys, sorrows, and discoveries powerful enough to convert a character who can no longer live to one who can" (166–67). The poet subordinates radically the praise of the dead to the *consolatio* of the living, and the *consolatio* "is itself but part of a vision which in the end draws the poem outside the traditional purlieus of elegy" (168).

Bishop (1968) 16–17, crediting Watts (1963), noted as a possible source for *Pearl* the *consolatio mortis*, Carmen xxxi of Paulinus of Nola, in which Paulinus consoles Pneumatius and his wife Fidelis after the death of their son Celsus. Bishop's presentation of this source reveals an author writing to console others over the loss of a beloved child.

Considering such a situation, we may have an answer to part of the mystery surrounding *Pearl*, for it is plausible to assume that the poet wrote to console someone else, as well, perhaps, as himself. Milroy (1971) 208 reconciled various arguments when he suggested that the author could have been "an unmarried cleric writing the poem as a *consolatio* for a friend, a brother, or a local dignitary, for whose bereavement he felt deeply, and assuming for that purpose a first person point-of-view." The observation of Pearsall (1981) 16, based on the likelihood of close contact between the world of aristocracy and the world of monastic learning, supports Milroy's statement. "It would be natural to suppose that clerks educated in monastic schools often moved out into the secular world as clerks or chaplains to noble households and there exercised their skills in alliterative verse on appropriate occasions."

It is conceivable, then, that *Pearl* was written for a nobleman who had lost a young daughter, a man who was perhaps the poet's patron. The father, in grieving over the death of his daughter, questions the ways of God, and this prompts the poet to put himself in the father's place to console him and to attempt to bring him to an understanding of the Lord's ways. In doing this, he becomes so involved in his verse, his own emotions enter in, and he thinks of the girl as someone he loved too, as, perhaps, he did in real life.

Among the many scholars who studied *Pearl* as a *consolatio*, Fowler (1984) 202 stated that the poem "provides an unmistakenly Boethian consolation in the teaching of the maiden," who "assures the dreamer that his beloved is happy in heaven." Cherniss (1987), viewing *Pearl* as a Boethian Apocalypse, argued that it "employs a Boethian vision to console its narrator for what he initially sees as personal worldly misfortune, the loss of a beloved child" (151). Like Boethius' *De Consolatio Philosophiae* and its progeny, "*Pearl*'s purpose is not mystical or controversial but practical. . . . The narrator's vision of the pearl-maiden is intended to restore his ability to live in the temporal world" (152).

However, *Pearl* is more than mere *consolatio*, for no one genre can account for its multi-faceted beauty. As an elegy, it praises a loved one who had died; as a dream-vision allegory, the pearl in the opening stanzas symbolizes the dead maiden who later represents purity, innocence, grace, and humility; as a theological treatise, it defends the teaching of the Church in fourteenth-century England, emphasizing the importance of divine grace and revealing how all are equally happy in God's kingdom though their positions vary within the hierarchical system; and, finally, as a *consolatio*, *Pearl* lifts the spirits of those who have lost loved ones, for above all, this sublime masterpiece makes lucid the unknown and the unreachable.

Theme and Structure

Boitani (1982) 113, in calling *Pearl* an elegy, a search for the lost

Eden, a parable of salvation, a *consolatio*, a theological debate, and a spiritual vision, stated: "With this poem, English literature acquires a 'classic' altogether different from *Piers Plowman*, one of which the language is not that of humble, ordinary speech but finely wrought and mounted in a setting of rigorous construction. *Pearl* tends, in miniature, towards the kind of poetry Dante created in *The Divine Comedy*."

Just as there is no one genre in the poem, and yet the reconciliation of its various genres widens its scope, there is no single theme, and yet the multiple concepts merge and unify in one great vision. *Pearl* is about purity, innocence, and grace, justice and faith, salvation realized and salvation desired, and, finally, consolation. Like the pure pearl-maiden, innocent children enter heaven through God's grace, their salvation quickly realized; like the dreamer, souls who live beyond the age of innocence, who often cannot understand God's justice, must endure earth's trials with simple faith and acceptance of his will, consoled in knowing that the gift of salvation has been given and is there to be received.

Pearl begins, "Perle plesaunte to prynces paye" (1); it concludes, "Ande precious perleȝ vnto his pay. Amen. Amen" (1212). In between, the dreamer moves from despair in an *erber grene* (38) to a new awakening in that *erber wlonk* (1171). At start and finish, he is in the waking world of reality, but in the beginning he cannot attain that *saȝt* 'peaceful' state (52); after his vision, he realizes it is easy for the good Christian to *sete saȝte* (1201).

Scholars who have studied the structure of *Pearl* do not always agree on the division of its parts, but none will deny that the themes and symbols are better understood when examined as elements woven into the poem's intricate form.

Robertson-C (1950b) 25–26 related theme and symbol by interpreting *Pearl* according to the fourfold level of biblical exegesis. "Literally, the Pearl is a gem. Allegorically, as the maiden of the poem, it represents those members of the Church who will be among the 'hundred' in the celestial procession, the perfectly innocent. Tropologically, the Pearl is a symbol of the soul that attains innocence through true penance and all that such penance implies. Anagogically, it is the life of innocence in the Celestial City."

Concerning structure, various scholars have pointed to tripartite divisions in *Pearl*. Everett (1955) 87 stated: "Of the twenty equal sections of the poem the first four are mainly devoted to presenting the dreamer's state of mind and to description of the dream country and of Pearl herself; argument and exposition occupy the central twelve sections, and the last four again contain description, this time of the new Jerusalem, and end with the poet's reflections."

Bishop (1968) 32–34 refined Everett's summary by setting off the first stanza-group and the last, noting the balancing descriptions at beginning (Groups II–IV) and end (XVII–XIX), and dividing the central portion of twelve groups into eight (V–XII), "concerned with the maiden's claim to be a queen in heaven," and four (XIII–XVI), "her assertion that she is a bride of the Lamb."

Blenkner-C (1968) 266–67 classified the first and last stanza-groups as the 'erber' frame and the dream-vision of eighteen groups in three parts: earthly paradise (II–IV), theological dialogue (V–XVI), and heavenly city (XVII–XIX). "The triple division of the dream corresponds to the theologian's division of the soul's ascent to God into three stages (from *without* to *within* to *above*), which may be roughly equated to man's three sources of knowledge (sense, intellect, and inspiration)."

While Everett, Bishop, and Blenkner, discussed *Pearl* according to tripartite divisions, some scholars presented different plans. Cohen (1976) argued that the allegory and structure of the poem are based upon the musical mode system in two separate movements: the Song of Earth (first twelve stanza-groups), and the Song of Heaven (last eight stanza-groups).

Olmert (1987), recalling the medieval board game (or "race game") as it related to the race game of life, contended that the poet cast *Pearl* in the shape of this game, a general layout of two halves of fifty stanzas each, with stanza 51 in the middle. According to Olmert, the stanzas in each half "are linked together to emphasize a constant progression on the part of the dreamer (or any player of the game of life) from ignorance to understanding" (388).

Harwood-BMW (1991) saw the structure of *Pearl* as chiastic, with an interlacing of Stanza-Groups X and XI, IX and XII, VIII and XIII, and all the other pairs working back to I and XX. "When the poem is read back and forth in this way, it divides into two halves of ten groups each" (61). Harwood theorized that the poet was influenced by the English ivory diptych, pictures depicted on two tablets connected by hinges, where a hierarchical distinction is made between the represented subjects, the superior of the two being on the wing to the viewer's right. Thus, the stanza-groups on the right in the second half of *Pearl* are superior in supporting heavenly values to the groups on the left in the first half.

While Cohen, Olmert, and Harwood structured *Pearl* outside the realm of three components, other scholars adhered to tripartite schemes. Ovitt (1979), similar to Everett (1955) 87, divided the twenty stanza-groups into four, twelve, and four, with the central twelve further divided threefold in the following way: (1) Groups V–VI, "where the dreamer is rebuked by Pearl for seeing only with his earthly eyes;" (2) Groups VII–XIII, "where the central question of the poem—the qualification of Pearl for salvation—is discussed;" (3) Groups XIV–XVI, "where the 'Lamb' is praised and where a discussion of the earthly Jerusalem leads to the climactic discussion of the Heavenly Jerusalem."

Chance-BMW (1991), recalling the interpretation of Robertson-C (1950b) 25–26 according to the fourfold level of biblical exegesis, presented, on p. 38, a tripartite division in the following way: (1) The moral or tropological sense dominates Groups II through most of VII, stanzas 6–33, concerning "the relationship between the Pearl-Maiden (representing reason) and the Dreamer (representing the literalist, fallen will or passion);" (2) the allegorical sense dominates part of Group VII and all those through XIII, stanzas 34–65, dealing with "the Parable of the Vineyard, drawn from the life of Christ as represented in the Gospel and signifying the nature of salvation;" (3) the anagogical sense pertains to Groups XIV–XIX, stanzas 66–96, "the Vision of the Heavenly Jerusalem." Group I provides "a preface stressing the literal or historical sense." Group XX provides a coda returning the reader to the literal sense from which the poem began, "but with the difference that the narrator has been educated, illumined, and convinced of a higher spiritual reality."

Clopper (1992), like Chance, based his structure on the fourfold level of biblical exegesis but in a different way. Noting first that his sections are not rigid and that transitional passages between them ease movement from one part to another, he presented, on pp. 233–34, the following plan:

(1) *Littera*, Group I, world of the dreamer in the garden, followed by transition to tropology in Groups II–IV, a picture of the garden in the opening scene "in a superessential but recognizable form," along with the appearance of the pearl-maiden.

(2) *Tropology*, Groups V–XII, where the dreamer is "in search of an understanding of the moral life requisite for salvation [in heaven] and the kind of life that is enjoyed there," followed by transition to typology (allegory) in Group XIII, a return to the question of the maiden's position in heaven.

(3) *Typology*, Groups XIV–XV, where the maiden's "concordance of Scripture seems intended to provide a way into the more difficult reading of Apocalypse," followed by transition to anagogy in Group XVI, where the link-word 'mote' has the "mystical multitude of senses that we associate with anagogy, the mode of Apocalypse."

(4) *Anagogy*, Groups XVII–XIX, where the dreamer sees the New Jerusalem and the Lamb. Group XX describes the awakening. The dreamer is "enlightened to some degree, but he is more conscious of the insubstantiality of his 'erbere.' "

There seems, then, to be much room for controversy in scholars' attempts to devise a structure for *Pearl*, just as there has been controversy, in the past, over the poem's genre and theme. However, in considering the last two elements, one may conclude that the disagreements have been reconciled, for the most part, since the poem contains more than one genre and multiple themes.

One factor that remains constant is the unification of themes that blend with the architectural plan of the work. The oneness of *Pearl* is in its circular structure, a total unity from beginning to end, the complex designs within bringing together the many ideas. As Nelson (1973) 26 stated, "The circular structure of *Pearl* is integral to our most vital experience of the poem and its vision. . . . Form and content in *Pearl* are not simply parallel or complementary—they are the same." Amoils (1974) 5–6 observed that *Pearl*, like its principal symbol, is "wemleȝ, clene, and clere,/And endeleȝ rounde" (737–38).

The following chart, which emphasizes tripartite divisions, makes no claim to read the poet's plan exactly but offers a convenient way to study *Pearl*. It may be called a triple-three structure, similar to the scheme devised by Vantuono (1984) for *Cleanness*. The Prologue and the Epilogue are clearly set apart from the Body—the Vision—which is also easily divisible into three parts. In addition, Part Two of the Vision, the Homiletic Center, is also apportioned triadically.

PROLOGUE
The Garden Setting (Group I)

BODY (Groups II–XIX + Lines 1153–70)

The Vision—Part One: Terrestrial Paradise and Pearl-Maiden (Groups II–IV)
The Vision—Part Two: Homiletic Center (Groups V–XVI)
    (1) Debate (V–VIII)
    (2) Parable of the Vineyard, with Explanation (IX–XII)
    (3) Perle Mascelleȝ, the Lamb, and the 144,000 Virgins (XIII–XVI)
The Vision—Part Three: The New Jerusalem and the Procession (Groups
                      XVII–XIX + Lines 1153–70)

EPILOGUE
Return to the Garden (Lines 1171–1212 of Group XX)

What may be considered the poet's greatest achievement from a structural standpoint is the nearly perfect symmetry of the parts. Within the twenty stanza-groups, not only is the Body, with its three main sections of the Vision, set well between Prologue and Epilogue, and not only is the large middle of the Body (Part Two—Groups V–XVI) centered in relation to what precedes and follows, but the middle of the third triad (IX–XII) forms a neat center also. This structural heart, which presents the Parable of the Vineyard, is the thematic heart of *Pearl*, a poem in which the roundness of the three in one form corresponds to the pearl itself, the symbol of salvation in heaven with the Holy Trinity

Marti (1991), who recognized the Parable of the Vineyard as a textual center, proposed that *Pearl* be read "according to a 'poetics of the body' governing not only the unity of the text itself, but the relationship of both author and reader to the text." He argued that the corporeal symmetry of the poem, "together with the corollary relation of each of its parts to the macrocosmic whole, constitutes an essential architectonic frame for any thematic interpretation" (85).

Within the circular structure, the concepts evolve naturally. The dreamer's visions of a heaven on earth and heaven itself, and his discussion with the maiden in between, move him from lamenting over death to trusting in resurrection; from ignorance to enlightenment, or, as Finlayson (1974) concluded, darkness to illumination; from rebellion to acceptance of God's will; from despair to consolation. Fritz (1980), in exploring the symbolic content of the numerical structure with regard to the thematic concerns of *Pearl*, stated, "Through form and content the reader could be led to see through the walls of the New Jerusalem, as the dreamer did, and see before him the joys of the celestial realm" (333–34).

Fleming (1981), discussing the 101 stanzas in the structure, noted that "the number of religious consolation is not an isolated hundred, but one hundred and one" (88)—a hundredfold increase—and called *Pearl* a poem of centuple consolation about "worldly loss and heavenly gain" (97). Petroff (1981), like Finlayson (1974), analyzed the changing mood of the dreamer as he views the various landscapes, for, after his experience, when he looks again at the garden, "he can see its nature with the eyes of the spirit, and realize its beauty as a promise of heaven, its dryness as a fact of the human condition" (191).

Bogdanos (1983), who viewed *Pearl* as "an incarnational symbol of God's universe" (12), dealt "especially with the artistic problem of representing the apocalyptic and the ineffable" to show "how the medieval symbol, often thought of as a static, self-enclosed metaphoric unit, can be transformed in the hands of a master poet into vital drama and therefore vital art" (1).

One gains the stability of heaven by enduring on this unstable earth, but this is only one of the lessons the dreamer must learn before he can attain peace. The joy he had felt in traversing the terrestrial paradise and in first seeing the pearl-maiden across the stream is quickly shattered when she tells him he cannot cross that stream and be with her. The idea of death for the body and resurrection for the soul is obscured in his dream. He still needs to grasp the spiritual concept of *Cortaysye*, the lesson of the Parable of the Vineyard, and God's system of *ryȝte* 'justice'.

At the start of Stanza-Group VIII, when the dreamer questions the maiden's queenship in heaven, a position he believes can belong only to Mary, the *Quen of Cortaysye* (432), the maiden answers that Mary is the supreme Queen; yet, everyone who enters heaven is a queen or king, living in perfect harmony. *Cortaysye* connotes primarily divine grace, but also charity and pity, and Mary is the mediatrix between God and those souls who seek his mercy.

The dreamer's earthbound view is developed further (lines 489–92) when he again questions the maiden's high estate, saying he believes she could be a countess but not a queen. This prompts the maiden to relate the Parable of the Vineyard (501–72), which only confuses the dreamer more, for, like the laborers who put in more hours than those who came into the vineyard late, he cannot understand how all receive one penny for pay, that God's spiritual justice is not worldly justice. As Horgan (1981) noted, the latter rewards workers according to their labor, but God, who owes man nothing, acts justly in merely keeping his commitment—the promise of salvation, which one cannot claim by right but must gain through mercy and grace.

The Parable of the Vineyard and the explanation of it, centrally located in *Pearl* in Stanza-Groups IX–XII, demonstrate why the maiden, who lived such a short time on earth (the vineyard), received the same reward (the penny symbolic of salvation) as those who endured a lifetime of struggle. In fact, due to her innocence and God's grace, her rank is higher than many.

The difficulty of interpreting the parable has led some scholars astray. For example, Brown (1904) initiated one of the early controversies over *Pearl* when he asserted that the poet defended the complete equality of heavenly rewards, but later scholars showed how unlikely it is that the poet would have followed the fourth-century heretic Jovinian in this matter, and there are passages in the poem that prove their point, such as lines 601–4 where the maiden tells the dreamer there is no confusion concerning more and less in heaven, for there all are paid in full, whether the reward be little or much.

Robertson-C (1950a) 295 translated part of Saint Augustine's "Sermo LXXXVII" in *Patrologia Latina* 38.533 to explain the doctrine of hierarchy in heaven: "We shall all be equal in that reward, the last like the first, and the first like the last. For that penny is eternal life, and all will be equal in eternal life. Although they will be radiant with a diversity of merits, one more, one less, that which pertains to eternal life will be equal to all." As Fisher (1961) 151–52 commented in discussing *Pearl*, the doctrine of hierarchy in heaven is "mystically resolved into equality."

In Stanza-Group XI, the emphasis on grace in the refrain, "For þe grace of God is gret inoghe," anticipates Group XII, especially the climactic concept, extending into XIII, of souls' not being able to enter heaven unless they come there as children (709–28).

The double-entendre of the link-word *ryȝte* is the key to comprehending Group XII. In lines 684, 696, and 720, when the pearl-maiden says, "Þe innocent is ay saf by ryȝte," she evidently means, as Gordon (1953) 150 noted in his glossary, the privilege the innocent have through justification by divine grace. This privilege applies with certainty to the innocent child who dies at an early age. In line 708, *ryȝte* concludes a stanza dealing with the righteous who should not presume to enter heaven on the grounds of strict justice, but must first come like the innocent child dependent on God's mercy.

When the dreamer questions the maiden's position as bride of the Lamb in the last stanza of Group XIII, one realizes that he has still not been able to grasp the deepest mysteries of the spiritual life. As Stiller (1982) observed, beautiful sights affect him, but throughout the central portion of the poem, he is inaccessible to logic and theology (407). It is mainly his vision of phenomenal beauty that brings him "as close to transcendence as a human being can come" (409).

The maiden tells him about the Lamb and the 144,000 virgins as a prelude to his vision of the New Jerusalem, which begins in Stanza-Group XVII. Then the dreamer is so enraptured by the sight of the Celestial City, especially when he sees his *lyttel quene* (1147) among the 144,000 in procession, that he attempts to plunge into the stream to reach her. The shock awakes him from his dream, and he finds himself back in the garden.

Only then, in his newly-found state of enlightenment, can he perceive, to a degree, the mysteries of eternal life, stop lamenting over the maiden's death, and start rejoicing in her resurrection, even though he is still in earth's *doel-doungoun* (1187). Only then can he comprehend the futility of rebelling against the inevitable, of opposing God's will: "Lorde, mad hit arn þat agayn þe stryuen,/Oþer proferen þe oȝt agayn þy paye" (1199–1200). Only then can he understand God's spiritual justice and know that faith and endurance in this mortal existence will gain for him the maiden's reward, for there is peace in contemplation of future bliss, in pleasing the Prince, "A God, a Lorde, a Frende ful fyin" (1204). Thus has his mood of despair turned to one of consolation.

PREFACE TO TEXT, TRANSLATION, AND NOTES

Text

The text of this edition first appeared in my Volume 1 of *The Pearl Poems: An Omnibus Edition* (1984). It was done in three main stages: (1) Transcription of the facsimile of the MS, published by the Early English Text Society in 1923; (2) Study of the original MS in the British Library, with the help of a grant of $600.00 in 1977 from the American Philosophical Society in Philadelphia; (3) Collation of my text with those of Morris (1864), Osgood (1906), Gollancz (1921), Chase (1932), Gordon (1953), Hillmann (1961), Cawley (1962), DeFord (1967), Moorman (1977), and Andrew & Waldron (1978). In studying the original MS in the British Library, I used an ultraviolet lamp to clarify many letters and words that are faded or stained.

In this edition, the folios are numbered according to the new foliation; therefore, the text of *Pearl* starts with f. 43, but one may note 39, the old number in ink, crossed out and 43 written below it in pencil. Illuminated letters mark the beginning of each of the 20 stanza-groups in the MS, and an additional letter *M* of *Moteleʒ* (961) starts the last stanza of Group XVI. These 21 illuminated letters are set in larger print in this edition.

The MS also contains many majuscules, but the scribe did not use capitalization according to a consistent practice. Though he began many lines with a majuscule, most lines have an initial miniscule. He did not always capitalize proper nouns, and sometimes he capitalized words within a line that need not have been capitalized. For example, within line 118 *Emerad* has a capital *E*, in contrast to *emerade* within line 1005. It seems, therefore, that much of what the scribe did in such matters must be considered decorative. I have used capitalization according to Modern English practices.

Punctuation, lacking in the MS, has been supplied. The spellings have been retained, except for *i-I* to *j-J* when the latter sound is intended. The scribe's long *I* does not always represent either the pronoun 'I' or the sound of *j*. For example, *I wysse* within a line is spelled *iwysse* in this edition. (See line 151.)

Contracted forms in the MS have been expanded. For example, the form *wᵗ* is written *wyth*, *&* is written *and*, and the crossed *q* is written *quoth*. The scribe used many abbreviations. (See the text of *Gawain* by Madden

[1839] for the printing of such forms as they appear in the MS.) The acute accent to mark a final weakly stressed *e* is added to words like *countré* (*Pearl* 297).

In the MS, numerous compounds are not joined, syllables of words are separated, and words frequently run together. In the text of this edition, all forms are printed as they would be in Modern English. For example, MS *luf daungere* (11) appears as *luf-daungere*, *my seluen* (52) as *myseluen*, and *inthis* (65) as *in this*. The scribe often placed the indefinite article *a* with the following noun or modifier as in *amyry* (23), printed *a myry*.

Emendations of the MS have been made in the following 12 places: *Is* to *is* 309; *perleʒ* to *perle* 335; *bẏgyner* to *Bygynner* 436; *wanig* to *waning* 558; *out out* to *out* 649; *hylleʒ* to *hylle* 678; *sor* to *For* 700; *lonbe* to *Lombe* 861; *As þise* to *As Johan þise* 997; *glode* to *golde* 1111; *quykeʒ* to *quyke* 1179; *Tf* to *If* 1185.

Translation and Notes

The translation keeps as close to the original as possible. The use of words with denotations different from the poet's does not change the essential meaning and mood of the poem. The notes list the literal sense of the Middle English vocabulary wherever changes that are not easily recognizable have occurred; thus one may examine the process of translating the original work into Modern English verse. Wherever extensive changes have been made, a literal rendering of the line or lines involved is provided.

Other verse translations of *Pearl* are by Coulton (1906), Jewett (1908), Mead (1908), Weston (1912), Kirtlan (1918), Chase (1932), Stone (1964), Gardner (1965), DeFord (1967), Williams (1967), Tolkien (1975), Borroff (1977), Vantuono (1987), and Finch (1993). Translations that are either literal or partly in verse are by Gollancz (1891, 1918, and 1921), Hillmann (1961), Crawford (1967), Eller (1983), and Vantuono (1984). Osgóod (1907) translated *Pearl* into prose; Turville-Petre (1984) has a prose translation at the bottoms of the pages of his modernized text of *Pearl*. Translations into foreign languages are by Decker (1916), German; Olivero (1926 and 1936) and Giaccherini (1989), Italian; Kalma (1938), Frisian; Miyata (1954), Terasawa (1960), and Naruse (1971), Japanese.

The poet occasionally used imperfect rhymes: *runnen* 26—*sunne* 28; *clot* 789—*hyl-coppe* 791; *men* 802—*Jerusalem* 804; *swatte* 829—*prophete* 831. As Northup (1897) 334 noted, *runnen* may be an example of apocope. The translation has imperfect rhymes: *loath* 377—*wroth* 379; *company* 542—*blame me* 544; *begin* 581—*him* 583; *came* 1119—*rain* 1121; *him* 1208—*thin* 1209.

Grant, Peterson, & Ross (1978) 175 noted the following self-rhymes: *spenud* 49—*spenned* 53; *tryed* 702, 707; *clere* 735, 737; *wale* 1000, 1007;

lambe-ly3t 1046—*ly3t* 1050; *wasse* 1108, 1112; *melle* 1118—*in-melle* 1127. The translation has self-rhymes: *long* 533—*belong* 535; *list* 604—*enlist* 611; *delight* 642—*light* 644; *will* 674, 683; *tried* 702, 707; *enlive* 842—*alive* 844; *amass* 1108—*mass* 1115; *fault* 1156—*default* 1163.

It was not always possible to capture the poet's intricate word-play in his use of refrain and concatenation. For example, in Stanza-Group IX the Middle English link-word *date* signifies 'beginning, end, season, hour, dawning,' and 'time'. The translations do not carry so rich a variety. For a comprehensive discussion of the poet's verse techniques, see the Appendix, "Poetic Mastery in *Pearl*."

Concerning diction in the translation, I retained the following Middle English words, though they are now listed as chiefly dialect in the unabridged version of *Webster's Third New International Dictionary of the English Language* (Springfield, Massachusetts: Merriam, 1966): *slade* (valley) 141; *woodshaws* (groves) 284. *Woodshaws* does not appear as a compound in Webster, but there is *shaw* (a small grove of trees). My use of *gitterner* 91 comes from adding the suffix to *gittern* (medieval stringed instrument of the guitar family), which appears only in the latter form in Webster. *Citoler* 91 from *citole* (a small flat-backed lute of late medieval times) is listed in the dictionary.

The punctuation of the translation sometimes differs slightly from the punctuation of the Middle English text. The reason for any change is usually evident. For example, Middle English "To clanly clos in golde so clere" (2) requires no comma within the line, but it seems better to place a comma in the translation: "In golden setting, shining clear."

PEARL

Folio 41, the first four illustrations for *Pearl,* reproduced by permission of the British Library: The dreamer sleeps near what looks like mounds on either side of him, with plants and trees springing from them and around them. Gollanz (1923) 9 noted that the scallop-shaped streamer in blue extending upward from his head may represent the departing of his spirit into space, lines 61–64. The illustrations in the manuscript are colored green, red, blue, yellow, brown, and white.

Folio 41b, reproduced by permission of the British Library: The dreamer stands by the stream separating him from the New Jerusalem. The artist could not capture the beauty of the description in lines 107–20. Fish are shown in the stream, even though the poet did not describe any.

Folio 42, reproduced by permission of the British Library: The dreamer is shown conversing with the pearl-maiden across the stream. Gordon (1953) x noted that her white dress, high at the neck and with long hanging sleeves, is in the fashion of the end of the fourteenth, or beginning of the fifteenth, century. The maiden's gesture, as Gordon also noted, seems to express disapproval of the dreamer's words. See especially Stanza-Group V (lines 241–300).

Folio 42b, reproduced by permission of the British Library: The dreamer is looking upward across the stream at the maiden behind the wall of the New Jerusalem. The wall is circular, whereas the city is described as square in the poem (lines 1023–32) in keeping with the biblical source. Gordon (1953) xi noted that in the picture the city resembles a feudal manor, with a tower and a hall depicted behind the wall. The artist, like the poet, medievalized the New Jerusalem.

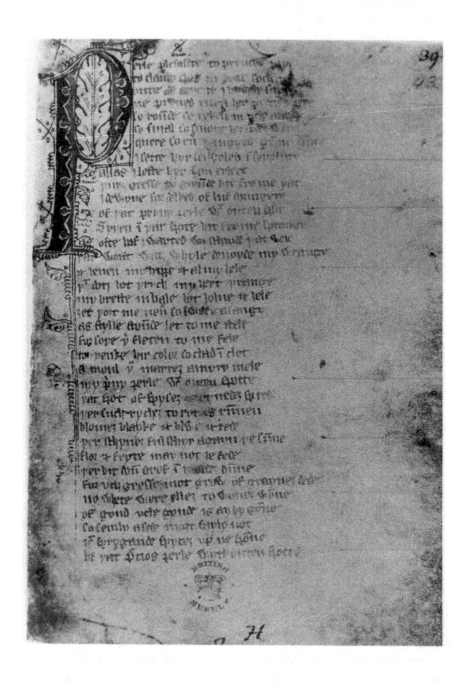

Folio 43, the first 36 lines of *Pearl,* reproduced by permission of the British Library. (The horizontal lines to the right of the text were drawn by me on my facsimile, from which this photograph was made. They are not in the original manuscript.)

I

f. 43   1   Perle plesaunte to prynces paye,
                   To clanly clos in golde so clere,
                   Oute of Oryent, I hardyly saye,
4   Ne proued I neuer her precios pere.
                   So rounde, so reken in vche araye,
                   So smal, so smoþe her sydeȝ were.
                   Queresoeuer I jugged gemmeȝ gaye,
8   I sette hyr sengeley in synglure.
                   Allas, I leste hyr in on erbere;
                   Þurȝ gresse to grounde hit fro me yot.
                   I dewyne, fordolked of luf-daungere,
12   Of þat pryuy perle wythouten spot.

         2   Syþen in þat spote hit fro me sprange,
                   Ofte haf I wayted, wyschande þat wele
                   Þat wont watȝ whyle deuoyde my wrange,
16   And heuen my happe and al my hele.
                   Þat dotȝ bot þrych my hert þrange,
                   My breste in bale bot bolne and bele.
                   Ȝet, þoȝt me neuer so swete a sange
20   As stylle stounde let to me stele.
                   Forsoþe, þer fleten to me fele
                   To þenke hir color so clad in clot.
                   O moul, þou marreȝ a myry juele,
24   My priuy perle wythouten spotte.

1 PAYE pleasure (The translation 'sway' is used here in the sense of 'dominion'. The earthly prince in line 1 foreshadows Christ the Prince in whose dominion the pearl-maiden will later be found. See the Commentary to line 1.)   2 TO CLANLY CLOS for [a] splendid setting   6 SYDEȜ WERE sides were   8 SENGELEY IN SYNGLURE apart as unique   9 LESTE lost   10 YOT slipped

PROLOGUE: THE GARDEN SETTING

I

f. 43   1
Pearl so pleasant in prince's sway,
In golden setting, shining clear,
Out of the Orient, I heartily say,
4   I never discovered her precious peer.
So round, so royal in each array,
So small, so smooth, with beauty sheer,
Wherever I gleaming gems did weigh,
8   I set her solely, singly to endear.
In arbor she from me did veer,
Slipping from grip to grassy lot.
I bear within love's pangs severe
12   For that special pearl without a spot.

    2
Since in that spot it from me fell,
I have often pondered, in pining for
My pearl that anguish used to quell
16   And make my heart toward heaven soar.
My mind is oppressed with mournful knell;
Pain sears my breast at sorrow's door.
Yet, I never heard a song's sweet swell
20   As the silent hour let me explore.
Truly, there carried many an encore
To call to mind her color in clot.
O earth, you destroy the jewel I adore,
24   My special pearl without a spot.

11 I lament, grief-stricken by frustrated love,   14 WYSCHANDE ÞAT WELE desiring that splendid pearl   15–16 That previously was accustomed to dispel my distress,/And increase my joy and all my well-being.   17–18 It does yet oppress my heart grievously,/Yet swell and burn my breast with anguish. 20 STELE slip   21 Truly, there floated to me many   23 MYRY beautiful

<table>
<tbody>
<tr><td>3</td><td>Þat spot of spyseȝ mot nedeȝ sprede,</td></tr>
</tbody>
</table>

3   Þat spot of spyseȝ mot nedeȝ sprede,
Þer such rycheȝ to rot is runnen.
Blomeȝ, blayke and blwe and rede,

28   Þer schyneȝ ful schyr agayn þe sunne.
Flor and fryte may not be fede
Þer hit doun drof in moldeȝ dunne,
For vch gresse mot grow of grayneȝ dede;

32   No whete were elleȝ to woneȝ wonne.
Of goud vche goude is ay bygonne;
So semly a sede moȝt fayly not,
Þat spryg ande spyceȝ vp ne sponne

36   Of þat precios perle wythouten spotte.

f. 43b   4   To þat spot þat I in speche expoun
I entred, in þat erber grene,
In Auguste, in a hyȝ seysoun,

40   Quen corne is coruen wyth crokeȝ kene.
On huyle þer perle hit trendeled doun,
Schadowed þis worteȝ, ful schyre and schene,
Gilofre, gyngure, and gromylyoun,

44   And pyonys powdered ay bytwene.
Ȝif hit watȝ semly on to sene,
A fayr reflayr ȝet fro hit flot.
Þer wonys þat worþyly, I wot and wene,

48   My precious perle wythouten spot.

5   Bifore þat spot my honde I spenud,
For care ful colde þat to me caȝt.
A deuely dele in my hert denned,

52   Þaȝ resoun sette myseluen saȝt.
I playned my perle þat þer watȝ spenned,
Wyth fyrte skylleȝ þat faste faȝt.

---

28 FUL SCHYR very brilliantly   29 FEDE wasted   31 GRAYNEȜ DEDE dead grains   32 TO WONEȜ WONNE taken to barns   34 SEMLY A SEDE excellent a seed   35 VP NE SPONNE would not spring up   39 IN A HYȜ SEYSOUN on a holy occasion   41 TRENDELED rolled   42 These plants, very bright and shiny, provided shade,

	3	That spot with spices is surely spread,
		Where such richness to ruin has run.
		Blossoms, white and blue and red,
28		There shine in splendor against the sun.
		Flower and fruit have never fled
		From where it mixed with molds of dun;
		Good plants must grow from grains' deathbed,
32		Or no sprouts would be for wheat barns won.
		From good each good is always begun;
		To fail to flourish this seed can not,
		Since shrubs and spices are purely spun
36		From that precious pearl without a spot.

f. 43b	4	At that spot which I in speech expound
		I entered, in that arbor green,
		In August, when a holy time came round,
40		When corn is cut with sickles keen.
		Where pearl lay pressed beneath that mound,
		Shade was scattered where plants careen;
		Gillyflower, ginger, and gromwell abound,
44		With peonies powdered in between.
		They richly rose with royal sheen,
		With fragrance fair, without a blot.
		There lies, I realize, that gem so clean,
48		My precious pearl without a spot.

[handwritten marginalia: plants & flowers grow from pearl, like a seed (consolatory) & it's also like a grave]

	5	Before that spot clasped hands expressed
		The care full cold inside me caught.
		A dismal grief my heart depressed,
52		Though reason reached for restful thought.
		I mourned for my pearl, below mound's crest,
		With frightful views that fiercely fought.

45–46 If it was beautiful to look upon,/A pleasant fragrance also wafted from it.   47 There lies that worthy gem, I realize, indeed,   49 SPENUD clasped   51 DENNED dwelled   52 SETTE MYSELUEN SA3T would have made me peaceful   53 SPENNED enclosed

Þaȝ kynde of Kryst me comfort kenned,
56 My wreched wylle in wo ay wraȝte.
I felle vpon þat floury flaȝt;
Suche odour to my herneȝ schot.
I slode vpon a slepyng-slaȝte
60 On þat precos perle wythouten spot.

THE VISION—PART ONE:
THE TERRESTRIAL PARADISE AND THE PEARL-MAIDEN

II

6   Fro spot my spyryt þer sprang in space;
        My body on balke þer bod in sweuen.
    My goste is gon in Godeȝ grace
64 In auenture þer meruayleȝ meuen.
    I ne wyste in þis worlde quere þat hit wace,
    Bot I knew me keste þer klyfeȝ cleuen.
    Towarde a foreste I bere þe face,
68 Where rych rokkeȝ wer to dyscreuen.
    Þe lyȝt of hem myȝt no mon leuen,
    Þe glemande glory þat of hem glent,
    For wern neuer webbeȝ þat wyȝeȝ weuen
72 Of half so dere adubmente.

f. 44 7 Dubbed wern alle þo downeȝ sydeȝ
    Wyth crystal klyffeȝ so cler of kynde.
    Holtewodeȝ bryȝt aboute hem bydeȝ,
76 Of bolleȝ as blwe as ble of ynde.
    As bornyst syluer þe lef onslydeȝ,
    Þat þike con trylle on vch a tynde.

55 Though [the] character of Christ would have shown me solace,   56
WRAȝTE moved   58 HERNEȝ brains   59 SLEPYNG-SLAȝTE deep slumber
62 BALKE mound   64 To [an] adventure where miracles transpire.   65 HIT
WACE it was   66 CLEUEN were cleft

12

Though kindly Christ filled comfort's quest,

56 My wretched will with woe was fraught.
To that flowery turf I fell, distraught;
Such odor to my head then shot.
Subdued was I by sleep's onslaught

60 Near that precious pearl without a spot.

THE VISION—PART ONE:
THE TERRESTRIAL PARADISE AND THE PEARL-MAIDEN

II

6 From that spot my spirit sprang into space, A
While my body stayed on earth asleep. B
My soul has gone in God's good grace, A

64 Moving swiftly in miraculous sweep. B
I knew not where in the world I would race, A
But I soon was cast where cliffs are steep. B
Toward a forest then I turned my face, A

68 Where rocks enriched the sylvan deep. B
Their lovely light to eyes did leap;
Their gleaming glory was heaven-sent.
Tapestries never were found in a heap

72 Of half so dear an adornment.

f. 44   7   Adorned was every soft hillside
With crystal cliffs clearly aligned.
Forests bright around them bide

76 With boles as blue as indigo's kind.
Like burnished silver sheer leaves slide,
Trailing on branches, there enshrined.

68 WER TO DYSCREUEN were to be seen   69 No man could believe the
light of them,   70-71 The gleaming glory that shone from them,/For [there]
were never tapestries that men wove   73 DOWNE3 hills'   74 KYNDE sub-
stance   76 BLE hue   77 ONSLYDE3 hang   78 TYNDE branch

Quen glem of glodeȝ agaynȝ hem glydeȝ,
Wyth schymeryng schene ful schrylle þay schynde.
Þe grauayl þat on grounde con grynde
Wern precious perleȝ of Oryente,
Þe sunnebemeȝ bot blo and blynde
In respecte of þat adubbement.

8

The adubbemente of þo downeȝ dere
Garten my goste al greffe forȝete.
So frech flauoreȝ of fryteȝ were,
As fode, hit con me fayre refete.
Fowleȝ þer flowen in fryth in fere,
Of flaumbande hweȝ, boþe smale and grete.
Bot, sytole-stryng and gyternere
Her reken myrþe moȝt not retrete,
For quen þose bryddeȝ her wyngeȝ bete,
Þay songen wyth a swete asent.
So gracos gle couþe no mon gete
As here and se her adubbement.

9

So al watȝ dubbet on dere asyse
Þat fryth þer fortwne forth me fereȝ.
Þe derþe þerof for to deuyse
Nis no wyȝ worþé þat tonge bereȝ.
I welke ay forth in wely wyse,
No bonk so byg þat did me dereȝ.
Þe fyrre in þe fryth þe feier con ryse
Þe playn, þe plontteȝ, þe spyse, þe pereȝ,
And raweȝ, and randeȝ, and rych reuereȝ;
As fyldor fyn her bukes brent.
I wan to a water by schore þat schereȝ;
Lorde, dere watȝ hit adubbement.

---

80 With shiny shimmering they shone very clearly.   81 GRYNDE mingle
83 BLO AND BLYNDE dark and lusterless   85 ÞO DOWNEȜ DERE those
delightful hills   86 AL GREFFE FORȜETE forget all grief   88 Like food,
they sweetly did refresh me.   89 IN FRYTH IN FERE in [the] forest in flocks
92 Could not imitate their beautiful melody,

When gleams through clearings against them glide,
80   They shine and shimmer as they unwind.
Pebbles on the ground that one could find
Were precious pearls from the Orient;
Sunbeams are dark, I then divined,
84   In comparison to that adornment.

8   The adornments there my being thrilled,
And made my soul's mad grief abate.
Fragrances fresh from fruit instilled
88   Food for peace, my fortunate fate.
Fluttering fowls the forest filled,
In flaming hues in them innate.
Neither citoler nor gitterner skilled
92   Their moving melodies could imitate;
For when those birds did wings rotate,
They sang their songs in sweet assent.
Such gracious glee no persons rate
96   As to hear [their song] and see their adornment.

9   With rich adornment under royal skies
Was forest floor where fortune fares.
The splendor there no sage can devise,
100   With worthy wording, however he dares.
I wandered onward in happy wise,
No hill so high, no path with snares.
Farther in the forest fairer did rise
104   Plains and spices, and trees with pears,
Hedgerows on lands, and rivers through lairs;
Their currents gleamed like fine gold filament.
I strolled to a stream displaying its wares;
108   Lord, dear was its adornment.

93 BETE beat   95 GETE obtain   97 DERE ASYSE royal style   98 FRYTH
forest . . . FERE3 carries   99–100 No man who has tongue is capable/Of
depicting the glory of it.   102 DID ME DERE3 made obstacles for me   104
PLONTTE3 saplings   105 RANDE3 strands   107 SCHERE3 flows

10   The dubbemente of þo derworth depe

                Wern bonkeȝ bene of beryl bryȝt.

                Swangeande swete, þe water con swepe

112   Wyth a rownande rourde, raykande aryȝt.

                In þe founce þer stonden stoneȝ stepe,

                As glente þurȝ glas þat glowed and glyȝt,

                A stremande sterneȝ, quen stroþe-men slepe,

116   Staren in welkyn in wynter nyȝt;

                For vche a pobbel in pole þer pyȝt

                Watȝ emerad, saffer, oþer gemme gente,

                Þat alle þe loȝe lemed of lyȝt,

120   So dere watȝ hit adubbement.

III

11   The dubbement dere of doun and daleȝ,

                  Of wod and water and wlonk playneȝ,

                Bylde in me blys, abated my baleȝ,

124   Fordidden my stresse, dystryed my payneȝ.

                Doun after a strem þat dryȝly haleȝ,

                I bowed in blys, bredful my brayneȝ.

                Þe fyrre I folȝed þose floty valeȝ,

128   Þe more strenghþe of joye myn herte strayneȝ.

                As fortune fares þeras ho frayneȝ,

                Wheþer solace ho sende oþer elleȝ sore,

                Þe wyȝ to wham her wylle ho wayneȝ

132   Hytteȝ to haue ay more and more.

12   More of wele watȝ in þat wyse

                Þen I cowþe telle, þaȝ I tom hade,

                For vrþely herte myȝt not suffyse

136   To þe tenþe dole of þo gladneȝ glade.

109 DERWORTH DEPE splendid depths   111 SWETE pleasantly   112 ROURDE sound   113–14 At the bottom there shone bright stones,/That glowed and glinted like flashes through glass,   116 STAREN gleaming   117 POLE stream . . . PYȜT placed   118 GENTE excellent

10   The adornments dear in depths that glow
Revealed fair banks of beryl bright.
Swirling freely, the stream did flow,
112   Whispering en route, whirling aright.
Biding at bottom, stones bestow
Glistening beams, void of blight,
Like stars which woodsmen sleep below,
116   Streaming in sky on winter's night;
For each jewel joined under floods in flight
Was emerald, sapphire, or pearl affluent,
Lending that brook its luminous light,
120   So dear was its adornment.

III

11   The adornments dear of hills and dales,
Of wood and water and wonderful plains,
Built in me joy, abated my bales,
124   Abolished distress, dispelled my pains.
Down by the stream that sadness curtails,
I strolled in bliss, brimful my brains.
The further I followed those water-filled vales,
128   More ardor of joy my heart attains.
As fortune directs wherever she reigns,
Whether solace she send or sorrows sore,
The mortal she leads to her life's lanes
132   Happens to have always more and more.

12   More of good was in that guise
Than I could tell, though time I made,   *but he was*
For mortal mind could not apprise
136   The tenth part so richly arrayed.

119 LO3E LEMED water gleamed   125 DRY3LY HALE3 incessantly flows
128 STRAYNE3 stirs   129 FRAYNE3 desires   130 OÞER ELLE3 SORE or
sorrow instead   131 The man upon whom she urges her will   133 WYSE
array   135 SUFFYSE suffice   136 GLADNE3 GLADE rich delights

		Forþy, I þoȝt þat Paradyse
		Watȝ þer oþer gayn þo bonkeȝ brade.
		I hoped þe water were a deuyse
140		Bytwene myrþeȝ by mereȝ made.
		Byȝonde þe broke, by slente oþer slade,
		I hope þat mote merked wore,
		Bot þe water watȝ depe; I dorst not wade,
144		And euer me longed a more and more.

f. 45	13	More and more, and ȝet wel mare
		Me lyste to se þe broke byȝonde,
		For if hit watȝ fayr þer I con fare,
148		Wel loueloker watȝ þe fyrre londe.
		Abowte me con I stote and stare;
		To fynde a forþe faste con I fonde,
		Bot woþeȝ mo, iwysse, þer ware
152		Þe fyrre I stalked by þe stronde;
		And euer me þoȝt I schulde not wonde
		For wo þer weleȝ so wynne wore.
		Þenne nwe note me com on honde,
156		Þat meued my mynde ay more and more.

	14	More meruayle con my dom adaunt.
		I seȝ byȝonde þat myry mere
		A crystal clyffe ful relusaunt.
160		Mony ryal ray con fro hit rere.
		At þe fote þerof þer sete a faunt,
		A mayden of menske, ful debonere.
		Blysnande whyt watȝ hyr bleaunt.
164		I knew hyr wel; I hade sen hyr ere.
		As glysnande golde þat man con schere,
		So schon þat schene anvnder schore.

138 BRADE broad   139–40 I supposed the water were a division/Between delights created alongside streams.   142 MERKED WORE would be situated 145 MARE more   148 FYRRE LONDE more distant land   150 FASTE eagerly . . . FONDE endeavor   151 IWYSSE indeed . . . WARE were   152 STRONDE shore   153 WONDE shrink

Therefore, I thought that Paradise
Was there or past those shores unscathed.
I assumed the streams did rise
140   To divide delights on each side displayed.
Beyond the brook, by slope or slade,
I imagined a castle of great splendor,
But the water was deep; I dared not wade,
144   And I constantly craved much more and more.

a dreamer's mind creating the dream

f. 45   13   Of more and more I was aware
And wished to see beyond the stream,
For if it were fair where I did fare,
148   More splendid did that distant land seem.
I stopped and round about did stare,
To find a ford and follow that dream,
But perils more increased my care
152   The farther I stepped along shore supreme;
I should not shrink, I then did deem,
From woe and all that wealth ignore.
Then a new marvel came near with gleam,
156   That moved my mind still more and more.

14   More marvels now amazed my mind,
As I gazed beyond those currents clear
To a crystal cliff with rays refined,
160   Each royal beam a radiant spear.
At the base a child sat enshrined,
A maiden of dignity in glowing gear,
Her attire by dazzling white defined;
164   I had seen her before in different sphere.
Like glistening gold that one does shear,
So shone that gem on distant shore.

eternal infant

154 From adversity where riches so precious were.   155 ON HONDE close
by   158 MYRY MERE pleasant brook   159 RELUSAUNT radiant   160
CON did . . . RERE rise   161 FAUNT child   162 DEBONERE gentle   163
BLYSNANDE gleaming . . . BLEAUNT silk attire   164 ERE before   166
SCHENE bright child . . . SCHORE cliff

On lenghe I loked to hyr þere;
168 Þe lenger, I knew hyr more and more.

15 The more I frayst hyr fayre face,
Her fygure fyn quen I had fonte,
Suche gladande glory con to me glace,
172 As lyttel byfore þerto watȝ wonte.
To calle hyr lyste con me enchace,
Bot baysment gef myn hert a brunt.
I seȝ hyr in so strange a place;
176 Such a burre myȝt make myn herte blunt.
Þenne vereȝ ho vp her fayre frount,
Hyr vysayge whyt as playn yuore.
Þat stonge myn hert, ful stray atount,
180 And euer þe lenger, þe more and more.

IV

f. 45b 16 More þen me lyste my drede aros;
I stod ful stylle and dorste not calle.
Wyth yȝen open and mouth ful clos,
184 I stod as hende as hawk in halle.
I hope that gostly watȝ þat porpose;
I dred onende quat schulde byfalle,
Lest ho me eschaped, þat I þer chos,
188 Er I at steuen hir moȝt stalle.
Þat gracios gay wythouten galle,
So smoþe, so smal, so seme slyȝt,
Ryseȝ vp in hir araye ryalle,
192 A precos pyece, in perleȝ pyȝt.

17 Perleȝ pyȝte of ryal prys

169 FRAYSTE scrutinized   170 FONTE perceived   171 GLACE glide   172
As shortly before [it] was also accustomed [to do].   173 LYSTE desire . . .
ENCHACE impel   174 But bewilderment struck my heart a blow.   176 Such
a shock could render my mind senseless.   178 PLAYN smooth

20

Looking at length at that child dear,
I sensed I knew her more and more.

15 The more I followed her faultless face,
And on her figure fine did gaze,
Such gladdening glory did me embrace,

172 As the custom carried in former days.
I wished to call that girl of grace,
But my mortal mind was in a maze.
I saw her in so strange a place;

176 The shock sped forth confusion's phase.
Then she her lovely face did raise,
Her visage, ivory white to adore.
That stung my mind astray in daze,

180 And ever the longer, the more and more.

IV

f. 45b 16 More than I wished my dread arose;
I stood so still and dared not call.
With eyes wide open, mouth closed, I froze,

184 And stood on hand like a hawk in a hall.
I imagined a spiritual matter God knows;
I feared whatever would befall,
Afraid she would escape, she whom I chose,

188 Before I could signal and make her stall.
Then that girl, so quick to enthrall,
So smooth, so small, slender and straight,
Royally arrayed, rises tall,

192 A precious pearl in pearls ornate.

17 Pearls ornate of royalty

179 STRAY ATOUNT dazed uncontrollably 184 HENDE reserved 185 PORPOSE meaning 186 ONENDE concerning 188 AT STEUEN with speech 189 GAY bright maiden . . . GALLE blemish 190 SEME SLY3T suitably slender 192 PYECE damsel . . . PY3T adorned 193 PRYS value

Þere moȝt mon, by grace, haf sene
Quen þat frech, as flor-de-lys,
196 Doun þe bonk con boȝe bydene.
Al blysnande whyt watȝ hir beau mys,
Vpon at sydeȝ and bounden bene
Wyth þe myryeste margarys, at my deuyse,
200 Þat euer I seȝ ȝet with myn yȝen,
Wyth lappeȝ large, I wot and I wene,
Dubbed with double perle and dyȝte.
Her cortel of self sute schene
204 Wyth precios perleȝ al vmbepyȝte.

18 A pyȝt coroune ȝet wer þat gyrle,
Of marjorys, and non oþer ston,
Hiȝe pynakled of cler quyt perle,
208 Wyth flurted flowreȝ, perfet vpon.
To hed hade ho non oþer werle.
Her lere-leke al hyr vmbegon,
Her semblaunt sade for doc oþer erle;
212 Her ble more blaȝt þen whalleȝ bon.
As schorne golde schyr her fax þenne schon,
On schyldereȝ þat leghe vnlapped lyȝte.
Her depe colour, ȝet, wonted non
216 Of precios perle in porfyl pyȝte.

f. 46 19 Pyȝt watȝ poyned and vche a hemme,
At honde, at sydeȝ, at ouerture,
Wyth whyte perle, and non oþer gemme;
220 And bornyste quyte watȝ hyr uesture.
Bot, a wonder perle wythouten wemme
Inmyddeȝ hyr breste watȝ sette so sure,

194 There could one, through good fortune, have seen   197 All shining white
was her excellent cloak,   198 BENE beautifully   199 AT MY DEUYSE in
my opinion   200 SEȜ saw . . . YȜEN eyes   201 I WOT AND I WENE I
know, indeed   202-3 Adorned and set with paired pearls./Her kirtle of [the]
same gleaming pattern   204 AL VMBEPYȜTE was completely surrounded

22

Amazingly might one assay,
When that maiden fair, like fleur-de-lis,
196   Down the slope did stroll straightway.
Her cloak of white, set glowingly,
Open at the sides, revealed an array
Of the finest pearls from distant sea
200   That I ever saw on any tray;
The large, loose sleeves, a fine display,
Were doubly adorned with pearls to mate.
Her kirtle showed that same great ray
204   Of precious pearls, pure and ornate.

    18   An ornate crown yet wore that girl,
Of margarites, and no other stone,
Pinnacled high with clear white pearl,
208   With flowers fashioned there, full-blown.
No other circlet was set awhirl;
On face was cambric, finely sewn.
Her semblance suited a duke or earl,
212   That ivory visage, whiter than whale's bone.
Like shorn gold sheer her hair then shone,
Lying on shoulders in stylish state.
Her collar wide lacked not the tone
216   Of precious pearls on borders ornate.

f. 46   19   Ornate was every wristlet and hem,
At hands, at sides, at each aperture,
With pearls of white, and no other gem,
220   And shining white was her vesture.
Besides, the greatest pearl none could condemn
Amid her breast was set so sure,

208 PERFET VPON perfectly spread   209–10 On [her] head she had no other circlet./Her face-cambric encompassing her [cheeks] completely,   212 BLE complexion . . . BLA3T white   214 Which lay lightly unclasped on [her] shoulders.   215 WONTED NON was not void   221 WONDER marvelous . . . WEMME flaw

23

A manneʒ dom moʒt dryʒly demme

224 Er mynde moʒt malte in hit mesure.

I hope no tong moʒt endure

No sauerly saghe say of þat syʒt,

So watʒ hit clene, and cler and pure,

228 Þat precios perle, þer hit watʒ pyʒt.

20 Pyʒt in perle, þat precios pyse

On wyþer half water com doun þe schore.

No gladder gome, heþen into Grece,

232 Þen I quen ho on brymme wore.

Ho watʒ me nerre þen aunte or nece;

My joy, forþy, watʒ much þe more.

Ho profered me speche, þat special spyce,

236 Enclynande lowe, in wommon lore,

Caʒte of her coroun of grete tresore,

And haylsed me wyth a lote lyʒte.

Wel watʒ me þat euer I watʒ bore,

240 To sware þat swete in perleʒ pyʒte.

THE VISION—PART TWO: THE HOMILETIC CENTER

V

21 "**O** perle," quoþ I, "in perleʒ pyʒt,

Art þou my perle þat I haf playned,

Regretted by myn one on nyʒte?

244 Much longeyng haf I for þe layned,

Syþen into gresse þou me aglyʒte.

Pensyf, payred, I am forpayned,

And þou in a lyf of lykyng lyʒte,

223-24 A man's mind might incessantly be frustrated/Before [his] reason could conceive of its value   226 To say any enthusiastic word of that sight, 228 PYʒT adorned   229 PYSE damsel   230 WYÞER HALF opposide side 231 GOME man   232 Than I when she was at [the] edge.

Mortal minds in imagining's realm
224 Could not conceive of its measure.
I truly think no tongue could endure
To speak of that shining treasure great,
So elegant it was, and clear and pure,
228 That precious pearl among pearls ornate.

20 In ornate pearls, that child of peace
Beyond the brook strolled down the shore.
No gladder soul breathed, from here to Greece,
232 To see her stand by stream's decor.
She was nearer to me than aunt or niece;
My joy, therefore, was much the more.
She proffered me speech, special release,
236 Bowing low, like a lady of lore,
Took off her crown, that treasure she wore,
And hailed me happily from her estate.
Born well was a spirit sent to soar,
240 To answer that pearl in pearls ornate.

THE VISION—PART TWO: THE HOMILETIC CENTER

V

21 "O pearl in ornate pearls of light,
Are you my pearl whose loss I lamented,
Mourning by myself alone at night?
244 In longing for you I have never relented,
Since you descended on grassy site.
Pensive, in pain, I am tormented,
While you bide in bliss on exuberant height,

235 SPYCE damsel   236 LORE way   238 LOTE LY3TE cheerful voice   239
Well was [it] for me that ever I was born,   240 SWETE sweet girl   241 PY3T
adorned   244 Much longing have I concealed for you,   245 AGLY3TE
slipped away   247 OF LYKYNG LY3TE of delight are settled

language fails

Eden, eternal infant, innocence, spirit, pre-birth wisdom pre-loss

248		In Paradys erde, of stryf vnstrayned.
		What wyrde haꝫ hyder my juel vayned
		And don me in þys del and gret daunger?
		Fro we in twynne wern towen and twayned,
252		I haf ben a joyleꝫ juelere."

f. 46b	22	That juel, þenne, in gemmeꝫ gente,
		Vered vp her vyse wyth yꝫen graye,
		Set on hyr coroun of perle orient,
256		And soberly after þenne con ho say:
		"Sir, ꝫe haf your tale mysetente,
		To say your perle is al awaye,
		Þat is in cofer so comly clente,
260		As in þis gardyn, gracios gaye,
		Hereinne to lenge foreuer and play,
		Þer mys nee mornyng com neuer here.
		Her were a forser for þe, in faye,
264		If þou were a gentyl jueler.

	23	"Bot, jueler gente, if þou schal lose
		Þy joy for a gemme þat þe watꝫ lef,
		Me þynk þe put in a mad porpose,
268		And busyeꝫ þe aboute a raysoun bref,
		For þat þou lesteꝫ watꝫ bot a rose
		Þat flowred and fayled as kynde hyt gef.
		Now þurꝫ kynde of þe kyste þat hyt con close,
272		To a perle of prys hit is put in pref;
		And þou hatꝫ called þy wyrde a þef,
		Þat oꝫt of noꝫt hatꝫ mad þe cler.
		Þou blameꝫ þe bote of þy meschef;
276		Þou art no kynde jueler."

248 OF STRYF VNSTRAYNED freed from strife   249–50 What fate has sent my jewel here/And forced me into this sadness and severe frustration?   251 Since we were pulled apart and separated,   253 GEMMEꝫ GENTE splendid gems   257 MYSETENTE misdirected   259 COMLY CLENTE fittingly enclosed   260 GRACIOS GAYE beautifully bright   261 PLAY exult   262 MORNYNG lamentation   263 Here would be a coffer for you, in truth,

248   In land of Paradise, sweetly scented.
                          To what fate has my lovely jewel consented,
                          While frustrated my woe cannot be crueler?
                          To be severed from you I have never assented;

252   I have only become a joyless jeweler."

f. 46b   22   That jewel, then, that gorgeous girl,
                          Raised her face with eyes of gray,
                          Put on her crown of oriental pearl,

256   And soberly after she then did say:
                          "Sir, you your words do wrongly hurl,
                          To say your pearl has gone away,
                          She in a coffer, snugly in furl,

260   As in this garden, here to stay,
                          Herein to linger beyond all clay,
                          Where loss nor longing never enter.
                          From stronghold sure you would never stray,

264   If you were a gentle jeweler.

          23   "Now, gentle jeweler, if you shall lose
                          Your joy for a gem that from you veered,
                          You apply your mind to maddening views,

268   And trouble yourself with transience bleared.
                          The rose you lost, your heavy heart rues,
                          Flowered and faded, was suddenly seared.
                        Through this kind of coffer it now ensues

272   As a pearl of price, forever endeared;
                        And you have called fate thief, and feared,
                        When it has shown you something surer.
                        You censure the remedy that has appeared;

276   You are no gracious jeweler."

consolation

266 ÞE WATꝫ LEF was dear to you   267 [It] seems to me you apply [yourself] to a foolish purpose,   268 RAYSOUN BREF transient matter   270 KYNDE HYT GEF nature directed it   271 HYT CON CLOSE does enclose it   272 PUT IN PREF established with certainty   273 WYRDE A ÞEF fate a thief   274 That has clearly made for you something from nothing.   275 MES-CHEF misfortune

24
A juel to me, þen, watʒ þys geste,
And jueleʒ wern hyr gentyl saweʒ.
"Iwyse," quoþ I, "my blysfol beste,

280
My grete dystresse þou al todraweʒ.
To be excused I make requeste;
I trawed my perle don out of daweʒ.
Now haf I fonde hyt, I scal ma feste,

284
And wony wyth hyt in schyr wodschaweʒ,
And loue my Lorde and al his laweʒ,
Þat hatʒ me broʒ þys blys ner.
Now were I at yow byʒonde þise waweʒ,

288
I were a joyfol jueler."

f. 47   25
"Jueler," sayde þat gemme clene,
"Wy borde ʒe men? So madde ʒe be!
Þre wordeʒ hatʒ þou spoken at ene;

292
Vnavysed, forsoþe, wern alle þre.
Þou ne woste in worlde quat on dotʒ mene;
Þy worde byfore þy wytte con fle.
Þou says þou traweʒ me in þis dene

296
Bycawse þou may wyth yʒen me se.
Anoþer, þou says in þys countré
Þyself schal won wyth me ryʒt here.
Þe þrydde, to passe þys water fre—

300
Þat may no joyfol jueler.

VI

26
"I halde þat jueler lyttel to prayse
Þat loueʒ wel þat he seʒ wyth yʒe,
And much to blame and vncortoyse,

304
Þat leueʒ oure Lorde wolde make a lyʒe,
Þat lelly hyʒte your lyf to rayse,

277 GESTE child   278 SAWEƷ words   279 BESTE most noble maiden   280
TODRAWEƷ dispel   282 DON OUT OF DAWEƷ was deprived of life   283
MA FESTE rejoice   286 Who has brought me near this bliss.

28

24 A jewel to me, then, was this child at rest,
 Each gentle word a jewel without flaws.
 "Indeed," said I, "my maiden blest,
280 My cold distress your comfort thaws.
 To be excused I make request;
 I deemed my pearl in dust that gnaws.
 Finding it here, no longer oppressed,
284 I shall dwell with it in sheer woodshaws,
 And honor my Lord and all his laws,
 So merry has he made this thankful viewer.
 Were I beyond this brook that awes,
288 I would be a joyful jeweler."

f. 47 25 "Jeweler," said that jewel clean,
 "Men who are mad speak erroneously.
 Three statements by you from right did lean;
292 Unwise, indeed, were all these three.
 You know not what in the world they mean;
 Your words before your wit do flee.
 You say you believe I exist in this scene
296 Because your eyes have lit on me.
 Second, you say in this country
 You from me shall never sever.
 The third, to cross this stream you see
300 Cannot now be, joyful jeweler.

you cannot join the dead

must mourn, be consoled by the vision & move on

VI

26 "I judge that jeweler little to praise,
 Who honors well what he sees with eye,
 And much to blame, with discourteous ways,
304 Who believes our Lord would tell a lie.
 He loyally vowed your spirit to raise,

287 WAWE3 waves 290 BORDE do speak lightly 291 AT ENE simultaneously 295 DENE valley 298 [You] yourself shall dwell with me right here. 299 FRE splendid 300 That may no joyful jeweler [do].

Þaʒ fortune dyd your flesch to dyʒe.
Ʒe setten hys wordeʒ ful west ernays,
308 Þat loueʒ noþynk bot ʒe hit syʒe;
And þat is a poynt o sorquydryʒe,
Þat vche god mon may euel byseme,
To leue no tale be true to tryʒe,
312 Bot þat hys one skyl may dem.

27 "Deme now þyself if þou con dayly,
As man to God wordeʒ schulde heue.
Þou saytʒ þou schal won in þis bayly;
316 Me þynk þe burde fyrst aske leue,
And ʒet of graunt þou myʒteʒ fayle.
Þou wylneʒ ouer þys water to weue;
Er most þou ceuer to oþer counsayl.
320 Þy corse in clot mot calder keue,
For hit watʒ forgarte at Paradys greue.
Oure ʒorefader hit con mysseʒeme.
Þurʒ drwry deth boʒ vch ma dreue
324 Er ouer þys dam hym Dryʒtyn deme."

f. 47b 28 "Demeʒ þou me," quoþ I, "my swete.
To dol agayn þenne I dowyne.
Now haf I fonte þat I forlete,
328 Schal I efte forgo hit er euer I fyne?
Why schal I hit boþe mysse and mete?
My precios perle dotʒ me gret pyne.
What serueʒ tresor bot gareʒ men grete
332 When he hit schal efte wyth teneʒ tyne?
Now rech I neuer for to declyne,

307 WEST ERNAYS idle pledge   308 You who honor nothing unless you see
it.   309 SORQUYDRYʒE pride   310 EUEL BYSEME ill befit   311 TO
TRYʒE to be considered   313 DAYLY speak courteously   314 HEUE present
315 BAYLY domain   317 GRAUNT consent   318 WYLNEʒ desire . . .
WEUE cross   319 CEUER submit . . . COUNSAYL plan   320 KEUE sink
321 FORGARTE condemned . . . GREUE grove   322 MYSSEʒEME forfeit
323 DREUE pass

Though destiny condemned your body to die.
You think untrue the words he says,

308   If you honor only what is not on high.
Pointless pride breaks the heavenly tie,
Fot it ill befits each being's dream
To believe no tale true, never to try,

312   Except what his reason alone can deem.

27   "Deem now yourself if you did speak
With words to God he should receive.
You say you shall dwell upon the peak;

316   I think you first should ask his leave,
And still you might fail to get what you seek.
Crossing this water you wish to achieve,
But first you must follow counsel bleak.

320   Your corpse to clot must coldly cleave,
For it was damned by Adam and Eve
When our old father did forfeit love's beam.
Through dreary death must each man weave

324   Before he can cross, as God will then deem."

f. 47b   28   "Deem me unworthy, my damsel sweet.
Then great sorrow is again all mine.
Finally finding my bliss complete,

328   Must I again lose that joy benign?
To find you and lose you is doom and defeat;
My precious pearl does sorrow assign.
Deceiving is treasure, forever fleet,

332   When one must surrender it, with soul supine.
I care not about falling from fortune fine,

324 DAM stream . . . DEME will direct   325 DEME3 censure   326 DOL
sorrow . . . DOWYNE must languish   327 FONTE found . . . FORLETE had
lost   328–29 Must I again surrender it before I die?/Why must I both lose and
find it?   330 DOT3 causes . . . PYNE anxiety   331–32 What does treasure
avail if [it] makes men lament/When they must afterwards surrender it with
sufferings?   333 FOR TO DECLYNE about falling from fortune

31

Ne how fer of folde þat man me fleme.
When I am partleȝ of perle myne,
336 Bot durande doel what may men deme?"

29 "Thow demeȝ noȝt bot doel-dystresse,"
Þenne sayde þat wyȝt. "Why dotȝ þou so?
For dyne of doel of lureȝ lesse,
340 Ofte mony mon forgoȝ þe mo.
Þe oȝte better þyseluen blesse,
And loue ay God, and wele and wo,
For anger gayneȝ þe not a cresse,
344 Who nedeȝ schal þole. Be not so þro,
For þoȝ þou daunce as any do,
Braundysch and bray þy braþeȝ breme,
When þou no fyrre may, to ne fro,
348 Þou moste abyde þat he schal deme.

30 "Deme Dryȝtyn; euer hym adyte.
Of þe way a fote ne wyl he wryþe.
Þy mendeȝ mounteȝ not a myte,
352 Þaȝ þou, for sorȝe, be neuer blyþe.
Stynst of þy strot and fyne to flyte,
And sech hys blyþe ful swefte and swyþe.
Þy prayer may hys pyté byte,
356 Þat mercy schal hyr crafteȝ kyþe.
Hys comforte may þy langour lyþe,
And þy lureȝ of lyȝtly leme;
For marre oþer madde, morne and myþe,
360 Al lys in hym to dyȝt and deme."

334 FOLDE land . . . FLEME may banish   335-36 When I am deprived of my pearl,/What can men expect but enduring distress?"   338 DOTȜ ÞOU SO do you [behave] so   339-40 For cries of mourning concerning insignificant losses,/Many men often forsake the greater happiness.   343 NOT A CRESSE nothing at all   344 ÞOLE suffer . . . ÞRO perverse

Nor how far I am flung from lands I esteem.
When I am parted from pearl divine,
336 Enduring distress is what I deem."

29 "You deem nothing but doleful distress,"
That damsel then said. "Why carry on so?
With cries of grief, men often digress,
340 Forsaking their happiness amid life's flow.
You would do better yourself to bless,
And love God always, in weal and woe,
For anguish gains you less and less,
344 When you must suffer on earth below;
For though you may writhe like any doe,
Brandish and bray, with bitterness steam,
When you can go no further, to nor fro,
348 You must endure what he shall deem.

30 "Deem God cruel in your earthly pit;
Stray he will not one step from his plan.
Your consolations increase not a bit,
352 Though you sit in sorrow, ungracious man.
Cease from strife, disputing quit,
And seek his bliss in this life's span.
Your prayer for pity is not unfit;
356 Mercy's virtues may your turmoils ban.
His solace your misery may softly fan,
And among misfortunes gently gleam;
For fret or fume as fierce as you can,
360 All lies in him to determine and deem."

346 BRAÞEȜ BREME fierce agonies 349 "Blame God; accuse him continually. 350 WRYÞE turn 352 BLYÞE glad 353 FYNE TO FLYTE stop disputing 354 SWEFTE AND SWYÞE swiftly and sincerely 355 BYTE arouse 356 So that mercy shall reveal her virtues. 357 LYÞE soften 359 MORNE AND MYÞE mourn and mutter

f. 48   31   Thenne demed I to þat damyselle:
                "Ne worþe no wrathþe vnto my Lorde,
                If rapely raue, spornande in spelle.
364   My herte watȝ al wyth mysse remorde,
                As wallande water gotȝ out of welle.
                I do me ay in hys myserecorde.
                Rebuke me neuer wyth wordeȝ felle,
368   Þaȝ I forloyne, my dere endorde,
                Bot lyþeȝ me kyndely your coumforde,
                Pytosly þenkande vpon þysse:
                Of care and me ȝe made acorde,
372   Þat er watȝ grounde of alle my blysse.

        32   "My blysse, my bale, ȝe han ben boþe,
                Bot much þe bygger ȝet watȝ my mon.
                Fro þou watȝ wroken fro vch a woþe,
376   I wyste neuer quere my perle watȝ gon.
                Now I hit se; now leþeȝ my loþe.
                And, quen we departed, we wern at on,
                God forbede we be now wroþe.
380   We meten so selden by stok oþer ston.
                Þaȝ cortaysly ȝe carp con,
                I am bot mol and marereȝ mysse;
                Bot Crystes mersy, and Mary and Jon—
384   Þise arn þe grounde of alle my blysse.

        33   "In blysse I se þe blyþely blent,
                And I a man al mornyf mate.
                Ȝe take þeron ful lyttel tente,
388   Þaȝ I hente ofte harmeȝ hate;

361 DEMED said   362 "Let [there] be no offense against my Lord,   363
SPORNANDE IN SPELLE stumbling in speech   364 WYTH MYSSE
REMORDE afflicted with loss   365 WALLANDE pouring   366
MYSERECORDE mercy   367 FELLE austere   368 FORLOYNE go astray .
. . ENDORDE golden maiden

f. 48   31   Then I deemed to answer that damsel:
"I do not intend to offend my Lord,
If rapidly I rave in a ranting spell.

364   Missing you so, remorse in me soared
And sprang forth, spilling like water from well.
Often his mercy my heart has restored.
Rebuke me never with words that tell

368   How I blundered so, my gold maiden adored,
But soothe me softly with solace implored,
Piteously thinking now upon this:
Between care and me you made accord,

372   You who were the ground of all my bliss.

32   "My bliss, my bale, you have been both,
But much the greater was my moan.
When pearl was parted from peril's growth,

376   I knew not where in whatever zone.
Seeing you now, to lament I am loath.
If we were one, in joy full-blown,
God forbid we be now wroth.

380   We meet so seldom by stock or stone.
Though courteous speech you do condone,
I am mere mold and vitality miss;
But Mary, John, and Christ's mercy shown—

384   These are the ground of all my bliss.

33   "To bliss I see you have been sent,
While I mourn and miss my dearest mate.
Concern for me is scarcely spent;

388   My suffering sighs you only berate.

375 WOÞE tribulation   377 LEÞEȜ MY LOÞE my sorrow is soothed   378 If, when we were parted, we were in harmony,   381 CARP CON can speak 385 "I see you eagerly engulfed in bliss,   386 MORNYF MATE mournfully subdued   387–88 You pay very little attention to it,/Though I am often caught by cruel misfortunes;

Bot now I am here in your presente,
I wolde bysech, wythouten debate,
ȝe wolde me say, in sobre asente,
392   What lyf ȝe lede erly and late,
For I am ful fayn þat your astate
Is worþen to worschyp and wele, iwysse.
Of alle my joy, þe hyȝe gate,
396   Hit is in grounde of alle my blysse."

f. 48b   34   "Now blysse, burne, mot þe bytyde,"
Þen sayde þat lufsoum of lyth and lere,
"And welcum here to walk and vyde,
400   For now þy speche is to me dere.
Maysterful mod and hyȝe pryde,
I hete þe, arn heterly hated here.
My Lorde ne loueȝ not for to chyde,
404   For meke arn alle þat woneȝ hym nere;
And when in hys place þou schal apere,
Be dep deuote, in hol mekenesse.
My Lorde þe Lamb loueȝ ay such chere,
408   Þat is þe grounde of alle my blysse.

35   "A blysful lyf þou says I lede;
Þou woldeȝ knaw þerof þe stage.
Þou wost wel when þy perle con schede,
412   I watȝ ful ȝong and tender of age,
Bot my Lorde þe Lombe, þurȝ hys Godhede,
He toke myself to hys maryage,
Corounde me quene in blysse to brede
416   In lenghe of dayeȝ þat euer schal wage;
And sesed in alle hys herytage
Hys lef is. I am holy hysse,
Hys pyese, hys prys; and hys parage

389 PRESENTE presence   391 IN SOBRE ASENTE with serious intention
394 Has come, indeed, to honor and well-being.   395 HYȜE GATE special
kind   397-98 "Now may bliss befall you, sir,"/Then said that lovely one of
figure and face,   399 VYDE wade   402 HETERLY intensely

36

But since I am here, asunder rent,
I would beseech, without debate,
You tell me now, with true intent,
392   What life you lead, early and late,
For I am glad your glorious estate
In honor is nestled and never amiss.
Of all my joy of highest rate,
396   This is the ground of all my bliss."

f. 48b   34   "May blessed bliss now be your guide,"
Said she of slender beauty sheer.
"Be welcome to walk and wade on your side,
400   For now your speech is to me dear.
Masterful mood and pompous pride,
I assure you, surely are hated here.
My gracious Lord cares not to chide,
404   For meek are all to him so near;
And when in his place you shall appear,
Be deeply devout; with meekness kiss.
My Lord the Lamb does love such cheer;
408   He is the ground of all my bliss.

        35   "A blissful life you say I lead;
You wish to know thereof each stage.
You know when your pearl did fall to seed,
412   I was full young, on life's first page,
But my Lord the Lamb fulfilled my need;
In marriage he did me engage,
Crowned me queen, a sacred deed,
416   Where days endure beyond earth's cage.
Endowed with his heritage in every age,
I am his beloved, wholly his,
His pearl, his prize, his to assuage;

404 WONEƷ HYM NERE dwell near him   406 HOL complete   407 AY
always . . . CHERE behavior   411 CON SCHEDE slipped away   415
BREDE dwell   416 WAGE endure   417 SESED endowed   418 LEF beloved
419 His maiden, his honored one; and his lineage

420   Is rote and grounde of alle my blysse."

                              VIII

        36   "Blysful," quoþ I, "may þys be trwe?
                    Dyspleseӡ not if I speke errour.
                    Art þou þe quene of heueneӡ blwe,
424   Þat al þys worlde schal do honour?
                    We leuen on Marye, þat Grace of grewe,
                    Þat ber a Barne, of Vyrgyn Flour.
                    Þe croune fro hyr quo moӡt remwe,
428   Bot ho hir passed in sum fauour?
                    Now, for synglerty o hyr dousour,
                    We calle hyr Fenyx of Arraby,
                    Þat, freles, fleӡe of hyr Fasor,
432   Lyk to þe Quen of Cortaysye."

f. 49   37   "Cortayse Quen," þenne syde þat gaye,
                    Knelande to grounde, folde vp hyr face,
                    "Makeleӡ Moder and myryest May,
436   Blessed Bygynner of vch a grace!"
                    Þenne ros ho vp and con restay,
                    And speke me towarde in þat space.
                    "Sir, fele here porchaseӡ and fongeӡ pray,
440   Bot supplantoreӡ none wythinne þys place.
                    Þat Emperise al heuenӡ hatӡ,
                    And vrþe and helle in her bayly.
                    Of erytage, ӡet, non wyl ho chace,
444   For ho is Quen of Cortaysye.

        38   "The court of þe kyndom of God alyue
                    Hatӡ a property in hyt self beyng.
                    Alle þat may þerinne aryue
448   Of alle þe reme is quen oþer kyng,

429 Now, because of [the] singularity of her sweetness   433 GAYE fair
maiden 434 FOLDE covering 435 MYRYEST MAY brightest Virgin

                              38

420   He is root and ground of all my bliss."

                        VIII

        36   "Blissful girl, can this be true?
                Be not displeased if I now err.
                Are you the queen of the heavens blue,
424   On whom all the world must honor confer?
                We accept only Mary, from whom Grace grew,
                Who bore a child, the Virgin's Flower.
                Unless she surpassed her in some virtue,
428   Who could remove the crown from her?
                Now, seeing her singly sweet manner,
                We call her Phoenix of Araby,
                Who, without fault, flew from her Maker,
432   Just like the Queen of Courtesy."

f. 49   37   "Courteous Queen," that maiden did say,
                Kneeling and holding her hands over her face,
                "Matchless Mother, bright Virgin of May,
436   Blessed Beginner of every grace!"
                Then she arose and did delay,
                And spoke to me at a pleasant pace.
                "Sir, many reach here to gain God's ray,
440   But no supplanters are in this place.
                That Empress has heaven as ruling base,
                And earth and hell in her supremacy.
                Yet, none from their heritage will she chase,
444   For she is Queen of Courtesy.

        38   "The court of the kingdom of God alive
                Has an attribute in its very being.
                Each soul who may therein arrive
448   Of all the realm is queen or king,

438–39 And spoke to me after that interval./"Sir, many strive for here and
receive [the] reward,   442 BAYLY jurisdiction

And neuer oþer ʒet schal depryue;
Bot, vch on fayn of oþereʒ hafyng,
And wolde her corouneʒ wern worþe þo fyue,
452   If possyble were her mendyng;
Bot my Lady, of quom Jesu con spryng,
Ho haldeʒ þe empyre ouer vus full hyʒe,
And þat dyspleseʒ non of oure gyng,
456   For ho is Quene of Cortaysye.

39   "Of courtaysye, as saytʒ Saynt Poule,
Al arn we membreʒ of Jhesu Kryst.
As heued and arme and legg and naule
460   Temen to hys body, ful trwe and tyste,
Ryʒt so is vch a Krysten sawle
A longande lym to þe Mayster of Myste.
Þenne loke what hate oþer any gawle
464   Is tached oþer tyʒed þy lymmeʒ bytwyste.
Þy heued hatʒ nauþer greme ne gryste
On arme oþer fynger, þaʒ þou ber byʒe.
So fare we alle wyth luf and lyste
468   To kyng and quene by cortaysye."

f. 49b   40   "Cortaysé," quoþ I, "I leue,
And charyté grete be yow among,
Bot my speche þat yow ne greue—
472   . . . .
Þyself in heuen ouer hyʒ þou heue,
To make þe quen, þat watʒ so ʒonge.
What more honour moʒte he acheue,
476   Þat hade endured in worlde stronge,
And lyued in penaunce hys lyueʒ longe,
Wyth bodyly bale hym blysse to byye?
What more worschyp moʒt ho fonge

453 OF QUOM JESU CON SPRYNG from whom Jesus did spring   455
GYNG assemblage   460 FUL TRWE AND TYSTE fully secure and joined
462 A member belonging to the Master of Spiritual Mysteries.   463 GAWLE
envy   464 Is rooted or fastened among your limbs.

	And yet shall never others deprive,
	For each one is happy with others' having,
	And would wish their crowns were then worth five,
452	If possible were their improving;
	But my Lady, chosen from Christ's beginning,
	Rules the empire, indeed, supremely,
	And that displeases none of us seeing
456	That she is Queen of Courtesy.

	39	"Due to courtesy, as says Saint Paul,
		We are all members of Jesus Christ.
		As head and limbs and navel all
460		Belong to his body, so highly priced,
		Just so is each soul for Christ to enthrall
		A marvelous member, to the Master enticed.
		Now see if hate or any gall
464		Is attached where bodily branches tryst.
		No ire or envy has head, the highest,
		Against arm or finger in fine jewelry.
		Thus all of us live with love unbiased
468		As kings and queens with courtesy."

f. 49b	40	"Courtesy clean, I firmly believe,
		And charity great to you have clung,
		But since my speech does you not grieve,
472		[I will speak again where words have sprung.]
		Yourself in heaven too high you heave,
		To claim to be a queen so young.
		What more honor might one achieve
476		Who endured on earth, though often stung,
		And lived in penance, lifelong unsung,
		Through bodily bale securing glee?
		What more esteem to a soul is swung

465 GREME NE GRYSTE anger nor resentment   466 BER BY3E wear jewelry   467 LYSTE happiness   476 STRONGE steadfastly   477 HYS LYUE3 LONGE throughout the length of his life   478 To secure happiness for himself through human suffering?   479 HO FONGE he obtain

480 Þen corounde be kyng by cortaysé?

IX

41 "That cortaysé is to fre of dede,
3yf hyt be soth þat þou coneȝ saye.
Þou lyfed not two ȝer in oure þede.
484 þou cowþeȝ neuer God nauþer plese ne pray,
Ne neuer nawþer Pater ne Crede,
And quen mad on þe fyrst day!
I may not traw, so God me spede,
488 Þat God wolde wryþe so wrange away.
Of countes, damysel, par ma fay,
Wer fayr in heuen to halde asstate,
Oþer elleȝ a lady of lasse aray;
492 Bot a quene—hit is to dere a date!"

42 "Þer is no date of hys godnesse,"
Þen sayde to me þat worþy wyȝte,
"For al is trawþe þat he con dresse,
496 And he may do noþynk bot ryȝt.
As Mathew meleȝ in your messe
In sothfol Gospel of God Almyȝt,
Insample he can ful grayþely gesse,
500 And lykneȝ hit to heuen lyȝte.
'My regne,' he saytȝ, 'is lyk on hyȝt
To a lorde þat hade a uyne I wate.
Of tyme of ȝere þe terme watȝ tyȝt,
504 To labor vyne watȝ dere þe date.

f. 50 43 " 'Þat date of ȝere wel knawe þys hyne.
Þe lorde ful erly vp he ros
To hyre werkmen to hys vyne,

487 TRAW believe . . . SPEDE may bless   488 WRYÞE turn   489 PAR MA
FAY by my faith   490 ASSTATE rank   492 DERE A DATE glorious a
beginning   493 DATE end   494 WYȜTE maiden   497 MELEȜ tells

480   Than to be crowned king through courtesy?

IX

41   "That courtesy is to free in deed,
If it be true what you do say.
Not two years in our land did your life exceed.

484   You could never either please God or pray,
Not ever either Pater or Creed,
And queen you became on the first day!
I cannot concede the God we heed

488   Would turn and wander so wrongly away.
As a countess, damsel, perhaps you may
Fairly hold rank in heaven's estate,
Or else a lady of lesser array,

492   But for queen it seems too soon a date."

42   "Dateless, indeed, is his goodness,"
Then said that worthy maiden in white,
"For only truth does he address,

496   And what he reveals is always right.
As Matthew in your mass does stress
In the Gospel great of the God of Might,
This parable Christ does skillfully express,

500   And likens it to the heaven of light.
'My realm,' he says, 'up on that height
To a lord and his vineyard does relate.
In season set on vineyard's site,

504   To cultivate, it was a splendid date.

f. 50   43   " 'These households know well that date in the year.
The lord full early then arose
To hire workmen for his vineyard dear.

498 SOTHFOL truthful   499 He does very fittingly devise [a] parable,   502
WATE know   503 TERME period . . . TY3T appointed   504 The season was
excellent to cultivate [the] vineyard.

508   And fyndeȝ þer summe to hys porpos.
         Into accorde þay con declyne
         For a pené on a day, and forth þay gotȝ,
         Wryþen, and worchen, and don gret pyne,
512   Keruen, and caggen, and man hit clos.
         Aboute vnder þe lorde to marked totȝ,
         And ydel men stande he fyndeȝ þerate.
         "Why stande ȝe ydel?" he sayde to þos.
516   "Ne knawe ȝe of þis day no date?"

44   " ' "Er date of daye hider arn we wonne."
         So watȝ al samen her answar soȝt.
         "We haf standen her syn ros þe sunne,
520   And no mon byddeȝ vus do ryȝt noȝt."
         "Gos into my vyne; dotȝ þat ȝe conne."
         So sayde þe lorde and made hit toȝt.
         "What resonabele hyre be naȝt be runne
524   I yow pray, in dede and þoȝte."
         Þay wente into þe vyne and wroȝte,
         And al day þe lorde þus ȝede his gate,
         And nw men to hys vyne he broȝte
528   Welneȝ wyl day watȝ passed date.

45   " 'At þe day, of date of euensonge,
         On oure byfore þe sonne go doun,
         He seȝ þer ydel men, ful stronge,
532   And sade to hen wyth sobre soun,
         "Wy stonde ȝe ydel þise dayeȝ longe?"
         Þay sayden her hyre watȝ nawhere boun.
         "Gotȝ to my vyne, ȝe men ȝonge,
536   And wyrkeȝ and dotȝ þat at ȝe moun."
         Sone þe worlde bycom wel broun;

509 DECLYNE submit   510 GOTȜ go   511 DON GRET PYNE exert great
effort   512 MAN HIT CLOS make them (the vines) secure   513 VNDER the
third hour   514 FYNDEȜ ÞERATE finds in that place   517 DATE OF
DAYE dawning of day . . . WONNE come   518 SOȜT given   520 RYȜT
NOȜT anything at all   521 DOTȜ ÞAT ȜE CONNE do what you can

508	Finding there some, his plan he shows,
	And they all agree to contract clear
	For a penny a day, their time to dispose.
	They twist and toil, travailing with gear,
512	Cut and bind where each branch grows.
	About nine the lord to market goes,
	And idle men standing he does berate.
	"Why do you stand idle?" he said to those.
516	"Do you not know the hour on this date?"

	44	" ' "Before dawn on this date here did we run."
		Together they gave the answer he sought.
		"Here have we stood since rose the sun,
520		And no one has our labor bought."
		"Go into my vineyard in unison."
		So said the lord, his statement taut.
		"What reasonable service by night may be spun
524		I ask of you, in deed and thought."
		They went to the vineyard, no longer distraught,
		And all day the lord, at leisurely rate,
		New men to his vineyard steadily brought,
528		As the day drove near its ending date.

	45	" 'That day at date of evensong,
		One hour before the sun goes down,
		He saw there idle men, full strong,
532		And asked these workers in the town,
		"Why are you idle this day so long?"
		No hiring was arranged they said with frown.
		"Go to my vineyard where men belong,
536		And work in there to win renown."
		Soon the earth grew dark and brown;

522 TO3T binding   523 BE NA3T BE RUNNE may be discharged by night
525 WRO3TE worked   526 3EDE HIS GATE went his way   528 Almost
until [the] day had passed [its] end.   532 HEN laborers . . . SOBRE SOUN
serious voice   534 BOUN arranged   536 And work and do that which you
can."   537 BROUN dark

Þe sunne watȝ doun, and and hit wex late,
To take her hyre he mad sumoun.
540   Þe day watȝ al apassed date.

X

" 'The date of þe daye þe lorde con knaw;
            Called to þe reue: "Lede, pay þe meyny.
        Gyf hem þe hyre þat I hem owe,
544   And, fyrre, þat non me may reprené,
        Set hem alle vpon a rawe,
        And gyf vch on inlyche a peny.
        Bygyn at þe laste þat standeȝ lowe,
548   Tyl to þe fyrste þat þou atteny."
        And þenne þe fyrst bygonne to pleny,
        And sayden þat þay hade trauayled sore.
        "Þese bot on oure hem con streny.
552   Vus þynk vus oȝe to take more.

        47   " ' "More haf we serued, vus þynk so,
        Þat suffred han þe dayeȝ hete,
        Þenn þyse þat wroȝt not houreȝ two;
556   And þou dotȝ hem vus to counterfete!"
        Þenne sayde þe lorde to on of þo:
        "Frende, no waning I wyl þe ȝete.
        Take þat is þyn owne and go.
560   And I hyred þe for a peny, agrete,
        Quy bygynneȝ þou now to þrete?
        Watȝ not a pené þy couenaunt þore?
        Fyrre þen couenaunde is noȝt to plete.
564   Wy schalte þou, þenne, ask more?

        48   " ' "More, weþer, louyly is me my gyfte,

539 HYRE payment . . . SUMOUN summons   540 The day had entirely
passed [its] end.   541 DATE OF ÞE DAYE time of the day   548 ATTENY
reach   549 PLENY complain   551 STRENY strain

The sun was down, and when it became late,
He prepared to pay them, their day to crown,

540   For the day had passed on that wearisome date.

X

      " 'The time on that date the lord did know;
He called to his reeve: "Man, pay the company.
Give the workers the wage I owe,

544   And, furthermore, so none may blame me,
Set them all upon a row,
And pay each one fully a penny.
Go from the last who stand there low

548   Up to the first; do not neglect any."
Then the first called this uncanny,
And said they had travailed sore.
"These strained one hour, unlike so many;

552   It seems to us we should have more.

        47   " ' "We deserve more, we say to you,
Having endured the long day's heat,
Than these who toiled not hours two;

556   And you call their work like ours complete!"
Then said the lord to one of the crew:
"Friend, I truly do not mistreat.
Receive your wage and do not rue.

560   If I hired you for a penny, replete,
Arguing now is indiscreet.
Was not a penny your pact before?
To exceed that pay would be unmeet.

564   Why shall you, then, be seeking more?

        48   " ' "Still more gracious from me is the gift,

556 And you consider them to be like us!"   557 ON OF ÞO one of them   558
"Friend, I intend to do you no harm.   560 AGRETE all told   561 ÞRETE
wrangle   562 ÞORE then   563 TO PLETE to be claimed

To do wyth myn quatso me lyke3,
Oþer elle3 þyn y3e to lyþer is lyfte
568 For I am goude and non byswyke3?"
'Þus schal I,' quoþ Kryste, 'hit skyfte.
Þe laste schal be þe fyrst þat stryke3,
And þe fyrst þe laste, be he neuer so swyft,
572 For mony ben calle, þa3 fewe be myke3.'
Þus pore men her part ay pyke3,
Þa3 þay com late and lyttel wore,
And þa3 her sweng wyth lyttel atslyke3,
576 Þe merci of God is much þe more.

f. 51 49 "More haf I of joye and blysse hereinne,
Of ladyschyp gret and lyue3 blom,
Þen alle þe wy3e3 in þe worlde my3t wynne,
580 By þe way of ry3t to aske dome.
Wheþer welnygh now I con bygynne
In euentyde, into þe vyne I come.
Fyrst of my hyre my Lorde con mynne.
584 I wat3 payed anon, of al and sum.
3et, oþer þer werne þat toke more tom,
Þat swange and swat for long 3ore,
Þat 3et of hyre noþynk þay nom,
588 Paraunter no3t schal to 3ere more."

50 Then more I meled and sayde apert:
"Me þynk þy tale vnresounable.
Godde3 ry3t is redy and euermore rert,
592 Oþer Holy Wryt is bot a fable.
In Sauter is sayd a verce ouerte,
Þat speke3 a poynt determynable.
'Þou quyte3 vch on as hys desserte,

567 LYÞER malice 568 BYSWYKE3 deprive 569 HIT SKYFTE arrange it
570 STRYKE3 enters 572 MYKE3 chosen ones 574 LYTTEL WORE
expend little effort 575 And though their labor may slip away with little
result, 580 In seeking judgment through the means of justice. 583 My Lord
did think of my reward first.

48

		In doing with mine whatever I please,
		Or do your eyes toward envy lift
568		Because I am good to all employees?"
		'Thus,' said Christ, 'such is my drift.
		The last shall be first in heavenly ease,
		And the first the last, be he ever so swift,
572		For many are called, but few chosen from these.'
		Thus humble men their share do seize,
		Though they come late after little dolor,
		And though their work ends like a waning breeze,
576		The mercy of God is much the more.

f. 51   49   "More glory and bliss have I herein,
             Of ladyship great and life in bloom,
             Than all the mortals in world might win,
580   In seeking judgment and justice presume.
             Though I quickly did begin
             Near eventide in vineyard's room,
             The Lord's favor first came to me from him;
584   I was paid at once where love does loom.
             Yet, others there were in earthly gloom,
             Laboring long with little in store,
             Who still reward could not assume,
588   And perhaps shall not for some years more."

         50 Then more I spoke with speech alert:
             "Your story seems unreasonable.
             God's right is readily in concert,
592   Or Holy Writ is but a fable.
             The Psalter shows a verse overt,
             Which decrees a point determinable.
             'You give to each his just desert,

584 OF AL AND SUM in every respect   585 TOM time   586–87 Who formerly had labored and sweat for [a] long while,/Who had yet received nothing of [their] reward,   589 APERT openly   591 RERT fixed   593 OUERTE simple   594 Which relates a definite point.   595 QUYTE3 reward . . . DESSERTE merit

596		Þou hyȝe Kyng, ay pertermynable.'
		Now he þat stod þe long day stable,
		And þou to payment com hym byfore,
		Þenne þe lasse in werke to take more able,
600		And euer þe lenger, þe lasse, þe more."

XI

	51	"Of more and lasse in Godeȝ ryche,"
		Þat gentyl sayde, "lys no joparde,
		For þer is vch mon payed inlyche,
604		Wheþer lyttel oþer much be hys rewarde;
		For þe gentyl Cheuentayn is no chyche,
		Queþersoeuer he dele nesch oþer harde.
		He laueȝ hys gyfteȝ as water of dyche,
608		Oþer gotȝ of golf þat neuer charde.
		Hys fraunchyse is large þat euer dard
		To hym þat matȝ in synne rescoghe.
		No blysse betȝ fro hem reparde,
612		For þe grace of God is gret inoghe.

f. 51b	52	"Bot, now þou moteȝ, me for to mate,
		Þat I my peny haf wrang tan here.
		Þou sayȝ þat I þat com to late
616		Am not worþy so gret lere.
		Where wysteȝ þou euer any bourne abate,
		Euer so holy in hys prayere,
		Þat he ne forfeted by sumkyn gate
620		Þe mede, sumtyme, of heueneȝ clere?
		And ay þe ofter þe alder þay were
		Þay laften ryȝt and wroȝten woghe.

596 PERTERMYNABLE judging perfectly   599-600 Then those who work less are able to receive more,/And increasingly, the less [they do], the more [they receive]."   601 RYCHE kingdom   602 JOPARDE confusion   603 PAYED INLYCHE fully compensated   605 CHYCHE miser   606 NESCH OÞER HARDE gently or firmly   607 LAUEȜ pours forth

596 High King of perfect judgment capable.'
     If one has stayed the long day stable,
     And you for payment come before,
     Then less of work makes one more payable,
600 And ever onward, less work gets more."

                    XI

51   "Of more and less in God's realm rich,"
     That damsel said, "no disorders exist,
     For each receives full pay in his niche,
604 Whether little or much is on his list;
     For the Chieftain from giving will never switch,
     Whether dealing gently or with firm fist.
     His gifts flow swiftly like floods in a ditch,
608 Or currents in whirlpools that never desist.
     His reward is great who transcends earth's mist;
     He beckons all sinners, being mild, not gruff.
     In perfect bliss, in heaven they enlist,
612 For the grace of God is great enough.

f. 51b 52 "Enough am I vexed when you now claim
     I wrongly won my penny here.
     You say that I who too late came
616 Am not worthy of this dwelling clear.
     Was there ever a human, humbly without blame,
     Ever so holy, with prayers to endear,
     Who did not forfeit, within life's frame,
620 The reward, sometime, of heaven's cheer?
     And always more often the older appear
     To stray from right, so their souls grow rough.

608 CHARDE varied   609–10 His privilege is great who always stood in
awe/Of him who brings salvation from sin.   611 BET3 will be . . .
REPARDE withheld   613 MOTE3 claim . . . MATE disconcert   614 TAN
obtained   616 LERE abode   617 Where did you ever know any man to bow
humbly,   619 SUMKYN GATE some kind of way   622 WOGHE wrong

Mercy and grace moste hem þen stere,

624   For þe grace of God is gret innoȝe.

53   "Bot, innoghe of grace hatȝ innocent.
As sone as þay arn borne by lyne,
In þe water of babtem þay dyssente.

628   Þen arne þay boroȝt into þe vyne.
Anon, þe day, wyth derk endente,
Þe niyȝt of deth dotȝ to enclyne.
Þat wroȝt neuer wrang er þenne þay wente

632   Þe gentyle Lorde þenne payeȝ hys hyne.
Þay dyden hys heste; þay wern þereine.
Why schulde he not her labour alow—
Ȝys, and pay hym at þe fyrst fyne?

636   For þe grace of God is gret innoghe.

54   "Inoȝe is knawen þat mankyn grete
Fyrst watȝ wroȝt to blysse parfyt.
Oure forme-fader hit con forfete

640   Þurȝ an apple þat he vpon con byte.
Al wer we dampned, for þat mete,
To dyȝe in doel, out of delyt,
And syþen wende to helle hete,

644   Þerinne to won wythoute respyt;
Bot þeron com a bote as-tyt.
Ryche blod ran on rode so roghe,
And wynne water, þen, at þat plyt.

648   Þe grace of God wex gret innoghe.

f. 52   55   "Innoghe þer wax out of þat welle,
Blod and water of brode wounde.
Þe blod vus boȝt fro bale of helle,

652   And delyuered vus of þe deth secounde.

626 BY LYNE through lineal descent   627 DYSSENTE descend   629 WYTH
DERK ENDENTE adorned by dusk   630 Does yield to the night of death.
632 HYS HYNE as his servants   633 HESTE bidding   635 Yes, and
recompense them with the first group completely?

624 Then mercy and grace must them steer,
For the grace of God is great enough.

53 "Enough of grace have the innocent.
After their birth in lineal line,
And baptismal blessing excellent,
628 They are brought into the yard of vine.
Soon, the day, toward darkness bent,
To night of death does then incline.
Who never did wrong before they went
632 The kind Lord pays, a blissful sign.
They bowed to his behest divine.
Should he not allow their labor tough,
And payment full to them consign?
636 The grace of God is great enough.

54 "Enough is it known that mankind proud
First was made for bliss full bright.
Our foremost father shamefully bowed
640 Through the forbidden apple that he did bite.
Damned were we then in sinful crowd,
To die in distress, away from delight,
And then sent to hell, no heaven allowed,
644 Therein to dwell, devoid of light.
The came a cure through God's great might,
When rich blood ran on rood on bluff,
And pure water, then, during that plight.
648 The grace of God flowed great enough.

f. 52 55 "Enough there gushed from that great well,
Blood and water from wound not bound.
The blood saved us from searing hell,
652 And from second death's pursuing hound.

638 WRO3T created . . . PARFYT perfect   641 METE meal   643 WENDE
to go . . . HETE heat   644 WON remain . . . RESPYT respite   645 But after
that a pardon came quickly.   651 BALE torments   652 And delivered us from
the second death.

Þe water is baptem, þe soþe to telle,
Þat folȝed þe glayue so grymly grounde,
Þat wascheȝ away þe gylteȝ felle
656   Þat Adam wyth inne deth vus drounde.
Now is þer noȝt in þe worlde rounde
Bytwene vus and blysse, bot þat he wythdroȝ,
And þat is restored in sely stounde,
660   And þe grace of God is gret innogh.

XII

56   "Grace innogh þe mon may haue,
       Þat synneȝ þenne new, ȝif hym repente,
    Bot wyth sorȝ and syt he mot hit craue,
664   And byde þe payne þerto is bent;
    Bot resoun of ryȝt þat con not raue
    Saueȝ euermore þe innossent.
    Hit is a dom þat neuer God gaue,
668   Þat euer the gyltleȝ schulde be schente.
    Þe gyltyf may contryssyoun hente,
    And be þurȝ mercy to grace þryȝt,
    Bot he to gyle þat neuer glente
672   At inoscente is saf and ryȝte.

57   "Ryȝt þus, þus, I knaw wel in þis cas,
    Two men to saue is God, by skylle,
    Þe ryȝtwys man schal se hys face,
676   þe harmleȝ haþel schal com hym tylle.
    Þe Sauter hyt satȝ þus in a pace:
    'Lorde, quo schal klymbe þy hyȝ hylle,
    Oþer rest wythinne þy holy place?'

653 SOÞE truth   654 FOLȜED ÞE GLAYUE resulted from the spear   655 GYLTEȜ FELLE bitterness of sin   656 With which Adam drowned us in death.   658 BOT ÞAT HE WYTHDROȜ except what he (Adam) rescinded 659 SELY STOUNDE blessed hour   664 PAYNE penalty . . . BENT attached 665 But [the] cause of justice which can not err

54

Baptismal water in wellspring's swell
Is due to spear so keenly ground;
It washes away guilt's wicked spell,
656   Unwound from Adam's sin unsound.
Now there is nothing in this world round
To block our bliss, for his rebuff
Is restored when one with baptism is crowned,
660   For the grace of God is great enough.

XII

56   "Grace enough gets the man so grave,
Who sins anew, if he repent;
With regret and grief he must it crave,
664   And abide the pain and penalty sent.
Unerring justice a path does pave
To always save the innocent.
Doleful doom God never gave,
668   To send the guiltless to punishment.
The guilty who for sins lament
Are immersed in mercy, with grace in sight;
But who never groveled in guile's ferment
672   With the innocent is redeemed by right.

57   "Rightly so, I know in this case,
If to save two souls it is God's will,
The righteous one shall see his face,
676   The innocent near his throne shall thrill.
The Psalter sets the scene apace:
'Lord, who shall climb your great, high hill,
Or rest within your holy place?'

667 DOM sentence   668 SCHENTE punished   669 HENTE obtain   670 ÞRYƷT thrust   671 GYLE deceit . . . GLENTE deviated   672 Is redeemed and justified with [the] innocent.   673 RYƷT ÞUS, ÞUS, rightly so, therefore, 674 SKYLLE agreement   676 The innocent person shall go to him.   677 SATƷ says . . . PACE passage

680	Hymself to onsware he is not dylle:
	'Hondelyngeӡ harme þat dyt not ille,
	Þat is of hert boþe clene and lyӡt,
	Þer schal hys step stable stylle.'
684	Þe innocent is ay saf by ryӡt.

f. 52b   58   "The ryӡtwys man also sertayn
Aproche he schal þat proper pyle—
Þat takeӡ not her lyf in vayne,
688   Ne glauereӡ her nieӡbor wyth no gyle.
Of þys ryӡtwys, saӡ Salamon playn
How kyntly oure con aquyle.
By wayeӡ ful streӡt he con hym strayn,
692   And scheued hym þe rengne of God awhyle.
As quo says, 'Lo, ӡon louely yle!
Þou may hit wynne if þou be wyӡte.'
Bot, hardyly, wythoute peryle,
696   Þe innocent is ay saue by ryӡte.

59   "Anende ryӡtwys men, ӡet saytӡ a gome,
Dauid in Sauter, if euer ӡe seӡ hit:
'Lorde, þy seruaunt draӡ neuer to dome,
700   For non lyuyande to þe is justyfyet.'
Forþy, to corte quen þou schal com,
Þer alle oure causeӡ schal be tryed,
Alegge þe ryӡt, þou may be innome
704   By þys ilke spech I haue asspyed.
Bot, he on rode þat blody dyed,
Delfully þurӡ hondeӡ þryӡt,
Gyue þe to passe, when þou arte tryed,
708   By innocens, and not by ryӡte.

60   "Ryӡtwysly quo con rede

680 DYLLE slow   682 LYӡT brave   683 STABLE STYLLE settle
permanently 685 SERTAYN certainly 686 PROPER PYLE perfect dwelling
689 SAӡ reveals . . . PLAYN clearly 690 How kindly mercy did prevail.
691 HYM STRAYN direct himself 692 SCHEUED appeared

680   He himself answers with speed and skill:
    'Who never with hands has done any ill,
    Who is perfectly pure within God's sight,
    There shall he settle, forever will.'
684   The innocent one is redeemed by right.

f. 52b 58 "The righteous man may certainly deign
    To approach that place in proper file,
    Having taken not his life in vain,
688   Nor cheated his neighbor through any guile.
    This righteous man, Solomon did explain,
    Secured sweet mercy with splendid smile.
    On paths full straight he did remain,
692   And to him appeared God's reign for awhile.
    As one may say, 'Behold, that lovely isle,
    Which you may win with brave foresight!'
    But, truly, without any perilous trial,
696   The innocent one is redeemed by right.

    59 "Concerning righteous men, yet says a man,
    David in Psalter, where truths preside:
    'Lord, spare your servant from judgment's plan,
700   For no one living is, before you, justified.'
    So when you come to his court's clan,
    Where all our causes shall be tried,
    To allege your right yourself you ban,
704   Due to that speech I have applied.
    But, he on rood who bloodily died,
    His pure hands pierced with pain in that plight,
    May permit you to pass, when you are tried,
708   Through innocence, and not by right.

    60 "Who righteously have ever read

694 WYȝTE courageous 695 HARDYLY certainly 698 SEȝ saw 699
DRAȝ bring . . . DOME judgment 703 INNOME trapped 704 ILKE same .
. . ASSPYED noted 706 DELFULLY painfully . . . ÞRYȝT pierced 708
RYȝTE justice 709 RYȝTWYSLY correctly

He loke on bok and be awayed
How Jhecu hym welke in areþede,

712 And burneȝ her barneȝ vnto hym brayde
For happe and hele þat fro hym ȝede.
To touch her chylder þay fayr hym prayed.
His dessypeleȝ, wyth blame, let be hym bede,

716 And wyth her resouneȝ ful fele restayed.
Jhecu þenne hem swetely sayde:
'Do way! Let chylder vnto me tyȝt;
To suche is heuenryche arayed.'

720 Þe innocent is ay saf by ryȝt.

XIII

f. 53   61   "Ihecu con calle to hym hys mylde,
And sayde hys ryche no wyȝ myȝt wynne,
Bot he com þyder ryȝt as a chylde,

724 Oþer elleȝ neuermore com þerinne.
Harmleȝ, trwe, and vndefylde,
Wythouten mote oþer mascle of sulpande synne,
Quen such þer cnoken on þe bylde,

728 Tyt schal hem men þe ȝate vnpynne.
Þer is þe blys þat con not blynne,
Þat þe jueler soȝte þurȝ perré pres,
And solde alle hys goud, boþe wolen and lynne,

732 To bye hym a perle watȝ mascelleȝ.

62   "This makelleȝ perle þat boȝt is dere,
Þe joueler gef fore alle hys god,
Is lyke þe reme of heuenesse clere.

736 So sayde þe Fader of folde and flode;

710 AWAYED informed   711 WELKE IN AREÞEDE walked among ancient
folk   712-13 And people brought their children to him/For [the] blessings and
healings that flowed from him.   714 FAYR courteously   715 LET BE HYM
BEDE ordered to let him be   716 FUL FELE RESTAYED restrained very
many   718 TYȜT come   727 BYLDE edifice

May look on the book before them laid,
And see how Jesus strode ahead
712   Where people then their young displayed
To gain the blessed balm he bred.
To touch their children they humbly prayed.
His disciples said to stop instead,
716   Restraining many with statements made.
Jesus then them sweetly bade:
'Step away! Let children come without fright;
For such is heaven's realm arrayed.'
720   The innocent child is redeemed by right.

XIII

f. 53   61   "Jesus called his disciples, so mild,
And said his realm no soul could win,
Unless he rightly arrive as a child,
724   Or else nevermore will he enter therein.
Innocent, honest, and undefiled,
Without stain or spot of polluting sin,
When such there knock, far from earth's wild,
728   Keepers shall quickly the gate unpin.
Therein is bliss in constant spin,
That the jeweler sought through gems to assess,
Selling his wool, and linen thin,
732   To purchase a pearl so spotless.

62   "This peerless, spotless pearl bought dear,
For which the jeweler gave all on hand,
Is like the realm of heaven clear.
736   So said the father of sea and land;

729 BLYNNE cease (Translating 'spin' at the end of this line accords with the description of encircling souls in heaven in line 1186. See the Commentary to that line.)   730 PERRÉ PRES precious stones   733 MAKELLE3 peerless   734 GOD wealth   735 HEUENESSE CLERE heaven's brightness   736 FOLDE AND FLODE land and water

For hit is wemleʒ, clene, and clere,
And endeleʒ rounde, and blyþe of mode,
And commune to alle þat ryʒtywys were.
740   Lo, euen inmyddeʒ my breste hit stode!
My Lorde, þe Lombe, þat schede hys blode,
He pyʒt hit þere in token of pes.
I rede þe forsake þe worlde wode
744   And porchace þy perle maskelles."

63   "O maskeleʒ perle in perleʒ pure,
Þat bereʒ," quoþ I, "þe perle of prys,
Quo formed þe þy fayre fygure,
748   Þat wroʒt þy wede, he watʒ ful wys.
Þy beauté com neuer of nature;
Pymalyon paynted neuer þy vys,
Ne Arystotel nawþer, by hys lettrure,
752   Of carpe þe kynde þese propertéʒ.
Þy colour passeʒ þe flour-de-lys;
Þyn angel-hauyng so clene corteʒ.
Breue me, bryʒt, quat-kyn offys
756   Bereʒ þe perle so maskelleʒ?"

f. 53b   64   "My makeleʒ Lambe þat al may bete,"
Quoþ scho, "my dere Destyné,
Me ches to hys make, alþaʒ vnmete
760   Sumtyme semed þat assemblé.
When I wente fro yor worlde wete,
He calde me to hys bonerté.
'Cum hyder to me, my lemman swete,
764   For mote ne spot is non in þe.'
He gef me myʒt and als bewté.
In hys blod he wesch my wede on dese,

737 CLERE sparkling   738 BLYÞE OF MODE fair in appearance   739
RYʒTYWYS WERE would be righteous   740 HIT STODE its position   743
REDE advise . . . WODE mad   746 PRYS price   747 Whoever formed your
fair figure for you,   748 WROʒT ÞY WEDE designed your vesture   751
LETTRURE writing

For it is flawless, pure, of great cheer,
Perfectly round, so fair and grand,
And common to all who right revere.

740   Amid my breast it now does stand;
My Lord, the Lamb, whose blood death banned,
Placed it there, his peace to impress.
Forsake this world with madness spanned,

744   And purchase your pearl so spotless."

63   "O spotless pearl in pearls so pure,
Who bears," said I, "the pearl to prize,
Whoever fashioned your fine vesture

748   And figure fair was fully wise.
Never in nature was such beauty sure;
Pygmalion your visage did never devise,
Nor did Aristotle either, in works that endure,

752   To such perfect properties ever give rise.
Your color the fleur-de-lis decries;
Your angelic demeanor accords no less.
Tell me, bright maiden, what royal ties

756   Maintains the pearl so spotless?"

f. 53b   64   "My peerless, spotless Lamb I met,"
Said she, "my precious Destiny,
Chose me as bride, my bliss to get,

760   Although unmeet was I formerly.
When I rose above earth's maddening net,
He called me to him graciously.
'Come, fair darling; do not fret.

764   No stain spoils your supremacy.'
He gave me might and great beauty.
On dais he washed in blood my dress,

752 Speak of the character of these qualities.   754 SO CLENE CORTE3
accords so completely   755 QUAT-KYN OFFYS what kind of position   757
MAKELE3 peerless . . . BETE comfort   759 VNMETE unsuitable   760
ASSEMBLÉ union   761 WETE maddened   762 BONERTÉ goodness   763
LEMMAN SWETE sweet darling   764 For stain or spot is not in you.'

| | | And coronde clene in vergynté, |
| 768 | | And pyȝt me in perleȝ maskelleȝ." |

	65	"Why, maskelleȝ bryd, þat bryȝt con flambe,
		Þat reiateȝ hatȝ so ryche and ryf,
		Quat-kyn þyng may be þat Lambe
772		Þat þe wolde wedde vnto hys vyf?
		Ouer alle oþer so hyȝ þou clambe,
		To lede wyth hym so ladyly lyf.
		So mony a comly anvnnder cambe
776		For Kryst han lyued in much stryf;
		And þou con alle þo dere out dryf,
		And fro þat maryag al oþer depres,
		Al-only þyself, so stout and styf,
780		A makeleȝ may, and maskelleȝ!"

XIV

	66	"Maskelles," quoþ þat myry quene,
		"Vnblemyst I am, wythouten blot,
		And þat may I wyth mensk menteene,
784		Bot 'makeleȝ Quene' þenne sade I not.
		Þe Lambes vyueȝ in blysse we bene,
		A hondred and forty þowsande flot,
		As in þe Apocalyppeȝ hit is sene.
788		Sant Johan hem syȝ al in a knot
		On þe hyl of Syon, þat semly clot.
		Þe apostel hem segh in gostly drem,
		Arayed to þe weddyng in þat hyl-coppe,
792		Þe nwe cyté o Jerusalem.

| f. 54 | 67 | "Of Jerusalem I in speche spelle, |

769 CON FLAMBE does sparkle 770 Who possesses royal powers so rich and abundant, 772 VYF wife 773 CLAMBE climbed 774 SO LADYLY LYF life so exalted 775 So many a noble lady beneath [her] headdress 777 And you did drive out all those noble women,

Crowned me clean in virginity,
768 And adorned me in pearls so spotless."

65 "Why, spotless bride, who brightly glows,
With royalty rich, so rifely hale,
What kind of Being is the Lamb who chose
772 To make you wife, a maid so frail?
Above all others so high you rose,
To lead a life without travail.
So many noble ladies, God knows,
776 Have lived for Christ in strife and bale;
And above them all you did prevail,
Beyond them all you did transgress,
Solely by yourself in nuptial veil,
780 A matchless maiden, and spotless!"

XIV

66 "Spotless," said that splendid queen,
"Unblemished I am, without a blot,
As here I appear in honor clean,
784 But 'unequalled Queen' then said I not.
The Lamb's wives we are with lovely sheen,
A hundred and forty thousand got,
As in the Apocalypse it is seen.
788 Saint John did see them all without spot
On the hill of Sion, that highland plot.
In spiritual dream the apostle saw them,
Arrayed for the wedding upon hill's lot,
792 The new city of Jerusalem.

f. 54 67 "Of Jerusalem I in speech shall tell,

778 And exclude all others from that marriage,   779 STOUT AND STYF
proud and firm   783 WYTH MENSK MENTEENE maintain with honor   785
VYUE3 wives . . . BENE are   786 FLOT in company   788 KNOT throng
789 SEMLY CLOT beautiful knoll   791 HYL-COPPE hilltop

63

If þou wyl knaw what-kyn he be,
My Lombe, my Lorde, my dere Juelle,
796 My Joy, my Blys, my Lemman fre.
Þe profete Ysaye of hym con melle,
Pitously, of hys debonerté,
Þat gloryous Gyltleȝ þat mon con quelle
800 Wythouten any sake of felonye.
As a schep to þe slaȝt þer lad watȝ he;
And as lombe þat clypper in lande men,
So closed he hys mouth fro vch query
804 Quen Jueȝ hym jugged in Jherusalem.

68 "In Jerusalem watȝ my Lemman slayn,
And rent on rode wyth boyeȝ bolde.
Al oure baleȝ to bere ful bayn,
808 He toke on hymself oure careȝ colde.
Wyth boffeteȝ watȝ hys face flayn,
Þat watȝ so fayr onto byholde.
For synne, he set hymself in vayn,
812 Þat neuer hade non hymself to wolde.
For vus he lette hym flyȝe and folde,
And brede vpon a bostwys bem.
As meke as lomp þat no playnt tolde,
816 For vus he swalt in Jerusalem.

69 "Jerusalem, Jordan, and Galalye—
Þeras baptysed þe goude Saynt Jon,
His wordeȝ acorded to Ysaye.
820 When Jhecu con to hym warde gon,
He sayde of hym þys professye:
'Lo, Godeȝ Lombe, as trwe as ston,
Þat dotȝ away þe synneȝ dryȝe,
824 Þat alle þys worlde hatȝ wroȝt vpon!'

794 If you wish to know what kind [of Being] he is,   796 LEMMAN FRE
noble Spouse   797 OF HYM CON MELLE of him did speak   798
DEBONERTÉ meekness   799 QUELLE slay   802 And like [a] lamb that
shearers in fields appraise,   807 BALEȝ sins . . . FUL BAYN fully prepared

64

If you wish to know his sovereignty,
My Lamb, My Lord, my precious Jewel,
796 My Joy, my Bliss, the Spouse for me.
The prophet Isaias, while speaking well,
Compassionately described his modesty,
That guiltless Christ cruel men did quell
800 Without any reason related to felony.
Like a sheep to slaughter led was he;
Like a lamb appeared that glorious Gem,
With mouth closed tight after each query
804 When the Jews judged him in Jerusalem.

68 "In Jerusalem was my Beloved slain,
And rent on rood by ruffians bold.
Willing to bear our sins that stain,
808 He assumed himself our cares full cold.
His face such bruises did retain,
That which was so fair to behold.
For sin, he suffered searing pain,
812 He who never had one to unfold.
He let himself be laid on mold,
And stretched upon a sturdy stem.
As meek as a lamb, as was foretold,
816 He died for us in Jerusalem.

69 "Jerusalem, Jordan, and Galilee—
Where John baptized in water's flow,
His words with Isaias were in harmony.
820 When Jesus up to him did go,
He said of him this prophecy:
'As true as stone does God's Lamb glow,
Who saves us from the sins we see,
824 Wrought in all this worldly woe!'

809 FLAYN bruised   811 Because of sin, he submitted himself to contempt,
812 WOLDE subdue   813 For us he allowed himself to be whipped and laid
low,   814 BEM beam   815 NO PLAYNT TOLDE sounded no lament   823
DRY3E burdensome   824 HAT3 WRO3T VPON has committed openly

Hymself ne wroȝt neuer ȝet non;
Wheþer, on hymself he con al clem.
Hys generacyoun quo recen con,
828 Þat dyȝed for vus in Jerusalem?

70 "In Jerusalem, þus, my Lemman swatte;
Twyeȝ for Lombe watȝ taken þare
By trw recorde of ayþer prophete,
832 For mode so meke and al hys fare.
Þe þryde tyme is, þerto, ful mete,
In Apokalypeȝ wryten ful ȝare.
Inmydeȝ þe trone þere saynteȝ sete,
836 Þe apostel Johan hym saytȝ as bare,
Lesande þe boke with leueȝ sware,
Þere seuen syngnetteȝ wern sette in seme;
And at þat syȝt vche douth con dare,
840 In helle, in erþe, and Jerusalem.

XV

71 "Thys Jerusalem Lombe hade neuer pechche
Of oþer huee bot quyt jolyf,
Þat mot ne masklle moȝt on streche
844 For wolle quyte so ronk and ryf.
Forþy, vche saule þat hade neuer teche
Is to þat Lombe a worthyly wyf,
And þaȝ vch day a store he feche,
848 Among vus commeȝ no noþer strot ne stryf.
Bot, vch on enlé we wolde were fyf;
Þe mo þe myryer, so God me blesse!
In compayny gret, our luf con þryf
852 In honour more, and neuer þe lesse.

826 WHEÞER nevertheless . . . CLEM claim 827 RECEN recount 829
SWATTE suffered 832 FARE ways 833 METE suitable 834 ȜARE clearly
836 HYM SAYTȜ AS BARE tells about him just as plainly 837 LESANDE
opening 838 Where seven seals were set on [the] border;

Though he never one did show,
He seized them all, himself to condemn.
His generation who can know,
828   He who died for us in Jerusalem?

f. 54b   70   "In Jerusalem my Dear did perish;
He was revealed as the Lamb twice there
In record true of two prophets to cherish,
832   Due to his mood so meek and fair.
The third time, thus, is easy to furnish,
Written in Apocalypse beyond compare.
Amid the throne where mild saints flourish,
836   The apostle John proclaims with care,
How he opened the book, with pages square,
With seven seals set as the border's emblem;
And at that sight souls bowed with flare,
840   In hell, on earth, and in Jerusalem.

XV

71   "This Jerusalem's Lamb had never a patch
Of other hue but white to enlive,
Where stain or spot might ever attach
844   To the wool so white, so bright and alive.
Each soul who never guilt did catch
Is for that Lamb a wife to revive,
And though each day he gathers a batch,
848   Among us none do strive to connive.
Besides, we would wish each one were five;
The more the merrier, may God me bless!
In company large, our love does thrive
852   With honor more, and never the less.

839 VCHE DOUTH CON DARE each group did bow in awe   842 QUYT
JOLYF beautiful white   843 STRECHE spread   844 RONK AND RYF rich
and abundant   845 FORÞY therefore . . . TECHE guilt   847 STORE group
848 STROT NE STRYF contention or discord   849 ON ENLÉ single one

"Lasse of blysse may non vus bryng
Þat beren þys perle vpon oure bereste,
For þay of mote couþe neuer mynge,
Of spotleȝ perleȝ þa beren þe creste.
Alþaȝ oure corses in clotteȝ clynge,
And ȝe remen for rauþe wythouten reste,
We þurȝoutly hauen cnawyng.
Of on dethe ful oure hope is drest.
Þe Lombe vus gladeȝ; oure care is kest.
He myrþeȝ vus alle at vch a mes.
Vch oneȝ blysse is breme and beste,
And neuer oneȝ honour ȝet neuer þe les.

f. 55   73   "Lest les þou leue my talle farande,
In Appocalyppece is wryten in wro.
'I seghe,' says Johan, 'þe Loumbe hym stande
On þe mount of Syon, ful þryuen and þro,
And wyth hym maydenneȝ, an hundreþe þowsande,
And fowre and forty þowsande mo.
On alle her forhedeȝ wryten I fande
Þe Lombeȝ nome, hys Fadereȝ also.
A hue fro heuen I herde þoo,
Lyk flodeȝ fele laden runnen on resse,
And as þunder þroweȝ in torreȝ blo,
Þat lote, I leue, watȝ neuer þe les.

74   " 'Nauþeles, þaȝ hit schowted scharpe,
And ledden loude alþaȝ hit were,
A note ful nwe I herde hem warpe;
To lysten þat watȝ ful lufly dere.
As harporeȝ harpen in her harpe,

855-56 For they who wear the diadem of spotless pearls/Could never think of quarreling.   857 IN CLOTTEȝ CLYNGE decay in clods   859-60 We possess understanding completely./Our hope has been fully realized through one death   861 GLADEȝ comforts . . . KEST cast away   862 MYRÞEȝ gladdens . . . MES festive gathering   865 "Lest you should believe my splendid story false,

72   "Less of bliss may no one bring
To us who bear this pearl on breast.
With wrangling words we never sting;

856   Our crown of pearls fulfills our quest.
Although our corpses to clods do cling,
And you groan in grief without a rest,
Our knowing is always in full swing;

860   One death has drawn us to heaven's crest.
By the comforting Lamb we are caressed;
At gatherings he gives us great gladness.
Each one's bliss is wondrous and best,

864   And never one's honor yet ever the less.

f. 55   73   "Lest you make less my story's trend,
The Apocalypse follows the factual flow.
'I saw,' says John, 'the Lamb, our Friend,

868   Standing on Sion, nobly aglow,
And with him virgins, a hundred thousand,
And forty-four thousand more in a row.
On their foreheads was written a blend,

872   The fair Lamb's name, his Father's also.
A voice from heaven I then heard grow,
Like the sound of streams in springing excess,
And as thunder peals over peaks below,

876   That sound, I believe, was never the less.

74   " 'Nevertheless, though not distant or dim,
And though that loud voice had no peer,
A canticle quite new then came with vim;

880   To listen to it was lovingly dear.
Like harpers harping, happy, not grim,

866 WRO passage   867 HYM STANDE himself standing   868 ÞRYUEN
AND ÞRO noble and steadfast   870 MO more   871 FANDE found   873
THOO then   874 Like [the] voice of many waters running in [a] rush,   875
IN TORRE3 BLO among leaden peaks   877 SCHOWTED SCHARPE
sounded sharply   878 LEDDEN LOUDE loud voice   879 WARPE sing

69

Þat nwe songe þay songen ful cler,
In sounande noteȝ, a gentyl carpe;
884 Ful fayre þe modeȝ þay fonge in fere.
Ryȝt byfore Godeȝ chayere,
And þe fowre besteȝ þat hym obes,
And þe aldermen so sadde of chere,
888 Her songe þay songen neuer þe les.

75 " 'Nowþelese, non watȝ neuer so quoynt,
For alle þe crafteȝ þat euer þay knewe,
Þat of þat songe myȝt synge a poynt,
892 Bot þat meyny. Þe Lombe þay swe,
For þay arn boȝt fro þe vrþe aloynte
As newe fryt, to God ful due;
And to þe gentyl Lombe hit arn anjoynt,
896 As lyk to hymself of lote and hwe,
For neuer lesyng ne tale vntrwe
Ne towched her tonge for no dysstresse.
Þat moteles meyny may neuer remwe
900 Fro þat maskeleȝ Mayster neuer þe les.' "

f. 55b 76 "Neuer þe les let be my þonc,"
Quoþ I, "my perle, þaȝ I appose.
I schulde not tempte þy wyt so wlonc;
904 To Krysteȝ chambre þat art ichose.
I am bot mokke and mul among,
And þou so ryche, a reken rose;
And bydeȝ here by þys blysful bonc,
908 Þer lyueȝ lyste may neuer lose.
Now, hynde, þat sympelnesse coneȝ enclose,
I wolde þe aske a þynge expresse,
And þaȝ I be bustwys, as a blose,
912 Let my bone vayl, neuerþelese.

---

884 They followed the modes in unison very skillfully.   886 OBES obey   887
SADDE OF CHERE dignified in mood   891 POYNT note   892 SWE follow
893 ALOYNTE distant   895 HIT ARN ANJOYNT they have been joined
896 LOTE AND HWE speech and appearance

That song so new they sang full clear,
With melodious notes, a noble hymn,
884 Following the modes so pleasing to hear.
Before God's throne, that Lord so near,
And the four beasts who obedience stress,
And the ancients of such elegant cheer,
888 They sang their song never the less.

75 " 'Nevertheless, none were ever so clever,
Despite all the skills they ever knew,
To make singing that song a successful endeavor,
892 Except that group of spotless hue.
Purchased from earth, with the Lamb forever,
First fruits are they, to God full due;
From the gentle Lamb they will never sever,
896 Being similar to him in pure virtue,
For never did lying nor tale untrue
Touch their tongue in any address.
Separation that assembly never will rue,
900 Being one with the Master never the less.' "

f. 55b · 76 "Never the less let me now thank
My Pearl," said I, "though my inquiry grows.
Your sparkling wit is supreme in rank;
904 To Christ's bridal chamber you are one who goes.
I am but dirt and dust so dank,
And you are so noble, a beautiful rose,
Biding here on this blissful bank,
908 Where life's pleasure purely flows.
Gracious girl, whom simplicity does enclose,
I would ask of you a thing express,
And though boisterous I may be in my pose,
912 Let my plea avail, nevertheless.

898 FOR NO DYSSTRESSE under any circumstance   899–900 That spotless
assembly can never be separated/From that spotless Master any the less.' " 902
APPOSE inquire   903 WLONC superb   905 AMONG together   908 LOSE
fade   911 BUSTWYS boisterous . . . BLOSE blast of wind

77   "Neuerþelese, cler I yow bycalle,
     If ȝe con se hyt be todone;
   As þou art gloryous, wythouten galle,

916   Wythnay þou neuer my ruful bone.
   Haf ȝe no woneȝ in castel-walle,
   Ne maner þer ȝe may mete and won?
   Þou telleȝ me of Jerusalem, þe ryche ryalle,

920   Þer Dauid dere watȝ dyȝt on trone,
   Bot by þyse holteȝ hit con not hone;
   Bot in Judee hit is, þat noble note.
   As ȝe are maskeleȝ vnder mone,

924   Your woneȝ schulde be wythouten mote.

78   "Þys moteleȝ meyny þou coneȝ of mele,
   Of þousandeȝ þryȝt, so gret a route,
   A gret ceté, for ȝe arn fele,

928   Yow byhod haue, wythouten doute.
   So cumly a pakke of joly juele
   Wer euel don schulde lyȝ þeroute;
   And by þyse bonkeȝ þer I con gele,

932   And I se no bygyng nawhere aboute,
   I trowe alone ȝe lenge and loute,
   To loke on þe glory of þys gracous gote.
   If þou hatȝ oþer bygyngeȝ stoute,

936   Now tech me to þat myry mote."

f. 56   79   "That mote þou meneȝ in Judy londe,"
   Þat specyal spyce þen to me spakk,
   "Þat is þe cyté þat þe Lombe con fonde

940   To soffer inne sor for maneȝ sake,

914 TODONE revealed   916 You would never refuse my compassionate request.   918 METE AND WON meet and linger   919 RYALLE royal   921 HONE be situated   922 NOTE city   923 MASKELEȜ spotless   924 WONEȜ abodes . . . MOTE spot   925 ÞOU CONEȜ OF MELE you do speak of   926 ÞRYȜT gathered . . . ROUTE crowd   927 FELE many

77   "Nevertheless, clearly on you I call
To have your splendid city shown;
Since you are glorious, without any gall,
916   To refuse my request you are not prone.
Have you no halls within castle wall,
Nor manors made of sturdy stone?
You tell me of Jerusalem, a realm not small,
920   Where noble David was adorned on throne,
But in these woods it is not known;
Only in Judea is that place remote.
Since under moon you bear pure tone,
924   Spotless must be this city you note.

78   "This spotless group that you now name,
In throngs of thousands, forever devout,
Must need a city of noble fame,
928   For you are many, without a doubt.
Such gorgeous jewels would wane in shame
In open air, in rain or drought,
And on these shores I surely claim
932   I see no structures round about.
I imagine you alone are out
To scan this splendid stream afloat.
If you have buildings, big and stout,
936   Show me that spotless city of note."

f. 56   79   "That spotless city in Judea's land,"
Said that girl across the lake,
"Is the dwelling where by Lamb's demand
940   He suffered in sorrow for mankind's sake,

928 BYHOD would oblige   929 CUMLY comely . . . JOLY elegant   930
WER EUEL DON would be unfavorably affected   931 CON GELE do linger
933 LENGE AND LOUTE stay and stroll   934 GOTE stream   936 Lead me
now to that excellent city."   937 MOTE city . . . MENE3 mention   938
That special damsel then said to me,   939 CON FONDE did seek

þe olde Jerusalem to vnderstonde,
For þer þe olde gulte watȝ don to slake;
Bot þe Nwe þat lyȝt of Godeȝ sonde,

944 Þe apostel in Apocalyppce in theme con take.
Þe Lompe þer wythouten spotteȝ blake
Hatȝ feryed þyder hys fayre flote,
And as hys flok is wythouten flake,

948 So is hys mote wythouten moote.

80 "Of moteȝ two to carpe clene,
And Jerusalem hyȝt boþe, nawþeles,
Þat nys to yow no more to mene

952 Bot 'Ceté of God' oþer 'Syȝt of Pes'.
In þat on, oure pes watȝ mad at ene;
Wyth payne to suffer þe Lombe hit chese.
In þat oþer is noȝt bot pes to glene,

956 Þat ay schal laste, wythouten reles.
Þat is þe borȝ þat we to pres,
Fro þat oure fresch be layd to rote,
Þer glory and blysse schal euer encres

960 To þe meyny þat is wythouten mote."

81 "Moteleȝ may, so meke and mylde,"
Þen sayde I to þat lufly flor,
"Bryng me to þat bygly bylde,

964 And let me se þy blysful bor."
Þat schene sayde: "Þat God wyl schylde.
Þou may not enter wythinne hys tor.
Bot, of þe Lombe I haue þe aquylde

968 For a syȝt þerof, þurȝ gret fauor.
Vtwyth to se þat clene cloystor
Þou may, bot inwyth, not a fote.

942 DON TO SLAKE made to abate   943 LYȝT descended . . . SONDE dispensation   945 SPOTTEȜ BLAKE black spots   946 FERYED led . . . FLOTE company   947 FLAKE blemish   948-49 So is his city without spot./"To speak clearly of two cities,   953 MAD AT ENE settled immediately 954 CHESE chose   956 RELES cessation

The old Jerusalem, you understand,
Where for our guilt he stood at stake;
But the New Jerusalem, God's glory grand,
944 The apostle in Apocalypse for theme did take.
The noble Lamb, without stain or ache,
There led his group, the apostle wrote,
And as his flock no filth does take,
948 Spotless too is his city of note.

80 "A spotless city and an earthly scene,
And both named Jerusalem, nevertheless,
No more than this to you should mean:
952 'City of God'—'Sight of Peacefulness'.
Our salvation in one was certainly seen;
The Lamb dwelled there in great distress.
In the other there is only peace to glean,
956 That will endure without duress.
That is the place to which we press,
After our flesh with death is smote,
Where glory reigns without recess
960 For the spotless group in this city of note."

81 "Spotless maiden, meek and mild,"
Then said I to that lovely flower,
"Show me to that city, child,
964 And let me see your blissful bower."
That damsel said: "Your scheme is wild.
You may not enter within God's tower,
But I spoke to the Lamb, who sweetly smiled;
968 Thus his grace on you will shower.
From without, that place your eyes may devour;
From within, you may no walk promote.

958 FRESCH young bodies . . . ROTE decay   959 ENCRES increase   960
MEYNY assembly . . . MOTE spot   963 BYGLY BYLDE stately city   965
SCHENE bright damsel . . . SCHYLDE prevent   966 TOR kingdom   967-68
However, I have prevailed upon the Lamb for you/For a sight of it, through
great favor.   969 CLOYSTOR city   970 FOTE foot

75

To strech in þe strete þou hatȝ no vygour,

972
Bot þou wer clene wythouten mote.

THE VISION—PART THREE
THE NEW JERUSALEM AND THE PROCESSION

XVII

82   "If I þis mote þe schal vnhyde,
    Bow vp towarde þys borneȝ heued,
    And I, anendeȝ þe on þis syde,
976
    Schal sve tyl þou to a hil be veued."
    Þen wolde no lenger byde,
    Bot lurked by launceȝ so lufly leued,
    Tyl on a hyl þat I asspyed,
980
    And blusched on þe burghe, as I forth dreued,
    Byȝonde þe brok fro me warde keued;
    Þat schyrrer þen sunne wyth schafteȝ schon.
    In þe Apokalypce is þe fasoun preued,
984
    As deuyseȝ hit, þe apostel Jhoan.

    83   As Johan þe apostel hit syȝ wyth syȝt,
    I syȝe þat cyty of gret renoun,
    Jerusalem, so nwe and ryally dyȝt,
988
    As hit watȝ lyȝt fro þe heuen adoun.
    Þe borȝ watȝ al of brende golde bryȝt,
    As glemande glas burnist broun,
    Wyth gentyl gemmeȝ anvnder pyȝt
992
    Wyth banteleȝ twelue on basyng boun.
    Þe foundementeȝ twelue of riche tenoun;
    Vch tabelmente watȝ a serlypeȝ ston,

972 MOTE spot   973-74 "If I shall reveal this city to you,/Go up toward [the] head of this stream,   976 VEUED directed   978 LURKED slipped . . . LAUNCEȝ branches   979 ASSPYED discovered   980 BLUSCHED gazed . . . DREUED strode   981 Set down opposite me beyond the brook;

972   To stride in the street you have no power,
Unless spotless you be in that city of note.

THE VISION—PART THREE
THE NEW JERUSALEM AND THE PROCESSION

XVII

f. 56b   82   "This spotless city God shall not hide,
If you stroll toward this great stream's head,
And I, across from you on this side,
976   Shall follow until to a hill you tread."
Desiring then no longer to bide,
I sped through lovely leaves there spread,
Till I, on a hill, saw magnified,
980   That brilliant borough by light beams fed.
Set down beyond the brook, it shed
Its rays that made the sun seem wan.
To this vision in the Apocalypse I was led,
984   Its beauty portrayed by the apostle John.

      83   As John the apostle saw the sight,
I saw that city of sterling fame,
Jerusalem new, in royal flight,
988   As it from heaven downward came.
The city shone, gold and bright,
Like gleaming glass in glistening frame,
With precious stones below, alight,
992   Twelve tiers, established with sturdy aim,
Foundations twelve, all there to name.
Each tier was a stone I gazed upon,

982 SCHYRRER more radiant . . . SCHAFTE3 rays   983 FASOUN appearance   987 DY3T embellished   988 LY3T come   989 BRENDE pure 990 BURNIST BROUN burnished brightly   991 PY3T adorned   992 BOUN built   993 TENOUN jointings   994 SERLYPE3 separate

| | | As derely deuyseȝ þis ilk toun |
| 996 | | In Apocalyppeȝ, þe apostel Johan. |

	84	As Johan þise stoneȝ in Writ con nemme,
		I knew þe name after his tale.
		Jasper hyȝt þe fyrst gemme,
1000		Þat I on the fyrst basse con wale;
		He glente grene in þe lowest hemme.
		Saffer helde þe secounde stale.
		Þe calsydoyne, þenne, wythouten wemme,
1004		In þe þryd table con purly pale.
		Þe emerade, þe furþe, so grene of scale,
		Þe sardonyse, þe fyfþe ston,
		Þe sexte, þe rybé—he con hit wale
1008		In þe Apocalyppce, þe apostel Johan.

f. 57	85	Ȝet joyned Johan þe crysolyt,
		Þe seuenþe gemme in fundament,
		Þe aȝtþe, þe beryl, cler and quyt,
1012		Þe topasye twynne-how, þe nente endent;
		Þe crysopase, þe tenþe, is tyȝt,
		Þe jacyngh, þe enleuenþe gent,
		Þe twelfþe, þe gentyleste in vch a plyt,
1016		Þe amatyst purpre, wyth ynde blente.
		Þe wal abof þe bantels bent,
		Of jasporye, as glas þat glysnande schon.
		I knew hit by his deuysement
1020		In þe Apocalyppeȝ, þe apostel Jhan.

	86	As Johan deuysed, ȝet saȝ I þare
		Þise twelue degrés wern brode and stayre.
		Þe cyté stod abof, ful sware,
1024		As longe, as brode, as hyȝe, ful fayre.

995 ILK same   998 TALE account   999 HYȜT was called   1000 WALE per-
ceive   1001 HEMME fringe   1002 STALE position   1003 WEMME stain
1004 Did truly glow dimly on the third tier.   1005 SCALE surface   1007
WALE perceive   1009 JOYNED enumerated

| | | As he skillfully portrayed, his spirit aflame, |
| 996 | | In Apocalypse, the apostle John. |

	84	As John did name these stones in Scripture,
		I knew each one in neat rotation.
		The gem of jasper, the first to treasure,
1000		I saw formed there on firm foundation;
		It glistened greenly in lowest measure.
		Sapphire was set in second station.
		Chalcedony then, a spotless pleasure,
1004		Glowed pale and pure, third in formation.
		The emerald, the fourth, a green creation,
		The sardonyx, the fifth, a stone put on,
		The sixth, the ruby, he saw with elation
1008		In the Apocalypse, the apostle John.

f. 57	85	John then saw the chrysolite,
		The seventh gem in ornament,
		The eighth, the beryl, clear and white,
1012		The twin-hued topaz, ninth in ascent,
		The tenth, the chrysoprase, set there tight,
		The jacinth, eleventh, heaven-sent,
		The twelfth, the gentlest in that site,
1016		The amethyst purple, with indigo blent.
		The rising wall's embellishment
		Was jasper pure; like glass it shone.
		I knew it by his development
1020		In the Apocalypse, the apostle John.

	86	As John described, yet saw I there
		These twelve, great steps were broad and steep.
		The city above, completely square,
1024		Was long and high, and of wide sweep,

1010 FUNDAMENT foundation   1012 ENDENT adorned   1013 TY3T fastened   1014 GENT splendid   1015 PLYT setting   1017–18 The wall of jasper, that glisteningly shone/Like glass, rose above the tiers.   1019 DEUYSEMENT description   1024 FUL FAYRE very equally

Þe streteȝ of golde, as glasse, al bare;
Þe wal of jasper, þat glent as glayre.
Þe woneȝ wythinne enurned ware
1028 Wyth alle-kynneȝ perré þat moȝt repayre.
Þenne helde vch sware of þis manayre
Twelue forlonge space er euer hit fon
Of heȝt, of brede, of lenþe to cayre,
1032 For meten hit syȝ, þe apostel Johan.

XVIII

87 As Johan hym wryteȝ, ȝet more I syȝe.
Vch pane of þat place had þre ȝateȝ;
So twelue in poursent I con asspye.
1036 Þe portaleȝ pyked of rych plateȝ,
And vch ȝate of a margyrye,
A parfyt perle þat neuer fateȝ.
Vch on in Scrypture a name con plye
1040 Of Israel barneȝ, folewande her dateȝ,
Þat is to say, as her byrþ-whateȝ;
Þe aldest ay fyrst þeron watȝ done.
Such lyȝt þer lemed in alle þe strateȝ,
1044 Hem nedde nawþer sunne ne mone.

f. 57b 88 Of sunne ne mone had þay no nede.
Þe self God watȝ her lambe-lyȝt,
Þe Lombe her lantyrne, wythouten drede.
1048 Þurȝ hym blysned þe borȝ al bryȝt.
Þurȝ woȝe and won my lokyng ȝede;
For sotyle cler, noȝt lette no lyȝt.
Þe hyȝe trone þer moȝt ȝe hede,

1025 BARE clear   1026 GLENT glistened   1027 ENURNED WARE were embellished   1028 PERRÉ jewelry . . . REPAYRE be gathered   1029 Then each square of this habitation contained   1030 FON ceased   1031 CAYRE extend   1033 SYȜE saw   1036 PYKED were adorned   1037 MARGYRYE pearl   1038 FATEȜ fades

With streets of gold, like glass so rare,
And jasper wall, like glair we keep.
The abodes within, adorned with flair,
1028   Had every jewel one finds in a heap.
Then each square of this stronghold deep
Held furlongs twelve before space was gone,
In height, in breadth, and great length to leap,
1032   As saw it measured the apostle John.

XVIII

87   As Saint John writes, more struck my eye.
Each side of that city had three gates;
So twelue in compass I did espy.
1036   These portals appeared with royal plates,
Each gate a pearl in heaven high,
A perfect pearl with precious traits.
Each one did Scripture's names supply
1040   Of Israel's children, following birth dates;
Accordingly each one correlates.
The first inscription was the eldest's boon.
Such light illumined heaven's estates,
1044   They needed neither sun nor moon.

f. 57b   88   Of sun or moon they had no need,
Since gracious God was their lamplight.
The Lamb their lantern, there indeed,
1048   Made that city especially bright.
Through wall and city my sight did speed;
Sheer clearness meant no obstacle might
Make my vision of throne recede,

1039 PLYE yield   1041 BYRÞ-WHATEȜ dates of birth   1042 DONE engraved   1043 LEMED shone . . . STRATEȜ streets   1047 DREDE doubt 1048 BLYSNED sparkled   1049 ȜEDE passed   1050–51 Because of [the] tenuous transparency, nothing obstructed any light./You could see the high throne there,

1052		Wyth alle þe apparaylmente vmbepyȝte,
		As Johan þe appostel in termeȝ tyȝte.
		Þe hyȝe Godeȝ self hit set vpone.
		A reuer of þe trone þer ran outryȝte;
1056		Watȝ bryȝter þen boþe þe sunne and mone.

	89	Sunne ne mone schon neuer so swete
		A þat foysoun flode out of þat flet.
		Swyþe hit swange þurȝ vch a strete,
1060		Wythouten fylþe oþer galle oþer glet.
		Kyrk þerinne watȝ non ȝete,
		Chapel ne temple þat euer watȝ set.
		Þe Almyȝty watȝ her mynyster mete,
1064		Þe Lombe, þe Sakerfyse, þer to reget.
		Þe ȝateȝ stoken watȝ neuer ȝet,
		Bot euermore vpen at vche a lone.
		Þer entreȝ non to take reset,
1068		Þat bereȝ any spot anvndeȝ mone.

	90	The mone may þerof acroche no myȝte.
		To spotty ho is, of body to grym;
		And also, þer ne is neuer nyȝt,
1072		What schulde þe mone þer compas clym
		And to euen wyth þat worþly lyȝt
		Þat schyneȝ vpon þe brokeȝ brym?
		Þe planeteȝ arn in to pouer a plyȝt,
1076		And þe self sunne ful fer to dym.
		Aboute þat water arn tres ful schym,
		Þat twelue fryteȝ of lyf con bere ful sone.
		Twelue syþeȝ on ȝer þay beren ful frym,
1080		And renowleȝ nwe in vche a mone.

f. 58	91	Anvnder mone so gret merwayle

1052 With all the heavenly retinue arrayed round about,   1053 IN TERMEȜ
TYȜTE set [it] down in words   1054 HIT SET VPONE sat upon it   1058
FOYSOUN blessed . . . FLET source   1063 MYNYSTER METE proper
cathedral

1052	Or draw my eyes from heavenly hosts in sight.
	As John the apostle of this scene did write,
	The great God graced the throne in tune.
	A river from that throne there ran outright,
1056	Brighter than both the sun and moon.

89	Sun or moon shone never so sweet
	As that flowing flood, void of grime.
	Swiftly it sped through every street,
1060	Without smut or scum, or slippery slime.
	No church rose there for souls' retreat,
	Chapel or temple with bells that chime.
	The Almighty was cathedral complete,
1064	The Lamb, the Sacrifice, always in prime.
	Gates, closed never in that clime,
	Were always open in that commune.
	No one enters to rest in time,
1068	Who bears a spot resembling the moon.

90	The moon can gain therein no might.
	Too spotty she is, so dull and stark;
	And besides, where there is never night,
1072	Why should the moon arise in arc
	And there compete with that glorious light,
	Beaming on brook with brilliant spark?
	The planets are in too poor a plight,
1076	And the sun itself full far too dark.
	Around that water, bright trees with bark
	Twelve fruits of life produce so soon.
	Twelve times a year they bloom in park,
1080	And renew again at every moon.

f. 58   91   Beneath the moon no heart so hale

1064 TO REGET to be received again   1065 STOKEN locked   1066 LONE
byway   1067 RESET refuge   1074 BROKE3 BRYM water of the brook
1077 SCHYM bright 1079 FRYM abundantly 1081 MERWAYLE miracle

No fleschly hert ne myȝt endeure,
As quen I blusched vpon þat baly,
1084   So ferly þerof watȝ þe fasure.
I stod as stylle as dased quayle,
For ferly of þat freuch fygure,
Þat felde I nawþer reste ne trauayle,
1088   So watȝ I rauyste wyth glymme pure;
For I dar say wyth conciens sure,
Hade bodyly burne abiden þat bone,
Þaȝ alle clerkeȝ hym hade in cure,
1092   His lyf wer loste anvnder mone.

XIX

92   Ryȝt as þe maynful mone con rys,
    Er þenne þe day-glem dryue al doun,
So sodanly, on a wonder wyse,
1096   I watȝ war of a prosessyoun.
Þis noble cité of ryche enpresse
Watȝ sodanly ful, wythouten sommoun,
Of such vergyneȝ, in þe same gyse,
1100   Þat watȝ my blysful anvnder croun;
And coronde wern alle of þe same fasoun,
Depaynt in perleȝ and wedeȝ qwyte.
In vch oneȝ breste watȝ bounden boun
1104   Þe blysful perle wythouten delyt.

93   Wyth gret delyt, þay glod in fere
On golden gateȝ þat glent as glasse.
Hundreth þowsandeȝ I wot þer were,
1108   And alle in sute her liuréȝ wasse.
Tor to knaw þe gladdest chere.

1082 FLESCHLY human   1083 BALY city   1084 FERLY marvelous . . .
FASURE appearance   1086 FERLY wonder . . . FREUCH FYGURE bril-
liant vision   1088 GLYMME spiritual light   1090 ABIDEN ÞAT BONE
experienced that revelation   1097 ENPRESSE glory

That miracle could ever endure,
As when I saw that city unveil,
1084   So marvelous was its spiritual lure.
I stood as still as a dazed quail,
In wonder with my eyes on tour,
Feeling neither rest nor travail,
1088   So entranced was I by vision pure;
For I dare say with conviction sure,
Had mortal man been granted that boon,
Though all the clerks took him for cure,
1092   His life would be lost beneath the moon.

XIX

92   Just as the mighty moon does rise,
Before the sun sinks, settling down,
So suddenly, in a wonderful wise,
1096   I saw a great procession in town.
This splendid city, a noble prize,
Was suddenly full of souls of renown,
A group of virgins in the same guise
1100   As was my girl beneath the crown,
Crowned the same, not one with a frown,
Arrayed with pearls and robes of white.
Bound on the breast of each one's gown
1104   Was the blissful pearl beyond delight.

93   With great delight, they did appear
On golden roads that gleamed like glass.
Hundreds of thousands, all so dear,
1108   With attire alike, did there amass,
Proceeding surely with similar cheer.

1098 SOMMOUN summons 1100 BLYSFUL beautiful maiden 1101
FASOUN fashion 1103 BOUN firmly 1105 GLOD IN FERE proceeded in
company 1107 WOT know 1108-9 And their clothes were all alike./[It was]
difficult to discover the happiest expression.

Þe Lombe byfore con proudly passe,
Wyth horneʒ seuen of red golde cler.

1112 As praysed perleʒ his wedeʒ wasse.
Towarde þe throne þay trone a tras;
Þaʒ þay wern fele, no pres in plyt,
Bot mylde as maydeneʒ seme at mas,

1116 So droʒ þay forth wyth gret delyt.

f. 58b 94 Delyt þat hys come encroched
To much hit were of for to melle.
Þise aldermen, quen he aproched,

1120 Grouelyng to his fete þay felle.
Legyounes of aungeleʒ, togeder uoched,
Þer kesten ensens of swete smelle.
Þen glory and gle watʒ nwe abroched;

1124 Al songe to loue þat gay Juelle.
Þe steuen moʒt stryke þurʒ þe vrþe to helle,
Þat þe Vertues of heuen of joye endyte,
To loue þe Lombe his meyny in-melle.

1128 Iwysse, I laʒt a gret delyt.

95 Delit, þe Lombe for to deuise,
Wyth much meruayle, in mynde went.
Best watʒ he, blyþest, and moste to pryse,

1132 Þat euer I herde of speche spent.
So worþly whyt wern wedeʒ hys,
His lokeʒ symple, hymself so gent,
Bot a wounde, ful wyde and weete, con wyse

1136 Anende hys hert, þurʒ hyde torente.
Of his quyte syde his blod out sprent.
Alas, þoʒt I, who did þat spyt?

1110 CON PROUDLY PASSE did pass proudly   1112 WEDEʒ WASSE gar-
ments were   1114 Though they were many, [there was] no crowding in [their]
arrangement,   1117 COME ENCROCHED approach aroused   1120
GROUELYNG prostrate   1121 UOCHED called   1123 NWE ABROCHED
proclaimed anew   1124 All sang to honor that noble Jewel.   1126 ENDYTE
chant

The Lamb in front of highest class
Had seven horns of red gold clear,
1112   And garments like prized pearls in grass.
They stepped in line, toward throne did pass,
So many assembled, an orderly sight.
Mild as maidens sweet at mass,
1116   So they drove forth with great delight.

f. 58b   94   The delight that set God's souls aflame
Would be too much for words to tell.
These aldermen, when near he came,
1120   Humbly at his feet they fell.
Legions of angels around did rain
Holy incense of sweetest smell.
Glory and glee all there did gain;
1124   All honored that Jewel with song's huge swell.
The sound could strike through earth to hell,
When the Virtues of heaven chant with might,
To praise the Lamb and his souls so well.
1128   Indeed, I experienced great delight.

       95   Delight in seeing the Lamb in stride
Amazed my mind, where marvels went.
Noblest was he, most graceful to guide,
1132   That ever I heard in speech intent.
A worthy white hue to his garments applied.
With humble appearance he was content,
But a wound, full wide and wet, did bide
1136   Beside his heart; his skin it rent.
From his white side streamed a bloody torrent.
Alas, thought I, who would act with such spite?

1127 HIS MEYNY IN-MELLE in the midst of his company   1129 FOR TO
DEUISE in observing   1131 BLYÞEST most gracious . . . PRYSE esteem
1132 SPENT described   1133 WEDEȝ garments   1134 GENT noble   1135
WYSE show   1136 ÞURȝ HYDE TORENTE torn through [the] skin   1137
SPRENT spurted   1138 SPYT outrage

		Ani breste for bale aȝt haf forbrent
1140		Er he þerto hade had delyt.

	96	The Lombe delyt non lyste to wene.
		Þaȝ he were hurt and wounde hade,
		In his sembelaunt watȝ neuer sene,
1144		So wern his glenteȝ gloryous glade.
		I loked among his meyny schene
		How þay wyth lyf wern laste and lade.
		Þen saȝ I þer my lyttel quene
1148		Þat, I wende, had standen by me in sclade.
		Lorde, much of mirþe watȝ þat ho made
		Among her fereȝ, þat watȝ so quyt.
		Þat syȝt me gart to þenk to wade,
1152		For luf-longyng in gret delyt.

XX

f. 59	97	Delyt me drof in yȝe and ere;
		My maneȝ mynde to maddyng malte.
		Quen I seȝ my frely, I wolde be þere
1156		Byȝonde þe water, þaȝ ho were walte.
		I þoȝt þat noþyng myȝt me dere,
		To fech me bur and take me halt,
		And to start in þe strem schulde non me stere,
1160		To swymme þe remnaunt, þaȝ I þer swalte.
		Bot, of þat munt I watȝ bitalt.
		When I schulde start in þe strem astraye,
		Out of þat caste I watȝ bycalt.
1164		Hit watȝ not at my Prynceȝ paye.

1139 Any breast ought to have burned with misery   1141 LYSTE TO WENE would wish to doubt   1144 GLENTEȜ glances   1145 MEYNY SCHENE bright company   1146 LASTE AND LADE filled and charged   1148 WENDE believed . . . SCLADE valley   1150 ÞAT WATȜ SO QUYT she who was so white   1154 TO MADDYNG MALTE was reduced to madness 1155 FRELY lovely maiden

1140

Any breast should have burned in baleful torment
Before it had seized such violent delight.

96

The Lamb's delight was lucid and keen.
Though the wound upon him heavily weighed,
In his semblance it was never seen,

1144

For his glorious glances never did fade.
I saw where his company did convene
A spiritual vibrance sweetly displayed.
Then saw I there my little queen

1148

Who in the vale had me delayed.
Lord, much of mirth was what she made
Among her friends; she was so white.
That vision made me wish to wade,

1152

Due to love's longing for great delight.

XX

f. 59   97

Delight then entered through eye and ear
To my mortal mind in maddening vault.
Seeing that girl beyond water clear,

1156

I would be there, though she would find fault.
I thought that nothing could make me veer,
Cause me grief, or make me halt,
Restrain me here, or wrongly steer

1160

My swimming swiftly in frenzied revolt.
But myself too high I did exalt,
For starting in the stream meant going astray,
And so I was stalled, my scheme in default.

1164

It pleased not my Prince in powerful sway.

1156 WALTE upset   1157 DERE thwart   1158 TAKE ME HALT cause me
to waver   1159–60 And no one would restrain me from starting into the
stream,/To swim the remainder, even if I would perish there.   1161 MUNT
intention . . . BITALT startled   1162 ASTRAYE impetuously   1163 CASTE
purpose . . . BYCALT called back   1164 PAYE liking (See the note to line 1
on page 8 for translating 'sway' in the sense of 'dominion'.)

	98	Hit payed hym not þat I so flonc	
		Ouer meruelous mereȝ, so mad arayde.	
		Of raas, þaȝ I were rasch and ronk,	
1168		Ȝet, rapely þerinne I watȝ restayed,	
		For ryȝt as I sparred vnto þe bonc,	
		Þat brathe out of my drem me brayde.	
		Þen wakned I in þat erber wlonk.	**Epilogue:**
1172		My hede vpon þat hylle watȝ layde,	**Return**
		Þeras my perle to grounde strayd.	**to the**
		I raxled and fel in gret affray,	**Garden**
		And, sykyng, to myself I sayd,	
1176		"Now al be to þat Prynceȝ paye."	

	99	Me payed ful ille to be out fleme
		So sodenly of þat fayre regioun,
		Fro alle þo syȝteȝ so quyke and queme.
1180		A longeyng heuy me strok in swone,
		And, rewfully þenne, I con toreme.
		"O perle," quoþ I, "of rych renoun,
		So watȝ hit me dere þat þou con deme
1184		In þys veray avysyoun.
		If hit be ueray and soth sermoun
		Þat þou so stykeȝ in garlande gay,
		So wel is me in þys doel-doungoun,
1188		Þat þou art to þat Prynseȝ paye."

f. 59b	100	To þat Prynceȝ paye hade I ay bente,
		And ȝerned no more þen watȝ me geuen,
		And halden me þer in trwe entent,
1192		As þe perle me prayed, þat watȝ so þryuen,
		As helde drawen to Goddeȝ present,

1165 PAYED pleased . . . FLONC would rush   1166 MEREȝ streams . . .
MAD ARAYDE madly resolved   1167 Though I would be swift and strong in
racing,   1168 RAPELY immediately . . . RESTAYED restrained   1169
BONC shore   1170 BRATHE violent movement . . . BRAYDE drew   1171
WLONK beautiful   1176 PAYE liking   1177 [It] pleased me very poorly to
be driven out   1179 QUYKE AND QUEME vivid and pleasing

	98	It pleased him not that I sway and blunder
		Beyond that brook, in madness bound.
		Rash and rank, mind rent asunder,
1168		Stopped was I, I surely found,
		For just as I sprang to plunge thereunder,
		That shock did shake me from vision's round.

I then awoke in that arbor of wonder,   **Epilogue:**
My head there laid upon that mound,   **Return**
Where my pearl had strayed into the ground.   **to the**
I rose, then dropped in great dismay,   **Garden**
And sighing, I said what I now expound:
"All must please that Prince in sway."

1172

1176

        99   Displeased to lose that sway I held,
              To be taken from that rare terrain,
              From all those sights so firmly jelled,
1180   Deep longing seared my soul with pain,
              And, sorrowfully then, my yearning swelled.
              "O Pearl," said I, "in royal train,
              What you declared my doubts dispelled,
1184   In vision dear God did ordain.
              If it is true you there remain,
              Set within the garland's spray,
              This dungeon drear I will not disdain,
1188   Because you please that Prince in sway."

f. 59b   100   To Prince's sway had I pleasingly bent,
               And desired no more than he had given,
               And maintained myself with true intent,
1192   As pearl implored, who there has thriven,
               When drawing toward God's firmament,

1180 A heavy yearning sent me into [a] swoon,   1181 CON TOREME did
lament   1184 In this truthful vision.   1185 UERAY AND SOTH SERMOUN
reliable and true speech   1186–87 That you thus are set within [the] noble gar-
land,/Then [it] is well with me in this miserable prison   1188 PAYE liking
1192 ÞRYUEN beautiful   1193 HELDE certainly . . . PRESENT presence

To mo of his mysterys I hade ben dryuen;
Bot ay wolde man of happe more hente

1196 Þen moȝten by ryȝt vpon hem clyuen.
Þerfore, my joye watȝ sone toriuen,
And I kaste of kytheȝ þat lasteȝ aye.
Lorde, mad hit arn þat agayn þe stryuen,

1200 Oþer proferen þe oȝt agayn þy paye.

101 To pay þe Prince oþer sete saȝte,
Hit is ful eþe to þe god Krystyin,
For I haf founden hym, boþe day and naȝte,

1204 A God, a Lorde, a Frende ful fyin.
Ouer þis hyul þis lote I laȝte,
For pyty of my perle enclyin,
And syþen to God I hit bytaȝte,

1208 In Krysteȝ dere blessyng, and myn,
Þat, in þe forme of bred and wyn,
Þe preste vus scheweȝ vch a daye.
He gef vus to be his homly hyne,

1212 Ande precious perleȝ vnto his pay. Amen. Amen.

1195-96 But man always would wish to seize more of happiness/Than could
be allotted to him with justice. 1198 KYTHEȜ lands 1200 Or present to you
anything against your liking. 1201 PAY please . . . SETE SAȜTE to be made
peaceful

To mysteries more I could have driven;
But man's wish for bliss is never spent,
1196 And he seeks beyond what fate has written.
Therefore, my joy was soon all riven,
And cast I was from spheres that stay.
Lord, mad are they who have ever striven
1200 To oppose or displease their Prince in sway.

101 Pleasing the Prince in sway supreme
Brings peace to Christians cleansed of sin;
Day and night I dwell in esteem
1204 For that God and Lord, a Friend to win.
Upon this mound my adventurous dream
Streamed through pity for pearl therein,
And then I left her amid God's gleam,
1208 With Christ's dear blessing, and mine through him
Whom, in the form of wine and wafer thin,
The priest does show to us every day.
May he let us be his serving kin,
1212 And precious pearls within his sway. Amen. Amen.

1202 EÞE easy   1204 FYIN excellent   1205 LOTE adventure . . . LA3TE
experienced   1206 ENCLYIN humble   1207 BYTA3TE entrusted   1208
MYN mine   1211 May he allow us to be his gracious servants,   1212 PAY
liking

COMMENTARY

Names of previous editors whose books were used in this study appear without date. For full listings, see s.v. the following in Bibliography I: Morris (1864), Osgood (1906), Gollancz (1921), Chase (1932), Gordon (1953), Hillmann (1961), Cawley (1962), DeFord (1967), Moorman (1977), and Andrew & Waldron (1978). References to other works have the name of the author, the date in parentheses, and page number(s), when needed. An *a*, *b*, or *c* after a date indicates more than one work in the same year by the same author. Again, for full listings, see Bibliography I. Notes involving meanings of words refer to the literal meanings, usually found at the bottoms of the pages of text and translation, not to the verse translation when the denotation of a word has been changed for poetic effect.

1–60 Elliott (1961) 70 referred to this opening stanza-group to show how the poet, in keeping with two rhetorical aspects stressed by Matthew of Vendôme in his *Ars Versificatoria* (c. 1175), linked his description to the mood of the story and enhanced the beauty of the poem. "Sixty lines suffice to create not merely an apt setting heavy with melancholy, but to introduce the theme of life and death and rebirth which is at the heart of *Pearl*."

Luttrell (1978), in "The Introduction to the Dream in *Pearl*," traced in ll. 1–60 the courtly love elements turning to the Christian concept of *Consolatio Mortis* in the Death and Resurrection theme.

1 As Gordon noted, the first two lines are probably not an apostrophe to the pearl. Schofield (1909) 600 stated, "Like the lapidaries in general, our poem opens with the name of the gem to be described." Marbodus' *De Gemmis* was the basis for all medieval lapidaries. *Pearl* symbolism also appears in *Cleanness* 553–56, 1067–68, 1116–32, and in *Gawain* 2364–65.

Osgood, pp. xxxii–xxxiii, suggested that the poet was familiar with the prologue to the life of Saint Margaret of Antioch in Jacobus de Voragine's *Legenda Aurea*. Like Gollancz, he argued that the maiden was perhaps the poet's daughter, named Margaret or Margery. See Earl (1972) for a study of the possible relationship between "Saint Margaret and the Pearl Maiden," and cf. the notes to 199, 206, and 1036–38.

Hoffman-C (1960) 91, refuting Hillmann-C (1945) on her interpretation of the pearl in the opening stanza as a material gem, argued that the first mean-

95

ing of the pearl is carried throughout the poem in stanzas 24, 28, 32, 76, 98, 99, and 100. "It is the pearl lost in human terms, in worldly and fleshly terms."

Krieg (1978), in his interpretation of the levels of meaning represented by the pearl image, started with the first level in the opening, the physical "in the form of an actual pearl" (21), and ended with the highest level, the pearl as a "symbol for Christ himself: perfect, spotless sacrifice, the only true gate into the Kingdom" (23).

Osgood and Gollancz believed *prynces* refers to Christ. Gordon noted here it means literally a prince of this world and symbolically Christ. Line 1 anticipates the last stanza-group where the reference to Christ the Prince is direct in 1164, 1176, 1188, 1189, and 1201.

Paye, the link-word in the last stanza-group, ends the first and last lines of the poem, lines that contain similar vocabulary and phrasing. See Ebbs (1958) 523 and Vantuono (1971) 67–68 for discussion of this rhetorical device not only in *Pearl* but also in *Cleanness*, *Patience*, and *Gawain*.

2   Osgood and Gollancz glossed *to* 'too'. Gordon and subsequent editors considered *to clanly clos* a split infin. Wright (1939) 2–3 suggested the reading given here: *To clanly clos* 'For (a) splendid setting' parallels *to prynces paye*. See *clĕnlī* adj. and *clŏs* n. Sense 3a of the latter defines 'the mansion of heaven, (Christ's) abode', with citation from *Glade us maiden* 12: "Crist up stey..He bar him seluen into is clos." As Wright observed, the first two lines foreshadow the pearl-maiden's appearance on the golden roads of heaven (1105–6).

Osgood, relating *golde* to the "coffer, i.e. Paradise" (259–72), believed l. 2 may contain an allusion to the maiden's tomb. He cited *The Gest Hystoriale of the Destruction of Troy* (13791–94) to prove that golden tombs and reliquaries were common in Northern alliterative poems.

Blanch-B (1965) 87 noted that gold, the usual setting for gems described in the medieval lapidaries, symbolizes the divine kingdom.

Bishop (1968) 83–84 traced this setting image through *Pearl* to the *garlande gay* of l. 1186, believing there may be allusion there to a golden *corona*, which, "in the ecclesiastical art of the time, symbolized the New Jerusalem." (See also 1186n.)

3   Origen, in his Commentary on Matt. 13.45–46, a passage paraphrased by the poet in 730–35, contrasted the less perfect British pearl with the Indian pearl, "rounded off on the outer surface, very white in colour, very translucent, and very large in size" (*The Ante-Nicene Fathers*, tr. of *The Writings of the Fathers down to A.D. 325*, ed. Allan Menzies, Vol. 9 [New York, 1912], p. 417).

Stern-C (1955) 75 noted that the Orient is the "eastern direction literally representative of the most priceless gems and anagogically representative of sun, light, Christ, and Jerusalem."

4 Hillmann read *proued . . . her* 'tested its' to support her view that a real jeweler and gem are designated here. For *proued* 'discovered', see *MED prẹven* v., sense 4a. Gordon compared the fem. pronouns denoting 'pearl' in *Cleanness* 1119–28.

5 Peck (1980), who viewed the structure of *Pearl* as an interlacement of circles, emphasized the roundness of the pearl. That, rather than linear analogies, "is perhaps the most important quality one should consider, for both Pearl and her poem are indeed round" (48). The largest circle is the whole poem, beginning with the dreamer meditating in his garden and ending where he began, "albeit with a different sense of garden than when he set out in his dream" (49). The smallest circles are the individual stanzas, which contain key words repeated in the first and last lines, except for the first line of the opening stanza in each group. In the 20 stanza-groups, there is a key word in the last line linked to a key word in the first line of the following group, except for the movement from Group XII to XIII. *Pay(e)* ends the first and last lines of the poem. Thus, as Peck commented, "not only is the plot round in its return to the garden where it began, but the overall structure forms a round as well" (49).

6 Gordon, comparing 190, showed such descriptions may apply to female figures. Hillmann considered them applicable only to a jewel. Kean (1967) 157, after referring to Lydgate's *Life of St. Margaret*: "And smal she was by humylite," related this virtue to 722–23 to show that the pearl is a proper symbol for children entering heaven.

8 Cf. *synglerty* 429, referring to the unique sweetness of Blessed Mary. Fick (1885), in his prefatory notes, proposed changing *synglure* to *synglere*. Osgood, Gollancz, Chase, Gordon, Cawley, and Moorman followed him, but Hillmann noted that emendation is unnecessary since *-ure* varies with *-ere* in words of French origin, as in *gyngure* 43. Variant spellings in the MS do not necessarily mean that the pronunciations were different.

9 *Erber(e)* appears again in 38 and 1171. The *MED* cited *Pearl* s.v. *hĕrbĕr* n.1, sense a, 'pleasure garden'. Gordon glossed 'grassy place in a garden, often among trees', a meaning comparable to *MED*, sense f, 'a grassy plot, a patch of greensward'. More than one sense fits *Pearl*. Note b, 'herb garden', in relation to the *erber* of lines 35–44.

Wellek-B (1933) 22 believed the poet fell asleep on a grave, "clearly pictured in the illustration to lines 57–64" on f. 41.

Hamilton-B (1955) 39, comparing the Garden of Eden, "where the maiden soul of man fell to earth and was lost," saw the dreamer asleep on the sloping crest of a hill, shadowed by trees and flowers, not "on or beside a grave or clump of plants" (48). The illustration is not precise in its details, but what looks like mounds may be represented on either side of the prostrate form of the dreamer.

Hillmann supposed the poet was talking about an expert jeweler who lost his gem while examining it in the outdoor light.

Luttrell-B (1965) 82–83, in discussing the *erber grene* 38 and the *huyle* 41 where the pearl rolled down, stated that the *erber* remains both a grass-plot and a garden so that the poet could apply allegory and give scope to garden imagery. "The garden and the turfed mound, in the context of the loss, *could* be a graveyard and a grave" (84).

Kean (1967) 16 associated the *erber* with the *hortus conclusus* of Song of Songs 4.12, the 'enclosed garden' that figuratively represents Christ's church containing faithful souls.

10 The usual reading of *yot* as a variant of *ʒode*, pt. of *gon*, seems adequate, since unvoicing of *-d* to *-t* suits the rhyme scheme. For other examples of unvoicing, see the notes to 460, 754, and 761.

Greene (1925) 821–22, comparing line 245 and the tone of lament in that stanza, believed the figure of a child lost in infancy was employed "as a literary device to impart the spiritual lesson of divine grace" (826).

Hamilton (1958) 179–80, thinking of how the pouring out of one's soul suited her allegorical interpretation, derived *yot* from *OED yet* 'pour, gush forth'.

11 Hillmann and Moorman took *dewyne* as a weak pt. without *-d*, since the narrator is here recalling the time when his pearl was lost, but 'lament' is fitting either as a switch to the historic pr. t. or to give the impression that, although he has already had the reconciliatory dream he is about to relate, he may still miss his pearl. (Cf. 17–18.)

Gollancz emended *fordolked* to *for-do[k]ked* and tr., "I pine, robbed by Love's severing power." Luttrell (1978) 275–77 supported Gollancz' emendation, but with a different interpretation: the narrator laments because he is deprived of the pearl's *luf-daungere*, her sweet thraldom.

Gordon and Moorman accord with the citation of *Pearl* by the *MED* s.v. *lŏve* n.1, 4b, *luf-daungere* 'the power of love', but senses 4 and 5 of *MED daunǧĕr* substantiate 'frustrated love'. Cf. *daunger* 'frustration' 250, and see Barron (1965) 13–15. Andrew & Waldron defined 'aloofness, distance of the beloved'.

Schofield (1904) 182–83 believed line 11 echoes *Le Roman de la Rose* 2968ff., where Danger drives the Lover away from the Rose. Hillmann thought *luf-daungere* denotes the dominion the pearl exercises over the affections of the jeweler—"in other words, his inordinate love for his earthly treasure," but Pilch-C (1964) 168 stated, "Here it becomes apparent for the first time that the pearl has a symbolic meaning and represents a beloved human being."

Kean (1967) 16 compared Song of Songs 2.5, *quia amóre lángueo* 'because I languish with love', and 5.7–8, where the Bride and Bridegroom are separated, pointing out that the mingling of biblical allusion with the diction of secular love poetry was not unusual for a medieval poet. Note, for example,

Christ's words to the pearl-maiden: "Cum hyder to me, my lemman swete" (763).

12-13 Macrae-Gibson-C (1968) 205, discussing link-words in the thematic structure, noted that because the pearl without *spot* 'blemish' could not be found in a particular *spot* 'place' on earth, the dreamer must leave the *erber* in the second stanza-group to rediscover his spiritual pearl in heaven. "Thus the refrain- and echo-words of the first stanza-group lay the foundation for much of the later development of the poem."

McGalliard (1969) 279-90 showed how the link-words and thought are "wedded in an unusually ordered but harmonious partnership. . . . Instead of announcing the content of the poem, [the links] organize it, focus it, concentrate it around a series of nuclei of attitude and emotion" (290).

Tomasch (1989) 11-20 traced *spot* 'place' and 'blemish' throughout *Pearl* as changes rung on two meanings by the use of *traductio, adnominatio,* and *expolitio.* Punning wordplay carries theme and builds structure. "Just as sound and sense become almost inseparably conjoined by the end of the poem, so too theme and structure finally appear as aspects of the same truth, facets of one whole. . . . The structure of *Pearl*, in its concatenation, stanza form and number, framework, circularity, and manifold repetitions of words and phrases serves to lead the reader through a series of images and a sequence of ideas to an understanding of the place of this work within an overall scheme that the poet has not so much imagined as imitated" (20).

13-24 Ginsberg (1988) 737 cited this stanza after pointing out that as in Dante, "dialectic becomes the scene of knowledge in *Pearl*, the environment where we see what otherwise cannot be known." In "Place and Dialectic in *Pearl* and Dante's *Paradiso*," he concluded that in "*Pearl*, places and arguments speak with the same voice; in the *Divine Comedy*, Dante's scrutiny of the locality of dialectic exposes its shortcomings as a way to describe paradise" (751).

14 'Pondered' seems more suitable than most editors' rendering of *wayted* as 'watched'. Cf. *OED wait* v.1, 3b, 'to watch mentally, consider attentively'. For *wele* 'splendid pearl', cf. *weal* sb.1, 2d, applying to a person. Gordon, Moorman, and Andrew & Waldron tr. 'precious thing', Hillmann 'wealth'.

15 Hillmann surmised the jeweler's absorption in his treasure caused him to overlook his *wrange* 'sin' of covetousness, but Gordon's *wrange* 'sorrow' accords with the tone of lament in this stanza. 'Distress' also suits the context.

17 As Gordon noted, *þat* refers to the mental action of l. 14, the dreamer's saddened state due to the loss of his pearl.

Gollancz and Chase added -*e* to *hert*. Emerson (1921) 134, also seeking to make the line regular, imputed carelessness to the scribe. Savage (1956b) 127 refuted this viewpoint, noting that the poet apparently had a choice of pronunciation with or without -e.

17-24 Cf. the dreamer's conflict described in 51-56.

18 The usual reading *bele* 'burn' (OI *bǽla*) seems fitting here. Cawley tr. 'festers', apparently following Luttrell (1955) 207-9 who argued for 'to suppurate', possibly from Old Swedish *bulin, bolin* 'swollen' (presuming a lost Scandinavian verb **bela*).

19-22 Gollancz compared *euensonge* (vespers) 529; so *sange* may denote the chanting of vespers. (See 529n.)

Osgood and Gordon suggested the poet was describing the genesis of *Pearl*. Gordon commented, "Though the poet felt grief, the sweetest of verse would come into his mind." Hamilton (1958) 182, in agreement with Wright (1940) 315-16, refuted this interpretation, seeing in these lines the first sense of peace to come, developed more fully in the next stanza.

Kean (1967) 42 related the theme to the *erber* in association with the Garden of Eden where Adam and Eve heard the voice of God, and the *hortus conclusus* of the Song of Songs, especially 2.14: "Sonet vox tua in áuribus meis: vox enim tua dulcis, et fácies tua decóra." ("Let thy voice sound in my ears: for thy voice is sweet, and thy face comely.")

Blenkner-C (1968) 237-39, believing the *sange* must come from within or above, noted that it presages the song of the birds (91-94), the 144,000 virgins (877-88), and the angels (1124-27).

Andrew & Waldron, following the interpretation of Davenport (1974) who contrasted the dreamer's past consolation and present desolation, translated: "Never yet did a song seem to me to have such sweetness as a moment of peace let steal over me. In truth there used to come fleetingly to me many (such moments). To think of her colour clad, as now, in mud!"

Gollanz' suggestion illumines the dreamer's reflections on his loss, for, in the chanting of vespers, whose liturgy deals with the promise of the Lord, verse 36 of the opening Ps. 104 touches upon death: "Et percússit omne primogénitum in terra eórum, primítias omnis labóris eórum." ("And he slew all the firstborn in their land: the firstfruits of all their labour.") In l. 894 the maiden is among the 144,000 virgins, "As newe fryt, to God ful due." It is only after his vision that the dreamer is able to accept fully the Lord's promise of resurrection.

21 Donaldson (1972) 80-82 suggested emending *Forsoþe* 'Truly' to *Forþoȝtes* 'Regrets', so that *fele* 'many' may refer to a specific n., but relating *fele* to the 'many (melodies)' heard at the silent hour makes good sense.

22 Osgood compared images of the grave in 320 and 857. Kean (1967) 23 added l. 958 in discussing the relationship of these images to the *memento mori* poems of the fourteenth century.

23 See Chapman (1945) 17-18 for other examples of personification in the *Pearl* poems. Morris read *mele* 'discourse' at the end of the line; Gollancz considered it an emendation: *myry mele* 'joyous thing'. However, the mark over the first minim denotes *i* equalling *j* in *juele*.

25   Osgood and Pilch-C (1964) 172-74 compared Thomas de Hale's "Love Ron" in which the unsullied maiden is called "swetture þan eny spis" (l. 168). The pearl-maiden is called *special spyce* in 235 and 938. Pilch, while noting representation of the bride as a *hortus conclusus* with spices springing forth in Song of Songs 4.12-16, pointed out that the details of the garden of spices in *Pearl* 43-46 remind one more of the orchard of *Deduiz* 'Pleasure' in *Le Roman de la Rose* 1341-44.

26   Dunlap (1977) 183-84 pointed to the double-entendre of *rot—rote*. The maiden's body, having sunk into *rot* 'decay', has run to Christ, the *rote* 'root' (420) of all her bliss, for only after the body is laid away to *rote* 'decay' (958) can the soul enter heaven. In discussing vegetations puns in *Pearl*, Dunlap noted that the "growth of the human soul, like that of plants, is based on regeneration, in kind, through death, and is cultivated by God" (181).

Northup (1897) 334 called *runnen* an example of apocope (the dropping of a final letter, syllable, or sound). Most editors emended to *runne*, but even if the *-n* were pronounced, one may retain the MS reading as an example of imperfect rhyme. See the notes to 791 and 802 for others.

27-28   Gollancz compared the Chaucerian *Romaunt of the Rose*: "Agayn the sonne an hundred hewes,/Blewe, yelowe, and reed, that fressh and newe is" (1577-78).

Gollancz and Hillmann glossed *blayke* 'pale', Andrew & Waldron 'white, pale'. Most editors favored Gordon's 'yellow', perhaps thinking of the citation from the Chaucerian *Romaunt*, but for *blayke* 'white', see *MED bleik* adj., sense b, where *Pearl* is cited.

Hillmann tr. *schyneȝ* 'will shine'. Andrew & Waldron followed Luttrell-B (1965) 71 who suggested emending to *schyne* to make the v. an infin. dependent on *mot* 'must' (25) so that the whole stanza would be an argument, "the narrator saying that spices, flowers, and fruit *ought* to spring from the pearl," but, as Bishop (1968) 141 noted, one may assume that the spices have already sprung from the pearl. Lines 41-44 of the next stanza support Bishop's view.

29   The flower later symbolizes both mortality and immortality. In 269-70 the maiden is compared to a rose that *flowred and fayled*; in 906 she is called a *reken rose*, in 962 a *lufly flor*. The symbols of pearl and flower come together in 269-72 in a context that deals with death and resurrection. *Fryte* 29 anticipates the reference to the maiden among the 144,000 virgins purchased from the distant earth, "As newe fryt, to God ful due" (894).

Gordon, Moorman, and Andrew & Waldron tr. *fede* 'faded', Hillmann 'withered' (OF *fade*). The *MED*, following Gollancz, cited *Pearl* s.v. *fēde* ppl. (OI *feyja* 'to rot, decay'), but sense 2 s.v. *fāde* adj. 'wasted' (OF *fade*) is suitable, if one considers that the poet switched the vowel from *a* to *e* for rhyme. (Cf. *ware* in rhyme position instead of *were* in 151 and 1027.)

Vasta-C (1967) 191–93, questioning such a vowel shift and noting the narrator's "interior disharmony," suggested *feden* 'to feed': the narrator wishes that "flower and fruit may not be permitted to feed on his Pearl. . . . Thus he desires that the natural process of corruption-generation should suspend itself."

However, this stanza focuses more on the idea of life coming from death. Kean (1967) 68–70 discussed the concept of blossoms of immortality springing from mortality, citing St. Bonaventura's *Vitis Mystica* which relates the flowers to virtues, the white lily to chastity, the blue violet to humility, and the red rose to patience and love. (Cf. *Pearl* 27.)

31–32 Gordon noted these lines are closely paralleled in *Piers Plowman*, C-Text, XIII, 179–81, but direct relationship is uncertain since both passages are based on John 12.24–25 where Christ speaks figuratively of his approaching death and resurrection. Cf. also 1 Cor. 15.36–37.

Johnson-C (1953) 34 associated *grayneʒ* with pearls. See *MED grain*, 3b, 'precious stone'. Richardson (1962) 312–13 related the harvest theme to the wine-harvest in the Parable of the Vineyard (501–72), and considered it fitting that *Pearl* should conclude with a reference to the bread and wine of the Eucharist (1209). *Woneʒ* 'barns' anticipates symbolically the *woneʒ* 'abodes' (1027) of the New Jerusalem.

35 Hillmann and DeFord separated MS *sprygande* to *spryg ande*. The emendation of all other editors to *spryngande* seems unnecessary, since the scribe sometimes ran words together. Cf., for example, *tomy* 58, *onbalke* and *þerbod* 62 in *Pearl*, and the separation of *glaumande* to *glaum ande* in *Gawain* 46, made by most editors of that poem.

37–48 Wrenn (1943) 31–32, noting that the flowers are symbols of powers of spiritual healing, discussed this stanza in relation to the April Eclogue of Spenser's *Shepheardes Calender*, ll. 136–44. On p. 48, he compared Spenser's *madding mynd* 25 to *Pearl* 1154. Cf also *garres . . . greete* in the opening line of the April Eclogue to *Pearl* 331.

39–40 For *hyʒ* 'holy', see *MED heigh* adj., 2d. For *seysoun* 'occasion, time', see *MED sēsǒun* n., 1d, 'the time of the year in which a particular festival or holy day occurs'. *Pearl* is cited there.

Osgood, p. xvi, Schofield (1909) 616, and Hillmann identified the *hyʒ seysoun* as the Assumption of the Virgin, August 15, because it relates to the comparison the poet makes later (421–56) between the pearl-maiden and the Blessed Mary.

Gollancz, Gordon, and Andrew & Waldron favored Lammastide, August 1, because of the emphasis on the cutting of corn. Gordon noted the poet may have been suggesting the "gathering of the Lord's harvest, with the Pearl as one of the 'first-fruits'; cf. 894."

Knightley (1961) 97, following the suggestion of Madeleva (1925), supposed the poet was referring to the feast of the Transfiguration, the 8th day, "which in biblical exegesis signifies the last day and therefore eternity."

Bishop (1968) 86, feeling the whole month of August provides the cue for mentioning the action of reaping, stated, "The poet is alluding to the traditional 'occupations of the months'—an iconographical commonplace in medieval miniatures, sculptures and stained glass."

Moorman surmised that *hyȝ* may be a variant (or possibly scribal error) for *híȝ* or *héȝ* 'hay', and tr. *hyȝ seysoun* 'hay season' when the grain is cut with sharp sickles.

Burke (1980) summed up the arguments on the Assumption, the Transfiguration, and Lammastide, and favored none of them. Instead, he identified *hyȝ seysoun* as a "Temporal Metaphor" and connected the harvest image with baptism. With reference to Bishop (1968) 86, he argued that the phrase refers not to any one feast but to the entire month of August. At the start of the poem, the maiden has "realized the promise of baptismal reaping," but the dreamer must still grow in "awareness, foreshadowed in the harvest image, to the meaning of his baptismal heritage" (47).

However, the poet in l. 39 appears to be pointing to a specific time within the month of August, and Lammastide seems appropriate. There are many vegetation symbols in *Pearl* associating the maiden with spice, flower, fruit, and seed. In the early English Church, Lammas (from 'loaf-mass') was kept as a harvest festival when loaves of bread made from the new grain were consecrated. *Pearl* begins with vegetation imagery and ends with a reference to the Eucharist (bread-wheat and wine-grapes), and in between there is the presentation of the Parable of the Vineyard (501–72).

41 The *huyle* is evidently the particular spot to be associated with *floury flaȝt* 57 and *balke* 62. Gordon glossed 'mound (overgrown with plants)', recalling Gollancz' association of the word with modern dialect *hile*, current in southeast Lancashire (Rochdale). Hillmann tr. 'hillock' (OE *hyll*), a likely place to lose a pearl, but hardly suggesting the "appearance of a well-kept grave-mound." However, if one recalls the image of the dead grain in the ground bringing forth growth (29–36), figuratively depicting Christ's death and resurrection, 'mound' with the connotation 'grave-mound' suits the context of 41, as well as those containing *hylle* 1172 and *hyul* 1205.

43 Gollancz compared the Chaucerian *Romaunt of the Rose* 1367–72. Stern-C (1955) 76 interpreted these spices as earthly manifestations of heaven's beneficence: gillifower, an aromatic and *healing* clove; ginger, an aromatic and *energizing* anti-irritant; gromwell, bearing "polished white, stony nutlets very much like pearls."

Gollancz (1891c) 109 noted that medieval man compared gromwell seeds to pearls. Wintermute (1949) suggested the poet placed the word in climactic position because of the resemblance. Bishop (1968) 87–88 cited *MED grŏmil* n., sense a, *Agnus Castus*: "It haȝt qwyt seed lyk a perle ston."

Wilson (1971a) pointed out that though *pearl-plant* as a synonym for *gromwell* is not found in English until the late sixteenth century, a Latin term for *gromwell* current in the poet's time was *margarita rusticorum.*

44 Cf. *powdered* to *poudred* in *Gawain* 800, describing the dispersal of pinnacles on Bercilak's castle. Reisner (1973) noted the word was employed in the technical language of heraldry. Recalling Cargill and Schlauch (1928), he suggested identification of the *Pearl*-poet with John Prat, a clerk attached to the household of John, Duke of Lancaster, since families that bore the name of Prat in fourteenth-century Europe "had arms with fields either powdered or charged with a variety of floral devices."

46 Andrew & Waldron, following Gollancz (1891c), assumed the word division of the MS may be wrong, changed *fayr reflayr* to *fayrre flayr*, and tr. 45-46: "If it was lovely to look at, still fairer was the scent that floated from it." However, as.Gordon noted, the sense is satisfactory as the text stands.

47 Cf. the verse tag *wot and wene* in 201.

49-60 Russell (1978) 21-23 noted that Augustine, in *De genesis ad literam* XII, vii, identifies three kinds of dreams: *somnium naturale, somnium animale,* and *somnium coeleste.* The first two have earthly causes; only the third has value as revelation. Russell argued that *Pearl*, along with *Piers Plowman* as another typical Middle English dream vision, is a *somnium animale* because it springs from the anxiety and perturbation of the dreamer's waking mind. He cited Macrobius' *Commentary on the Dream of Scipio* to support his view, and opposed Spearing (1970) 112 who classified *Pearl* as a *somnium mentis*, a dream occurring in Scripture in such a way as to "make it clear that sleeping and dreaming are used as images referring to mystical states." See also 790n.

Champion (1992) argued that in terms of the self and the self's conflicts with the narrative's many norms, "the world of *Pearl* is more novelistic . . . than the more orthodox *Piers Plowman*." *Pearl* is "private, multi-levelled, psychologically complex," whereas the spiritual pilgrimage in *Piers* is "closer to the shared anxieties of a folk-community" (632). As an example, she noted, p. 633, the images in this stanza 5 of clenched hands, anguish within the heart, and the sense of inner collapse.

49 *Spenud*, with a bar over the *e* denoting a following *n*, may be the MS form, rhyming vocally with *denned* 51. Cf. suffixes with other than *e* vowel in *coruon* (*Gawain* 797) and *flemus* (*Cleanness* 31). The scribe's two minims for both *n* and *u* sometimes cause confusion. (Morris, for example, read *denely* 'loud' instead of *deuely* in l. 51.) Most editors emended to *spenned*. Andrew & Waldron read *spennd*.

51 Hillmann tr. *deuely* 'wicked', feeling the grief of the "jeweler" should be defined as such, but Gordon's 'dreary' accords better with *care ful colde* 50 and *playned* 53. One may consider word-play, since medieval man considered it sinful to mourn excessively over the death of a person.

52 Bishop (1968) 73-74, disagreeing with Gordon's contention that *resoun* does not echo *Le Roman de la Rose* 2997f., compared the *Roman*'s Lady Reason, who has much in common with Boethius' Lady Philosophy.

Sette . . . saȝt occurs again in 1201 after the dreamer has been made peaceful by the maiden's teaching and the vision of the New Jerusalem that was granted to him.

53 Andrew & Waldron, believing the poet usually avoided identical rhyme, adopted Gollancz' emendation of *spenned* to *penned*. (They also followed Gollancz in emending *tryed* 702 to *cryed* because *tryed* appears in l. 707.) However, *spenned*, the same v. as *spenud* 49 (ON *spenna*) but with slightly different connotation, seems suitable. (Cf. 702n.)

Hamilton (1958) 183 suggested *OED spend* v.1 (OE *spendan*) 'lost' to accord better with her "lost pearl equals lost grace" interpretation. One may consider word-play: the dreamer has 'lost' grace because of too much mourning over his pearl 'enclosed' there.

Fletcher (1921) long ago demonstrated a multi-level approach to *Pearl* and the possibility of reconciling the elegiac and allegorical theories.

Allen (1971) 137–39, with reference to Fletcher and Wellek-B (1933), noted that the letter and the spiritual allegory need not be in opposition, since "biblical and historical people may be understood as figures without denying their existence."

54 Hillmann, rejecting emendation to *fyrce* (made by Gollancz, Gordon, Cawley, Moorman, and Andrew & Waldron), glossed *fyrte* 'violence' and tr., "With violence which swiftly reasonings fought." MS *fyrte* may also be retained by taking it from *MED fēren* v.1, 'fear', where *fērt* is listed as a pp.

55-56 Johnson-C (1953) 34 noted word-play on *kynde*, "both nature and kindness." As Hillmann observed, the 'character of Christ' implies Christ's virtues, including his humble suffering on earth, which should teach the dreamer acceptance of God's will.

57 Luttrell-B (1965) 70 defined *floury flaȝt* 'flowery slab of turf', rejecting the 'flowery mead' identification of Elliott (1951). Citations s.v. *MED flaught* n. point toward Luttrell's view.

58-59 Kean (1967) 18 compared Song of Songs 5.1-2, which describes aromatical spices in the *hortus conclusus*, sleep, and the voice of the beloved beckoning.

Blanch (1973) 61, pointing ahead to *ensens of swete smelle* (1122) scattered by angels in the New Jerusalem, noted that sweet-smelling spices and flowers "are conventionally emblematic of heaven and God's grace."

59 *Slode* literally denotes 'slid'. One may translate *slepyng-slaȝt* 'deep slumber' (as it is in Volume 1 of my 1984 omnibus edition of the *Pearl* poems) or 'sleep's onslaught' (given in the verse translation here). Gordon, who noted that the usual meaning of *slaȝt* is 'a violent or sudden blow', glossed *slepyng-slaȝt* 'sudden onset of sleep'. Andrew & Waldron glossed 'sudden heavy sleep' but pointed out that "the metaphor could suggest either a sleep like death, or else sleep which descends with the suddenness of a blow." Fowler (1984) 206-7 favored 'sleeping-blow' and freely paraphrased: "I was slugged into sleep."

60 All editors emended MS *precos* to *precios*. For retention of *precos*, cf. omission of *i* in *graco(u)s* 95, 934 and *precos* 192. Four occurrences may indicate a variant spelling. *MED grāciŏus* lists a form without *i*.

61 Osgood's 'space', adopted by DeFord, was supported by Bloomfield (1969) 302: "In the fourteenth century it was believed that one's spirit did travel in space in a vision or even in sleep." Hillmann tr. *in space* 'at once'; Gordon glossed 'after a time', with Cawley, Moorman, and Andrew & Waldron in agreement.

62 Gordon's *sweuen* 'sleep (or dream)' represents the readings of editors. Spearing (1970) 111, following Kean (1967) 29, suggested placing a semicolon after *bod*, translating *sweuen* 'vision', and running l. 62 into 63, but *auenture* 64 may be associated with the vision. Andrew & Waldron placed a period after *bod* but still translated *sweuen* 'sleep'.

65 Gordon, comparing 293, tr., "I had no idea at all where it was," but Hillmann's literal reading seems fitting here. Andrew & Waldron, crediting Pearsall & Salter (1973) 56, cited Honorius of Autun's reference to paradise as a delightful place in the Orient (*PL* 172.1117).

67 The superb imagery of the terrestrial paradise prevails to l. 120. Schofield (1904) 189-90 compared Ch. 33 of *Mandeville's Travels*. Osgood, pp. 57-58, compared similar imagery in the *Troy* and *Alexander* romances. M. Williams (1970) discussed "Oriental Backgrounds & the *Pearl*-Poet." See also Curtius (1948) 195-200 for discussion of descriptions of the *locus amoenus* in Latin poetry of the Middle Ages, Patch (1950) 190 for a comparison of *Pearl* to "other world" descriptions, Blanch-B (1965) 87 for reminiscences of the Garden of Love in *Le Roman de la Rose*, and Finlayson (1974) for a study of how the three *loci* in *Pearl*, garden, earthly paradise, and heaven, relate to the development of the dreamer' soul from darkness to illumination.

69-70 These lines show a variation of the formula which states that something is too difficult to describe. Here the dreamer is saying no man could believe what he saw. See 99-100n on the inexpressibility topos.

73-77 Blanch-B (1965) 87, noting that crystal and silver in the medieval lapidaries were considered inferior reflections of gold, hence appropriate for a terrestrial paradise setting, showed how the poet underscored the difference between this region and the New Jerusalem described in ll. 980-1092.

78 Gordon, Hillmann, Moorman, and Andrew & Waldron gave the sense of 'quiver' for *trylle*, but *OED trill* v.2, sense 3, 'trail' is fitting here.

79 Hillmann tr. *glodeȝ* 'glades'; Moorman and Andrew & Waldron adopted Gordon's 'clear patches of sky' (*MED glāde* n.1, sense b). However, the description seems to be of sunlight coming through 'open spaces (clearings)' in trees (*MED*, sense a).

80 Robinson (1984) 226 would tr. *schrylle* 'shrilly', but this entire stanza appeals to the sense of sight, not sound, and it is difficult to justify a description of leaves shining 'shrilly'. The *MED* cites only *Pearl* s.v. *shril(le* adv., sense c, 'brightly, sharply'.

81 Editors gave the sense of sound for *grynde* 'grind, crunch', but 'mingle' as an extension of *MED grīnden* v.1, 1d, continues the description of the dreamer's seeing the landscape around him. As with *schrylle* 80, it seems the poet changed the denotation of a word that usually referred to sound to refer to sight. Besides, what can make a grinding sound on the *grauayl* but physical footsteps, and the dreamer is out of his body, as ll. 61–62 indicate.

Tajima (1975), examining the poet's use of *con* as a periphrastic auxil., concluded that it is almost always used to place the infin. in rhyming position. For other linguistic studies, see Tajima (1970, 1971, 1972, 1976, and 1978).

82 See 3n on the dreamer's Oriental pearl. Tristman-C (1970) 279 saw the image of pearls here anticipating the dreamer's view of the 144,000 virgins in procession (1096–1104).

83 Cf. 1076. Neither sun nor moon is needed in the New Jerusalem.

87–88 Blenkner (1971) 38–42 discussed vegetation imagery in *Pearl*. These lines recall 29, 46, and 58, and foreshadow the description of the fruit-bearing trees of life in 1077–80, based on Rev. 22.2.

95 Editors emended *gracos* to *gracios*, but see 60n.

98 See Patch (1950) 222–29 for discussion of the allegorical tradition of the Goddess Fortuna, and Kean (1967) 237–39 and Bishop (1968) 74–76 for the poet's use of *fortune* in *Pearl* in ll. 98, 129, 306, as it differs in meaning from *wyrde* 249, 273 and *Destyné* 758. The pearl-maiden utters *Destyné* as a synonym for Christ, *wyrde* is a power God exerts, but, as Kean noted, *fortune* is used "for the particular turn which events take in the world."

99–100 Boitani (1982) 105 compared these lines to Dante's *Paradiso* I, 4–6: "Nel ciel che puì della sua luce prende/fu' io, e vidi cose che ridire/né sa né può chi di là su discende." ("I have been in the heaven that most receives His light and I have seen things which whoso descends from up there has neither knowledge nor power to re-tell.") Stating that something is difficult to describe was not uncommon in medieval literature. Cf. in *Pearl* ll. 133–36, 223–26, and 1117–18, and see Vantuono (1971) 65–67 for use of the formula in *Patience, Cleanness,* and *Gawain,* as well.

Schotter (1984) 29 cited ll. 99–100 and 223–26 as examples of the inexpressibility topos and then developed the idea that human language is valid as a means of communication between God and man but must be doomed to failure because words are insufficient to convey a true picture of the Divine. "By using language which warns against itself, the poet is able to achieve a poetic incarnation on the Augustinian model—to suggest the Divine Word through the limited medium of his own words" (32).

Watts (1984) studied the inexpressibility topos in 99–100, 133–36, 223–26, and 1117–18, pointing out that the first and last are brief and bound the dream at beginning and end. "The dreamer says each of the four" (26). In comparing Dante, she noted that the Italian poet joins failure of flesh and language, but this similarity to *Pearl* also reveals a crucial difference, for Dante, as in *Paradiso* I, 4–6, says, "I have been in the heaven," and "I have seen things." Thus, "his memory is less dark than other memories. *Pearl*'s dreamer has no such stance" (30), for he never enters heaven.

102 Hieatt (1965) 141 noted the dream psychology of doing easily what is impossible or painful in the real world.

104–5 Added to the vegetation imagery recalling 25–36 are the rivers of spiritual life, to be followed by *fyldor* (106) anticipating heaven. *Reuereȝ*, placed so close to *water* (107), the main stream, has caused some difficulty. Gollancz' 'river-meads' was favored by Gordon, Moorman, and Andrew & Waldron, but Hillmann's 'rivers' seems suitable, for the poet may have had in mind Genesis 2.10–14, where the river that waters Eden divides into four branches.

106 Editors read *b[o]nkes* instead of *bukes*, as if an *o* or part of it were missing, but the MS reading may be retained as a *b* followed by two minims representing *u*. See 49n on *n-u* confusion, and cf. *bukes* as a variant spelling of *MED bek* n.1, 'small stream', to the *u-e* variants of *lude-lede-leude* in *Gawain* 133, 126, 675. The spelling is *lede* 'man' in *Pearl* 542.

107 Gordon, after identifying *water* as the river of life (Rev. 22.1), flowing from heaven into the terrestrial paradise (see 974, 1055–60), defined *schereȝ* 'meanders along', stating, "The identity and sense of this word are uncertain." The v. may be a form of MED *chāren* 'move'. Cf. in *Gawain schere* 334 for the n. *chere*. Another initial *ch-sch* variant spelling in *Gawain* is *cheldeȝ* 1611 alongside *scheldeȝ* 1626.

113 Schofield (1904) 190 compared a description in *Mandeville's Travels* of pearls at the bottom of a lake in Ceylon. Osgood doubted the dependence of these verses on *Mandeville*, but *gemme gente* (118) may imply noble pearls. (See 118n.) Gollancz compared the Chaucerian *Romaunt of the Rose* 125–27. French *fo(u)ns* occurs in both *Mandeville* and *Le Roman de la Rose*. *Cleanness* 1026 has *founs* in a passage which Brown (1904) 149–50 showed is dependent on the French *Mandeville*.

Gollancz tr. *stonden* 'shone'. Revard (1962) supported this reading with reference to *OED stand* v., sense 33, observing that 'shone' rather than 'stood' is in "accord with the poet's heightened language." Gordon glossed 'stand' pr. t. Andrew & Waldron emended to *stoden* 'shone' because "this portion of the narrative is consistently in the pa. t.," but *stonden* as a pt. pl. with *-en* may be compared to *weuen* (71).

114 The image of glass appears here and in ll. 990, 1018, 1025, and 1106. Phillips (1984), in her study of "Medieval Glass-Making Techniques and the Imagery of Glass in *Pearl*," concluded, p. 212, that the glass images occur at all the points of greatest emotional intensity. "As the dreamer moves toward a state of deep inner illumination the predominant colours of the poem become those of the great windows of the fourteenth-century churches and cathedrals, golden yellow and a brilliant pearly whiteness."

115 MS *a*, gliding to the *s* of *stremande*, may be a shortened form of *as*. Note the omission of the final letter of monosyllabic words in 144, 309, 429, 792, and 1058. Editors emended to *as*.

Strothe 'wooded' is used attrib. in *Gawain* 1710. Gordon gave to *strope-men* the generalized poetic sense 'men of this world'. The literal 'woodsmen' is also suitable here. Elliott (1979) 61–62, after noting the cognate OE *strōd* 'marshy land overgrown with brushwood' and the emphasis on water in this passage, stated that *strope-men*, while it may literally mean 'dwellers in a marshy woodland', is singularly fitting in this stanza as a "symbol of country people, like Hardy's Woodlanders."

116 For pr. p. *staren* 'gleaming', a form different from the usual *-ande* in this MS, cf. *runnen* 874, *drawen* 1193, and see Mustanoja (1960) 569–70 for similar examples in ME.

118 The phrase *gemme gente* perhaps denotes pearls, as it does in 253. Blanch-B (1965) 88–89 noted that *beryl* (110) signifies rebirth into a new and purer life, *emerad* signifies good faith and suggests chastity, and *saffer* symbolizes hope, truth, and wisdom. All three jewels "point to the prerequisites for heavenly existence." For cleansing symbols involving blood and water in relation to Christ's death on the cross and the sacrament of baptism, see 649–56 and 766.

127 Osgood's *floty* 'watery' was adopted by most editors and the *MED*. Moorman favored Hillmann's 'undulating'.

129-32 See 98n on the allusion to the Goddess Fortuna. Osgood compared 1195 in a stanza that deals with the conflict between man's desire and God's will.

Macrae-Gibson-C (1968) 206 noted the development of the dreamer's conflict with the use of the link-word *more* in Stanza-Group III. In X, the link-word is again *more*; the laborers in the vineyard think they deserve *more* than those who worked only one hour (551–53). In contrast, each soul in heaven, instead of envying others, wishes their crowns were worth five (451) and that every soul were five—*þe mo þe myryer* 850. (See also 1195n.)

131 Andrew & Waldron emended *her* to *his* and tr. 131–32: "The man to whom she sends his desire seeks to have more and more (of it) all the time." However, MS *her* may stand, for the poet is evidently saying that fortune may send more and more of either solace or sorrow, as she wills. At this point, the dreamer is receiving her benefits, but he has also experienced her sting in feeling sadness on earth.

133-36 See 99–100n on the inexpressibility topos.

136 Gollancz capitalized *Gladneʒ*, believing the poet was thinking of Dame Gladness in *Le Roman de la Rose*. Gordon, Hillmann, and Andrew & Waldron glossed 'joys, gladness' (*MED gladnes(se* n., 1c, 'source of joy'). Rendering *gladneʒ* 'delights' is fitting here. Moorman referred to Emerson (1927) 813 who took the word as the pl. of *MED glāden* n., 'cleared space in a wood'.

137 Gollancz compared *paradys erthly* in the Chaucerian *Romaunt of the Rose* 648. The garden of the *Roman*, that of Eden in Genesis, and the *hortus conslusus* of Solomon's Song of Songs all share common features of the *locus amoenus*. (See 67n.) Here and in 248 *Paradys(e)* may denote the divine kingdom, since the dreamer, though his conception is earth-bound, apparently feels he is approaching heaven. (Cf. 295–300n.)

138 All editors, except Morris, Hillmann, and DeFord, emended *oþer* to *over*, but Fowler (1960) 29 and Hillmann showed that MS *oþer* may be retained. The dreamer thinks that Paradise must be either on his side of the stream or on the opposite side.

139–40 Morris (1891a) 603 suggested emending *myrþeʒ* to *myrcheʒ* 'boundaries'. Osgood glossed *myrþeʒ* 'pleasance, pleasure garden' and *mereʒ* 'boundary-lines.' Gollancz' emendation to *mereʒ by Myrþe*, based on the Chaucerian *Romaunt of the Rose* 1409–16, where Déduit, the Lord of the Garden, is called *Mirthe*, was supported by Day (1934). Bone (1937) refuted Gordon & Onions (1932) 131 who rendered *myrþeʒ* 'pleasure-gardens'. Moorman followed Gordon who, in his edition, suggested: "I thought the stream was a division made by pools, separating the delights." Andrew & Waldron, except for their rendering of *myrþeʒ* as 'pleasure-gardens', agreed.

Fowler (1960) tr., "I thought that the water was a deception/Made by meres among the delights," feeling the dreamer may have thought that although the water seemed continuous and impassable, if he walked along the shore, he would eventually find an opening. Hillmann tr., "I supposed the water was a division/Between joyances with boundaries made," arguing that the dreamer here pictured Paradise as a "hierarchy of states of beatitude with boundaries fixed between them."

Gordon's reading seems best, except that *mereʒ* 'streams' is used in this edition, instead of 'pools', to depict the rushing currents of water. (Cf. the images in 111–12.) The dreamer sees the water as a division between the delights on his side and on the opposite side. (Note 137–38, 141–42, and 147–48.) *Mere(ʒ)* denotes water in ll. 158 and 1166. *By mereʒ made* 'created alongside streams' modifies *myrþeʒ* 'delights'.

142 *Hope* is a pt. with loss of -*d* before *þ*. Cf. 185, 286 (loss of -*t* before *þ*), 572, 752, and see Day (1919) and Gordon & Onions (1932) 132–36 for a discussion in relation to the other poems in the MS. All editors, except Osgood, Hillmann, DeFord, and Moorman, emended.

144 *Euer . . . a* may be a variant of *euer . . . ay* 'always'. See 115n.

110

151 The context of 151–54 favors *woþeʒ* 'perils' (ON *váði*), given by Osgood, Gollancz, Gordon, Moorman, and Andrew & Waldron. The dreamer is looking for a way to cross the stream, perilous because of its depth (143) and its swirling (111). Hillmann tr. *woþeʒ* 'searchings' from OE *wáþ*. (See also 375n on *woþe*.)

161–68 The figure of the maiden is central to the debate over elegy or allegory in *Pearl*, a debate tempered by the recognition of both genres in the poem. For a survey of scholarship on the subject from Wellek-B (1933) to the beginning of the 1970s, see Eldredge (1975) 172–78.

Piehler (1971), relating *Pearl* to Jungian dream psychology, viewed the maiden as a symbolic manifestation of the dreamer's lost innocence, but still concluded that the "text allows us little alternative to interpreting the maiden as primarily the poet's daughter; the symbolic roles we have distinguished are no more than aspects of her manifestation which enable us to see her as more than herself in a state of glory" (162). For negative criticism of Piehler's psychological interpretation, see Levine (1977).

Wright (1982) suggested that the chief inspiration for the part played by Pearl Prynne in Dimmesdale's conversion (in Hawthorne's *The Scarlet Letter*) came from Dante's *Divine Comedy* and *Pearl*. Dante's Beatrice and the pearl-maiden "inform Hawthorne's conception of Pearl Prynne throughout the novel. . . . To the end, therefore, in deed if not in word, Pearl continues to play the part of censor and guide which she inherited from Beatrice and the Pearl-maiden" (118).

161–62 Hillmann tr. *faunt* 'youthful being', believing, p. xx, that the jeweler's material pearl has now been transformed into his soul, symbolized by the maiden. Gollancz, Gordon, Moorman, and Andrew & Waldron tr. 'child'. *MED faunt* shows the word may mean 'young child' or 'infant', without specification of age. *Mayden of menske* qualifies the meaning in this context, and if one is to judge by the illustrations on folios 42 and 42b, she may be called a young child of advanced stature.

Osgood, p. xxv, referred to Saint Augustine's *The City of God* 22.14: "Quid ergo de infantibus dicturi sumus, nisi quia non in ea resurrecturi sunt corporis exiquitate, qua mortui; sed quod eis tardius accessurum erat tempore, hoc sunt illo Dei opere miro atque celerrimo recepturi" (*PL* 41.776). ("Now as touching infants, I say they shall not rise again with that littleness of body in which they died, but that the sudden and strange power of God shall give them a stature of full growth" [tr. John Healey, Vol. 2, p. 380].)

Marti (1993) 313, crediting Bishop (1968) 101, noted that l. 857, "Alþaʒ oure corses in clotteʒ clynge," makes clear that the maiden's body has not been resurrected, but it is necessary for her to assume a "visionary body," like the characters in Dante's *Divine Comedy*. This "visionary body," then, has the appearance of the one which, according to patristic authorities, a soul will assume after the General Resurrection. Like Dante, in order to facilitate poetic representation, the *Pearl*-poet "gives his afterworld figures bodies before they could really have them" (314). See Marti for a study of the seven traditional characteristics of the resurrected body in *Pearl*, four for the resurrected bodies of the just, *agilitas, claritas, subtilitas,* and *impassibilitas* (agility, clarity, subtlety, and impassibility), and three for the resurrected bodies of both the just and the wicked, *qualitas, integritas,* and *identitas* (quality, integrity, and identity).

163 Cf. 197. *MED blēaunt* defines 'silk fabric' for the garments worn in *Pearl* and *Gawain* 879 and 1928. Rev. 19.8 describes *byssino* 'fine linen' for the garment the bride of Christ wears, but the poet sometimes altered biblical details without changing the essential meaning. (Cf. 785–86n.)

166 *Schore* evidently denotes the 'cliff' of 159. Gordon, in his glossary, compared *schore* 'ridge' in *Gawain* 2161.

171–72 Cf. 15–16.

175–76 Hillmann, following Madeleva (1925) 131, believed these lines undermine the theory that *Pearl* is a lament for a dead child because the dreamer "could not reasonably, as a Christian, be surprised at seeing his little dead daughter there." Spearing (1970) 132 pointed out that one need not suppose the dreamer will always think and feel with reason. He failed to do so in the garden (51–56).

179 Andrew & Waldron followed Gollancz in emending *atount* to *astount*, arguing that the "alliteration would appear to support the emendation," but the poet did not use alliteration regularly in *Pearl*, and *atount* 'dazed', which Gordon derived from OF *ato(u)ner*, is suitable.

184 Hammerle (1936) compared *The Castle of Perseverance*, c. 1425: "As a hawke, I hoppe in my hende halle" (406).

Chapman (1945) 20, viewing the parallelism to 1085 as a Virgilian mannerism, listed 62 examples among the four poems in the MS.

Reichardt-BMW (1991) discussed the animal similes of *hawk* here, *do* 345, and *quayle* 1085, arguing that they "depict a composite portrait of the dreamer's emotional and spiritual character" (17). The hawk simile "ultimately points toward the dreamer's own temptation to seize the object of his desire (i.e. the pearl) just as a hawk would seize its prey" (19), the doe simile reveals his tendency "to avoid what is unpleasant or painful" (20), and the quail simile shows his attachment to carnal pleasures, "since the beast it invokes was proverbially linked to fleshliness and earth-bound existence" (22).

185 See 142n for retention of MS *hope*. Most editors adopted Osgood's *porpose* 'intended meaning', a sense different from 'purpose' (267, 508). The poet presents his persona as one who is predisposed to receive spiritual instruction and insights, like Saint John who had seen the heavenly procession *in gostly drem* (790).

Hendrix (1985) 462, in referring to this line and the poet's use of *gostly porpose*, stated, "It is in this section that the dreamer—and the reader with him—makes a first tentative leap toward the spiritual."

Thomas (1938) 222, following Gollancz, tr. *porpose* 'vision', but *MED* *purpōs* n. does not substantiate this reading.

Andrew & Waldron rendered *porpose* 'quarry' and translated the line: "I thought that the quarry was spiritual."

188 In view of 173-74 and 182-83, *steuen* 'speech' (Morris, Osgood, Hillmann) seems preferable to 'meeting' (Gollancz, Gordon, Andrew & Waldron).

190 Cf. the description of the pearl in 6.

192 See 60n for retention of MS *precos*.

193 See 745-46n for discussion of *perleȝ . . . prys*.

195 Osgood compared 753. Hoffman-C (1960) 99, tracing the flower imagery through 207-8, 269-70, 753, 906-8, and 961-62, noted the constant identification of flower, fruit, and jewel with the maiden, related to the "death-and-resurrection motif, which has a further presentation in the two Jerusalems and the figure of Christ." (See also 29n.)

197-220 Schotter (1979), after discussing "The Poetic Function of Alliterative Formulas of Clothing in the Portrait of the Pearl Maiden," concluded that while the poet depicts her with the language associated with romance heroines, he carefully omits the most gaudy formulas so that the "maiden's portrait can be seen, once the dreamer's focus on outward and visible signs has been overcome, to be perfectly appropriate to her role as one of the Brides of the Lamb" (195).

197 Cf. 163. *Mys* 'cloak' denotes the loose outer garment the maiden wears over her *cortel* (203). As Gollancz noted, l. 197 is not an exact repetition of 163, since the reference there is to the maiden's general attire. In 197-220 the poet depicts the details of her dress.

Osgood's emendation to *bleaunt of biys* is more radical than Gordon's *beau biys* 'fair fine linen', based on Rev. 19.8. MS *beaumys* seems better disconnected. (See 35n for other examples of words that run together in the MS.) Gollancz (1891c) first read *beau mys*. *Mys* is a shortening of *MED amit* n., (variant *amis*). See 802n for other examples of aphetic forms of OF words. Hillmann read *beaumys* 'mantle', deriving it from *be* 'around' + *aumys*.

199 Cf. *marjorys* 206, *margyrye* 1037, and *margerye-perle* symbolizing the pure soul in *Cleanness* 556. M. Williams (1970) 104, referring to the Vulgate's *margarita*, commented that the triple meaning of jewel, flower, and a girl's name is played upon in *Pearl*.

Ginsberg (1983) 184, with reference to Gordon, pp. xxvii-xxix, noted the preface to the legend of Saint Margaret in Jacobus de Voragine's *Legenda Aurea*: "Margarita dicitur a quandam pretiosa gemma, quae margarita vocatur, quae gemma est candida, parva, et virtuosa. Sic beata Margareta fuit candida per virginitatem." ("Margaret takes her name from a certain precious gem which is called the pearl [Latin 'margarita'], which gem is white, small and of great merit. Thus St Margaret was white in her virginity.") Ginsberg added that the tradition was a commonplace throughout the Middle Ages. (See also 1n.)

201 Gollancz correctly observed that *lappeʒ large* are depicted in the MS illustrations on folios 42 and 42b. However, as Gordon, p. 56, pointed out, the pictured details do not always agree with the poetic descriptions. For example, pearls are not clearly visible in the illustrations, and the maiden's hair is not hanging loose. Gordon noted that in the poet's eyes, "Her costume is a simple form of the aristocratic dress of the second half of the fourteenth century. . . . Her golden hair flowed loose over her neck and shoulders, as befitted a maiden and a bride." (See also 213–14n.)

205 Gollancz commented on the crown as a symbol of virginity. Cf. 767: "coronde clene in vergynté." It is also a symbol of salvation in heaven. See 253–55n and 451n.

Fletcher (1921) 11, citing 205–6 and 217–19 to compare the maiden's adornment in pearls to the description of Mary in Albertus Magnus' *De Laudibus Beatae Mariae Virginis*, wrote, "The 'faithful soul' in the poem, the little child, is bedecked with but one gem, one virtue, the pearl of innocence." However, it may be that the many pearls described on the maiden's dress and crown (199–219) symbolize her virtues in general, such as innocence, purity, humility, and grace, all subordinate to the *wonder perle* (221) on her breast, Matthew's *perle of prys* (746), symbol of the heavenly kingdom.

206 By taking *gyrle* (205) in conjunction with *of marjorys*, one may consider word-play on the name of the maiden. (Cf. 199n.)

208 Editors rendered *vpon* as the adv. 'on it', but the adj. 'spread' fits the context also. Cf. *vpon* 'open' in 198.

209 Osgood emended to *herle* 'imbraided fillet', but Gordon explained MS *werle* as a synonym for crown, deriving it from *OED whirl (whorl)* sb. The idea is that the maiden wore no other 'circlet' to confine her hair. The *OED* cited only *Pearl* s.v. *werle* 'covering, attire', with derivation from *wear* v. + *-le*.

210 Morris and Gollancz emended MS *lere leke* to *here heke*, taking *heke* as a variant of *eke* 'also'. Osgood emended to *here-leke* 'locks of hair'. Moorman followed Gordon who also changed *lere* to *here* 'hair' but glossed *leke* as the pt. 'enclosed', with *semblaunt* (211) as its object: "Her hair, lying all about her, enclosed her countenance." However, since the maiden's hair is described in 213–14, it may be the poet described another feature here.

Hillmann tr. *lere leke* 'face-radiance', kept *vmbe gon* separate, and glossed *gon* 'beamed': "Her face-radiance all 'round her beamed." Andrew & Waldron agreed with Cawley who retained the MS forms with a reading that seems preferable: "Her face was enclosed all around (i.e. with a wimple)." The *MED* also suggested this reading s.v. ? *lẹre leke* n., '? face linen, wimple', deriving *leke* from *lāke* n.(2) 'fine linen, ? cambric' (MDu., MLG

114

laken). Cambric is a fine white linen used for the wimple worn by women in the late medieval period. Lucas (1978) also supported Cawley's reading.

212 Osgood noted, "Though from the walrus, ivory was generally called whale's bone." Gollancz compared the description of a banner in *Wynnere and Wastoure*: "Whitte als the whalles bone" (181).

213-14 Lucas (1977), after noting that in the second half of the fourteenth century it was customary for ladies to wear their hair bound and/or covered, stated: "Free-flowing hair is appropriate to the pearl-maiden firstly as an unmarried girl (the Dreamer's child), and also subsequently as a bride (of the Lamb) and as a queen (of the heavenly kingdom)."

215 Chase and Hillmann, following Cook (1908) 199, tr. *colour* 'collar'. See also Schofield (1909) 658-60, Hulbert (1927) 119, and Emerson (1927) 816. Gordon, with most editors in agreement, glossed *colour* '(white) complexion', but the poet described the maiden's *ble* 'complexion' in 212. Cf. the description of pearls on material in 197-204 and 217-19. For *depe* 'wide', see *MED dẹp* adj., 1c and 1d.

218 Cf. *Cleanness*: "And fetyse of a fayr forme, to fote and to honde" (174). The poet there explains the allegory of the Parable of the Wedding Feast in which clothes represent deeds and thoughts. In *Pearl*, too, the outer attire symbolizes the inner soul.

219 Cf. 206.

220 As Gollancz noted, *uesture* denotes the maiden's entire array. Cf. 163.

221-28 The *wonder perle* is the *perle of prys* (Matt. 13.45-46), mentioned first here, then a bit past the middle of the poem (732-46), and finally toward the end (854, 1103-4). (See 730-35n.)

223-26 Gardner (1977a) 176-77, in his study of Chaucer's "*The House of Fame*, or 'Dante in English' " (Ch. 5 in *The Poetry of Chaucer*), noted how both Chaucer and the *Pearl*-poet "make a point repeatedly of their inability to put their dream-experience into words." Cf., for example, Chaucer's lines in reference to his description of the castle: "That al the men that ben on lyve/Ne han the kunnynge to descrive" (1167-68), and "Ne kan I not to you devyse,/My wit ne may me not suffise" (1179-80). Cf., in *Pearl*, ll. 99-100, 133-36, and 1117-18, and see 99-100n.

229 Most editors emended *pyse* to *pyece* or *pece* (and *spyce* 235 to *spece*), apparently to rhyme with *Grece* and *nece*, but *e* sometimes varies with *i* (*y*). Note *enpresse* 1097 instead of *enpryse*, *geuen* 1190 instead of *gyuen*, and *hym* 'them' for *hem* 635.

231 Cf. *Gawain* 2023 where *Grece* is also in rhyme position.

233 *Nerre* is ambiguous. Osgood, Gollancz, and Gordon believed the poet was probably referring to his daughter. Hillmann glossed *nerre* adv. comp. 'nearer', stating, "not in relationship but in position, locality."

Since the word may express the idea of one's being simply more dear to another than any other person, it is possible the poet had in mind a little girl who was not related to him by blood, but to whom he had formed a close attachment. Those who support only the allegorical theory discount any autobiographical element. See, for example, Schofield (1909) 657.

On the other hand, the seemingly personal references in the poem are many. Greene (1925) 816-17 cited 41 lines with personal touches, among them 161-62, 164, 167-68, 233, 241-45, 378-80, and 483-85. Bishop (1968) 8, who favored Gordon's view, noted, nevertheless, that the maiden may have been a god-child, grandchild, or even a younger sister of the poet.

Milroy (1971) 208 suggested the poet may have been an "unmarried cleric writing the poem as a *consolatio* for a friend, a brother or a local dignitary, for whose bereavement he felt deeply, and assuming for that purpose a first person point-of-view."

235 See 229n for retention of MS *spyce*. The spice image is carried throughout *Pearl*. The spot where the pearl was lost is spread with spices (25, 35), the dreamer sees spices in the terrestrial paradise (104), and the maiden is again called *specyal spyce* (938). At the basis of this image is the symbolic death-and-resurrection seed that fell into the ground. (See 31-32n.)

Osgood compared the reference to the Virgin, "Heil spice swettist of sauour," 1. 29 of "Hail, Blessed Mary!" in *Hymns to the Virgin & Christ, The Parliament of Devils, and other Religious Poems*, ed. F.J. Furnivall, *EETS, OS* 24 (London, 1868).

245 Cf. similar images in 10, 30, and 41 to denote the loss of the pearl.

249-50 Cf. *luf-daungere* 11. As Bishop (1968) 75-76 noted, the dreamer eventually becomes content even though he considers himself in a *doel-doungoun* 1187. (See 1182-88n.)

Higgs (1974) studied the personal progress of the dreamer who learns "to see in present evil the prospects of eventual good through the power of God" (388).

252 Cf. the implied reference to a *juelere* in ll. 1-8. Hillmann supposed the dreamer is represented as an actual 'jeweler', but the link-word in this stanza-group is apparently used metaphorically. (See 730n.)

253-55 The pearl in pearls puts on her crown of pearls; the pure soul clothed in virtues puts on her crown of virginity and salvation. (See 205n and 451n.) In 745-46 the dreamer addresses the maiden as a spotless pearl in pure pearls, possessing the *perle of prys* (heaven).

Hoffman-C (1960) 90-91 discussed the multiple meanings of the pearl figure. Gordon viewed the pearl-maiden as a lost child's soul. Hillmann supposed the dreamer, at this point, is viewing his own soul safely enclosed in heaven, "were he a noble jeweler (264)."

Mahl (1966) equated the maiden with the "concept of the pure Church which, when it became corrupted in the world, [the dreamer] had lost" (28).

116

254 Emerson (1927) 817 compared Guenevere's *yȝen gray* in *Gawain* 82, also rhyming with *say*. *Graye*, a favorite color of women's eyes in ME poetry, may denote a bluish gray.

257 Gross-BMW (1991) 79, after observing how the maiden reproaches the dreamer for misconceiving her death as the loss of a precious pearl, thus confounding the material and the spiritual, noted that this line "may equally be read as an accurate comment of the narrator's use of language, for throughout the poem he consistently 'tells his tale wrongly,' employing a courtly rhetoric inappropriate to the 'ghostly' matters that are or should be his concern." In contrast, the maiden's courtly rhetoric "provides an accurate indication of her spiritual state and the most nearly adequate vehicle for the expression of the ineffable" (80).

259 Gollancz compared the *cofer* in *Cleanness*, denoting the ark of salvation in 310, 339, and 492. It may also mean 'treasure chest' (*coferes, Cleanness* 1428, for the vessels in the temple of Jerusalem), 'casket' and 'treasure house'. The maiden describes herself as being in this *cofer*, the treasure chest of heaven. See 2n for possible allusion to her tomb. Andrew & Waldron referred to Piehler (1971) 145 who discussed the ambiguity between the senses 'treasure chest' and 'coffin'.

260 *Gardyn* occurs only here in *Pearl*, recalling the *erber(e)* of ll. 9 and 38, but the latter is the garden of loss whereas this garden represents heaven. The poet anticipates the theme of death for the body in the earthly garden and resurrection for the soul in the heavenly garden (265–76).

263 *Forser* as a metaphor for heaven relates to *cofer* 259 and *gardyn* 260. *Cofer* and the *forser* doubly enforce the concept of the pure soul like a jewel, safely encased in Christ's strongbox of heaven. The *gardyn* suggests a vegetation image with God as the Gardener who cares for one's soul. See *MED gardiner* n., sense b.

269–72 Flower and jewel imagery again merge in the death-and-resurrection theme. (See 29n.) *Rose* (269), the material pearl—the maiden's body, blossomed and decayed as nature directed, but from this decay rose the *perle of prys*, her soul. Lines 29–30 describe flower and fruit that cannot be wasted where the pearl drove down into dark molds, for from this loss comes the *reken rose* (906), the immortal maiden.

Cf. *kynde of the kyste* to *kynde of Kryst* (55). *Kyste*, the treasure chest of heaven, echoes *Kryst*, who cares for souls, and recalls *cofer* (259) and *forser* (263). The symbolic significance of *perle of prys* is different in 746. Here it signifies the maiden's soul; there the *perle of prys*, which the maiden wears on her breast, represents heaven. (See 745–46n.)

Hillmann, interpreting this stanza as an attack upon covetousness, tr. *put in pref* 'put to the test'. Gordon's 'has proved in fact to be' is the sense given by other editors.

273–76 Gordon's paraphrase of 274 clarifies the connotation: "has made an eternal pearl out of a short-lived rose." Kellogg-C (1956), seeing in this passage an allusion to the Augustinian doctrine of *creatio ex nihilo*, concluded that the "Pearl-maiden would not be saying that God has favored the dreamer by making his mortal rose into an immortal pearl, but rather that the Dreamer, instead of complaining against God for a presumed injustice, should be praising God for his very existence."

The context of this stanza, however, indicates that the Augustinian doctrine of *creatio ex nihilo* prevails here first in relation to the maiden who, like all mankind, was created by God from nothing, had to die and decay physically (269-70) because of Adam's sin, but then was spiritually revived (271-72) due to Christ's death on the cross. (See 637-60.) The dreamer should be thankful for the maiden's glorified state and accordingly for the opportunity he has of achieving it in the future.

Bishop (1968) 19 compared the 'life is a loan' consolatory topic quoted by Sister Mary Beyenka (*Consolation in St. Augustine* [Washington, D.C., 1950], pp. 102-4) from a Letter of Augustine to Probus: "God has taken nothing of yours, when He took His own possession; He is like a creditor to whom only thanks are now due." As Bishop noted, the dreamer will be consoled in the end, knowing the maiden is in the possession of her rightful owner.

277-78   Most editors rendered *geste* 'guest'. Hulbert (1927) 119 believed the alliteration suggests Morris' old reading. 'tale, saying' (*MED ğĕst(e)* n.1). Word-play may be involved, but the primary sense seems to relate to the maiden. The *MED* cited *Pearl* s.v. *gest* n., 3a, 'one newly arrived in a place', but 'newborn child', sense 1c, may apply in the figurative sense, newly born into Paradise. The maiden is called *faunt* 'child' in 161.

Rupp (1955) saw word-play in both lines: "A jewel (pearl) to me then was this guest (the Pearl-maiden) or tale (pearl), and jewels (pearls) were her gentle words (pearls)." Citing Matt. 7.6: "neque mittatis margarítas vestras ante porcos" ("neither cast ye your pearls before swine"), Rupp believed the dreamer, not aware of the irony in his words, may be classified as 'porcos', at this point, in need of the maiden's instruction, but the poet, "with his authorial foreknowledge," sees the complete relationship between dreamer and maiden.

279-88   Rupp's observation that a distinction must be made between the poet and his persona is supported by these lines, for the dreamer fails to understand the spiritual import of what the maiden has said. The poet creates such situations to lead to debate and homily, techniques which dominate the central portion of *Pearl*.

282   Hoffman-C (1960) 96-98 compared 23-24, 305-6, 319-22, 857-60, 957-58, and 1206 for images which emphasize a physical, literal death, not a figurative loss with symbolic interpretations.

286   For loss of -*t* in *broʒ*, due to the following *þ*, cf. 142n.

287   *Waweʒ* 'waves' denotes the tossing currents of the rapidly flowing stream. See 111–12.

289–300 Hill (1974) 157 compared the dreamer's dullness to that of Will in *Piers Plowman*. "Langland and the *Pearl* poet are in surprising fraternity: the dreamer in *Pearl* is very much like his dreaming literary cousin, Will. . . . The maiden in *Pearl*, furthermore, castigates the dreamer in tones reminiscent of Holy Church." Hill concluded that the *Pearl*-poet "believes in the limitations of his dreamer, much as he apparently ackowledges limitations to the expressibility of language" (168–69).

Fowler (1984) 212–13, in commenting on this stanza and the next one, pointed out how the maiden speaks like an adult rather than as a child who died in infancy, but her maturity "(if not indeed her omniscience) is perfectly in keeping with the common belief that spirits of the departed, whenever they choose to return and speak to men, are possessed of complete knowledge (1 Cor. 13.12: *then shall I know even as also I am known*." Cf. 161–62n on the maiden's advanced stature and l. 859: "We þurȝoutly hauen cnawyng."

295–300 Spearing (1970) 151–52, refuting the contention of Kean (1967) 128 that the dreamer thought the maiden was on earth, defined *dene* 295 as a sector of heaven, commenting that he should have believed the maiden was there without having seen her. The next stanza recalls Christ's words in John 20.29: "Quia vidísti me, Thoma, credidísti; beáti qui non vidérunt et credidérunt." ("Because thou hast seen me, Thomas, thou hast believed: blessed are they that have not seen, and have believed.") The dreamer, besides believing only what he sees, thought he could dwell in her region and, for that purpose, cross the stream. These are the three errors he utters in 282–88; the maiden refutes all three in the next two stanzas (301–24).

302 *Loueȝ* 'honors' here and in 308 recalls 285 and heightens the word-play with *leueȝ* 'believes' 304 and *leue* 311. Hamilton-B (1955) 42 favored retention of the MS form in 302. Most editors emended to *leueȝ* in 302 and 308.

307 Osgood emended *westernays* to *besternays* 'reversed' (OF *bestorneis*). Chase emended to *bestornays*. Most editors, following Henry Bradley (revision of *A Middle English Dictionary*, ed. F.H. Stratmann [Oxford, 1891], p. 708), retained *westernays* 'reversed, awry' as an altered form of *besternays*, "the alteration being due to the influence of *west*, since the word was applied to a church which faced west instead of east as was then usual" (Gordon).

Hillmann's division to *west ernays* 'empty pledge' seems suitable. (See 35n for similar examples of disjoining.) *OED weste* a. 'desolate' relates to *waste* a., sense 4, 'idle, vain' in relation to speech. *MED ĕrnes* n., sense 2, defines 'pledge'. Hillmann compared Ps. 88.35: "Neque profanábo testaméntum meum et quae procédunt de lábiis meis non fáciam írrita." ("Neither will I profane my covenant: and the words that proceed from my mouth I will not make void.") See also Hillmann (1943).

309 In 401–2 the maiden tells the dreamer arrogant pride has no place

119

in Paradise. See Blenkner-C (1968) 230 for discussion of three deadly sins noted in *Pearl*, pride (301-10), anger (341-60), and envy (613-16). Concerning envy, cf. also 445-68 and 845-52.

313 Gordon glossed *dayly* '*contend*' (ON *deila*), Hillmann 'speak lightly' (OF *dalier*), Andrew & Waldron 'speak'. Luttrell (1962a) 447-48 and Moorman favored 'to talk courteously', a suitable sense, since the maiden had referred to the dreamer as being *vncortoyse* (303).

321 *Paradys greue* is synonymous with the Garden of Eden. *Greue* evidently alludes to that specific part of the garden in which the apple tree grew. *Paradys(e)* in 137 and 248 apparently denotes the divine kingdom. (See 137n.)

322 In 639-60 the maiden tells of the *ʒorefader*'s (Adam's) sin and man's salvation through Christ's crucifixion.

323 Emendation of *ma* 'man' to *man* (Gordon, Cawley, Moorman, and Andrew & Waldron) seems unnecessary. Cf. s.v. *MED man* pron. indef., sense b, *Sir Ferumbras* 2828: "Ma calþ me Gyoun of Borgoygne."

326 Andrew & Waldron compared line 11.

331-32 For *he* 'they', cf. the forms *he (ho)* for the nom. pl. in *Cleanness* 62, 657, and 1267 (OE *hēo, hīe, hī*), and see *MED hẹ* pron. 3, 1a, 'of persons: they'. Gordon's interpretation of *men* as a sg. indef. pron. was adopted by subsequent editors.

334 Andrew & Waldron noted an "allusion to the theme of exile, common in OE poetry." See, for example, *The Wanderer* and *The Seafarer* in *Seven Old English Poems*, ed. John C. Pope (Indianapolis, 1966).

335 Hillmann retained MS *perleʒ* and tr. 'peerless one', but, as Gordon noted, the scribe probably repeated *ʒ* from *partleʒ*. Cf. similar repetitions in 678, where the MS has *hylleʒ* in rhyme position instead of *hylle*, and 1179 (*quykeʒ* instead of *quyke*).

336 Through the dreamer's lack of understanding, the poet advances the dramatic dialogue. Spearing (1970) 152 compared Chaucer's dreamer in *The Book of the Duchess*. (See also 279-88n.)

344-48 Cf. *Patience* 1-8, 524-31 and *Pearl* 349-60, 1199-1200. Osgood and Gordon observed that the call for patience and obedience to God's will is similar in both poems.

345 See 184n on animal similes in *Pearl*.

349 Gordon's *adyte* 'accuse' (OF *aditer*), previously noted by Emerson (1922) 67-68 and adopted by editors following Gordon, seems preferable to 'arrange, dispose' (OE *adihtan*), given by Osgood and Gollancz.

353 Savage (1956b) 127 noted that *stynst* is a correct form for the imper. sg. Gollancz, Chase, Gordon, Cawley, and Andrew & Waldron emended to *stynt*.

358 Emerson (1927) 819, refuting Osgood's "and lightly drive thy frowns away" (with *leme* from ON *lemja* 'beat'), and Gollancz' emendation of MS *&* to *þat alle* (with tr. of *lyʒtly leme* 'glance lightly off'), interpreted *of* 'among' as a prep. in postponed construction governing *lureʒ*, and *leme* as the v. 'shine'. Cf. the sense of *lemed* in 119 and 1043.

The *MED* cited *Pearl* s.v. *lẹmen* v.1, sense b, 'drive away', and accounted for Gordon's emendation to *fleme* 'banish' by adding [? read: *fleme*], but *lēmen* v.2, 1b, 'shine, radiate' substantiates Emerson's reading, followed by Hillmann and DeFord. Cawley, Moorman, and Andrew & Waldron followed Gordon.

Stanley (1990) 158–60 compared this stanza to the penultimate stanza of "The Three Foes of Man," a lyric in MS Harley 2253, No. 2 in G. L. Brook's *The Harley Lyrics* (4th edition; Manchester, 1968). Noting the line in the lyric—*for folkes fader al fleme*—he argued that the verb in *Pearl* is *offleme* and that *of lyʒtly leme* constitutes an unusual tmesis (separation of parts of a compound word by the intervention of one or more words). Since there would be no difference in sound between *offleme* and *ofleme*, Stanley concluded, p. 160, that by metanalysis (the analysis of words or groups of words into new elements) tmesis might lead to *of . . . leme* for *of . . . fleme*.

359 Gordon's *myþe* 'conceal (one's feelings)' from OE *mīþan* was adopted by subsequent editors, but the v. may be from the OE n. *mūþa* 'mouth' with *y* for *u* needed for rhyme. For other *i(y)-u* variants, cf. *huyle* 41—*hylle* 1172 and *gylteʒ* 655—*gulte* 942. The idea of concealment does not seem to be involved in the thought of this passage, whereas *myþe* 'mutter' is appropriate to the sense. Osgood, Gollancz, and Chase emended MS *marre* to *marred* and tr. *marred oþer madde* 'marred or made'.

363 Most editors inserted *I* before *raue*, but there is much ellipsis in the poems of this MS. Note, for example, *Pearl* 96 and 977, and see 977n. *I* appears at the start of this stanza.

364-65 Gollancz, comparing Lamentations 2.19 and Ps. 61.8, construed 365–66 together: "Like water pouring from a well, I readily resign myself to God's gracious will." Gordon's reading, adopted by subsequent editors, seems preferable. Cf. Ps. 21.15: "Sicut aqua effúsus sum." ("I am poured out like water."), and 362–63 to verse 14: "Aperuérunt super me os suum, sicut leo rápiens et rúgiens." ("They have opened their mouths against me, as a lion ravening and roaring.")

368 Andrew & Waldron followed Rønberg (1976) who, rejecting the usual reading *endorde* 'adored (one)'—OF *adorer*, with altered prefix—defined 'gold-adorned' (OF *endorer*). The maiden is compared to *glysnande golde* (165), and there are references to gold in ll. 2 and 213. The *MED* s.v. *endōren* v. records the word only in the restricted sense, 'to cover or coat (a roast or other dish) with a glaze (usually made from the yolks of eggs)', but Rønberg noted that in Godefroy's *Dictionnaire de l'Ancienne Langue Française*, there are several examples of *endorer* with the non-culinary meaning.

369 Osgood inserted *wyth* before *your*, but *coumforde* 'with (your) solace' may be interpreted as a synthetic dat. Cf. *perle* 'for (my) pearl' (53).

Emendation of *lype3* to *kype3* 'show' (Gollancz, Chase, Gordon, Cawley, and Andrew & Waldron) seems unnecessary.

375 Cf. 151n on *wope3* 'perils'. The *OED* s.v. *wothe* sb. and a., 'the condition of being exposed to or liable to injury or harm', cited *Pearl*. Morris and Gollancz tr. 'path', Hillmann and DeFord 'search'.

Wright (1939) 11–12 felt it would be contradictory for the dreamer to think the maiden had been delivered from peril and yet say he never knew where she had gone, but one must take into account the confused state of the dreamer. (See Hieatt [1965] 140.)

378–80 See 233n on personal touches in *Pearl*.

382 MS *marere3* has caused difficulty. Gollancz (1891c), following Morris' suggestion, emended to *marre3* v., took *mysse* as a n., and tr. 'grief woundeth me'.

Osgood retained *marere3* 'botcher's' and tr. "I am worth no more than a botcher's blunder, good for nothing." The *MED* s.v. *marrer* n. followed Osgood.

An anonymous reviewer of Gollancz' edition (*Athenæum* [1891] 185) and Holthausen (1893) 146 proposed emending to *manere3* 'manners'. Gollancz, in his 1921 edition, Chase, Gordon, Cawley, and Andrew & Waldron adopted this emendation.

Schofield (1909) 663 suggested *mariere3* or *margere3*: "I am but dust and lack margeries (pearls)," a reading accepted by Hamilton (1958) 185 and Moorman.

Smithers (1948–49) 60–62 argued to retain the MS form by translating *marere3 mysse* 'dung-raker's muck', deriving *marere3* from OF *marrier* 'a labourer who uses a *marre*' (tool employed for gardening), and *mysse* from MDu. *misse (messe)* 'manure, dung, dirt'.

Holman (1951), attempting to authenticate Osgood's reading by citing Jeremias 18.1–6, where the reference is to the potter making vessels of clay, paraphrased, "I am only clay and a botcher's mistake; for I was marred in the potter's hands."

Hillmann divided the word into *mare re3* 'great eloquence (onrush of speech)'—ME *resse* (*Pearl* 874) from OE *ræs*—believing the dreamer was referring to his lack of power of speech. (DeFord followed Hillmann.)

However, *marere3* '(spiritual) vitality' may be interpreted as a n. sg. variant of *MED marwe* n.1, senses 3b and 3c. (Many variant spellings are listed there.) In *Pearl*, *3* sometimes equals *w*: *fol3ed* 127—*folewande* 1040. The medial *e* of *marere3* is simply an intervening vowel. (Cf. *boro3t* 628 and *bereste* 854.)

There may be word-play involving *MED marwe* n.2, sense a, 'companion', for the dreamer is missing his pearl as a companion. Finally, one may compare 971 for the fig. application. There, when the maiden tells the dreamer he has no *vygour* 'power' to stride in the street of the New Jerusalem, she is referring to his lack of spiritual vitality.

383 Savage (1956b) 128 pointed to the "rood on its screen in the parish church, with the figures of Mary and John on either side of it."

Hamilton (1958) 185-86 thought it more likely that the line refers to Mary and the apostle as they are portrayed in scenes of the Last Judgment.

Coldstream (1981) 178, in agreement with Savage, noted how in the parish churches "the chancel was always divided from the nave by the rood screen, on which stood a carved representation of the crucifixion, with Mary and St John, associated by the *Pearl* poet."

393-96 Hamilton (1958) 186 felt that in the context of this stanza-group (361-420), 'bliss' can only mean eternal blessedness: "It goes without saying that a medieval Catholic would have been liable to ecclesiastical censure for asserting that the blessed condition of his child in heaven, or of any other creature, was the foundation of all his bliss, the highest way to his own beatitude." Because the maiden expresses unqualified approval in the next stanza, Hamilton believed the dreamer was addressing his own soul.

This interpretation, however, limits the sense of 'bliss', which can mean mortal joy as well as beatitude. The former sense apparently prevails in 372-73 and 396, the latter in 384-85, 397, 408, and 420. There does not seem to be anything erroneous in the dreamer's saying his greatest earthly happiness is knowing she is eternally blessed. This attitude shows his spiritual progress, foreshadowing the end when he again expresses satisfaction because of the maiden's blessed state (1185-88).

399 Editors read *byde* 'stay', but the first letter resembles a spread *v* or *b*, or even a badly made *w*. *Vyde* may be a variant of *wade* 143, 1151. The *OED* lists *wide* as a Scottish variant. The *v* of *vyde*, pronounced *w*, is comparable to *vyf* 'wife' 772; alliteration on *w* is retained in both lines.

In 143 the dreamer said he dared not 'wade' because the water was deep; in 1151 he wishes to 'wade'. In both instances, he is thinking of crossing over, but in this passage the maiden speaks, welcoming him to 'wade' on his side of the stream, which may relate to a symbolic act of cleansing in preparation for the time when he would be able to cross over. (Note l. 405.)

One is reminded of the concluding verses of Dante's *Purgatorio* (Canto 33), where the poet drinks from the stream in the terrestrial paradise to cleanse himself in preparation for his journey into *Paradiso*: "Io ritornai da la santissim'onda/rifatto sì come piante novelle/rinnovellate di novella fronda,/puro e disposto a salire a le stelle." ("From that most holy wave I came away/refashioned, like new plants no blemish mars,/made new again with new leaves: pure as they,/and ready now for mounting to the stars.") (The text and translation are taken from Geoffrey L. Bickersteth's *The Divine Comedy* [Harvard UP, 1965].)

401-2 Cf. 309n. 'Pride', the first of the seven deadly sins, contrasts with humility. In *Cleanness* 205-34, Lucifer's pride is the origin of sin. The maiden's approval of the dreamer in this stanza stems from the spiritual progress he has made. As Blenkner-C (1968) 267 stated, "The narrator's experience is presented in terms which reveal a markedly consistent progression from the worldly to the religious point of view." (See also the end of 393-96n.)

407 Reference to Christ as the sacrificial Lamb occurs here for the first time. The qualities of the Lamb such as innocence, spotlessness, meekness, and radiance are those qualities which the pearl-maiden possesses. In 795-96 the Lord is Lamb, Jewel, Joy, Bliss, and Spouse.

410 *MED stāge* n., 4c, 'state, condition', cites *Pearl*. Sense 4b, 'a hierarchical rank', is also fitting. The poet anticipates the view the dreamer will have of other souls in heaven, according to a hierarchical system. Note, for example, 453-66 and 1096-1128, and see 445-48n for further discussion.

411-12 Lines 10 and 245 present images of the pearl's slipping into grass. *Schede* may also denote 'depart', relating to death, or 'pour out', relating to loss of grace. Hamilton (1958) 180 favored the latter.

Supporters of the elegiacal theory see a personal reference in these lines. (Cf. 233 and 483-85, and see 233n.) The allegorists maintain that the pearl is here being identified with the dreamer's soul, "spiritually immature," as Hillmann says, when it fell to the ground.

413-14 Madeleva (1925) 152-54 applied these lines only to those in religious orders, but, as Hillmann noted, it is the "teaching of Catholic mysticism that Christ is the destined spiritual Bridegroom of all souls of good will." (See ll. 845-46.) In 785-87 the maiden refers to herself as one of the Lamb's wives of renown.

417 See 703n for other examples of the poet's use of legal terminology. Gordon compared *erytage* 443 and Rom. 8.16-17: "Ipse enim Spíritus testimónium reddit spirítui nostro, quod sumus fílii Dei. Si autem fílii, et herédes: herédes quidem Dei, coherédes autem Christi; si tamen compátimur, ut et conglorificémur." ("For the Spirit himself giveth testimony to our spirit, that we are the sons of God. And if sons, heirs also; heirs indeed of God, and joint-heirs with Christ: yet so, if we suffer with him, that we may be also glorified with him.")

Reisner (1975) discussed this passage and what follows in Stanza-Group VIII in relation to legal procedures in fourteenth-century England.

419 Editors read *prese* 'great worth' (Gordon) instead of *pyese* 'maiden', but what they took for an *r* in the MS looks more like the top of a *y*. For another example of *y* with its bottom illegible, see the *y* of *Kryst* (55) in the MS. The pearl-maiden is called *pyece* in l. 192.

422 Cf. 381-82 on the dreamer's awareness of his shortcomings..

423 Neilson (1902a) 72-74, in an article associating *Pearl*, *The Awntyrs off Arthure at the Terne Wathelyn*, and *Saint Erkenwald* as works of Huchown of the Awle Ryale, compared Gregory's mistaking his mother for the queen of heaven in the *Trentalle Sancti Gregorii*.

Matthews (1960) 208–9, noting similarities between *Gawain* and the *Awntyrs*, suggested these similarities may be due to the influence of *Gawain* on the latter poem.

Hanna (1974) 14–16 discussed similar verse techniques in *Pearl*, *Gawain*, and the *Awntyrs*. (On pp. 44–46, he noted parallels in the descriptions of the deer hunts in the two romances.)

425 *Grace* here refers to Christ. Hillmann, correcting Osgood's note, pointed out that, according to Catholic doctrine, Mary is sometimes called the "Channel of Grace," but the "Source of Grace" is God alone.

426 Whiteley (1931) wondered if *of Vyrgin Flour* meant 'out of a spotless virginity' or 'a child of purest excellence'. Fairchild (1931) supported the second meaning, favored only by Moorman among editors. See the citations s.v. *MED flŏur* n.1, fig., sense 1c (c), 'with reference to the Christ child'. *Flour* parallels *Grace* (425) in reference to Christ, whose qualities on a grand scale relate to those of the pearl-maiden on a smaller scale. She is both flower and gem, just as Jesus is called *Flour* here and *Juelle* in ll. 795 and 1124. (Cf. 269–72n and 407n.)

429–30 Osgood, p. xxi, noted that Blanche is called phoenix of Araby in Chaucer's *Book of the Duchess* (982). The phoenix, a bird of Egyptian legend, which burned itself and rose from its own ashes, is a medieval symbol usually representing Christ. However, as Fletcher (1921) 15–16 observed, Albertus Magnus compared Mary to the phoenix in *De Laudibus Beatae Mariae Virginis* VII, iii, 1: "Maria una sola est mater et virgo. Unde et comparatur phoenici, quae est unica avis sine patre."

431 Hillmann (1943) 43 first noted the analogy between Mary and the phoenix is that Mary, born free from original sin by divine grace, was immaculate at conception. She tr. *hyr* 'its', but the phoenix symbolized both Christ's death and resurrection and Mary's purity and virginity, and the context of 429–32 favors fem. usage.

Freles 'without fault' (*MED frēlēs* adj.), given by most editors, is fitting. Hamilton (1958) 187 suggested emending to *fer(e)les* 'without equal'; Luttrell (1962a) 448, Moorman, and Andrew & Waldron supported this reading. However, the sense 'faultless' applies well to the Immaculate Conception of Mary.

432 The form of *Cortaysye*, the link-word in this stanza-group, varies. Note *cortayse* adj. (433). In 445 *court* is the link-word. As Gordon noted, the primary meaning of *Cortaysye* is divine grace. Mary, "from whom Grace grew" (425), "Blessed Beginner of every grace" (436), may aptly be called "Queen of Courtesy." The pearl-maiden, too, possesses divine grace as one of the queens in heaven (468). *Cortaysye* also connotes charity and pity, and Mary is the mediatrix between God and men who seek his mercy. In ll. 467–68 souls in heaven live *wyth luf . . . by cortaysye*; ll. 469–70 refer to *cortaysé* and *charyté*.

125

Milroy (1971) 203 noted the significance of the *cáritas* expounded by St. Paul in 1 Cor. 13, closely related to 1 Cor. 12.12-27, upon which *Pearl* 457-66 is based. The absence of *gawle* 'envy' (463) in the heavenly souls points up their great *cortaysye*. As Paul says in 1 Cor. 13.4, "Cáritas non aemulátur." ("Charity envieth not.") For further discussion of the poet's use of *cortaysye*, see also Brewer (1966), Evans (1967), and Matsui (1971).

433 Editors emended MS *syde* to *sayde*, but *MED seien* v.1 lists *side* as a pt. form for 'said', and in this MS *i* varies with *y* and *i* (*y*) sometimes with *e*. (Cf. 229n.)

434 For *folde* 'covering' as a pp. tr. prog., cf. *vmbegon* 'encompassing' (210) and see Mustanoja (1960) 549-51. Gollancz thought the maiden was covering her face in the hanging folds of her garment. Andrew & Waldron followed Gordon who rendered *folde vp hyr face* 'with her face upturned'. Moorman agreed with Hillmann who suggested the maiden was "covering her face with her hands" in "horror at the jeweler's ignorant but blasphemous question" (423). Hillmann's gloss is fitting, but the maiden's movement may be taken as a gesture of humble adoration for Mary, not horror over the dreamer's question.

436 Mary is the 'Beginner' of every grace in that she gave birth to Jesus. (See 425n.)

439 Gordon compared the metaphor of the race in St. Paul's 1 Cor. 9.24-25. Oakden (1968) 345-46, discussing liturgical influence of the Septuagesima cycle, noted that the maiden has on the incorruptible crown of salvation mentioned by Paul. (See 451n.)

440 Metlitzki (1988) 200-1 stated that *supplantorez* should be translated 'supplanters', for it echoes the Vulgate's wording of Genesis 27.36 in the lament of the twice-cheated Esau: "Iuste vocátum est nomen eius Iacob; supplantávit enim me en áltera vice." ("Rightly is his name called Jacob; for he hath supplanted me lo this second time.") The *Pearl*-poet "uses the word 'supplanters' to denote those who chase a brother from his heritage."

444 The dreamer first called Mary *Quen of Cortaysye* (432), showing he was not ignorant of basic Christian doctrines. The poet presents his persona as one who needs to accept much of what he knows, but his emotions stand in the way. (See 51-56.) In the end he does accept. (See 1199-1200.)

Burnley (1979) 153, discussing Chaucer's use of *gentillesse* as a Christian virtue—"true *gentillesse* is associated with the example of Christ"— compared *Pearl* in which the "Virgin is celebrated as the queen of true *curteisie*. *Gentillesse* and *curteisie* are, already in the fourteenth century, treated as religious and philosophical ideals of a distinctly unworldly kind." (Cf. 432n.)

445-48 Fisher (1961) 151-52 cited these lines to point out in *Pearl* the recognition of grades in the hierarchy of heaven, a hierarchy "mystically resolved into equality." This stanza and the next anticipate the Parable of the

126

Vineyard (501–72), dealing with the concept that all receive the same reward regardless of how much work they do, a concept that is complicated by the difficulty of reconciling this "same reward" with the hierarchical doctrine. All attain salvation and are happy to the fullness of their capacity to be happy. In this sense, all are equally content. Yet, there are ranks in heaven, as ll. 453–66 and 1096–1128 show. (See also 603–4n.)

The maiden herself holds a special position as a young virgin. One may compare glasses of different sizes filled to the brim. The glasses are souls, and the liquid inside represents happiness. Though all are filled to capacity, the larger ones contain more than the smaller. For a similar comparison using the "pint-pot and the quart-pot" metaphor, Moorman (1968) 48 cited Dorothy L. Sayers, *Introductory Papers on Dante* (New York, 1954), p. 57. Gordon, pp. xxiv–xxv, refuted the view that *Pearl* contains heresy because it asserts that the heavenly reward is the same for all.

445-52 Blanch (1973) 74 compared "The London Lapidary of King Philip" in *English Mediaeval Lapidaries*, ed. Joan Evans and Mary S. Serjeantson, *EETS, OS* 190 (1933), pp. 19–20: "nyne ordres of angeles þat lyven in þat joye þat noon hath enuye of othre, þat is þe life corouned, in þe which shal noon entre but he be kyng corouned or quene, for all be corouned be name."

451 Osgood compared l. 849, where the concept and choice of the number five are similar. The crown, which represents the maiden's virginity in l. 767, here typifies the incorruptible crown of salvation. (See 205n, 253–55n, and 439n.)

453-56 Nicholls (1985) 110 noted that although Mary is the high Queen, this does not displease the maiden or her fellow souls because Mary is a gracious and courteous ruler. The poet "reaffirms courtesy as an expression of the love that binds God to man, and grace, acting through courtesy, as man's main hope of redemption" (111). Nicholls studied the poet's works "to elucidate aspects of the thematic and artistic design of the poems by reference to the ideals of contemporary and social practice in good manners and refined conduct" (4).

457-66 Pilch-C (1964) 177 observed that in this passage, based on 1 Cor. 12.12–27, the body of Christ, considered by its members, symbolizes the hierarchy of the heavenly society. The poet's method here is *abbreviatio*. He ordinarily employed *amplificatio*, as in ll. 501–72 paraphrasing Matt. 20.1–16. See Parr (1970) for a full discussion of "Rhetoric and Symbol in the *Pearl*."

Marti (1991) argued that the extensive reference here to the hierarchy of head and limbs in the *corpus mysticum*, and the prominent allusion to the sacrament of the Holy Eucharist at the poem's end (1209–10) "make it impossible to ignore the theology of the body as one of *Pearl*'s major themes" (84).

459 Only Morris and Osgood among the editors glossed *naule* 'nail'.

Osgood believed 'navel' offended poetic delicacy, but medieval writers did not regard the image in this way. As Fletcher (1921) 2 noted, Albertus Magnus compared the Virgin Mary's navel to a wine-cup in the hand of the Holy Ghost in *De Laudibus Beatae Mariae Virginis* V, ii, 68.

460 Osgood's retention of *tyste* as a variant of *tyȝte* 'tight' has not been accepted. Gordon, who emended to *tryste* 'faithfully', as did all other editors, noted that there is no instance in the MS of *st* for *ȝt*.

For *tyste* 'joined', cf. *OED tissed* ppl. a. (OF *tistre*), used in association with weaving. The citation in the *OED* is 1585, but *tissed* stems from *tissue* sb. and v., for which there are ME quotations. For other examples of unvoicing of *-d* to *-t*, see the notes to 10, 754, and 761. The poet may have related the sense 'joined' (or 'woven together') to parts of the body, as in 1 Cor. 12.24: "Deus temperávit corpus ei." ("God hath tempered the body together.")

462 Morris suggested *myste* 'mysteries' (*MED mist* n.2, 'spiritual mysteries'). Osgood, Gollancz, and Hillmann took *myste* as a variant of *myȝte* 'might', but Gordon, who again noted the unlikelihood of *st* being used for *ȝt*, glossed 'spiritual mysteries', comparing *spiritualibus* in 1 Cor. 12.1. Moorman and Andrew & Waldron adopted this reading.

Wright (1939) 12, following Emerson (1922) 70, interpreted *myste* (OF *miste* adj.) as a sb. adj. and tr. *Master of myste* 'Master of gentility'.

Murtaugh (1971), citing *OED mist* sb.3, a shortened form of *mister* sb.1, 'occupation, service', proposed 'Master of Ministries'. The poet may have been employing his characteristic word-play on more than one meaning, but there is sufficient evidence to support Morris' original suggestion as the primary sense.

472 Gollancz supplied: [Me þynk þou spekeȝ now ful wronge.] However, as Crawford (1967) 118 noted, the missing line is perhaps pre-scribal. "The poet may have avoided formal perfection for fear of excessive vanity offending God."

Nelson (1973) 33 stated: "*Pearl's* partial roundness, aching for completion, is the emblem of a flawed circle. It is an appropriate vehicle for our fallen perception—for the poet's expression of his vision and our experience of it."

Carlson (1991) agreed with Crawford and Nelson, noting that there is grammatical sense in the passage as it stands. The missing l. 472 "makes sense as a flaw that the *Pearl*-poet built into his poem, as a testament to a humble awareness on his part of the inevitableness of the failure of human effort, even in the instance of his own work, to attain to perfection" (60). (I believe the arguments of these critics may be correct, concerning the Middle English text; my inserting a line into the translation is simply for the sake of retaining the verse form in Modern English.)

479 For *ho* 'he', see *MED hē* pron. 1, where *ho* is listed as a variant spelling. Morris tr. *ho* 'she', paraphrasing, "He desires to know what greater honour she can have." Other editors emended *ho* to *he*.

483-85 Morris, Osgood, Gollancz, and Gordon believed these lines refer to a child who died before the age of two. Osgood noted that clergymen were instructed to teach people, especially children, the Pater Noster and the Creed.

Madeleva (1925) 160-64 argued that a novice in the religious life could be considered a child since she would know no more than the rudiments, after two years, in a series of spiritual meditations that needed to be learned along with the Pater and the Creed.

Hillmann maintained that the dreamer, in his confused state, thought he was addressing his lost material pearl imported from the Orient only two years before and personified in the maiden, who really represents his soul.

Carson (1965), noting that the learning of prayers would be required for a newly baptized adult who had come to England from another land, interpreted "*Pearl* as an elegy in which the poet laments not the loss of a two-year old daughter but that of a girl with whom his relationship is romantic rather than paternal" (17).

However, the statement in 483 that the maiden lived not two years in the land, taken with 412: "I watȝ ful ȝong and tender of age," does not seem to fit an adult. Though simple vocal prayers were recommended for the early stages of conversion, ll. 484-85 say that the maiden could not pray, "Not ever either Pater or Creed," and one might expect that after almost two years a convert or a novice would have learned something.

488 Gollancz compared l. 350. The poet continues to show the dreamer's obtuseness.

489 Spearing-B (1962) 113 compared l. 211, noting that a countess is the wife of an earl: the dreamer "is unable to conceive of a hierarchy in any other than these familiar terms."

492 Gollancz, Gordon, and Moorman rendered *date* 'goal', Hillmann 'term', Andrew & Waldron 'rank'. Cf. the sense 'beginning' to *date* 'dawning' 517. In 486 the dreamer doubted that the maiden could be made a queen on the first day.

497 *Messe* 'mass' occurs here and in the form *mas* in l. 1115. (See the note to *mes* in l. 862 for a different denotation there.) Phillips (1985) traced liturgical influences on the poem and attempted "to show that there is still much to be said for [the] original intuition of [Garrett (1918) concerning] the immediacy of the eucharist in *Pearl*" (475).

497-98 The reference is to the Gospel for Septuagesima Sunday. Oakden (1968) 343-45 and Bishop (1968) 124-25 discussed liturgical influence on *Pearl*. As Oakden noted, since Septuagesima forms the beginning of the second part of the ecclesiastical year comprising the seasons of Lent, Passiontide, and Easter, it fit the poem's theme of mortality, death, and resurrection. See also Gatta (1974) on "Transformation Symbolism and the Liturgy of the Mass in *Pearl*."

501-72 Placed near the center of the poem, the Parable of the Vineyard (Matt. 20.1-16) illustrates why the pearl-maiden, who lived such a short time on earth (the vineyard), received the same reward (the penny representing the Beatific Vision) as those who endured a lifetime of struggle. In fact, due to her innocence and God's grace, her rank in heaven is higher than many.

503-4 Osgood rendered *terme* 'end'. He believed the reference is to the grape-harvest in mid-autumn. Gordon's *terme* 'appointed period' and *date* 'season' appear to be the proper meanings.

Kean (1967) 52, citing the description of the work being done in l. 512, believed the season is March, as shown in *Très Riches Heures du Duc de Berry*. However, as Johnson-BMW (1991) argued, pp. 8 and 14, the time of the year may be September, the sign of Libra. She noted that Virgil, in the *Georgics* (Book II, 397ff.), recommended dressing the vines three or four times a year, contending that the soil should be broken up, the grove lightened of its foliage, and the vines cut and pruned into shape in the fall.

505 As Gordon noted, *þys* may be rendered 'these'. (Cf. *þis worteʒ* 'these plants' 42.) *Hyne* 'households' is then a coll. n. Gollancz' *hyne* 'household' may be the correct sense, but the poet's general meaning apparently includes all members of households. Cf. *MED hīne* n., 1b, 'a religious familia, monastic community' in place names. The *patrifamilias* of Matt. 20.1 means 'householder', the meaning given by Hillmann, but the poet sometimes altered biblical details. (Cf. 163n.) Osgood, Gordon, Moorman, and Andrew & Waldron rendered *hyne* 'laborers' in agreement with *MED* 2b.

512 *Keruen* denotes the pruning of the vines, which are also being bound and made secure. For coll. *hit* 'them', see *MED hit* pron., 2f. See 503-4n on the time of the year.

513 *Vnder* 'the third hour' is about nine o'clock in the morning.

523-24 Editors rendered *hyre* 'wage, reward', but *MED hīr(e* n., 2d, 'service', is fitting, and MS *pray* 'ask' may be retained. Hillmann construed 522-23 together as part of the narrative, retained *pray*, and tr. 524: "I call on you through bond and intent." All editors, except Hillmann and DeFord, emended *pray* to *pay*.

529 'Evensong' is the *undeciman* 'eleventh hour' (about 5 P.M.) of Matt. 20.6, the sixth in a system of seven canonical hours and the time for celebrating vespers. See 19-22n for discussion of the possibility that *sange* (19) denotes the chanting of vespers. The poet may have foreshadowed there the maiden's entrance into the vineyard (earth) about the eleventh hour (581-82) and her immediate reward (583-84). See 581-82n.

529-30 Johnson-BMW (1991) agreed that the 'eleventh hour' should be associated with the maiden as an individual baptized shortly before death, but suggested that we also "apply the parable to the dreamer whose life, like

130

any life, can be divided into twelve hours" (14). The "dreamer himself is in his eleventh hour" (10), Johnson stated, and concluded, p. 11, that the "August date of the poem [see l. 39] marks [him] as sorely in need of an eleventh-hour work permit." The maiden "urges upon him timely labor, August's spiritual work that must precede the balance scales of September."

532 MS *hen* may be retained as coll. usage of *MED hīne* n., 2b, 'a farm laborer'. The *MED* lists *hen(e* as a variant spelling. All editors emended *hen* to *hem* 'them'.

535 The words *ȝe* and *men* run together in the MS, but so do they in 290 where they obviously had to be separated. Editors tr. *ȝemen* 'hired laborers, yeomen'.

536 Gollancz defined *at* 'which' as a Northern rel. pron. from ON *at*. Gordon interpreted *þat at* as a development of *þat þat* because *at* "does not occur as a relative elsewhere in this group of poems." However, cf. *at* 'which' in *Gawain* 2205. (Editors of *Gawain* unnecessarily emended to *as*.)

538 Hillmann retained *and and* 'and when'. All other editors, except DeFord, emended to *and*, but see *MED and* conj. (& adv.), 6a.

545-48 Marti (1991) 86 stated, "Like the *Pearl* text, the workmen form a line (*rawe*), but the equivalence of first and last in both brings the ends together to create a circle." Marti saw the source for the meaning of *Pearl* at its structural center in the poet's paraphrase of the Parable of the Vineyard, which "recounts the events of a single day, but resonates simultaneously with the larger time frames of both the human lifespan and the whole of salvation history. As such it stands in striking microcosmic relation to the text containing it, a poem narrating both a single day from the life of the dreamer and, in its figural movement from the garden of loss to the New Jerusalem, the history of mankind" (87).

546 Most editors tr. *inlyche* 'alike, equally'. Hillmann followed Hamilton (1958) 188–89 who noted that *inlyche* is better rendered 'fully' here and in l. 603. This reading suits the interpretation of the Parable of the Vineyard more exactly, since each soul receives 'fully' the reward of salvation, even though there are ranks in the hierarchical system of heaven. (See 603–4n for further discussion.) The *MED* cited *Pearl* s.v. *inlīche* adv., 'alike, equally', but ll. 546 and 603 would be better listed s.v. *inlī* adv., 1c, 'wholly'. The variant spelling *inliche* appears there.

552 Macrae-Gibson-C (1968) 210 noted the significance of the link-word *more* in this stanza-group in relation to its use as the link in Group III. The dreamer then yearned for more and more (144–45). In 599–600 he will take up the complaint of the laborers who thought they should have received more, but by the end of the poem (1189–1200) he will accept God's will concerning *more and lasse* (601).

555 Matt. 20.12 reads: "Hi novíssimi una hora fecérunt." ("These last have worked but one hour.") The poet paraphrases this verse in 551 but adds

555 to remind us that the maiden "lyfed not two ʒer in oure þede" (483).

558 Morris emended MS *wanig* to *wrang*, which accords with Matt. 20.13: "Amíce, non fácio tibi iniúriam." ("Friend, I do thee no wrong.") Most editors emended to *waning* but tr. 'diminution, loss'. Hillmann retained *wanig* and tr., "Friend, I will not concede thee lacking," but her derivation of the word from OE *wan* plus *-ig* is doubtful.

Emerson (1927) 822 noted that OED *waning* vbl. sb. (OE *wanung*) could render the Vulgate's *iniúriam*. See sense 1b, 'damage inflicted by a person'. Emerson also suggested that ʒete 'to do' is the verb represented by *MED* gĕten v.1, for which the variant spelling ʒeten is listed.

Moorman followed Fowler (1959) 582 who took *waning* from OE wānung and tr., "Friend, I will allow thee no lamentation," but Emerson's interpretation seems preferable.

570-72 Cf. Matt. 20.16: "Sic erunt novíssimi primi, et primi novíssimi; multi enim sunt vocáti, pauci vero elécti." ("So shall the last be first, and the first last. For many are called, but few chosen.") The second part of the Vulgate's verse also appears in Matt. 22.14 at the end of the Parable of the Wedding Feast, paraphrased in *Cleanness* 51-160.

A key to the interpretation of *Pearl* may be in Augustine's "Sermo LXXXVII," *PL* 38.533, tr. by Robertson-C (1950a) 295: "We shall all be equal in that reward, the last like the first, and the first like the last. For that penny is eternal life, and all will be equal in eternal life. Although they will be radiant with a diversity of merits, one more, one less, that which pertains to eternal life will be equal to all." Augustine's writing, as Robertson noted, explains the doctrine of hierarchy in heaven: all receive salvation, but there are different degrees of glory in God's kingdom.

Mykeʒ, which renders the Vulgate's *elécti*, may have special significance for the pearl-maiden whose place in heaven is higher than many. See, for example, 577-80. Hamilton (1958) 187-88 supported Gordon's interpretation of *mykeʒ* as an aphetic form of *amike* 'friend' (L *amícus*), with the extended sense 'chosen companions of the Lord'. Hillmann tr. *mykeʒ* 'chosen ones', but suggested derivation from OE *mæcca* 'companion'.

574 Editors took *wore* as a variant of *were* and rendered *lyttel* 'lowly, unimportant', but *were* is pt., and this tense does not accord well with the tenses of the other verbs in 573-76. *Wore* 'expend' may be a variant of *OED ware* v.2, found in *Gawain* 402, 1235.

581-82 The pearl-maiden is one who toiled the least in the Vineyard, one who came at the eleventh hour, almost at the time of evening. (See 529n.) Osgood considered Augustine's interpretation in *PL* 38.533 an inversion of these lines because Augustine says the ones called at the eleventh hour are those who became Christians when they were decrepit. However, Robertson-C (1950a) 293-94, noting that later commentators frequently changed details without changing the basic meaning or *sentence*, cited and tr. Bruno Astensis, twelfth century, for an interpretation that fits *Pearl*: "But the eleventh hour is the hour at which one of whatever age begins to serve when he approaches his end and is near death. Not only the youthful and the aged, but also the children have this hour" (*PL* 165.237). As Robertson noted, the pearl-maiden is, therefore, simply stressing the fact that she was baptized only shortly before death. See also Bishop (1968) 122-25, who cited the interpretation of the Parable of the Vineyard by Honorius 'of Autun' in *PL* 172.858. Honorius specifically included those who die as infants in the same category as those who are converted "in decrepita aetate."

588 In contrast to the maiden who went to heaven immediately (584), those who lived longer and committed sin had a debt to pay. (See 617-22.) As Hillmann noted, the reference is apparently to purgatory where souls not entirely cleansed of sin must endure a fixed term. Most editors tr. *toȝere* 'this year', but *to ȝere more* 'for years more' seems preferable. (See 35n for examples of connected words in the MS that need to be separated.)

591 Emerson (1922) 74 suggested *rert* 'fixed, established' (Hillmann). Moorman and Andrew & Waldron favored 'upraised, supreme' (Gollancz and Gordon).

595-96 Cf. Ps. 61.12-13: "Semel locútus est Deus; duo haec audívi: quia potéstas Dei est,/et tibi, Dómine, misericórdia; quia tu reddes unicuíque iuxta ópera sua." ("God hath spoken once, these two things have I heard, that power belongeth to God,/and mercy to thee, O Lord; for thou wilt render to every man according to his works.")

In the MS, the line under *p* of *p(er)termynable* is the abbreviation for *er*. Though Gordon, following earliers editors and the *OED*, read *pretermynable* 'foreordaining', he suggested *pertermynable* from ME *termyne* v., with *per* as an intensive prefix, to express the concept *quia potéstas Dei est*.

The sense '(power of) judging perfectly' relates to God's justice being forever fixed (591). The reference is only to the *poynt* (594) concerned with God's power, not to the second point in Ps. 61.13 concerned with the Lord's mercy, for the dreamer must still learn, in the next stanza-group (601-660), that the grace of God is great enough for the innocent child.

Pertermynable 'judging perfectly' is derived from the *OED* prefix 1 *per-*, I.2, 'thoroughly' plus *terminable* a. from *termine* v., sense 1, 'to determine'. Kaske (1959) 418-21, supporting Gordon's suggestion, tr. 'speaking or declaring enduringly'.

Hillmann read *Pretermynable* 'Infinite (Before the terminable)', comparing, among other biblical verses, Ps. 73.12. Andrew & Waldron, crediting Kean (1967) 191, glossed *pertermynable* 'supreme in judgment'.

The *MED* cites only *Pearl* s.v. *pertermináble* adj., 'having power to determine all things; ? determining beforehand, preordaining'.

603-4 All editors, except Hillmann and Moorman, tr. *inlyche* 'alike, equally'. For tr. 'fully', see 546n. All are 'fully' compensated in having gained heaven, but 'little or much' may be the reward because various individuals have different ranks. For discussion of the system of hierarchy in heaven, see also the notes to 410, 445–48, 546, 570–72, and 862.

Brown (1904) 133–37 thought that the poet was following the fourth-century heretic Jovinian, who asserted that the heavenly rewards are equal. Osgood, pp. xxxix–xl, though he accepted Brown's interpretation, expressed some doubt when he stated it was "at variance with the poet's social ideas," especially since the orthodox view is implied in *Cleanness* 113–24.

Fletcher (1921) 17–19 refuted Brown, noting passages in *Pearl* that prove the poet was in accord with the prevalent Christian doctrine of graded heavenly rewards. See, for example, 577–80, where the pearl-maiden speaks of having more *blysse* than others, and 887, which indicates the *aldermen* are closer to God's throne than she is. For further discussion refuting Brown, see also Sledd (1940) 381, Hamilton (1943) 372, and Hillmann's 603–6n. For an attempt to revive Brown's argument, see Oiji (1961) 46–57.

606 *Nesch oþer harde*, as Gordon observed in his 603–4n, probably refers to God's way of meting out rewards and punishments. However, it does seem that the distinctuion here is between salvation and eternal damnation. *Harde* may imply punishment for sinners who must endure the penalty of atonement. (See 661–64.)

Wellek-B (1933) 25–26 discussed *gratia prima*, free grace given by God in baptism to remit original sin, and *gratia secunda*, additional grace given in proportion to one's merits. The grown-up person may lose his title to free grace by sinning or add to this title by performing good works. The maiden speaks of those who forfeit their title in 617–22.

607–8 Cf. the water symbolism here to the stream flowing from God's throne (107, 934, 974, 1055–60) and the baptismal water (627) springing from Christ's wound (647–55). In contrast, the simile involving water in 364–65 perhaps represents the dreamer's loss of grace, due to despair.

Gordon's "streams from a deep source that has never ceased to flow" (608) is fitting, but *goteȝ* may denote 'currents', as in *Cleanness* 413. *MED gŏulf*, sense b, defines 'whirlpool', and *chāren* v.1, 3a, lists 'to change or vary in character, condition, or attitude'. Cf. this simile depicting God's grace going around in a circle to pure souls with the description of the *garlande gay* (1186).

The image of water in a *dyche* (607) seems unpleasant unless one thinks of it as depicting life-giving waters in a moat surrounding the castle of heaven. Olmert (1987) 401, with reference to Owst (1926) 325, noted that the sermonist Bromyard described God's 'ditch' of protective waters in this way.

609–10 Gordon, with Osgood, Gollancz, and Hillmann in agreement, favored, "That man's privilege is great who ever stood in awe of Him who rescues sinners." Mitchell (1964) supported this reading, pointing to *MED* *fraunchīs(e* n., 1c, 'spiritual freedom; especially the privileged state of Adam and Eve before the fall'. *Dard* is the pt. of *dare* 'bow in awe' (839). *Hym* refers to the *gentyl Cheuentayn* (605), Christ who died on the cross to save mankind after the sin of Adam. (See 637-60.)

Visser-C (1958), by comparing other ME auxil. verbs used to connote motion, defined *dard* 'dared to go' and tr., "That man's privilege is great who (at a certain moment in his life) had the courage to go or turn to Him [God] who rescues sinners."

Kaske (1959) 422-25, basing his interpretation on John 1.14, 16-18, the concept of the Word made flesh, proposed the following sense: The liberality of Him who was ever hidden (God the Father) is abundant to Him (God the Son) Who makes rescue in sin.

Russom (1976) 26-28, with an interpretation that recalls one given by Morris (1891a) 602-3, argued that *to hym* is a preposed constituent of *þat*, having as its antecedent *vch mon* 603. He tr., "His grace is great which was ever a mystery, which makes *him* (each man) rescue in sin." See Russom for a study (in all four poems of the MS and in *Saint Erkenwald*) of a type of relative clause in which certain constituents of the clause appear immediately to the left of the relative pronoun.

612 The emphasis on God's grace in this Stanza-Group XI anticipates Group XII, especially the climactic concept, extending into XIII, of one's not being able to enter heaven unless he come there as a child (709-28).

Brown (1904) 129-30 noted that the poet, in stressing God's grace for salvation, sided with the English theologian Thomas Bradwardine (died 1349), whose *De Causa Dei contra Pelagium* opposed Semi-Pelagianism. The followers of Pelagianism held that merit acquired by right conduct was more important than divine grace to obtain salvation.

Mann (1983) examined 'enough' as a poetic link-word that "vibrates with emotional and intellectual connotations" (18). The "image of *innoghe* involves no renunciation, no settling for second-best, but rather an endlessly sufficient abundance" (29). Mann also studied the poet's use of *paye, more,* and *lasse* in *Pearl*.

613 Chase accepted the emendation of *now* to *inow* by Emerson (1927) 824, and Macrae-Gibson-C (1968) 210 supported it, but Gordon pointed out that the link is not broken, since *now* echoes *inoghe* 612 in sound. Cf. the echoing of sound, not a repetition of the same word, in *court* 445, following *Cortaysye* 444. (The spelling is *innoʒe* in *Pearl* 624 and *innowe* in *Gawain* 1401.)

613-16 Wood (1973), considering these lines in relation to 551-56, in which the early-comers to the vineyard complain, associated the dreamer with the early-comers and argued that critics, while overstressing his sorrow at losing his pearl, have "given too little attention to the resentment and envy with which he regards her present good fortune" (9). Wood compared the dreamer to Old Man (Adam) in relation to Old Law (Old Testament) concepts, until he learns the lesson of grace taught by the maiden.

616 Osgood, Gollancz, and Chase, following Morris' suggestion, emended *lere* to *here* (variant of *hyre* 'wage'). Gordon, followed by Cawley, Moorman, and Andrew & Waldron, emended to *fere* 'fortune, rank, dignity' (OF *afeire*). Hillmann tr. MS *lere* 'recompense', considering it a variant of *MED lūre* n.1. For *lere* 'abode', see *MED leir* n.1, sense e, 'a place where someone dwells'. The poet perhaps anticipates here *heueneȝ clere* (620), the maiden's abode.

617 Most editors considered *abate* a variant of *abyde* 'endure' (OE *abīdan*), but derivation from OF *abatre* seems preferable. Emerson (1922) 75, though he took *abate* as a pp. rather than an infin., suggested sense 1b, 'to bow humbly', s.v. *MED abāten, -i(en*, where *Pearl* is cited.

Hillmann tr. 'to lose zeal' (*MED* 4b), thinking it would be contrary to Christian teaching for the maiden to say that "no matter how prayerful a man's life may be, he will at some time fall into sin." However, the maiden is apparently merely asking the dreamer if he ever knew any man who did not sin during his lifetime, even though he prayed often, for men ordinarily lose their innocence as they grow older (621–22), whereas the maiden, having died soon after being baptized, never lost her innocence. (See 625–32.)

As Fletcher (1921) 4 observed, the grown person can humble himself like a child through contrition, but "he is not *by nature* one with the perfect exemplar of Innocence, Christ, as is the little child."

617–24 Russell (1983) 188 observed that the maiden's "notion that the older one gets, the more one sins is, though uncourteous, the perfect rejoinder to the narrator's position that long struggle is inherently more meritorious than innocence." Russell argued that the message of *Pearl* is the maiden's "persistent theme of heavenly 'courtesy,' the sweet, mysterious *gentilesse* that constitutes the poem's ultimate critique of eschatology" (185).

Baker (1984), analyzing the debate between the dreamer and the maiden in Stanza-Groups VIII–XIII, cited this passage to highlight the maiden's teaching that no one is saved by works alone. "The infants, restored to innocence by baptismal grace, have a right to heaven while the older Christians, having lost their baptismal right through personal sin, can only regain heaven by asking for God's mercy and grace in the sacrament of penance" (267). Baker, studying the episode about Trajan, the righteous heathen, in *Piers Plowman*, concluded that Langland agrees with the *Pearl*-poet. "Although both concede that the righteous man will be saved, they insist that he achieves salvation by grace, which makes good works meritorious" (273).

630 *To*, governing *niyȝt*, is in post. c. Gordon noted that the spelling *niyȝt* occurs in *Gawain* 929 and *Cleanness* 1779. Morris, Osgood, Gollancz, Chase, Hillmann, and DeFord read *myȝt*.

632 Cf. coll. *hyne* 'servants' (1211), and the idea at the end of the poem that God's 'servants' are 'precious pearls' *vnto his pay.*

635 Concerning the first word in this line, Osgood, who edited from photographs, wrote, "I am at a loss for the intended reading." Examination of the original MS under the ultra-violet lamp in the British Library substantiates Gollancz' ȝys in his 1921 edition. (He read ȝy[ld] in his 1891 edition.)

Gordon, Moorman, and Andrew & Waldron, following Wright (1939) 16, took *at þe fyrst* as an adv. phr., *fyne* as an adv., and tr. 'pay them first in full'. Hillmann adopted Gollancz' 'at the first day's close'. Revard (1964) interpreted *fyne* as a n. and tr. 'according to the original contract'. However, *fyne* 'completely' may be rendered adverbially, and *fyrst* as a n. refers to the 'first group' who came into the vineyard, *þe fyrst* (549) who began to complain when they learned that the others were going to receive a penny also.

Davis (1954) 98 noted that emendation of *hym* to *hem* is unnecessary, since *hym* is occasionally used as a pl. form in this MS. (See 229n.) Only Hillmann and Andrew & Waldron, among the editors, retained MS *hym* 'them'.

639 The *forme-fader* Adam is named specifically in 656. Osgood compared 639-45 to *Saint Erkenwald* 294-98. Cf. also *Cleanness* 235-48.

648 God's grace to cleanse and save mankind flowed in both the blood Christ shed at his crucifixion and the water mingled with blood spurting from his side (646-47). The maiden explains this symbolism in the next stanza, a symbolism that recalls the stream (107), separating the terrestrial paradise from the heavenly, and anticipates the Lamb's shedding of blood (741) and the pearl-maiden's garment being cleansed by this blood (766). See Rev. 7.14-17 and 22.14-17 for the basis of this blood and water symbolism, and Johnson-C (1953) 41 for discussion of the imagery.

652 The *deth secounde*, as Hillmann noted, refers to the condemnation of souls at the Last Judgment. See the following verses of the Apocalypse: 2.11, 20.6, 20.14, and 21.8.

654 As Gollancz observed, this incident in John 19.34 is amplified in the apocryphal gospel of Nicodemus. Longinus, whose name corresponds to the Greek term for 'lance', was the soldier who pierced Christ's side.

655 Editors rendered *gylteȝ* as a pl. n., but Otten (1971) suggested reading *gylteȝ* 'of sin' as a gen. and *felle* as a n. (Latin *fel* 'gall, bitterness'— MED *fel(le)* n.). Noting that the reference is to Adam's singular original sin, Otten compared *þe olde gulte* (942) and cited patristic and liturgical sources, among them Tertullian's *De Baptismo* in which baptismal water is mentioned in conjunction with the spear that pierced Christ's side.

658 Most editors took *he* as a reference to God, but Hillmann, with DeFord and Moorman in agreement, pointed out that the logical and grammatical antecedent of *he* is Adam (656).

659 As Hillmann noted, *sely stounde* 'blessed hour' refers to the time when baptism is received.

661-64 See Osgood's note (660ff.) for discussion of the doctrine. The person who, living in this world, sins after being baptized, commits what is called 'actual sin', different from the 'original sin' cleansed by baptism. 'Actual sin' is forgiven by the sacrament of penance, if the guilty one is contrite (669-70). The baptized innocent child is saved without need of penance, in contrast to the person who is always in danger of sinning the older he becomes (617-22).

665 Osgood glossed *resoun* 'fair consideration', noting that the personified *Resoun* in *Piers Plowman*, Passus IV, is distinguished for his justice. (See the A-Text, ll. 117-45). Gordon followed Gollancz' tr., "but Reason, straying not from right." Hillmann tr. 'sentence of justice'. Andrew & Waldron capitalized *Resoun* and commented, "God is here portrayed as a quasi-personification of reason." Rendering *resoun of ryȝt* 'cause of justice' also suits the context.

672 Gordon's *ryȝte* 'justified, sanctified by divine grace' reveals the double-entendre of this link-word, which can denote '(strict) justice' and 'justifiable claim, on legal or moral grounds, to have or obtain something' (one's privilege). In 684, 696, and 720, when the pearl-maiden says, "The innocent one (child) is always redeemed by right," she evidently means the privilege the innocent have through justification by divine grace. This privilege applies with certainty to the child who dies soon after being baptized. In 708 *ryȝte* 'justice' concludes a stanza that shows the ordinary man, so liable to sin on earth, should not presume to enter heaven on the grounds of strict justice, but must first become like the innocent child (717-28).

673-76 The poet apparently distinguishes between the righteous man who enters heaven through penance (661-64) and the innocent one who joins God immediately. The doctrine of hierarchy may be implied. The innocent one, like the pearl-maiden, has a higher rank in heaven. See Fletcher (1921) 17-18 on this point.

681 *Hondelyngeȝ* 'with hands' translates in part *innocens mánibus* 'the innocent in hands' of Ps. 23.4.

687-88 In the ME text, there is a switch from sg. *man . . . he* (685-86) to pl. *her* 'their'. Cf. the syntax of 609-11 and 617-23.

689 Osgood, Gollancz, Hillmann, and Moorman defined *saȝ* 'saw', but Gordon's 'says' seems preferable, since the reference is to the biblical writing attributed to Solomon. The 'righteous man' is Jacob. Gordon, comparing *sade* 532 instead of *sayde* as an example of an *a-ay* spelling variant, noted that MS *saȝ* may be retained. Andrew & Waldron emended to *sayz*.

690-92 Bradley (1890) 201 compared Wisdom 10.10: "Haec prófugam irae fratris iustum dedúxit per vias rectas et osténdit illi regnum Dei et dedit illi scientam sanctorum, honestávit illum in labóribus et complévit labóres illíus." ("She conducted the just, when he fled from his brother's wrath, and shewed him the kingdom of God, and gave him the knowledge of the holy things, made him honourable in his labours, and accomplished his labours.")

Emendation of l. 690 may be avoided with the following readings: *kyntly* 'kindly' as a variant of *MED kīndelī* adj. (cf. *dyt* 681 instead of *dyd*); *oure* 'mercy' from *MED ōr(e* n.2, sense 1a; *aquyle* 'prevail' (cf. the sense of *aquylde* 967). Granting that the poet altered the biblical verse (cf. 163n), one need not emend *he* to *ho* 'she' to agree with fem. Wisdom. Mercy did prevail for Jacob, for he was not only given a vision of heaven (Gen. 28.11-17) but was also permitted to escape the wrath of his brother Esau, who sought to murder him (Gen. 27.41-45).

See Rathborne (1963) for a summary of emendations. Gordon, Cawley, and Moorman followed Bradley (1890) 201 who changed *he* to *ho* and suggested, "How [koyntyse on]oure con aquyle." ("How wisdom obtained honor.") Osgood followed Gollancz (1890) 223: "How kyntly oure [kyng him] con aquyle." ("How kindly our King welcomed him.") In his 1921 edition, Gollancz substituted *Koyntyse* for *kyng*. Hillmann, reading *onre* instead of *oure*, and emending to *on[o]re*, tr. 690: "How fittingly honor [he] did receive." Andrew & Waldron emended *How kyntly* to *Hym Koyntyse* and tr. 690: "(that) our Wisdom received him." They read *He (Wisdom)* in 691, believing the poet changed the gender of the personification, "possibly to conform to the common medieval identification of Wisdom with Christ."

Rathborne (1963), noting liturgical influence on *Pearl* and the fact that *Dominus* occurs in liturgical texts dealing with Wisdom 10.10, favored the reading which appeared in Gollancz' 1891 edition: "How kyntly oure [lord hym] con aquyle."

702 Gollanz' emendation of *tryed* to *cryed*, adopted by Andrew & Waldron because of alliteration and the recurrence of *tryed* 707, seems unnecessary. (Cf. 53n.) Apparently the poet did not always avoid identical rhyme. *Clere* appears in rhyme position in ll. 735 and 737.

703 Interpreting *alegge* as imper., Osgood tr. 'urge your privilege', Gollancz 'renounce thy right'; both rendered *innome* 'received'.

Everett & Hurnard (1947), noting legal phraseology in this passage, argued for the reading adopted by Gordon and subsequent editors, and given here. *Innome* 'trapped' is a pp. *(MED inimen* v., 2c). Cf. legal terminology in 417, 563, 580, 594, and 613.

707-8 These lines anticipate 709-28. Even the righteous man must become like the innocent child through God's grace before he may enter heaven. The aspect of humility is implied here. (See ll. 401-8.)

721-32 Pattison (1978) 22 cited this passage , noting that the young girl of the poem, who died in infancy, "is at once a child, a pearl, and a maiden—or rather three aspects of one phenomenon, an innocence possible to all Christians. . . . Childhood is at once a state on a par with adulthood and one of spotless innocence," provided, of course, that the child has been baptized, as the poet makes clear in ll. 625-60. See 161-62n on Augustine's explanation of the advanced stature in heaven of the child who dies in infancy.

721 The link-word *ryȝt* of the preceding stanza-group does not appear here, the only place in the poem lacking concatenation. Macrae-Gibson-C (1968) 213, following Gordon's discussion (pp. 88–89), felt the missing link is due to textual corruption.

McGalliard (1969) 288, citing Medary (1916) 265 and noting that according to the conventions of "linking" poems, a link might be omitted if the line contained a proper name or if the link-word appeared in an adjacent verse, believed the poet may have availed himself of the latter privilege, since *ryȝt* does appear in l. 723.

Andrew & Waldron considered "unacceptable both syntactically and metrically" the suggestion of Emerson (1927) 825 to add *Ryȝt* 'Straightway' at the beginning of the line, but they did substitute *Ryȝt* 'Justice' for *Ihecu*, believing the poet intended to personify "Jesus as 'Justice', and that MS *Jesus* is a scribal substitution for the sake of greater explicitness."

However, the omission may be prescribal. Røstvig (1967) 326–32 argued that the poet, working with numerical symbolism, deliberately made a break here to divide *Pearl* into twelve stanza-groups, followed by eight, thereby making more prominent the fact that the last eight deal with the eternal bliss of those who are saved by the Lamb. The eighth day, according to biblical numerical symbolism, signifies eternity.

Casling & Scattergood (1974) 87–89, in agreement with Røstvig, also favored the view that the break in stanza-linking at this point was deliberately made by the poet.

Carlson (1991) argued that there is a failed link here, that it is authorial and served the poet to make a point, but he disagreed that the point is Røstvig's two divisions of twelve and eight. Instead, he concluded, p. 62, that the poet deliberately created the failed link to call attention to the pearl-maiden's point "that 'ryȝt' will lead the Dreamer nowhere, while Christ's mercy and grace could benefit him, indeed must benefit him if he is to have any hope for salvation; at just this point in her argument, 'ryȝt' as a link-word likewise turns out to lead nowhere formally, and in its place in the poet's formal scheme of things appears what the Dreamer ought to rely on instead of 'ryȝt', namely 'Iesus'."

Mylde is a sb. adj., evidently referring to Christ's 'humble disciples' (Gollancz, Gordon, Cawley, and Andrew & Waldron). Osgood suggested 'little child' (Matt. 18.2) but also noted the reference may be to the disciples (Mark 9.34). Hillmann and Moorman favored 'tender ones (children)', but the doctrinal pronouncement of 721–28 would be more appropriately directed to the disciples rather than to the children.

722-24 Fast (1992) 379 observed that this is the lesson of humility the dreamer must learn. He is advised by the maiden to forsake this world and purchase his spotless pearl (743–44), which is salvation. In discussing the relationship between the poet and his persona, the dreamer, Fast suggested that although the "poet is the artist deliberately restructuring his material, and therefore not to be identified entirely with the dreamer, he is also a mere human sharing the condition of the dreamer, and required to pay attention to the lessons of the dreamer" (373).

726 Bishop (1984) 455, after noting that *Pearl* employs and adapts several of the *topoi* associated with the ancient tradition of the *consolatio mortis*, compared this line to a statement made by King Edward III in a letter he wrote to the Queen of Castile, concerning the death of his daughter Joan: Christ joined Joan to himself while she was "innocentum et immaculatum, ab omni Carnis Spurcitia peregrinam." Joan, who was betrothed to the Infante Pedro, son of Pedro the Cruel, King of Castile, died of the plague on September 2, 1348, while she was on her way to Spain. Bishop cited passages of *solacia* in letters to the Infante, the King, and the Queen, and observed that although Joan was fifteen, she was, like the maiden in *Pearl*, "accorded the status, not only of Bride of Christ, but also that of Queen in Heaven" (456).

730 Spearing (1970) 160 noted pearl symbolism is resumed in this stanza-group from Group V. The jeweler (dreamer) of V is reintroduced here, as the poet, to retain the identification, alters Matt. 13.45 by calling the 'merchant' a 'jeweler'. (See 252n.)

730–35 See 221–28n. Matt. 13.45–46 reads: "Iterum símile est regnum caelórum hómini negotiatóri quaerénti bonas margarítas;/invénta autem una pretiósa margaríta, ábiit et véndidit ómnia quae hábuit et emit eam." ("Again the kingdom of heaven is like to a merchant seeking good pearls;/Who when he had found one pearl of great price, went his way, and sold all that he had, and bought it.")

Osgood (735–43n) gave the various patristic viewpoints concerning pearl symbolism. (See also Schofield [1909] 634–37.) The poet followed the Vulgate closely in making Matthew's 'pearl of price' (746) symbolize heaven itself, but, as Schofield observed, much of the thought of the Church Fathers comes into the entire structure of *Pearl*, for this gem, according to the Fathers, may also represent Christ, the Virgin, gospel teaching, purity, grace, and truth.

Osgood cited Ephrem's hymn on the death of children (*Select Hymns and Homilies*, tr. H. Burgess, p. 14): "Like pearls in diadems children are inserted in the kingdom." Hillmann rightly refuted Osgood's comment that the poet's interpretation of the pearl of great price "is somewhat confused." Representing *heuenesse clere* (735), this pearl is worn by the maiden on her breast in 222 and 740, and the image is extended to other souls in heaven in 854 and 1103. When the dreamer first saw it (221–28), he did not fully understand its significance. Now he is advised to abandon the mad world and purchase it (743–44).

732 See Macrae-Gibson-C (1968) 214 for a discussion of word-play on the link-words in this stanza-group. *Makelleʒ* replaces *mascelleʒ* in 733 and 757; in 780 the two come together. The dreamer is corrected (781–84), as he had been before (421–56), when the maiden says she is *maskelles* 'spotless' (781) but not *makeleʒ* 'unequalled' (784), for that title belongs only to the Virgin Mary. The pearl of price is both spotless and peerless (732–33). Gordon, in a long note to l. 733, showed that MS *makelleʒ* (733) and *makeleʒ* (757) should be retained, for there is similarity of sound in the two words, and the concatenation is not broken. See also Baird (1973) for arguments favoring retention of the MS forms in both places.

739 Cf. 675 and 685–88 on salvation for the righteous. For the intervening vowel in *ryʒtywys*, cf. *boroʒt* 628, *bereste* 854, and *mynyster* 1063. Editors emended to *ryʒtwys*.

740 Osgood and Gordon read *stode* 'stood' as a v. Gollancz and Hillmann interpreted *hit* as gen. 'its' and *stode* as a n. 'setting, position'. Moorman and Andrew & Waldron, following Hamilton (1958) 190, tr. 'shone'.

745–46 The spotless pearl (pure soul) adorned with pearls (virtues) possesses the pearl of price (heaven). See 253–55n and 855–56n for a similar fusing of pearl symbols, and 269–72n for discussion of the phrase *perle of prys* in that context. The phrasing of another occurrence differs slightly: "Perleʒ pyʒte of ryal prys" (193). The poet, therefore, employs *perle(ʒ)* . . . *prys* alliteration three times, first to denote the pearls (virtues) the maiden wears (193), secondly to represent the maiden's soul (272), and thirdly to denote the large pearl (heaven) she wears on her breast (746). All these symbols come together in 745–46.

749–52 Gordon thought it "highly probable" that the poet echoed *Le Roman de la Rose* (ed. Langlois 16013f.) where it is argued that neither philosophers like Plato and Aristotle "nor the artist, not even Pygmalion, can imitate successfully the works of Nature."

Pilch-C (1964) 165–67 opposed Gordon, noting that "Jean de Meun speaks of the superiority of nature to art, i.e., to man's creation," but the poet's point is not to contrast nature with art but to show "the inferiority of both to God."

751 *Lettrure* 'writing' (Osgood and Hillmann) seems preferable to 'learning, science' (Gollancz, Gordon, Moorman, and Andrew & Waldron).

752 See 142n on omission of *-d* in *carpe*. Gollancz, Chase, Gordon, Cawley, and Andrew & Waldron emended to *carped*.

754 Editors rendered *corteʒ* as an adj. corresponding to *cortayse*, but the words may be from *MED cŏrden* v.1, an aphetic form of *accorden*. For unvoicing of *d* to *t*, cf. *dyt* 681, *kyntly* 690, and *wete* 761.

755 Morris thought he was emending *oftriys* to *of priys* 'of value'. Gollancz rendered *triys* as a form of 'truce'—"What kind of peace bears as its symbol the spotless pearl" (755–56)? However, Gordon & Onions (1933) 180-

81, citing an anonymous reviewer of Gollancz' 1921 edition of *Pearl* in *TLS* (May 18, 1922), noted that *triys* 'truce' is "phonologically inadmissible," and then sparked the controversy over *ostriys* 'oysters' by pointing to Henry Bradley's notation on the margin of the staff copy of Morris' *Early English Alliterative Poems* in the Oxford Dictionary room. Osgood had read MS *offys* 'position', noting that the second *f* is spread on top, but Gordon accepted Osgood's reading only as a "happy emendation."

Davis (1954) 98–99, in his review of Gordon's edition, pointed out that after examining the MS anew, he saw *offys* as the true form, for the disputed mark read as the abbreviation for *ri* is a "plain tick, at the same angle as the off-stroke of *f*." My own viewing of the word under the ultra-violet lamp in the British Library supports Davis' observation. The top of an *f* is not always securely joined in the MS. Note, for example, the *f* of *of* in l. 752.

Hillmann and subsequent editors accepted *offys* as the MS reading, but Donaldson (1972) 75–79 argued again for *ostriys* not only as the MS reading— "What kind of oysters produce a pearl like you?"—but also as a type of allegory the poet might have used. Davis had commented, if only *offys* "can be accepted as the scribe's intention, we may be spared long notes about truce and oysters."

761 Moorman followed Hillmann who, disagreeing with *wete* 'wet' given by previous editors, derived the word from OE *wite* and tr. *worlde wete* 'world's woe'. However, *wete* may be the pp. of *OED wede* v. (Cf. pt. *wed* 'went mad' in *Cleanness* 1585.) For other examples of unvoicing of *d* to *t*, see the notes to 10, 460, and 754. *Worlde wete* corresponds in meaning, then, to *worlde wode* 743. Andrew & Waldron supported *wete* 'wet'.

763–64 See 11n on phrasing associated with secular love poetry. Christ is called *Lemman* 'Spouse, Beloved, Dear' in 796, 805, and 829. Cf. Song of Songs 4.7–8 and the application of those verses, with the refrain *Veni, coronaberis*, in "A Song of Great Sweetness to His Daintiest Dam," *Hymns to the Virgin and Christ*, ed. F.J. Furnivall, *EETS, OS*, 24 (1868), pp. 1–3.

765 This line helps to explain the matured state of the child's soul in heaven. See 161–62n.

766 Cf. Rev. 7.14 and 22.14. Lines 646, 705, and 801–16 refer to Christ's shedding his blood for man's salvation. See 218n on the garment metaphor.

767 The crown symbolizes both virginity and salvation. See 205n, 253–55n, and 451n. Luttrell (1962b) discussed the pearl as a symbol of virginity in other medieval works, among them *The Book of the Knight of La Tour-Landry* and the literature of John Gower.

768 *Pyȝt* 'adorned' echoes the link-word of Stanza-Group IV, and this line recalls the dominant image in that group of the maiden adorned with pearls representing virtues, such as power, beauty, purity, and virginity (765–67).

769 Osgood compared *bryd . . . flambe* to *flaumbande . . . bryddeʒ* 90–93. In the latter context the word denotes 'birds'. The pearl-maiden, bride of Christ, possesses qualities of the Virgin Mary, who was compared to the Phoenix of Araby in l. 430. In 94 the birds sing; in 882 the brides of the Lamb sing.

775 As Hillmann noted, *anvnnder cambe* is a conventional phrase, complimentary to ladies. Since the next line speaks of living for Christ in hardship, there may be an allusion to the religious life here.

Bloomfield (1969) 302 supposed the reference is to female martyrs whom the pearl-maiden surpassed in heaven's hierarchy.

777–80 The poet again presents the dreamer as confused and incredulous in order that the maiden may continue to reveal spiritual mysteries. She had already explained (433–56) she is not equal to Mary. Cf. *makeleʒ Moder* 435 to *makeleʒ Quene* 784, and see 279–88n and 444n on the distinction to be made between the poet and his persona.

781–84 Arthur (1989) 129 cited these lines to show how the maiden speaks as a master of logic. She is one of 144,000 virgins who is both *maskelles* 'spotless' (781) and *makeleʒ* 'peerless and husbandless'. The latter meaning, according to Arthur, is "revealed by the collocation of *vergynté* (767), *maskelleʒ bryd* (769), and *makeleʒ may* (780). . . . "If we must gloss, then, we need an entry such as *ma(s)kel(l)eʒ* 'spotless sinless virgin bride of Christ' to indicate the poet's quadrivial talent," and we "could therefore say that Pearl is *ma(s)kel(l)eʒ simpliciter*, but *ma(s)kel(l)eʒ quene* would mean 'without equal in her royal status' and so would be false."

785–86 Gordon and Cawley followed Gollancz in emending l. 786 so that 144,000 would be named, the number given in Rev. 14.1–3 and in ll. 869–70. (On the poet's altering of biblical details, see 163n.)

Hulbert (1927) 118, feeling the insertion of *fowre* into 786 made the meter clumsy, asked, "Could not the poet use a 'round number'?"

Robertson-C (1950b) 19 also supported the MS reading as a sort of poetic license, noting it was a familiar technique in sermons to suggest a familiar biblical passage by merely hinting at it, or by quoting it incompletely. (See 869–70n for a discussion of the 144,000 virgins in *Pearl* and in Revelation.)

789 As Clark & Wasserman (1979) 4 noted, the dreamer has recognized *clot* only as 'clay' (22), but the enlightened maiden, besides considering this meaning (320, 857), also refers to the New Jerusalem as *clot*. Thus, death in the earthly *clot* leads to resurrection in the heavenly *clot*. See Clark & Wasserman's "The Spatial Argument of *Pearl*: Perspectives on a Venerable Bead" for a study of how the poet, in having the maiden guide the dreamer from views of earthly appearance toward an understanding of spiritual truths, "grounds abstract principles in concrete physical circumstances, . . . creating a graphic doubleness, whereby moral stance is reflected and expressed by physical position and surroundings" (1).

790 Edward Wilson (1968) discussed "The 'Gostly Drem' in *Pearl.*" Of the three kinds of mystical visions—corporeal, spiritual, and intellectual—the dreamer's like the Apocalyptic vision of St. John, is classified formally as spiritual. Wilson, arguing that the dreamer was unready for a spiritual vision but in need of one, concluded: "Only after the maiden's instruction is his dream spiritual in terms of his interior disposition," and "only then does he have the ghostly vision of Jerusalem" (101). On this point, see also pp. 15-19 of Wilson's book, *The Gawain-Poet* (1976).

Spearing (1970) 110 also discussed these three kinds of religious visions, which Augustine (in *De Genesi ad Litteram, PL,* XXXIV, cols. 458ff.) distinguishes in the following way: (1) bodily vision "in which experience is received directly through the natural senses of the body;" (2) spiritual vision "in which spiritual forces affect the imagination as if they were sensory images;" (3) intellectual vision "in which God communicates directly with the human intellect in a way which is speechless and imageless and therefore ineffable." Spearing, with reference to Wilson (1968), noted, p. 111, that when the dreamer refers to St. John's vision as a 'gostly drem' (790), he is using that phrase as an equivalent to Augustine's 'spiritual vision'. The dreamer's experience is a 'gostly drem' or *somnium mentis,* and it leads him "into a contemplation of divine mysteries" (112). (See also 1090-92n.)

791 Only Chase adopted the emendation to *hyl-cot* of Emerson (1922) 77 for the sake of perfect rhyme, but Hillmann noted that *cot* in OE and ME generally referred to lowly dwellings. (On the poet's occasional use of imperfect rhymes, see 26n and 802n.)

797-804 Cf. the prophecy of the passion of Christ in Isaias 53, especially verse 7: "Oblátus est quia ipse vóluit et non apéruit os suum, sicut ovis ad occisiónem ducétur, et quasi agnus coram tondénte se obmutéscet et non apériet os suum." ("He was offered because it was his own will, and he opened not his mouth: he shall be led as a sheep to the slaughter, and shall be dumb as a lamb before his shearer, and he shall not open his mouth.") Osgood, Gollancz, Gordon, Hillmann, and Andrew & Waldron punctuated 799-84 as a quotation within a quotation, but since not all the words of these six lines are in Isaias, the passage may be taken as a continuation of the maiden's speech. Cf. her free paraphrase of Matthew in 730-35. See also Bishop (1968) 126-27 on the punctuation of this passage, and cf. 825-28n.

802 Editors' emendation of *men* to *nem* (OE *niman* 'seize') seems unnecessary. (See 26n and 791n on imperfect rhymes.) The detail of 'seizing' a lamb is not in Isaias 53.7, and *men* may be taken as an aphetic form of *MED âmen* v., sense 2, 'appraise' (OF *aesmer*). This Lamb was one to be appraised. For other examples of aphetic forms of OF words, cf. *mys* 197, *mykeʒ* 572, and *corteʒ* 754. There may also be word-play on senses 4 and 5 of *MED âmen,* 'intend (an injury), aim (a blow)', relating to Christ's crucifixion.

806 Moorman favored Hillmann's belief that the *boyeʒ* 'ruffians' refer to the two men who were hanged with Christ, but the sense of Gollancz' translation, followed by Gordon and Andrew & Waldron, seems preferable. Andrew & Waldron tr. *wyth boyeȝ bolde* 'by wicked ruffians' and compared *Patience* 95–96.

811 Editors rendered *set hymself in vayn* 'set himself at nought'. For *vayn* 'contempt', cf. *OED vain* a. and sb., II. 6a, in the phr *to take . . . in vain* 'to treat with contempt'.

812 Hillmann's *wolde* 'subdue' (OE *wealdan*) seems preferable to Gordon's 'possess, be responsible for'. Andrew & Waldron's *to wolde* 'in (His) possession' follows the reading of Wright (1939) 17.

815 Cf. *Lompe* 'Lamb' 945 and contrast *lambe-lyȝt* 'lamplight' 1046. As Gordon noted, such reverse spellings are characteristically Western. There may be word-play on the idea of Christ the Lamb, shedding his light as Lamp of the world.

817–18 The reference is to John the Baptist, to be distinguished from the apostle John, mentioned in 834–36 as the writer of the Apocalypse. Osgood, saying there is no "account of John's having preached or baptized elsewhere than in the region of Jordan," believed *þereas* must refer to *Jordan*, but the poet may have interpreted history loosely here for the sake of his verse. (Cf. 163n, 785–86n, and 837n on altering biblical details.)

822 Johnson-C (1953) 44 noted how the phrase *trwe as ston* "recalls the symbolic overtones of jewel-stone imagery" in *Pearl*. Christ is called *Juelle* in 795 and 1124, the maiden is named 'jewel' in 23, 249, 253, and 277, and in 929 souls in heaven are called 'jewels'. Gordon pointed out that *trewe as ston* is part of the couplet written above the illustration of Bercilak's wife visiting Gawain on f. 129 in the MS.

824 Editors did not regard *vpon* as an adv., but cf. the adjectives *vpon* 198, 208, and *vpen* 1066, and see *MED ŏpen* adv., sense a, where *Cursor Mundi* 26215 is cited: "His penance open most be schaun."

825–28 Cf. 797–804n on punctuation. Osgood, Gollancz, Gordon, Hillmann, Cawley, and Andrew & Waldron included these lines in the quotation beginning at l. 822, but, as both Emerson (1927) 826 and Bishop (1968) 126 noted, John does not speak these words.

826 Most editors tr. *clem* 'claim' (OF *clamer*), which suits the context well. (*MED claimen* v. lists *clemen* as a variant spelling.) Morris (1891a) 603, Hillmann, and Moorman favored 'smear' (OE *clǣman*).

829 Since the previous three stanzas refer to Christ's passion, MS *swatte* suits the context well as the pt. of *MED swēten* v., sense c, 'to bleed, sweat blood'. As Savage (1956b) 127 noted, emendation to the adj. *swete* 'sweet' (Osgood, Gollancz, Chase, Gordon, Cawley, and Andrew & Waldron) seems unnecessary. The pronunciation may have been different, but imperfect rhymes occur elsewhere. (See 802n.)

830–34 The first two places in which Christ is spoken of as the Lamb are Isaias 53.7 and John 1.29. (See 797–804 and 821–24.) The third place is the Apocalypse. As Gollancz observed, "From here to l. 1128 the Apocalypse is the main source of the poet's inspiration." Gordon noted that *ayber prophete* (831) refers to Isaias and John the Baptist, but the Baptist's words quoted in ll. 822–24 come down through the Gospel of the apostle John (1.29), who also wrote the Apocalypse. (See l. 836.)

836 Emendation of MS *saytȝ* 'tells' seems unnecessary. The apostle John did tell about his vision of the Lamb in the Apocalypse. Osgood and Chase emended to *syȝ* 'saw', and Gollancz, Gordon, Cawley, and Andrew & Waldron emended to *saȝ* 'saw'.

837 As Gordon, p. xxx, noted, the Book of Revelation was a scroll, but the poet describes it as a medieval book with square pages. On the poet's altering of biblical details, see the notes to the following lines: 163, 785–86, and 817–18.

839 *Dard* 'stood in awe' suits the context of 609; here *dare* 'bow in awe' accords well with Rev. 5.8, which describes the four living creatures and the twenty-four ancients falling down before the Lamb.

840 The Jerusalem mentioned here is the New Jerusalem, the heaven of the Apocalypse, to be distinguished from the Old Jerusalem on earth. See 937–60. The first time the link-word was used in l. 792 of this stanza-group it referred to the New Jerusalem. Thus Group XIV begins and ends with descriptions of the heavenly Jerusalem, and in between Christ's suffering in the earthly Jerusalem is depicted. The poet's circular structure is evident not only in *Pearl* as a whole but also in passages within the poem.

841 Gordon followed earlier editors in rendering *pechche* 'sin, impurity' (OF *pechè*). Hillmann followed Emerson (1922) 81–82 who argued for 'patch' (AN *peche*), which seems preferable.

852 Reading *neuer þe lesse* as three separate elements is appropriate here. Cf. 864, 876, 888, 900, and 901. Only in 912 and 913 does joining the elements and translating 'nevertheless' seem fitting. One cannot always go by MS authority because the scribe was often inconsistent in his connecting or disconnecting of syllables. For example *þelesse* appears in 852, and *lestles* needs to be separated in 865.

854 Again the *wonder perle*, worn on the maiden's breast (221–22), Matthew's *pretiosa margarita* (730–46), is mentioned, as it will be in 1103–4. The theme of salvation in God's kingdom spans the entire poem.

855–56 For *þa* 'who', see *OED tho* rel. pron., III. 5. The idea of there being no quarreling among the blessed was anticipated in 848. Cf. also 463–66.

Hillmann tr. *crest* 'best', as if the reference is to the pearl worn on the maiden's breast, but most editors defined 'crown', which seems preferable. It is noteworthy that the pearl of price (heaven) and the crown of pearls (salvation and virginity) are described in close proximity in these three passages:

205-28, 853-56, and 1100-4. In addition, the crown of *vergynté* (767) is mentioned fairly close to the *perle of prys* (746). The pearl-maiden, one of 144,000 virgins, has obtained salvation. See also 745-46n on fusing of pearl symbols.

859 Gordon compared 1 Cor. 13.11-12 and pointed out that Augustine in *De Peccatorum Meritis et Remissione* applied the promise of complete knowledge specifically to the baptized infant.

860 Osgood, Gollancz, Gordon, Moorman, and Andrew & Waldron agreed that *on dethe* refers to Christ's death on the cross, through which the hope of salvation has been realized.

862 Most editors rendered *mes* 'mass', but Hillmann's derivation from OF *mes* 'feast' seems preferable, since there is no mass in heaven, as it is known here on earth. The reference is to the symbolic heavenly banquet, the allegory of which is explained in *Cleanness* 161-62: "Thus comparisuneȝ Kryst þe kyndom of heuenn/To þis frelych feste þat fele arn to called."

Schotter (1981) noted that the medieval feast, because it traditionally involved seating according to rank as well as bountiful food, embodies the paradox of equality and hierarchy of reward in *Pearl*. "It thus serves as a metaphor for a heaven which is simultaneously equal in its reward and unequal in its rank" (172). In conclusion, pp. 177-78, Schotter cited ll. 603-8 to clearly show the idea of equality and hierarchy of reward in the poem. Cf. 603-4n where there are references to other notes that discuss this concept.

865 All editors, except Andrew & Waldron, emended MS *talle* 'story' to *tale*, but cf. *masklle* 843 and *talle* 'word' in *Cleanness* 48.

865-900 Cf. Rev. 14.1-5. Oakden (1968) 348-50, stressing liturgical influence on *Pearl*, noted that this biblical passage forms the Epistle for the Feast of Holy Innocents on December 28.

869-70 Cf. 785-86. *Maydenneȝ* renders *virgines* of Rev. 14.4 and may be tr. 'virgins'. As Gordon noted, "Many theologians understood the *virgines* to be celibates of the Church irrespective of their sex on earth." Robertson-C (1950b) 19 cited Augustine (*PL* 35.2437) for proof of this point.

MED maiden n., sense 2d, gives ME citations which denote men as virgins. In 785 Lamb's 'wives' are named, but every pure soul in heaven, male or female, is considered the bride of Christ. There is no reason to assume that the poet intended to portray everyone in the group as female, like the pearl-maiden. In 448 and 468 he refers to the souls in heaven as kings and queens. In 1099 he uses *vergyneȝ* to describe those in the procession. In 1115 *maydeneȝ* 'maidens', since it occurs in a simile, does not indicate that only females were among the 144,000.

Hart (1927), refuting Sister Madeleva's assertion that children had no place in the band of virgins, noted that at the time *Pearl* was written, virginity was upheld as a virtue even in a child. She cited Chaucer's "Prioress' Tale" in which the seven-year-old *clergeoun* is praised as a "gemme of chastite" (609), one who follows the Lamb as a "martir sowded to virginitee" (579).

148

881-84 Chapman (1931) 179-80, pointing to *mode3* 'modes' (884) especially, suggested that the poet had more than a passing knowledge of church music. Gordon glossed 'strains of music', thinking it doubtful that the technical sense of *mode3* existed in English before the sixteenth century, but the *OED* cites Chaucer's *Boethius* II. pr. i. 20 s.v. *mode* sb., I. 1a, 'a kind or form of scale; a particular scheme or system of sounds'.

Cohen (1976), taking up Chapman's suggestion, argued that the allegory and the structure of *Pearl* are based upon the musical mode system in two separate movements: the Song of Earth (first twelve stanza-groups), and the Song of Heaven (last eight stanza-groups).

885-88 Rev. 14.3 says only the 144,000 sang the canticle before the throne, the four beasts, and the ancients. (Cf. 889-92.) Hillmann noted that the *fowre beste3* represent animated nature: man, birds, cattle, and wild animals (Rev. 4.7).

Fletcher (1921) 16-17 pointed out that medieval theologians identified the 24 *aldermen* (Rev. 4.4), who appear again in 1119-20, as the 12 patriarchs of the Old Testament and the 12 apostles of the New Testament.

893-94 Hoffman-C (1960) 99-101 discussed the fruit-flower-jewel imagery relating to the theme of death and resurrection. For example, 894 recalls 29-35 and anticipates 1077-80. (See the notes to 19-22, 29, 195, 269-72, 906, 962, and 1077-80.)

901 Adam (1976) 3 noted the possibility of a pun, 'never (to) thee less'.

901-12 These lines form a sixth stanza in this group. All the other groups have five. Brink (1889) 349 suggested one should be omitted. Osgood (p. xlvi) and Gollancz (853-64n) suspected a scribe copied the second one by mistake. Gordon (p. 88) considered ll. 901-12 superfluous.

However, this sixth stanza seems authentic. Chapman (1939) 257, comparing numerical symbolism in Dante and *Pearl*, argued that the poet deliberately planned 101 stanzas, dividing the first 99 into three groups of approximately equal length and adding the last two as an epilogue.

Davis (1954) 100 pointed out that the extra stanza makes the total come to 101, the same as in *Gawain*.

Kean (1965) 50 did not find Chapman's tripartite division of *Pearl* convincing, but she did support his contention that the poet employed numerical symbolism. Adding the extra stanza makes the poem contain 1212 lines instead of 1200; $12 \times 12 = 144$, and there are 144,000 virgins in the heavenly procession; 12 and 12 is also appropriate to the ground plan of the New Jerusalem (992-1035). Cf. also the trees that produce 12 fruits of life 12 times a year (1077-80).

Bishop (1968) 28-29 supported Kean's views with more evidence. See also 992n on the poet's use of the number 12 in *Pearl* and the discussion of Peck (1980) 44-51 in "Number as Cosmic Language." For additional arguments favoring the authenticity of this stanza, see Greenwood (1956) 7–9, Røstvig (1967) 330, Nolan & Farley-Hills (1971) 298, Finkelstein (1973) 427–32, Adam (1976) 2–6, Nolan (1977) 197–98, and Carlson (1991) 62–64.

903 Donner (1988) 323 noted that Andrew & Waldron translate, "I should not so presumptuously test [your] wisdom," whereas Gordon, Hillmann, and Moorman are in agreement with the literal translation given by Vantuono (1984): "I should not try your intelligence so superb." Thus Andrew & Waldron take *wlonc* 'presumptuosuly' as an adv. modifying the v. *tempte* while the second translation employs *wlonc* 'superb' as a postposed adj. modifying the n. *wyt*.

Donner, noting that both interpretations are equally valid, since it is appropriate for the dreamer to compliment the maiden and to apologize for his presumptuousness, argued that the "poet intends both meanings, exploiting the ambiguity inherent in this kind of structure." See Donner (1988) for his study of "A Grammatical Perspective on Word Play in *Pearl*" and Donner (1989) on "Word Play and Word Form in *Pearl*," in which he again takes a linguistic approach, saying, in his conclusion: "Like so much else of the poem's artistry built on the poet's respect for structural detail, lexical artistry in *Pearl* has a firm foundation in his mastery of lexical structure" (181).

905 Osgood compared 382.

906 See 269–72n for discussion of the mortal rose that fades. This *reken rose*, which the pearl-maiden has become, is the immortal flower of heaven. (See 962n and 1186n.)

909 *Sympelnesse* typifies the innocent maiden, her lack of deceit, as Gordon suggested. (See 897–98.) Hillmann compared 2 Cor. 8.2, 9.11, 9.13, and especially 11.3 where Paul commends as a virtue the *simplicitáte quae est in Christo* 'simplicity that is in Christ'. The 144,000 virgins are like the Lamb in 'speech and appearance' (896).

911 Morris and Osgood glossed *blose* 'blaze, flame' (ON *blossi*). Gollancz emended to *wose* 'wild man' (OE *-wāsa* in the compound *wuduwāsa*). In agreement with Gollancz (1891c), Gordon, and Hillmann, the *MED* cites only *Pearl* s.v. *blōse* '? an uncouth person'.

Andrew & Waldron, following a suggestion made by Gordon, emended *blose* to *bose* 'peasant', a form of *MED bōce* n, 3d, "a 'lump of a man' (used disparagingly)."

Manes (1986) took *blose* as a syncopated by-form of ME *bolas* from OF *beloce*, which survives in Modern English as *bullace* 'a wild plum tree'. Arguing that the poet employs the image of "the gnarled boughs and scored bark of a fruit tree" (5), he tr., "And though I'm rough as a wild plum tree."

However, *blose* may be a variant spelling of *MED blǎs* n., sense a, 'blowing (of wind), a gust'. The vowel shift from *a* to *o* fits the rhyme scheme. Cf. *ware* 151 and *wore* 154 in rhyme position instead of *were*.

917–18 Gordon observed how the poet's verses and the illustration on

f. 42b medievalize the New Jerusalem. Cf. the use of *tor* 966, *woneʒ* and *manayre* in 1027–29, and calling the 'city' a *mote* in ll. 936, 948, and 973.

919–22 Here and in the next stanza, the dreamer asks foolish questions for a man who by now should know more about heavenly mysteries, but this is the technique the poet used to keep the plot moving. Hieatt (1965) 140–41, discussing how this "confusion and lack of logic, by waking standards," may be accouted for by the dream-vision psychology of medieval literature, compared the "dawsed" dreamer in Chaucer's *Book of the Duchess*. (Cf. 336n.)

923–24 *Maskeleʒ* recalls one of the link-words of Stanza-Group XIII. *Mone* anticipates the link for Group XVIII. In this group, the word-play on *mote* 'spot (stain)' and 'city' (New Jerusalem), merging in l. 948 of the central stanza, recalls the first group in *Pearl* with its play on *spot* (pearl without 'spot') and the 'spot' where she was buried. See Macrae-Gibson-C (1968) 215–17 for further discussion.

929–30 The poet extends his *juele* metaphor throughout the entire poem. The maiden is called a 'jewel' in l. 23 and Stanza-Group V, the dreamer is called a 'jeweler' in Group V, Matthew's merchant becomes a 'jeweler' in ll. 730 and 734, and Christ is called *Juelle* in 795 and 1124.

934 See 60n on retention of MS *gracous*. Editors emended to *gracious*.

935 Hillmann and DeFord, following Osgood, Gollancz, and Chase, read *lygyngeʒ* 'lodgings'. Other editors who printed *bygyngeʒ* considered it an emendation of the MS. However, the tiny bottom loop that completes the *b* may be faded, or perhaps, being squeezed against the *y*, it was not clearly made.

938 The pearl-maiden is called *special spyce* (235). Just as he echoed the jewel metaphor in 929–30, the poet does so with the spice symbol here. (See 31–32n, 43n, and 235n.)

942 *Olde gulte* denotes original sin created by the fall of Adam and Eve. (Cf. 655n.)

945 See 815n for discussion of *Lompe* 'Lamb'.

953 Editors rendered *pes* 'peace', but the precise denotation seems to differ slightly from 'peace' 955. For *pes* 'salvation', cf. *MED pĕs* n., sense 1e, 'a pardon granted to a person'. Hillmann tr. *at ene* 'formerly'; Gordon glossed *mad at ene* 'arranged, settled'. *At ene* 'immediately' indicates the poet may have been thinking of the exact time of Christ's death on the cross when mankind's salvation was accomplished.

958 *Fresch* looks like *fresth* in the MS, but the scribe's *c* sometimes resembles *t*. In view of the poet's frequent use of the sb. adj., editors' emendation of *fresch* 'young bodies' to *flesch* seems unnecessary. Cf. *frech* 'fair maiden' (195). *Layd to rote* recalls *to rot is runnen* (26).

961 The *M* of *Moteleʒ* is an extra illuminated letter, making the total 21 in *Pearl*.

962 The flower metaphor, relating to the death-and-resurrection theme, began with the mention of *flor* (29); it may be traced through 269 (mortal rose), 906 (immortal rose), and to the end of the poem. In 426 Jesus is the 'Virgin's Flower'; in 195 and 753 the color of the pearl-maiden is compared to 'fleur-de-lis'. In 1079 the fruit trees bloom; in 1186 the maiden is set within the *garlande gay*.

963–64 The dreamer desires that which cannot be fully realized, as in 283–88. Now, however, as the maiden explains (965–72), he will receive a vision of the New Jerusalem.

965–72 See Blenkner-C (1968) 250–51 for a discussion of how this preface to the final *visio* contains an allusion to the Blessed Trinity: *God* (the Father) 965, *Lombe* (the Son) 967, and *fauor* (grace of the Holy Spirit) 968. All-powerful God through his Son Jesus brings grace to men. Blenkner related this concept to the distinction of the three persons "according to power, wisdom, and goodness, who operate, dispose, and will."

Baldwin (1984) 140–41, after referring to Blenkner, argued that like Walter Hilton in *The Scale of Perfection*, the *Pearl*-poet used the Trinity as a structural principle. The *erbere* suggests the Garden of Eden, reminding us of God the Father who *clad* the pearl in *clot* (22). In the dream garden, the dreamer learns about God the Son, the bridegroom of the maiden (413–14). Finally, the dreamer's vision of heaven is a gift of the Holy Spirit, and the pearls which symbolize the souls of each maiden are now visible on *vch oneȝ breste* (1103).

966–68 Eckhardt (1980) 102 noted that *Pearl* incorporates the Boethian tradition of woman as intercessor. The dreamer is guided toward divine truth by the maiden "who (like Dante's Beatrice) takes part of her strength from her affective value, the personal emotional bond between herself and the narrator."

Bishop (1987), in his discussion of *Pearl, Piers Plowman*, and Dante's *Paradiso*, also compared the role of the maiden to that of Beatrice, but he noted a difference between the Italian poem and the English poems. For Dante, both "poem and vision cease simultaneously," because his "*alta fantasia* (*Paradiso*, XXXIII.142)—the human faculty that enables one to perceive a *somnium coeleste*—can no longer comprehend what it beholds." In the two English poems, the vision of the heavenly court is followed by an anti-climax. In *Pearl*, it is only after the dreamer awakes in his earthly garden that he begins to understand the maiden's message of salvation. In *Piers Plowman*, after "Piers' description of the 'court as cler as the sonne' [B-Text, Passus V, l. 594 in Skeat's edition], the poem descends, in Passus VI, to the unglamorous environment of the half-acre to begin a long and torturous quest for the way to salvation" (118).

967 Cf. *aquyle* 'prevail' (690). There may be word-play here, based on a hunting metaphor: *aquylde* 'pursued' the Lamb for a favor. *MED aquīlen*, sense b, defines 'to pursue (game)'. (See 1085n for reference to other hunting images in the poems of the MS.)

969 Morris and Gollancz tr. *cloystor* 'cloister'. Bloomfield (1969) 302 rejected 'enclosure' (Osgood, Gordon, Hillmann) because this denotation obscures the traditional image of heaven as a 'cloister'. Andrew & Waldron glossed 'city, city wall'. 'City' is fitting. Other synonyms the poet used for *cyty* are *bylde* (963), *mote(ȝ)* (936-37, 948-49, 973), and *won* (1049).

969-72 Johnson (1979), in discussing structural, thematic, and imagistic correspondences between *Pearl* and John 20.11-18, related the maiden's injunction to the dreamer not to cross the stream to the motif of the *Noli me tangere* 'Do not touch me' (Christ's words [in John 20.17] to the grieving Mary Magdalene when he appears to her by the sepulchre after his resurrection on Easter morning). Johnson noted the pre-eminence of spiritual knowledge over corporeal knowledge. "The final poetic resurrection of spirit and growth in faith is prepared for by the resurrection of Christ in a garden and His consolation to Mary, the garden changing with the awareness of the mourner" (105-6).

Johnson (1984) 146-61 discussed the *Noli me tangere* motif again, arguing that "it is central to the poet's purpose in *Pearl* and is, in many ways, a source of the poem's spiritual power" (146). (See ll. 289-324 for the first time the maiden tells the dreamer he cannot cross the stream.)

973-84 Andrew & Waldron (973-1032n) credited Kean (1967) 207-9 for comparison to Matilda, on the other side of the stream, directing Dante to his vision in the opening 18 lines of *Purgatorio*, Canto XXIX.

977 Editors inserted *I* after *wolde*, but the subject is often understood, especially if it appears elsewhere in the passage, as it does here in 979 and 980. See 363n on ellipsis.

979-81 Gollancz observed, "The poet does not see the city on a hill, but he, being on a hill, beholds the New Jerusalem." In Rev. 21.10, John is taken up to a high mountain to see the city coming down out of heaven from God. (Cf. 986-88.) Most editors accepted Gollancz' interpretation, but Moorman supposed the "poet, unlike the Apostle John . . . sees from a river valley the Heavenly City on a hill."

992 The wall rises above the *banteleȝ* (*fundaménta duódecim* 'twelve foundations' of Rev. 21.14). Cf. the *wal abof þe bantels bent* (1017). In the description of lidded goblets constructed like castles (*Cleanness* 1459), *bantelles* denotes tiers of masonry projecting from the top of a wall beneath battlements, but the picture in *Pearl* is different. Synonyms for *banteleȝ* (992) are *foundementeȝ* (993) and *degrés* (1022). The qualifying adj. 'twelve' occurs in all three instances. Editors have agreed with Gordon & Onions (1933) 184-85 on this interpretation. For an argument maintaining that the *banteleȝ* in *Pearl* are the highest parts of the fortification, see Kean (1967) 214-15. Viewing the illustration on f. 42b does not settle the argument, for there neither steps nor projecting outworks are shown, and the wall is round in contrast to the foursquare described in *Pearl* 1023 and Rev. 21.16.

The number twelve appears again in ll. 993, 1022, 1030, 1035, 1078, and 1079. Brewer (1983) 169 noted that the poet makes great use of twelve, a significant biblical and folkloric number, especially in the Apocalypse, "and in Gothic design (the first Gothic church, St Denis in Paris, was founded on twelve pillars because of the symbolic biblical significance, not structural utility, and King's College Chapel in Cambridge has twelve bays)." Each of the 101 stanzas of *Pearl* has twelve lines, making 1212 lines in the poem. (See also 901–12n on the poet's use of the number twelve.)

999–1016 On the naming of twelve stones, cf. the description of the goblets in *Cleanness* 1469–72. As Schofield (1909) 604–7 pointed out, what may seem like a mere catalogue to the modern reader held symbolic significance for the medieval person with some knowledge of the religious use to which lapidaries were put.

Stern-C (1955) 82–85, Blanch-B (1965) 91–96, and Blanch, once again, (1973) 69–75 discussed the following symbols in relation to *Pearl*: 1 jasper (faith), 2 sapphire (hope), 3 chalcedony (good works), 4 emerald (chastity), 5 sardonyx (repentance), 6 ruby (Jesus), 7 chrysolite (prophecies and miracles of Jesus), 8 beryl (resurrection), 9 topaz (nine orders of angels), 10 chrysoprase (earthly travail), 11 jacinth (safety in far places), 12 amethyst (Christ's purple robe).

Blanch-B (1965) 96–97, noting that gold symbolizes heaven, also referred to *streteȝ of golde* (1025), *golden gateȝ* (1106), and the Lamb's seven horns of *red golde cler* (1111). Cf. the description of the pearl in *golde so cler* (2), and see the note to line 2.

1001 Emerson (1927) 829 compared *Mandeville's Travels*, "where, in the description of the steps in the palace of Prester John, we have 'another of jasper grene.' " (See, for example, the edition of M.C. Seymour [Oxford UP, 1968], Ch. 30, p. 213.)

1007 Since Rev. 21.20 lists the sardius as the sixth stone, Gollancz emended *rybé* to *sarde*, but the poet sometimes altered biblical details. (See, for example, 163n and 785–86n.) As Gordon noted, *as her byrþ-whateȝ* (1041) indicates the poet connected the description of the New Jerusalem with the details of Aaron's ephod and breast-plate in Exodus 28.17–20, where the sardius is named as the first of twelve stones, and early commentators associated the sardius with the ruby. (See 1041n.)

1011 The beryl signifies resurrection. Osgood compared *Cleanness* 554–56, where the poet speaks of souls that must be as pure as the beryl and the pearl to enter heaven. (Cf. also *Cleanness* 1132.) In *Pearl* 110, the banks of the stream which separate the terrestrial paradise from God's kingdom are of *beryl bryȝt*, and in that stream are emeralds, sapphires, and *gemme gente* (118), perhaps pearls. (See 118n.) Røstvig (1967) noted that the eighth day signifies eternity. (See 721n.) The beryl is the eighth stone in the foundation.

1012 Gollancz and Gordon cited Bede's Commentary on Rev. (*PL*

93.200) which describes the double-color of the topaz, probably in reference to its yellow-green.

1015 Gordon pointed out that the London Lapidary says of the amethyst that it is *comfortable in all sorowes* (though the French original has *yvresse* 'drunkenness', not 'sorrows'), and in the Latin Lapidary in MS. Digby 13 the amethyst is "said to have protecting power against a long list of dangers and misfortunes." (See P. Studer and J. Evans, *Anglo-Norman Lapidaries* [Paris, 1924], p. 380.)

1025 Gordon noted that *bare* 'clear' does not mean the golden streets were transparent. As in the general idea of the simile in Rev. 21.21, they, being free from filth, only shone like transparent glass.

1026 Gollancz refuted Osgood's *glayre* 'amber'. In his glossary, Gordon noted that *glayre* was used in the illumination of manuscripts. (See *MED glaire* n., sense a, 'white of an egg, albumen'.) Gollancz' observation that the description in this line indicates the dreamer could see through the wall seems to be correct. (Cf. 1049–50n.)

1027 No mention is made of 'abodes' in Ch. 21 of Revelation. The poet apparently added these to make the city conform to a medieval stronghold. (Cf. 917–18n.)

1029–30 Because Rev. 21.16 gives a measurement of twelve thousand furlongs, Gollancz emended the MS text. Gordon thought the omission of *þowsande* may have arisen from "the poet's use of a commentary in which the verse explained was given in an abbreviated form." Moorman (1965) 72–73 noted that *twelue forlonge* accords better with the dimensions of a medieval *manayre*. See 917–18n and 1027n on the poet's altering of biblical details to make the city conform to a medieval structure.

1035 Chase, Hillmann, DeFord, and Moorman followed Osgood's *pourseut* 'succession', but *n* and *u* (made with two minims) cannot be distinguished in this MS, and *poursent* 'compass' is a more likely reading. Cf. *pursaunt* 'boundary' (1385) in *Cleanness*. Gordon noted that 'succession' as a meaning of *pursuit* is not known in ME.

1036–38 See 199n and 206n on the poet's use of *margarys* 'pearls'. As Ginsberg (1983) 144 noted, pearls "would have commonly brought to mind John's vision of the rewards of heaven for those who were chaste on earth." These lines are based on Rev. 21.21: "Et duódecim portae duódecim margarítae sunt per síngulas, et síngulae portae erant ex síngulis margarítis." ("And the twelve gates are twelve pearls, one to each: and every several gate was of one several pearl.")

1041 Morris and Osgood misinterpreted *byrþ-whateʒ*, making *whateʒ* equal *watʒ* 'was'. Gollancz defined 'birth omens', but Gordon's 'fortunes of birth, order of birth' provides the proper sense. Exodus 28.10 describes names engraved *iuxta órdinem nativitátis eórum* 'according to the order of their birth' in the description of the stones of Aaron's ephod. As Gordon noted, the passages in Exodus and Rev. 21 were "traditionally associated because of their similar lists of precious stones." (See also 1007n.)

1046 God in the person of Christ the Lamb (1047) sheds the light of the Holy Ghost like a lamp. (Cf. 815n on word-play.) Only Cawley, among editors, read *a* in *lambe-lyȝt* rather than *o*, but the MS shows *a* more clearly.

1049-50 No verse in Rev. 21 or 22 says the Apostle John looked through the wall, but this appears to be the poet's meaning. (Cf. 1026n.) Gordon tr. *For sotyle cler* 'For (all) being transparent and clear'.

1052 Hillmann's *apparaylmente* 'hosts of Heaven' (cf. Rev. 4.2-10 and 7.9-11) seems preferable to Gordon's 'adornment'. *MED appareil(le)ment* follows Gordon, but cf. *ap(p)areil*, 2a, 'martial array, a host'.

1055 This river is the source of the stream to which the dreamer strolled. (See 107n.)

1058 For retention of MS *a* 'as', see 115n.

1059 Cf. the description in 111.

1063 For retention of MS *mynyster*, see 739n on words with intervening vowels. Editors after Gordon adopted his emendation to *mynster*.

1064 Osgood glossed *reget* 'reproduce'. Gordon, Cawley, Moorman, and Andrew & Waldron adopted the emendation of Wright (1939) 20-21 to *refet* 'refreshment'. Hillmann followed Gollancz' 'get again, redeem', citing the description of the slain Lamb in Rev. 5.6-9. The reference in *Pearl* is to the meeting of the soul with Christ the Lamb in heaven, not to the reception of the Eucharist, for, as Hillmann noted in refutation of Osgood, there is no mass in heaven, as it is known on earth. (See 862n.) At these gatherings, the Lamb passes proudly in front, the visible wound in his side giving no pain but serving to recall his sacrifice on the cross. (See 1110-1144.)

1068 For retention of MS *anvndeȝ* 'comparable to, resembling', cf. *MED anent(es* prep., 5b. The moon is a defiled spot compared to the purity needed to enter heaven. (See 1070.) The *MED* lists *anundes* as a variant spelling. Editors emended to *an-vnder*.

1073 Gordon noted that *to* before *euen* is pleonastic because *to euen* is the second of two infinitives following the auxil. v. *schulde* (1072). The *worþly lyȝt* is the "glory of God," and the "Lamb is the lamp thereof" (Rev. 21.23). Cf. 1046-47.

1076 Cf. 83 which describes the sunbeams as dark and lusterless in comparison to the pearls on the ground of the terrestrial paradise. In the New Jerusalem neither sun nor moon is needed. (See 1044-45.)

1077-80 The *fryteȝ* image recalls 29, 87, and 894. In 29 fruit grows from the spot where the pearl sank into decay, in 87 the dreamer is refreshed by the fragrance of fruits growing in the terrestrial paradise, and in 894 the pearl-maiden is described as *newe fryt* purchased from the earth, *to God ful due*. See 938n for reference to jewel and spice metaphors and 962n for discussion of the flower metaphor.

1081-92 In 221-28 the pearl on the maiden's breast is beyond description. Now the dreamer says mortal man would not be able to endure the sight of the New Jerusalem. As the poem progresses, the imagery and concepts the poet attempts to convey become increasingly sublime and, in his own words, difficult to accomplish. See 1117-18 and 99-100n on the inexpressibility topos.

1085 Osgood compared Chaucer's *Clerk's Tale*: "couche as doth a quaille" (1206). Noting the animal similes in *Pearl* 184 and 345, he stated in his 345n, "Such allusions may arise from the poet's interest in the hunt." Cf. also 184n, 967n, the effective *houndeʒ of heuen* image in *Cleanness* 961, and the following passages in *Gawain*, noted by Osgood: 1126-77, 1319-71, 1412-70, 1561-1622, 1690-1732, and 1893-1921.

1086 Moorman adopted Gordon's emendation of *freuch* to *frelich* 'noble', suggested by Morris in his glossary. The *MED*, following Osgood, cited *Pearl* s.v. *frough* adj., 1b, 'delicate; ? delightful', but *freuch* may be a variant spelling of *frech* 195 and *fresch* 958, perhaps influenced by the French diphthong *eu*. (Cf. *endeure* 1082.) For the meaning 'brilliant', see *MED frĕsh* adj., 6b (a). Andrew & Waldron thought it necessary to emend to *frech*.

1087 Olson (1982) rightly refuted Gordon's interpretation of *reste ne trauayle* as implying "no bodily sensations," noting that of all the major editions of *Pearl* to his writing of the article, only Gordon offered any explanation of the phrase, but why should the radiance of the New Jerusalem cause the "narrator not to feel bodily sensation when he has been out of the body since the beginning of the vision." The words obviously refer to a mental condition. The translation of *trauayle* as 'travail' is employed in the Modern English sense, 'mental work or exertion'. As Olson concluded, the dreamer's soul "feels 'nawþer reste ne trauayle' because it is at once active with desire, moving with love toward the object of desire, and hence not at rest, and yet so delighted by the vision of the Holy City, so close to the experience of ultimate satisfaction, that it feels no weakening, senses no 'trauyale' as it would if it were engaged in the affairs of the active life" (425).

1088 Editors rendered *glymme* 'radiance, brightness', listing it separately from *glem* 79, and the *MED* cited only *Pearl* s.v. *glimme* n., but the word may be a variant of *glem*. For the meaning 'spiritual light', see *MED glĕm* n., fig., 2a, and cf. 1073n. For other examples of the *i (y)-e* variant, see 229n.

1090-92 Higgs (1974) 400 concluded that this passage implies the dreamer now realizes he must die before he can enter the New Jerusalem.

Spearing (1984) 237 remarked, "Like John in Revelation, but unlike Paul in Corinthians, he knows that while 'dreaming', he was out of the body. . . . His experience is in fact a mystical vision." John begins verse 2 of Chapter 4 in the Apocalypse with, "Et statim fui in spíritu." ("And immediately I was in the spirit.") Paul, in 2 Cor. 12.2, says, "Scio hóminem in Christo ante annos quattuórdecim, sive in córpore néscio sive extra corpus néscio Deus scit, raptum huiúsmodi usque ad tértium caelum." ("I know a man in Christ above fourteen years ago [whether in the body, I know not, or out of the body, I know not; God knoweth], such a one caught up to the third heaven.") The *Pearl*-poet's significant lines here are: "Fro spot my spyryt þer sprang in space;/My body on balke þer bod in sweuen" (61–62).

1093–96 Borroff (1982) 161 suggested separating MS *maynful* and translating *mayn ful mone* 'great full moon', but, as Gordon noted, *maynful* 'mighty' implies a full moon. Borroff, who traced images of roundness in *Pearl*, stated, "The simile of the 'maynful' (or 'mayn ful') 'mone' is significant in that it participates in a symbolic opposition between roundness and linearity that is thematically important in *Pearl*" (166–67).

A full, white moon bears resemblance to a pearl, and all the virgins wear the great pearl on their breast (1103–4). Cf. in Song of Songs 6.9 the second of four similes describing the appearance of Christ's spouse: "Quae est ista, quae progréditur quasi auróra consúrgens, pulchra ut luna, elécta ut sol, terríbilis ut castrórum ácies ordináta?" ("Who is she that cometh forth as the morning rising, fair as the moon, bright as the sun, terrible as an army set in array?")

1094 The time reference here anticipates the ending of the dreamer's vision. On this point, see Macrae-Gibson-C (1968) 216–17.

1097 Savage (1956b) 127 favored retention of MS *enpresse*. The *MED* s.v. *emprīse* lists *enprese* as a variant spelling. For other examples of the *i (y)-e* variant, see 229n. All editors, except Morris, DeFord, and Andrew & Waldron, emended to *enpryse*.

1101–4 This quatrain condenses the description of the pearl-maiden in 197–228. The *pretiosa margarita* is described there for the first time and here for the last time. See 730–35n for further discussion.

1104 Most editors emended *wythouten* to *with gret*, but Hillmann's *wythouten delyt* 'beyond delight' is fitting. See *OED without* B. prep., I. 2b, 'so as to exceed; beyond'.

Busse (1980) argued that emendation is unnecessary, but he would read *wythouten delyt* 'without delay', taking *delyt* 'delay' from *MED dēlīte* n. (2).

1106 Cf. 1025, and see 2n on golde as a symbol for heaven.

1107 The reference is to the 144,000 virgins. Cf. 785–86 and 869–70.

1110 The image of the Lamb leading the procession is based on Rev. 14.1–4. There is no detailed description given there, as in *Pearl* 1096–1116, but a procession is implied in verse 4: "Hi sequúntur Agnum quocúmque íerit." ("These follow the Lamb whithersoever he goeth.")

1111 This image requires a symbolic reading. Cf. in Rev. 5.6 the "Agnum stantem tanquam occísum, habéntem córnua septem et óculos septem, qui sunt septem spíritus Dei missi in omnem terram." ("Lamb standing as it were slain, having seven horns and seven eyes: which are the seven Spirits of

God, sent forth into all the earth.")

Blanch-B (1965) 97 noted that the number 'seven' may be "identified with the seven sacraments, the grace of which flow from the redemptive sacrifice of the Lamb as Christ." Cf. also the seven virtues and the eight Beatitudes which become seven, since the first and the last are similar. (See *Patience* 29-40.)

Gollancz observed that Christ's head is compared to gold in Song of Songs 5.11. Other examples in *Pearl* of striking images that must be viewed symbolically are the names of the Lamb and the Father written on the fore-heads of the 144,000 virgins (871-72), the four beasts before God's throne (886), and the blood spurting from the wounded side of the Lamb (1135-37).

1113-16 Rastetter (1992), seeing liturgical influence on *Pearl*, noted that *lectio* 8 in the Sarum Breviary contains a lesson about the virgins; it was read on All Saints' Day by one boy while five others, representing five wise virgins, proceeded in order from the vestry in surplices, with heads veiled in white amices. She argued, p. 146, that this vivid procession "would certainly impress itself upon those witnessing it at church, and perhaps the poet had these boys acting the part of virgins in mind when he described the orderliness of the procession in *Pearl*: 'mylde as maydeneʒ seme at mas' (1115)."

1115 Phillips (1985) 477 argued that just as the image of *quayle* 1085 recalls *hawk* 184, *mas* here echoes *mes* 862 in a passage where the maiden tells the dreamer about the joy of the heavenly company around the Lamb. Her argument may stand even though *mes* in l. 862 apparently denotes a festive gathering rather than a mass as it is known here on earth (see the note). The meanings merge if one thinks of the origin of the mass at the Last Supper where Christ and his apostles were gathered.

1115-16 This simile, which reminds one of *maydeneʒ* in an earthly church procession, does not indicate the poet believed the 144,000 were all females. (See 869-70n for a fuller discussion.)

1117-18 See 99-100n on the inexpressibility topos.

1119 See 885-88n on the poet's first reference to the *aldermen*.

1124-27 *Al* 1124 apparently refers to the singing of the 144,000 virgins (1113-16), the aldermen (1119-20), and the *legyounes of aungeles* (1121), though only one order of the last group is mentioned in 1126. This song is evidently not the same one the maiden describes to the dreamer in 877-92, for it is said in both the Bible (Rev. 14.2-3) and the poem that only the 144,000 virgins could sing that one. The dreamer, having heard the song of the birds in the terrestrial paradise (91-94), now hears a greater song coming from the New Jerusalem, one that was perhaps foreshadowed in ll. 19-22. (See the note.)

1126 Osgood noted that the *Vertues of heuen*, one of nine orders of angels, were first described in Ch. 8 of *De Cælesti Hierarchia*, a treatise attributed to Dionysius. Hillmann referred to Dante's *Paradiso* XXVIII, where all nine orders are described. On the casting out of heaven of the tenth and highest order led by Lucifer, see *Cleanness* 205–34.

1135–37 See 1111n for other examples of Apocalyptic images that should be read symbolically. This one, apparently suggested by the reference to the slain Lamb in Rev. 5.6, describes the Lamb's blood spurting from his side for the salvation of mankind. Cf. 649–56 which relates Christ's shedding of blood and water to the pouring out of God's grace. Rev. 7.14, like 22.14, speaks of those who "lavérunt stolas suas et dealbavérunt eas in sánguine Agni," ("have washed their robes, and have made them white in the blood of the Lamb"). Cf. the maiden's words to the dreamer: "In hys blod he wesch my wede on dese" (766).

Field (1986) 15 stated, "The mark of death is a cause of joy, worn as proudly and joyfully by the Lamb as the maidens each wear the pearl that marks them as his. . . . By affording a glimpse of the triumphal Lamb of the Apocalypse still bearing, so unexpectedly, the mark of Christ's human passion, the poet bridges the distance between human life and heavenly glory with an ease and dramatic boldness typical of his time" (16).

White (1987) argued that the Lamb, in spite of the description in ll. 841–44, can hardly be described as spotless (2). Christ has embraced the imperfections of those who are to be forgiven and thus brought about a new perfection, a higher one, "since the Lamb is the summit of the universe. So true perfection seems to be constituted with the help of imperfection. The validity of this paradox is perhaps guaranteed by the fact that the Lamb, even in heaven, is evidently happy with what seems to be his suffering," as ll. 1141–44 show (6).

1147 The dreamer's calling the maiden 'my little queen' indicates he has learned the lesson taught in ll. 421–68.

1151–52 While Blenkner-C (1968) 259–61 validly observed, especially in view of 1179–80, that the proper antecedent of *syȝt* is not just the sight of the pearl-maiden, but the "final *visio* in its entirety," it also seems true, in view of 1155–56, that the dreamer's seeing the maiden in the midst of all the splendor is the climactic motivating factor leading to his desire to cross the stream. *Luf-longyng* may be both compared and contrasted with *luf-daungere* (11). The dreamer is no longer frustrated in his love for his lost pearl, but he must necessarily be thwarted in his mad desire to take part in her delight.

1153–55 Hillmann, opposing Madeleva (1925) 46–47 who saw in these lines "the desire, which all mystics share, 'to die and leave the world' in order to enjoy eternal happiness with God," supposed l. 1154 records the "folly of the jeweler's uncontrolled passion for beauty." However, this entire stanza, especially l. 1160, may indicate a subconscious death wish on the part of the dreamer. In *Patience* 427, as in 488 and 494, Jonas wants to *swelt* 'perish' in order to be relieved of the world's ills. In the end, the dreamer learns acceptance, but that he is also conscious of tribulations on earth is proved by l. 1187.

160

1154 Hillmann tr. gen. *maneȝ*, literally 'man's', as the adj. 'mortal'.

1156 As Hillmann noted, the maiden had earlier (318–24) told the dreamer why he could not cross the stream.

1158 Moorman and Andrew & Waldron accepted Gordon's "by striking me a blow or stopping my advance." Hillmann, following Gollancz, tr., "To work up speed for myself and to spring high." The former interpretation seems preferable. For the tr. given here, see *MED bir(e* n.1, sense 4, 'an outburst (of grief)', and *halten* v., fig. 2b, 'to waver'.

1164 *Paye*, the link-word of this stanza-group, recalls line 1 where the reference to Christ the Prince was anticipated. (See 1n.)

Schless (1989) argued that the force of the opening and the closing of the poem is not fully realized until we understand that "princes paye" may be evoking a fundamental concept of the relatively recent discovery and glossing of Roman law, a celebrated absolutist tag from the *Institutes of Justinian—* "what pleases the prince has the force of law." The "legal maxim 'princes paye' at once establishes the poem's primary confrontations . . . between absolutist and comparative, between New and Old, between divine and human law" (183–84). According to Schless, this is carefully developed with the use of *deme* (judging) in Stanza-Group VI, *grace* in XI, and *ryȝt* in XII, where the themes "evoke an almost universal legalistic discussion." Here, in the center of the poem, "new law and old law, *grace* and *ryȝt*, are intertexed in a (literally) theological discussion that is bracketed by the poem's opening and closing evocation of 'quod principi placet legis habet vigorem' "(184).

1171 The scene reverts to the beginning. Cf. *erber(e)*, ll. 9 and 38.

1182–88 See Bishop (1968) 75–76 for a comparison of this passage to the first speech the dreamer addresses to the pearl-maiden (241–52). Both begin with *O perle*, and there is a correspondence between *del . . . daunger* (250) and *doel-doungoun* (1187). The dreamer, who was formerly a tormented man, is now content because of the maiden's glorified state. (See also 249–50n.)

1185 Among the four poems in the MS, the term *sermoun* occurs only here, reminding one that the long central portion of *Pearl* (Stanza-Groups V–XVI, ll. 241–972) is largely homiletic, in the tradition of *Cleanness* and *Patience*. Cf. this line to Rev. 22.6: "Haec verba fidelíssima sunt et vera." ("These words are most faithful and true.")

1186 Morris' suggestion, made in his glossary, to emend *stykeȝ* to *strykeȝ* 'walk, go' was followed by Osgood, Gollancz, Chase, and Andrew & Waldron in the belief that the *garlande* denotes the maiden's crown. However, as Gordon noted, comparing the use of *stykeȝ* in *Cleanness* 157 and 583, and crediting Hillmann-C (1945) 13–14, the *garlande* is apparently a metaphorical description of the circle of the blessed in heaven, conveying an image either of a jewelled coronet or of a flowered wreath.

Bishop (1957) and (1968) 30–31, 83–84, arguing that the *garlande* represents the final stage in the development of a lapidary metaphor begun in l. 2, saw it as a golden ecclesiastical *corona* typifying the New Jerusalem, with its gems symbolizing souls.

The *MED* s.v. *gerlŏnd* n. lists citations for 'wreath of flowers' s.v. sense 1a and 'coronet of gold' s.v. 2a where *Pearl* is cited, but Hillmann's reference to Dante supports the 'flowered wreath' metaphor: *ghirlanda (Paradiso* X, 92) and *ghirlande (Paradiso* XII, 20). In both passages, Dante pictures encircling souls as flowers, using *piante* 'blossoms' in the former and *sempiterne rose* 'sempiternal roses' in the latter.

Garbáty (1984) 752 favored Hillmann's interpretation when he noted, "The garland is also seen in Dante's *Paradiso* (X, 91–93), in the circle of the blessed."

Lines 1182–86 bring together the double image of the maiden as pearl and flower. She is addressed as *perle* in 1182 and then pictured within the garland, recalling that she had been described as a *reken rose* (906), 'a beautiful rose' of immortality, and a *lufly flor* (962). (See 962n for further discussion of the flower metaphor in *Pearl*.)

1189–1200 Bridges (1984), exploring expectations of an ending but frequent frustrations of those expectations in the literary form of the dream-vision, argued that even a "seemingly closed work like *Pearl* frustrates some of our expectations of closure" (84). Viewing features of closure in *Pearl* as ambiguous, she commented, "As for the reality to which the dreamer awakes, it is pervaded by a feeling of disappointment and loss that is in one sense heightened by the so-called consolatory vision." The affirmation of the didactic value of the vision, "while affording the poet consolation, is at the same time the occasion for him to lament his exile from the *fayre regioun* [1178] and to voice his frustration that the vision was so incomplete" (86–87).

1195 See 129–32n on the use of the link-word *more* in Stanza-Groups III and X. The dreamer now realizes that one must be humble to be led to *mo* 'more' (1194) of God's mysteries.

1196 Gollancz, Gordon, Cawley, and Andrew & Waldron emended *moȝten* to *moȝte*, but MS *moȝten*, a pl. form of the v., may stand in relation to *man* (mankind) and *more* 1195, interpreted collectively. Cf. *hit arn* 'they are' 1199, where the coll. pron. takes a pl. v. For *hem* 'to him', cf. the reverse *hym* 'them' 635 and see the notes to 229, 635, and 1088 on *i (y)-e* spelling variants. Hillmann interpreted *man* 1195 as pl. 'men' and *hem* as pl. 'to them'.

1199–1200 See 344–48n on the call for patience and acceptance of God's will. Sanderlin (1981), in discussing the poet's use of the negative exemplum throughout his work, commented that his protagonists "verge on being anti-heroes." In his characterizations of Jonas in *Patience*, Gawain in *Sir Gawain and the Green Knight*, and the dreamer, he "combines realistic observation of human weaknesses with amused compassion" (52). The dreamer, after he plunges into the stream and awakens, "accepts God's will for the Pearl and prays only 'to please that Prince.' This negative exemplum, negative in its revelation of human inability to comprehend the Divine, leaves the protagonist at least partly aware of his limitations" (53).

1201–12 Gradon (1971) 210 observed that in the opening stanza "the pearl is a precious jewel for the delectation of princes; in the last the pearl is those who live humbly in submission to the will of God." The refrain (in the last stanza-group) echoes *prynces paye* (1). "As the imagery evolves and devolves so we have the progress of the dreamer's mind from the earthliness, or cupidity, of the natural man to humility and spirituality."

Sanderlin (1985) 37 noted that the dreamer, consoled by his vision, is now resigned to his loss. "He is not without hope and displays a different spirit from what he had shown in the beginning." Sanderlin compared Jonas, Gawain, and the dreamer as protagonists facing three confrontations with "something more than man"—Jonas with God, Gawain with the Green Knight, and the dreamer with the maiden. In each case, the hero's "efforts lead to a final encounter which results in a final failure—but the hero is better off at the end than he was in the beginning because he has a truer image of himself (as fallible prophet, obtuse Christian, or imperfect knight)" (36).

Despres (1989) 92 argued that the didactic note at the end of *Pearl* tells us that the poem's function is not simply to evoke wonder but to instruct others. The dreamer's final resolution to conform his will to Christ (l. 1176) and take communal comfort in the sacraments "suggests that *Pearl* is not about the rare vision of a medieval contemplative but is concerned with the *via activa*." The dreamer's vision ends "not in the mystical bliss of spiritual beatitude but in an affective experience, reflection and a repentant heart. The poem, therefore, belongs to the widely encompassing tradition of late-medieval penitential literature." (See also the reference to Braswell in 1207–8n.)

1201 Cf. *sette . . . saȝt* (52). The dreamer could not be made peaceful then because of the grief that dwelled in his heart. The phrase is echoed now in a contrasting situation, for the dreamer has conquered his own *wreched wylle* (56).

1204 The concept of friendship with God is found in the Bible. Cf., for example, Song of Songs 5.16: "Ipse est amícus meus." ("He is my friend.") Hamilton-B (1955) 250 noted Wisdom 7.14 and John 15.15. In *Cleanness* 1229–32 the poet says had Sedecias been God's friend, misfortune would not have befallen. See also 570–72n on *mykeȝ*.

Robinson (1984) 233 commented that the dreamer's "reward for offering his Pearl and his grief up to God is at last the cure of suffering, not just by going past it as we do in life, but in being able to report that God is a 'frende ful fyin'."

1205 For a discussion of *hyul* and related words, see 41n. Osgood, Gordon, and Moorman rendered *lote* 'fortune', Hillmann tr. 'destiny', Gollancz defined 'vision', and Andrew & Waldron tr. 'happening, chance', noting the possibility of a pun on 'speech, word'. *MED lŏt* n.1 cites *Pearl* s.v. sense 1c, 'fortune, destiny, adventure'. The last seems fitting as the primary meaning, but other meanings come in as word-play.

It was characteristic of the poet to recall earlier parts of his poem as he drew toward the end. See, for example, the notes to 1182-88, 1201, 1207, and 1212. Here he may be recalling 61-64, where the dreamer's spirit leaves his body and proceeds *in auenture*. In both 64 and 1205, it is understood that the poet is denoting a spiritual adventure and that the words *auenture* and *lote* take in all that occurs from the time the dreamer falls asleep (59) to the time he awakens (1171).

Torti (1983) connected *auenture* (64), *cnawyng* (859), and *lote* (1205), noting, p. 59, that human reason cannot completely grasp the mysteries of God, for "the journey, the 'auenture', has only served to reconfirm the impossibility of reconciling on earth the experience of any one thing desired by the dreamer and the perfect 'cnawyng' of everything voiced by the maiden." Torti took the primary meaning of *lote* to be 'fortune', believed another meaning to be 'experience' or 'adventure', and then noted that in view of the poet's use of ambiguity and word-play, "it seems obvious . . . that the meanings of *fortune, adventure,* and *talk* or *song* are all present in this line." Taking up the suggestion of Gordon (p. 86), she argued that "*Pearl* thus points to the poet's reflection, however oblique and indirect, on his poetry" (60).

1206 Hoffman-C (1960) 96 tr., "For pity of my pearl lying prostrate." Editors who supplied translations of this line gave the following sense: "Lying prostrate for sorrow for my pearl" (Andrew & Waldron). However, rendering *enclyin* 'humble' in reference to the maiden accords with the poet's emphasis on submission to God's will (1199-1200). Humility is one of the lessons the maiden taught earlier (401-8). (See also 6n.) The *MED* cited *Pearl* s.v. *enclīn* adj., sense 1, 'bowed down; submissive, humble'.

1207 *Hit* recalls *hit* (10, 13), used alongside *her* (4, 6) and *hyr* (8, 9). Hillmann, who tr. all these forms as neuter in her belief that a material pearl was lost in the garden by an actual jeweler, wrote: "The concluding stanza shows the jeweler ready, through renunciation (*bytaʒte*, 1207), to enter upon the mystical life." (Cf. 4n.)

Bloomfield (1969) 301, in discussing the opening stanza, opposed Hillmann's interpretation, which he believed to be based on an "excessive literalism. . . . Rhetorical hyperboles about 'never finding (or even testing) its peer' need not be uttered by a jeweler to have validity."

1207-8 Because this formula was often used in the fifteenth and sixteenth centuries in addresses from parent to child, Davis-C (1966) felt these lines might indicate the poet was speaking of his child. However, in an appendix, pp. 329-34, he noted the same form of blessing in passages that do not contain addresses from parent to child.

Cowen (1978) revealed that the formula also appears in *Ipomedon*, ll.

7095-6, at the end of a comment by the narrator on the changeability of women's affections. It must be concluded, then, that ll. 1207-8 prove nothing definite about the relationship between the poet and the pearl-maiden.

Braswell (1983) 95 commented that the dreamer "attempts restitution: the Pearl maiden, whom he had earlier claimed in his selfishness, he now relinquishes in his selflessness and commits to God. . . . The character of the dreamer has acquired depth and poignancy through the use of the vocabulary and the emotional attitudes inherited by the poet from the penitential tradition." (See also the reference to Despres in 1201-12n.)

1208 Hillmann, Cawley, and DeFord followed Hamilton (1955) 124 who suggested *myn* 'memory'. However, reading *myn* 'mine' seems preferable, since this meaning relates to the dreamer's entrusting his pearl to God (1207).

1209-10 Garrett (1918) studied *Pearl* in relation to the teachings of the Eucharist, noting the symbolic connection between the gem and the Host.

Ackerman-C (1964) 157-61, discussing the allusion to the Parable of the Vineyard and specifically to the penny in Friar Lorens' exposition of the fourth petition of the *Pater Noster* in *Le Somme des Vices et des Vertues*, c. 1279, observed that Lorens equated the daily bread (the consecrated Host) with the penny of the parable.

Sklute (1973) noted that the dreamer has finally realized that he does not have to leave earth to approach the godhead, for it is "present for him in the Eucharist whose essential mystery is in its offer of the bliss of heaven here on earth" (679).

Eldredge (1978) compared William Woodford's images of the Eucharistic wafer in *De Sacramento Altaris* to the poet's descriptions of the pearl, notably roundness as a symbol of perfection, purity, and simplicity, and as a reflection of the shape of the penny paid to the workers in the Parable of the Vineyard.

Allen (1982) 50 commented that the poet goes further than Dante does in the last canto of *Paradiso* because *Pearl* includes the departure from the dream and the return to life, and in this return the dreamer is given the experience of Christ in the mass in the form of the Holy Eucharist which the priest shows us every day. Allen then added: "The same experience, of course, was Dante's once he left his poem. Both for Dante and the dreamer, this is as it should be, for it is in the mode and under the appearance of the Eucharist that the incarnation presents itself, as the continuing and continuously re-enacted spectacle at the centre of life, meaning, and society."

Phillips (1985) 479-80 argued that *Þat* beginning l. 1209 does not refer to *Krysteʒ* (1208) but rather to *hit* (1207)—"hit (the pearl) . . . Þat in þe forme of bred and wyn/Þe preste vus scheweʒ vch a daye." She saw in this reading a "delicate exchange of meaning . . . between Christ-pearl-bread and wine, and pearl and eucharist (bread and wine)." While there is certainly a symbolic connection between the gem and the Host, as Garrett (1918) noted, one need not accept Phillips' grammatical reading here to agree with her seeing a "delicate network of eucharistic allusions by which the poem is enmeshed," a poem whose structure "bears a strong resemblance to the structure of the mass" (484).

1211 Gollancz and Gordon interpreted pr. subj. *gef* 'may allow' as a variant spelling of *gyue*. Moorman and Andrew & Waldron followed Hillmann who glossed the v. as pt. 3 sg. 'gave, granted', rejecting the idea that *Pearl* ends with the conventional medieval prayer. However, this conclusion resembles those of *Cleanness* and *Gawain* which contain the conventional prayer.

The adj. *homly* 'gracious' (*MED*, sense 3a) appears only here in the MS. The *MED*, in accordance with the reading given by most editors, cites *Pearl* s.v. sense 1b with fig. application for *homly hyne*, 'belonging to a household (God's servants)'. Andrew & Waldron glossed 'humble, obedient (perh. also of [God's] household)'. The word conveys multiple meanings in this context, for souls in God's household are gracious, humble, and obedient.

F.E. Richardson (1962) 312 observed how the poet recalls the Parable of the Vineyard, paraphrased in 501–72, and applies the lesson to his audience by using *hyne*. Cf. the use of that word in 505 and 632. Good souls, both on earth and in heaven, are frequently called 'servants' in the Bible. Hillmann compared Ephesians 2.18–19 and Rev. 19.10. See also Rev. 7.3 and 22.3, 6, 9.

Tristram (1976) viewed *Pearl*—along with *Gawain*, *Piers Plowman*, Chaucer's poetry, and Dante's *Commedia*—as an affirmation of "the vision which lies at the end of an arduous pilgrimage" (212). The unremitting search leads to the Triumph of Life, associated with Christ and the Eternal Life. The poet reveals, in his conclusion, that servants of God on earth will become his servants in heaven, like the precious pearl.

The *Pearl*-poet's purpose may be compared to Dante's, as stated in the latter's letter to Can Grande della Scala: "The purpose of the whole [the *Comedy*] and of this portion [the *Paradiso*] is to remove those who are living in this life from the state of wretchedness, and to lead them to the state of blessedness." (See the Carlyle-Wicksteed translation of *The Divine Comedy*, p. 607.)

1212 The end echoes the beginning. (See 1n.) A similar technique is used in the other poems of the MS. In *Patience* the last line echoes the first, in *Gawain* l. 2525 (the last before the final bob and wheel) is like 1, and in *Cleanness* the theme is identified in beginning and end, with 1805–8 recalling 5–6 and 1809–10 recalling 27–28.

APPENDICES

Poetic Mastery in *Pearl*

Pearl contains 20 stanza-groups of 60 lines each, divided into 5 stanzas of 12 lines each, except for Group XV which has 6 stanzas equalling 72 lines. Thus there are 101 stanzas totalling 1212 lines. Stanza 76 (lines 901–12) in Group XV was apparently added by the poet as part of his elaborate numerological structure, for the numbers 101 and 1212 are significant in his scheme.

Sir Gawain and the Green Knight also has 101 stanzas, the Roman numeral for 101 is *CI*, and Greenwood (1956) 12 has noted that *CI* may relate to the last two letters of the name *Masci* and thus the possible identification of the poet. In addition, Fleming (1981) pointed out the importance of 101 as a number of religious consolation in *Pearl*, a poem of centuple consolation, since one hundred and one means a hundredfold increase. Considering the 1212 lines, Kean (1965) observed that 12 x 12 equalling 144 relates to the architecture of the New Jerusalem (1029–32) and there are 144,000 virgins in the heavenly procession (869–70).

The smaller poetic structures are masterfully arranged within the overall plan. Stanzas in each group have a refrain and a link-word, the groups themselves are joined by concatenation, and *paye*, the last word of the opening line, becomes the link-word in the last stanza-group, thus completing the circle. The refrain often varies slightly in wording. In Group I, for example, *pryuy perle wythouten spot* (12, 24) varies with *precios perle wythouten spotte* (36, 48, 60), but the last word *spot*, the C rhyme in the ABABABABBCBC end-rhyme pattern appears, usually as the first stress-word, in the opening line of the next stanza.

The concatenation, besides binding together each stanza in a group, also connects one group to the next, for the link-word appears in the opening line of the new group before the poet moves to a different refrain and link-word. For example, "On þat precos perle wythouten spot" (60) concludes Stanza-Group I, "Fro spot my spyryt þer sprang in space" (61) begins Stanza-Group II, and the new refrain in line 72 is "Of half so dere adubmente," with *adubmente* becoming the new link-word. A link-word occasionally varies in form, as with *Dubbed* beginning line 73.

167

"The refrain and *concatenatio* thus produce an effect of both pause and continuity between stanzas, which is one of the most charming external traits of the poem" (Osgood [1906] xlvi). The following exception to the rule is apparently by design, for among the 20 stanza-groups, the only point at which the linking fails is from XII to XIII. Røstvig (1967) argued that the poet may have deliberately omitted the link-word to show a division of twelve and eight. The last eight stanza-groups in *Pearl* are especially concerned with heavenly bliss, and the eighth day, according to biblical numerical symbolism represents eternity.

The poet combined native alliteration with foreign rhyme. Gordon (1953) 91 noted that the alliteration "is not systematic, and it varies considerably," sometimes on four stressed syllables (lines 1, 18, 40, 55, etc.), sometimes three (2, 4, 8, 11, 14, etc.), or two (7, 10, etc.), "and in many lines (roughly one in four) there is no alliteration at all." Words beginning with *h* may alliterate with words beginning with a vowel, as in line 3, and in these patterns the vowels may be unidentical. "Original *wh* (written *wh, w, qu*) probably alliterates with *w* in 15, 32, 65, 131, &c."

Northup (1897) 338, considering only stressed syllables as alliterating with one another, provided the following statistics: alliterating two stressed syllables (547 lines—45%); alliterating three stressed syllables (192 lines—16%); alliterating four stressed syllables (49 lines—4%); double, transverse, and introverted alliteration (37 lines—3%). The totals are 825 lines—68%.

Northup added: double alliteration (type aabb) occurs in 25 lines (e.g., 102, 593); transverse alliteration (abab) occurs in two lines (650, 956); introverted alliteration (abba) occurs in ten lines (56, 74, 143, 287, 290, 862, 960, 1027, 1093, 1171). Vowel alliteration is found in 46 lines (e.g., 261, 310, 545), and alliteration of a vowel with *h* occurs in about 25 lines (e.g., 58, 210, 614, 679).

The alliteration in the translation is not always in the same places and on the same letters, but it compares favorably with the amount of alliteration in the original. I included the types of vocalic alliteration the poet used, on unidentical vowels and with initial *h* in the patterns. I alliterated combinations like *sm* or *sp* with *s* or with other combinations beginning with *s*. Menner (1920) lvii stated. "In general, *sk, sp, st*, as in Old English, do not alliterate with *s*; and this is also the case with *sch* and *sm*." However, he did note exceptions in *Cleanness*, showing a mixture of combinations, such as *scheldeȝ— swyn—swaneȝ* (58), *schulde—syt—smyte* (566), and *standes—ston—salt* (999).

As Tolkien (1975) 148 commented, we "no longer habitually expect alliteration as an essential ingredient in verse, as the people of the North and West of England once did," but, as I worked on the translation, alliteration of some type, if not always the same as the poet's, often seemed to fall easily into place.

In dealing with rhythm, opinions of scholars sometimes cover a wide range of thought. The comment of Gardner (1965), "Few poets in English, and for that matter few poets anywhere, can surpass the music of the *Gawain*-poet" (90), is in sharp contrast with the viewpoint of Tolkien (1975) who felt the metrical effect of the whole of *Pearl* carries "a certain monotony" (147). Most critics today would agree with Gardner's statement.

There are also divided opinions concerning the affinity of the line in *Pearl* to either French poetry or Anglo-Saxon poetry. Tolkien (1975) 146 considered it a "French line, modified primarily (a) by the difference of English from French generally, and (b) by the influence of inherited metrical practices and taste, especially in the areas where the alliterative tradition was still strong." Gordon, however, believed the line "is probably more truly understood as a modification of the alliterative line than as a basically French line partly assimilated to the alliterative tradition" (91).

It would seem that Gordon is closer to the mark on this point, for the rhythm of *Pearl* is not consistently iambic tetrameter in an octosyllabic line. Scholars have recognized the varying number of syllables (from as little as seven to as many as thirteen, or possibly fourteen if one were to pronounce -*e* in some instances,) in a large proportion of the lines, along with the appearance of two or more unstressed syllables between stressed syllables.

While it is obvious that alliteration in *Pearl* associates the verse of that poem with *Cleanness, Patience,* and *Gawain,* it is less obvious that the rhythmic patterns in *Pearl* are also the same as those that appear in the long alliterative line of the other three poems. This is because the lines in *Pearl* are shorter, with a caesura frequently so slight that it is hardly noticeable. The rhythm is predominantly rising (iambic and anapestic), but the poet varied the flow of his lines effectively, with employment of initial stress, clashing rhythm, and falling rhythm (trochaic and dactylic) at appropriate points.

Pope (1966) 105–16, in discussing Old English versification, reviewed the classification of syllabic patterns, based on half-lines, made by Sievers (1885) and (1893): *Type A*—lift, drop, lift, drop; *Type B*—drop, lift, drop, lift; *Type C*—drop, lift, lift, drop; *Type D*—lift, lift, half-lift, drop, or a lift, lift, drop, half-lift; *Type E*—lift, half-lift, drop, lift. A 'lift' is one syllable that receives primary stress, a 'half-lift' is one syllable that receives secondary stress, and a 'drop' is the one or more unstressed syllables that come between those that have primary or secondary stress.

The following analyses, based on Old English antecedents, will combine a scansion of lines with marking of alliteration, drawing examples from the first 100 lines of *Pearl*. For the use of alliterative symbols beneath the line, I am indebted to Borroff (1967) 55–62. Oakden I (1930–35) 131–245, Pope (1966) 97–138, and Hieatt (1974) also provided essential information for the establishment of the working system found below.

The symbol [/] indicates primary stress and relates to the OE lift; [\] indicates secondary stress and relates to the OE half-lift. Unaccented syllables, which relate to the OE drop, are not marked. A slanted line between words indicates the caesura. The small letters 'a', 'b', and 'x' beneath the line mark the alliterative pattern. The 'x' appears under syllables of primary or secondary stress that do not alliterate. When an alliterating syllable does not carry primary or secondary stress, the (a) or (b) will be in parentheses.

The entire ME line will be cited in the following examples, but the choice in relation to the OE type is determined by either the on-verse, the first half line, or the off-verse, the second half line. The words 'on' or 'off' after the line number in parentheses will indicate the part that is being compared to the OE type. No such indication will appear when the rhythmic pattern is the same in both halves of the line. The comparison of the ME verse to the OE type is based only on rhythm.

Among the alliterative lines of *Cleanness, Patience,* and *Gawain,* and other alliterative ME poetry, one finds many extended lines—that is lines with the addition of an extra stressed syllable in the on-verse. Note, for example, *Patience* 63:

> Góddes glám to hym glód/þat hym vnglád máde.
> a   a   a   a   x

Such a line, carrying three primary stresses in the on-verse, was apparently influenced by OE hypermetric verses.

Borroff (1962) scanned extended lines with four primary stresses and one secondary stress. Hieatt (1974) 128, also reading extended lines with four primary stresses and one secondary, concluded that the Old English *D* and *E* verses "have not disappeared, but provide a more satisfactory explanation of the lines with more than four principal stresses than does the theory that they derive from the hypermetric." Note, for example, the on-verse of *Cleanness* 23, which may be scanned in relation to OE *Type E*—lift, half-lift, drop, lift.

> Krýst kỳdde hit hymsélf/in a cárp óneȝ.
> a   a   x   a x

In *Pearl,* however, since the lines are shorter than those in *Cleanness, Patience,* and *Gawain,* extended lines are rare. One example (line 75) follows:

> Hóltewòdeȝ brýȝt/abóute hem býdeȝ.
> x   x   a   a   a

In the on-verse, if the -*e* of *Holte* is not sounded, one may compare

Cleanness 23. Considering that the *-e* may be sounded, one then notes an expanded OE *Type E* with a drop between the lift and half-lift. (See Pope [1966] 116 for examples in OE.)

For *Pearl*, then, due to the almost complete absence of the extended line, the scansions below, in five categories, deal only with the normal verse that carries two main stresses: OE *Types A, B,* and *C,* and the combinations *BA* and *AB.* The corresponding Modern English translations will also be cited and discussed in relation to the Middle English. Because of the technical aspect of the subject and controversy over many of its points, one may view some of the lines below in different ways and may find other lines in *Pearl* that are exceptions to the rule in not fitting any of the five categories.

(I) *ME Falling Rhythm in Relation to OE Type A—Lift, Drop, Lift, Drop*

> (1) Oute of Oryent,/I hardyly saye.　　(3 on)
> 　　a　　a　　　　a　　x
>
> (2) Fowleȝ þer flowen/in fryth in fere.　(89 on)
> 　　a　　　a　　　　a　　　a
>
> (1) Out of the Orient,/I heartily say.
> 　　a　　　a　　　a　　x
>
> (2) Fluttering fowls/the forest filled.
> 　　a　　　a　　　a　　a

The poet used initial stress and a falling rhythm (trochaic and dactylic) often enough to keep his verse patterns from becoming monotonous. Note how he switches to the usual rising rhythm in the off-verse of both examples.

The translations follow the originals fairly closely. In 1, there are two unaccented syllables between the lifts; in the ME line there is probably only one, since the *-e* of *Oute* may not be sounded before the vowel beginning the next word *of.* In 2, the rhythm is different because *fowls* before the caesura is monosyllabic; thus the translation of the on-verse is *Type AB*—lift, drop, lift (falling-rising rhythm).

(II) *ME Rising Rhythm in Relation to OE Type B—Drop, Lift, Drop, Lift*

> (1) Þurȝ gresse to grounde/hit fro me yot.　(10)
> 　　a　　　a　　　　x　　x

(2) And héuen my háppe/and ál my héle.   (16)
    a   a   a   a

(1) Slípping from gríp/to grássy lót.
   x   a   a   x

(2) And máke my héart/toward héaven sóar.
    x   a   a   x

The common rising rhythm runs through the whole line in both ME examples. Less prominent words carry stress fairly often in *Pearl*. Note *fro* in 1 and *al* in 2. There is no alliterative pattern in the second half of 1, but the poet did not strive for alliteration regularly in this poem. Example 2 reveals an aaaa vocalic pattern on unidentical vowels and with initial *h* involved. Alliterating on unidentical vowels follows the OE practice; having initial *h* in the pattern is contrary to OE practice, for OE *h* alliterates only with itself.

It should be noted that if *-e* were sounded in *grounde, happe*, and *hele*, there would be no stressed syllable before the caesura in 1 and 2, and no stressed syllable at the end of 2. The question of the pronunciation of final *e* has been controversial, but it seems safe to say that it is not sounded before the caesura in these examples because the following words begin with *h (hit)* and a vowel *(and)*.

The *-e* in *hele* is another matter, since the word is in rhyme position, matching other words with final *e*. Borroff (1977) 34 presented evidence which implies that *-e* is "not pronounced in rhyme-words in *Pearl*, even when it is present in all the members of a rhyming group." Not sounding final *e* makes the usage accord with what was taking place in the spoken language of the poet's dialect.

The translation of the on-verse of 1 is *Type AB*—lift, drop, lift—instead of *Type B*. Alliteration on *g* in this line is retained, but it is positioned differently. In line 2, the rhythm is the same, but the alliteration is lost on two syllables, unless one were to consider alliteration on the *m* of *make* and the *m* of *my* and thus mark an a(a)b/bx pattern on *máke my héart/. . . héaven sóar*. The poet sometimes used an unstressed syllable in an alliterative pattern.

(III) *ME Clashing Rhythm in Relation to OE Type C—Drop, Lift, Lift, Drop*

(1) Where rých rókkeʒ/wér to dyscréuen.   (68 on)
  (a)   b   b   a   x

(2) So fréch fláuoreʒ/of frýteʒ wére.   (87 on)
    a   a   a   x

(1) Where rócks enríched/the sýlvan deép.
     a   a   x   x

(2) Frágrances frésh/from frúit instílled.
  a   a   (a)   a   x

Difficulty again arises because of the question of final *e*. Emerson (1921), (1922), and (1927) suggested numerous changes for *Pearl* involving final *e*, attributing what he called errors to a careless scribe. Gordon (1953) 90 noted that Gollancz (1921) and Chase (1932) avoided clashing stress in their editions by altering the text wherever possible. However, since the poet was familiar with alliterative verse where clashing stress occurs, there seems to be no reason to deny that he would use it in *Pearl*.

Gollancz and Chase emended *rych* to *ryche*, but they did not change *frech*, apparently because *rych* (OE *rīce*) had -*e* at an earlier stage of the language but *frech* (OE *fersc*) did not. Such matters cannot be settled with certainty, but under the circumstances, it seems reasonable to go by what the MS contains, considering that the poet would have used -*e* or not used it in accordance with what prosodic effects he wanted at a certain point, not with the form of the early language.

The translation of 1 contains a different rhythm, *Type B*—drop, lift, drop, lift. It is the same in both halves of the line. The alliteration is only on two syllables. In 2, the rhythm of the on-verse is *Type AB*—lift, drop, lift—instead of *Type C*. The alliteration is increased.

(IV) *ME Rising-Falling Rhythm—Type BA—Drop, Lift, Drop, Lift, Drop*

(1) Ne proúed I neúer/her précios pére.   (4 on)
 (a) b   a   b   b

(2) So roúnde, so réken/in vche araýe.   (5 on)
  a   a   x   a

(1) I néver discóvered/her précios peér.
  x   x   a   a

(2) So roúnd, so róyal/in eách arraý.
  a   a   x   a

Tolkien & Gordon (1925) 119 called these *Type AB*, noting this kind already existed in OE as *Type A* with an introductory syllable (anacrusis). See

Pope (1966) 109 for examples. Davis (1967) 148 changed Tolkien and Gordon's designation to *BA*. Oakden I (1930–35) 174–75 pointed out how the increased use of the 'auftakt' (upbeat) with the falling rhythm produced the new rising-falling rhythm, which passed from late OE verse into ME and became very common. The alliteration of *Ne . . . neuer* may be accidental.

In the translation of 1, the rhythm is the same, but some alliteration is lost. In 2, the translation is the same as the original in both rhyme and alliteration.

(V) *ME Falling-Rising Rhythm—Type AB—Lift, Drop, Lift*

(1) Syþen in þat spote/hit fro me sprange. (13 on)
   a   a   x   a

(2) Blomeʒ, blayke/and blwe and rede. (27 on)
   a   a   a   x

(1) Since in that spot/it from me fell.
   a   a   b   b

(2) Blossoms, white/and blue and red.
   a   x   a   x

The falling-rising rhythm in these on-verses occurs because the *-e* of *spote* is elided before *hit*, as is the *-e* of *blayke* before *and*.

In both translations, the rhythm is the same. In 1, alliteration is increased in a different pattern; in 2, alliteration is lost on one syllable.

Though one must account for differences in *Pearl* because of the shorter line that contains end-rhyme throughout, the rhythms are comparable to those found in the alliterative lines of the other three poems in the manuscript— *Cleanness, Patience,* and *Sir Gawain and the Green Knight.* These rhythms from OE antecedents, in combination with the many alliterative patterns, place *Pearl* strongly in the Anglo-Saxon tradition.

Dialect and Language

Lancashire, Derbyshire, Staffordshire, and Cheshire are four counties in the Northwest Midland area to which *Pearl* and the other poems in the manuscript have been assigned. For example, Morris (1864) xxi–xl, in examining details of dialect and grammar, leaned toward Lancashire, Serjeantson (1927)

327–28 favored Derbyshire, and McIntosh (1963) 5 said of *Gawain* that it "can only *fit* with reasonable propriety in a very small area either in SE Cheshire or just over the border in NE Staffordshire."

While it is difficult to determine a specific locale for the composition of the poems, controversy concerning the general area has ceased. After Hulbert (1921) argued that one cannot tell if *Gawain* was composed in the East or the West of the North Midlands, Menner (1922), without pinpointing any specific county, refuted his contention and established with sound evidence the Northwest Midland dialect for *Pearl, Cleanness, Patience,* and *Gawain.* (See also Menner [1926] and Gordon [1953] xliv–lii on this point.)

There are many features that favor the Northwest Midland dialect. The following examples are all from *Pearl*: (1) *eʒ* (or *es*) endings for some pr. pl. forms of verbs—*schyneʒ* 'shine' 28; (2) pr. p. ending in *ande—durande* 'enduring' 336; (3) dropping of inflectional endings—*Lombe* 'Lamb's' 1141, an uninflected genitive; (4) use of the auxil. v. *con* 'did' 313; (5) retention of *aw* from OE *āw—knawen* 'known' 637 [OE *cnāwan*]; (6) unvoicing of final plosives—*lomp* 'lamb' 815; (7) rounding of *a* to *o* before nasal consonants—*hondeʒ* 'hands' 706; (8) development of OE *eo* to *u—burne* 'man' 1090 [OE *beorn*]; (9) representation of OE *ȳ* (or *ȳ*) as *u—gulte* 'guilt' 942 [OE *gylt*].

The vocabulary of *Pearl* is mainly Anglo-Saxon. Gordon noted that there are about 130 words of Scandinavian origin (p. 97) and more than 500 words of French origin (p. 101). Considering the four poems in the manuscript together, a rough estimate on a percentage basis follows: Anglo-Saxon 60%; French 30 %; Scandinavian 10%.

Concerning spelling and phonology, the following examples from *Pearl* reveal only some unusual forms. The letters *i (y)* and *e* are sometimes interchangeable. For example, *him (hym)* 'him' and *hem* 'them' are the usual forms for the sg. and pl. pronouns, but in line 635 *hym* denotes 'them', and in line 1196 *hem* denotes 'him'.

The letters *u, v,* and sometimes *w* are interchangeable phonologically. A *v* appears initially even when the sound is *u*, as in words like *vnder* 923, *vp* 35, and *vpon* 57 from Old English *under, up,* and *upp-on.* In words of French derivation, initial *v* usually represents its Modern English sound, as in *veray* 'truthful' 1184 [OF *verai*], but in the next line 1185, the spelling is *ueray*, even though the pronunciation is the same. Initial *v* may appear in place of *w*, as in *vyf* 'wife' 772 instead of *wyf* 846 [OE *wīf*]. The alliteration in line 772 shows the proper sound: "Þat þe wolde wedde vnto hys vyf." In *blwe* 'blue' 27, *w* has the sound of *u*. Within a word, the graph *u* may represent consonantal *v—pryuy* 'special' 12 [OF *privé*].

A *qu* often appears instead of *wh—quo* 'who' 678 instead of *who* 1138 [OE *hwā*]. Initial *wh* from OE *hw* alliterates with *w* even when it is spelled *qu*: "I ne wyste in þis worlde quere þat hit wace" (65).

Of the two graphs that are not found in Modern English, *þ* (*thorn*) causes no difficulty because it always represents *th*, as in *þe* 'the', but *ȝ* was used for a variety of sounds. In the first three categories below, *ȝ* is called *yogh*.

(1) The sound of Modern English *y* in initial position is found in a word like *ȝet* 'yet' 585. After the vowels *e* or *i (y)*, the sound is found in words like *yȝe* 'eye' 302 and *hiȝe* 'high' 207.

(2) The *w* sound is represented in the following groups, with the spelling *gh* sometimes coming in: *folȝed* 'followed' 127—*folewande* 'following' 1040; *innoȝe* 'enough' 624—*inogh* 612. (See 613n in the Commentary on the echoing of the sound of *inoghe* in *now* for concatenation.)

(3) Before *t* and after *e, i (y)*, the graph *ȝ* has the voiceless fricative sound (front palatal) of German *ich*—*ryȝt* 'right' 684 [OE *riht*]. Before *t* and after the back vowels *a* and *o*, *ȝ* represents the voiceless fricative sound (back velar) of German *doch*—*soȝte* 'sought' 730 [OE *sōhte*]. The same sound occurs finally in a word like *þaȝ* 'though' 52 [OE *þē(a)h, þah*].

(4) in this fourth category, the graph *ȝ*, from the letter *z*, has the sound of Modern English *z* in *ȝeferus* 'Zephyrus' (*Patience* 470 and *Gawain* 517). The graph does not appear initially with this sound in any word of *Pearl*. It seems that *ȝ* and *s* in final position were sometimes used interchangeably for the voiced and voiceless spirants /z/ and /s/; the *ȝ* was probably voiced in a word like *aungeleȝ* 'angels' 1121.

The ending *tȝ*, from OF *tz* (representing the sound /ts/ which was later simplified to /s/), appears in words like *gotȝ* 'go' 510 and *watȝ* 'was' 45, the usual ending, but there are variant spellings such as *gos* 521 and *wace* 65, *wasse* 1108, 1112. (The last two examples are in rhyme position.) The sound of final *tȝ* in the poems of this manuscript is usually presumed to be /s/, but McLaughlin (1963) 99–100, noting that the graphic sequence *tȝ* is not used only for the voiceless spirant /s/, argued that there is enough evidence to favor its interpretation as the voiced spirant /z/.

Sources and Analogues

The poet's main and certain source was the Vulgate, but scholars have argued that he was influenced by other material, such as the writings of the Church Fathers, the liturgy of the mass, medieval lapidaries based on Marbodus' *De Gemmis*, illustrated Apocalypse manuscripts, *Mandeville's Travels*, *Le Roman de la Rose*, Boethius' *De Consolatio Philosophiae*, Dante's *Divine Comedy*, and Boccaccio's *Olympia*. The Commentary contains many references to scholars who have dealt with sources and analogues. More will appear in this section, which concludes with a listing of biblical correspondences.

Schofield (1904) 203–15 argued that the poet knew Boccaccio's *Olympia*, a Latin eclogue (c. 1360) on the death of the author's five-and-a-half-year-old daughter, Violante. Osgood (1906) xxiii–xxv favored Schofield's view. Gollancz (1921), in his edition of *Pearl*, printed the whole of Boccaccio's text and commented, p. 244, that "such parallels as might be discovered in the two poems might be due to the poets' common knowledge, ideas, and belief." Gordon (1953) xxxv favored Gollancz' view, but Finlayson (1983), who also presented comparisons between *Pearl* and Petrarch's *Trionfo della Morte*, argued in favor of Schofield's thesis. Carlson (1987) opposed Finlayson, saying that the "evidence of the manuscript tradition of Boccaccio's poem suggests that the *Pearl*-poet could not have had access to a copy of *Olympia* in England by the end of the fourteenth century" (182).

Manzalauoi (1965) studied what he considered to be Arabic influences on *Pearl*, through French and Latin translations. Lasater (1974) 69–95 also argued for Islamic influence.

Wimsatt (1970) 117–33 studied *Pearl* in relation to several medieval authors, among them Boethius, Dante, Thomas Usk (*Testament of Love*), and the French scholar Jean Gerson (*Consolation of Theology*). Niemann (1974) 218–25 related *Pearl* not only to *The Divine Comedy* but also to the twelfth-century Middle English *Vision of Tundale*.

Whitaker (1981), comparing descriptions in *Pearl* to illustrated Apocalypse manuscripts, argued that the poet's sources were visual, as well as verbal. It "does not seem far-fetched to propose that the image of the Pearl-maiden is composed of elements drawn from artists' depictions of the angel-guide, Drusiana, the Woman clothed with the sun, and the Bride of the Lamb" (187). (Drusiana was a convert whose baptism by Saint John led to his persecution and exile to Patmos, where he had his vision.) Whitaker also compared the poet's descriptions of the Lamb in *Pearl* to depictions of the Lamb in the illustrated Apocalypse manuscripts, and the terrestrial paradise and New Jerusalem settings to manuscripts with landscapes containing images from the real world of nature.

Stanbury (1984), with reference to Whitaker, argued that the poet was familiar with illustrated Apocalypse books of the thirteenth and fourteenth centuries and with commentaries on the Apocalypse. She noted typical features that suggest similarities with *Pearl*, such as the bleeding Lamb, the city that is twelve furlongs instead of the 12,000 of Revelation 21.16, a river that separates John from the New Jerusalem, and an angel-guide that leads and directs him.

Rastetter (1992) saw in the liturgy for the feast of All Saints on November 1 material for a thematic interpretation of the climax of *Pearl*, for this is where the poet employed readings from the Apocalypse that served as the epistles for All Saints' Day and Eve. The ninth and most important reading in the Sarum Breviary deals with numerous themes identical to those of *Pearl*, such as no one's being angry or envious in heaven, the New Jerusalem as a place of tranquillity and rest, as well as a place of light where no sun is needed, the washing of robes in the blood of the Lamb, descriptions of the heavenly host comprising angels, saints, patriarchs, apostles, martyrs, and virgins, and finally the exhortation of "Christians to follow in the saviour's footsteps that they may join the ranks of the blessed" (152). (For comprehensive coverage of the subject, see Rastetter's doctoral dissertation, "The Liturgical Background to the Middle English *Pearl*," University of Manchester [1989].)

O'Mara (1992a and 1992b) argued that the *Pearl*-poet was indebted to the theologian Robert Holcot (c. 1300–1349), a Dominican priest who wrote *Moralitates* (c. 1340), a small collection of moralized legends and tales intended for preachers.

Tables such as the one presented below, showing the correspondences between lines in *Pearl* and verses in the Vulgate, are in the editions of Osgood (pp. 98–100) and Gordon (pp. 165–67). I am indebted to them and to other researchers for what follows. Some comparisons include the poet's elaborations; lines 501–72, for example, add to Matt. 20.1–16. Parentheses around an entry mean the poet seems to have known and may have used that source, but the correspondence is not close enough to tell for sure.

Pearl	*Vulgate*	*Pearl*	*Vulgate*
(11)	(Song 2.5, 5.8)	(439)	(1 Cor. 9.24–25)
(19–22)	(Song 2.14)	(440)	(Gen. 27.36)
(25–28,		(451)	(1 Cor. 9.25; James
41–46)	(Song 4.12–16)		1.12; 1 Peter 5.4)
31–32	John 12.24–25;	457–66	1 Cor. 12.12–27
	1 Cor. 15.36–37	501–72	Matt. 20.1–16
(39–40)	(Rev. 14.13–16)	595–96	Ps. 61.12–13
(57–60)	(Song 5.1–2)	(612, 624,	
(103–6)	(Gen. 2.9–14)	636, 648,	
107	Rev. 22.1	660)	(2 Cor. 12.9)
163, 197	Rev. 19.8	(646–48)	(Rev. 7.14–17,
(205–8)	(Ps. 20.4)		22.14–17)
(285)	(Ps. 118.97, 118.163–65)	650, 654	John 19.34
(301–12)	(John 20.29)	(652)	(Rev. 2.11, 20.6,
(304–5)	(Titus 1.2; Heb. 10.23)		20.14, 21.8)
(307)	(Ps. 88.35)	(656–59)	(1 Cor. 15.22)
(362–63)	(Ps. 21.14)	(675–76)	(Ps. 23.5–6; Matt.
(364–65)	(Ps. 21.15)		5.8; 1 Cor. 13.12;
(401–4)	(1 Peter 5.5–6)		Rev. 22.4)
(413–14)	(Rev. 19.7)	678–83	Ps. 23.3–4, 14.1–2,
(416)	(Ps. 22.6)		14.5
(417)	(Gal. 4.7; Rom. 8.16–17)	(683)	(Ps. 120.3)

Pearl	Vulgate	Pearl	Vulgate
(685–86)	(Matt. 25.46)	897–900	Rev. 14.5
687–88	Ps. 23.4, 14.3	(909)	(2 Cor. 11.3)
690–92	Wisdom 10.10	943	Rev. 21.2
(692–94)	(Gen. 28.11–17)	(952)	(Heb. 12.22; Rev.
699–700	Ps. 142.2		3.12; Ezec. 13.16)
711–24	Matt. 18.1–3, 19.13–15;	966, 970,	
	Mark 10.13–16;	972	Rev. 21.27, 22.14
	Luke 18.15–17	979–81	Rev. 21.10
(721)	(Mark 9.34)	982	Rev. 21.11, 21.23
727–28	Luke 11. 9–10	985–88	Rev. 21.2, 21.10
730–35	Matt. 13.45–46	989–94	Rev. 21.14, 21.18–19
763–64	Song 4.7–8	999–1016	Rev. 21.19–20
766	Rev. 7.14, 22.14	1007	Rev. 21.20; Exodus
(767–68)	(Isaias 61.10)		28.17
786–89	Rev. 14.1, 14.3	1017–18	Rev. 21.18
785, 791–92	Rev. 19.7	1023–24	Rev. 21.16
801–3	Isaias 53.7	1025	Rev. 21.21
803	Matt. 26.63, 27.12;	1026	Rev. 21.18
	Mark 14.61, 15.5	1029–32	Rev. 21.15–16
805–16	Isaias 53.4–10; Matt.	1034–35	Rev. 21.12–13
	26–67; Mark 14.65	1036–38	Rev. 21.21
817–18	Matt. 3.13; Mark 1.4–5,	1039–42	Rev. 21.12; Exodus
	1.9; Luke 3.3; John 1.28		28.9–11; Ezec.
819	Isaias 40.3; Matt. 3.3;		48.31–34
	Luke 3.4; John 1.23	1043–48	Rev. 21.23, 22.5
820–24	John 1.29	1051–54	Rev. 4.2–10, 7.9–11
822–24	Isaias 53.4–10	1055–60	Rev. 22.1
825	Isaias 53.9	1061–63	Rev. 21.22
826	Isaias 53.4–7, 53.10–12	1064	Rev. 5.6, 5.9, 5.12
827–28	Isaias 53.8	1065–66	Rev. 21.25
835–40	Rev. 5.1, 5.6–8, 5.13–14	1067–68	Rev. 21.27
(841–44)	(Dan. 7.9; 1 Peter 1.19;	1069	Rev. 21.23
	Rev. 1.14)	1071	Rev. 21.25, 22.5
(845–46)	(Rev. 14.5, 19.7)	1072–76	Rev. 21.23, 22.5
(859)	(1 Cor. 13.11–12)	1077–80	Rev. 22.2
(860)	(Heb. 10.10, 10.12, 10.14)	(1093–96)	(Song 6.9)
867–72	Rev. 14.1	1099	Rev. 14.4
869–70	Rev. 14.3–4	(1100–1)	(1 Cor. 9.25; James
873–81	Rev. 14.2		1.12; 1 Peter 5.4)
882–96	Rev. 14.3–4	(1102)	(Rev. 7.9, 7.14)

Pearl	Vulgate	Pearl	Vulgate
1106	Rev. 21.21	(1124)	(Song 5.11, 5.14–15)
(1107)	(Rev. 5.11)	(1126)	(1 Peter 3.22)
1110	Rev. 14.1, 14.4	(1135–37)	(Rev. 5.6, 5.9)
1111	Rev. 5.6; (Song 5.11)	(1146)	(Rev. 7.17, 22.14
1119–20	Rev. 5.8, 5.14	(1183–85)	(Rev. 22.6)
1121	Rev. 5.11; (Matt. 26.53)	(1204)	(Song 5.16; Wisdom
1122	Rev. 5.8, 8.3–4		7.14; John 15.15)
1123–27	Rev. 5.11–13	(1211)	(Rev. 7.3, 22.3, 22.6)

ABBREVIATIONS

Grammatical Terms and Other Terms

a.	adjective	infin.	infinitive
abbr.	abbreviation	infl.	inflected *or* influenced
acc.	accusative	intens.	intensive
adj.	adjective	interj.	interjection
adv.	adverb, adverbial	interrog.	interrogative
art.	article	masc.	masculine
assoc.	associated	n	note in Commentary
attrib.	attributively	n.	noun
auxil.	auxiliary	neg.	negative
c.	*circa* 'about'	neut.	neuter
cent.	century	nom.	nominative
cf.	*confer* 'compare'	num.	number, numeral
cl.	clause	obj.	object
coll.	collective	pa. t.	past tense
comp.	comparative	pass.	passive
conj.	conjunction	perf.	perfect
correl.	correlative	perf. p.	perfect participle
corresp.	corresponding	perh.	perhaps
dat.	dative	phr.	phrase
def.	definite	pl.	plural
demons.	demonstrative	poss.	possessive
dial.	dialect	post. c.	postponed
emph.	emphatic		construction
f.	folio	pp.	past participle
f., ff.	and the following	ppl.	past participle
fem.	feminine	ppl. a.	participial adjective
fig.	figurative	pr.	present
fut.	future	pr. p.	present participle
gen.	genitive	pr. t.	present tense
ger.	gerund	prec.	preceding
imper.	imperative	pred.	predicate
impers.	impersonal	pref.	prefix
indef.	indefinite	prep.	preposition

prob.	probably	suf.	suffix
prog.	progressively	suff.	suffix
pron.	pronoun	sup.	superlative
pt.	preterite (past tense)	superl.	superlative
refl.	reflexive	t.	tense
rel.	relative	tr.	translated
s.v.	*sub verbo* or *voce*		translation
	'under the word	ult.	ultimately
	or heading'	v.	verb, verbal
sb.	substance	v., vv.	verse, verses
sb. adj.	substantival adjective	var.	variant
sg.	singular	vbl.	verbal
subj.	sunjunctive	voc.	vocative

Languages and Dialects

A	Anglian (dialects of OE)	ML	Medieval Latin
AF	Anglo-French	MLG	Middle Low German
AL	Anglo-Latin	Mn. Scot.	Modern Scottish
AN	Anglo-Norman	Mod. E.	Modern English
CF	Central French	Nhb.	Northumbrian (dialect of OE)
Dan.	Danish	Norw.	Norwegian
Du.	Dutch	OA	Old Anglian
EFris.	East Frisian	ODan.	Old Danish
EWS	Early West Saxon	OE	Old English
F	French	OF	Old French
G	German	OFris.	Old Frisian
Gmc.	Germanic	OHG	Old High German
Gr.	Greek	OI	Old Icelandic
Icel.	Icelandic	OIr.	Old Irish
K	Kentish (dialect of OE)	ON	Old Norse
L	Latin	ONF	Old Northern French
LG	Low German	OS	Old Saxon
LOE	Late Old English	OScot.	Old Scottish
LWS	Late West Saxon	OSwed.	Old Swedish
MDu.	Middle Dutch	Scand.	Scandinavian
ME	Middle English	Swed.	Swedish
Merc.	Mercian (dialect of OE)	WFris.	West Frisian
MHG	Middle High German	WS	West Saxon (dialect of OE

Parts of the Bible

Cor.	Corinthians	Heb.	Hebrews
Dan.	Daniel	Matt.	Matthew
Ezec.	Ezechiel	Ps.	Psalm
Gal.	Galatians	Rev.	Revelation
Gen.	Genesis		(Apocalypse)
		Rom.	Romans

Periodicals, Dictionaries, and Serial Volumes

(The abbreviations *N.S.* and *UP* designate *New Series* and *University Press.*)

ABR	*American Benedictine Review*
AN&Q	*American Notes and Queries*
AnM	*Annuale Mediaevale*
Archiv	*Archiv für das Studium der Neueren Sprachen und Literaturen*
BJRL	*Bulletin of the John Rylands University Library of Manchester*
ChauR	*Chaucer Review: A Journal of Medieval Studies and Literary Criticism*
CHEL	*Cambridge History of English Literature*
CHum	*Computers and the Humanities*
DQR	*Dutch Quarterly Review of Anglo-American Letters*
E&S	*Essays and Studies by Members of the English Association*
EETS	*Early English Text Society* (This abbreviation alone indicates Original Series.)
EETS, ES	*Early English Text Society, Extra Series*
EETS, OS	*Early English Text Society, Original Series*
EGS	*English and Germanic Studies*
EIC	*Essays in Criticism: A Quarterly Journal of Literary Criticism*
ELH	*Journal of English Literary History*
ELN	*English Language Notes*
EngR	*The English Record*
ES	*English Studies*
ESC	*English Studies in Canada*
FCS	*Fifteenth-Century Studies*
JCulS	*Journal of Cultural Science* (Kobe University of Commerce)
JEGP	*Journal of English and Germanic Philology*
JEngL	*Journal of English Linguistics*
JLDS	*The Journal of the Lancashire Dialect Society*
JMH	*Journal of Medieval History*
JPC	*Journal of Popular Culture*

LingS	*Linguistic Science* (Kyushu University)
LM	*Les Langues Modernes*
LQ	*Language Quarterly* (University of South Florida)
MÆ	*Medium Ævum*
M&H	*Medievalia et Humanistica: Studies in Medieval and Renaissance Culture*
MCR	*The Melbourne Critical Review*
MED	*Middle English Dictionary*
MLN	*Modern Language Notes*
MLQ	*Modern Language Quarterly*
MLR	*Modern Language Review*
MP	*Modern Philology*
MS	*Mediaeval Studies*
MSE	*Massachusetts Studies in English*
N&Q	*Notes and Queries*
Neophil	*Neophilologus*
NM	*Neuphilologische Mitteilungen*
NMS	*Nottingham Mediaeval Studies*
OED	*The Compact Edition of the Oxford English Dictionary* (This work is sometimes designated *NED.*)
OPLiLL	*Occasional Papers in Linguistics and Language Learning*
PG	*Patrologia Graeca*
PL	*Patrologia Latina*
PMLA	*Publications of the Modern Language Association of America*
PQ	*Philological Quarterly*
PRPSG	*Proceedings of the Royal Philosophical Society of Glasgow*
RES	*The Review of English Studies*
RPh	*Romance Philology*
RR	*Romanic Review*
SAC	*Studies in the Age of Chaucer: The Yearbook of the New Chaucer Society*
SELit	*Studies in English Literature* (English Literary Society of Japan)
SHumF	*Studies in the Humanities* (Fukuoka Women's University)
SIcon	*Studies in Iconography*
SMC	*Studies in Medieval Culture*
SN	*Studia Neophilologica*
SoQ	*The Southern Quarterly: A Journal of the Arts in the South*
SP	*Studies in Philology*
StHum	*Studies in the Humanities* (Indiana University of Pennsylvania)
TGAS	*Transactions of the Glasgow Archaeological Society)*
TLS	*The Times Literary Supplement* (London)
USFLQ	*The University of South Florida Language Quarterly*
YWES	*The Year's Work in English Studies*

BIBLIOGRAPHY I

Most references in this book are short: last name of author, date in parentheses, and page number(s), when needed. The reader is, therefore, directed to the alphabetical listing of this Bibliography I for full information. An *a, b,* or *c* after a date indicates more than one work in the same year by the same author.

The symbols *B, BMW, C,* and *HZ* after names refer to the following four volumes of collected articles: Blanch (1966); Blanch, Miller, & Wasserman (1991); Conley (1970); Howard & Zacher (1968). References to these volumes will add: *Blanch Collection; Blanch, Miller, & Wasserman Collection; Conley Collection; Howard & Zacher Collection.* The articles in the *Blanch, Miller, & Wasserman Collection* are original. Paginal listings are to the reprints in the other three volumes, not to the journal or book in which the material first appeared.

Bibliography II, which comes after this Bibliography I, contains references in the following categories: (1) Bibles; (2) Concordance, Dictionaries, Grammars, and Index of Names; (3) Facsimile of the Manuscript; (4) Texts and Translations: French, Greek, Italian, Latin (Non-Religious), Latin (Religious), and Old English and Middle English; (5) Yearly Bibliographies and Other Bibliographical Listings.

ACKERMAN-C (1964), Robert W. "The Pearl-Maiden and the Penny." *RPh* 17. In *Conley Collection*, pp. 149–62.

ADAM (1976), Katherine L. *The Anomalous Stanza of Pearl: Does It Disclose a Six-Hundred-Year-Old Secret?* Medieval Series 1. Fayetteville, Arkansas: Monograph Publishers.

ALLEN (1971), Judson Boyce. *The Friar as Critic: Literary Attitudes in the Later Middle Ages.* Nashville: Vanderbilt UP.

ALLEN (1982), J.B. *The Ethical Poetic of the Later Middle Ages: A Decorum of Convenient Distinction.* Toronto: Toronto UP.

AMOILS (1974), Eugenie R. "The 'Endeleʒ Rounde': Poetic Diction and Theme in *Pearl*." *Middeleeuse Studies/Medieval Studies*, pp. 3–34. Johannesburg: Rand Afrikaans University (1975).

ANDREW (1981), Malcolm. *"Pearl,* Line 161." *Explicator* 40, 4–5.

ANDREW & WALDRON (1978), Malcolm & Ronald. Ed. *The Poems of the Pearl Manuscript: Pearl, Cleanness, Patience, Sir Gawain and the Green Knight.* York Medieval Texts, second series. London: Arnold; Berkeley: California UP (1979); revised edition, University of Exeter (1987).

ARTHUR (1989), Ross G. "The *Pearl*-Poet as Master of Logic." *ESC* 15, 123–33.

ATTREED (1983), Lorraine C. "From *Pearl* Maiden to Tower Princes: Towards a New History of Medieval Childhood." *JMH* 9, 43–58.

BAIRD (1973), Joseph L. *"Maskeleȝ, Makeleȝ:* Poet and Dreamer in *The Pearl." AN&Q* 12, 27–28.

BAKER (1984), Denise N. "Dialectic Form in *Pearl* and *Piers Plowman." Viator* 15, 263–73.

BALDWIN (1984), A.P. "The Tripartite Reformation of the Soul in *The Scale of Perfection, Pearl* and *Piers Plowman."* In *The Medieval Mystical Tradition in England.* Exeter Symposium III. Papers Read at Dartington Hall, July 1984. Ed. Marion Glasscoe. Cambridge, England: Brewer, pp. 136–49.

BARRON (1965), W.R.J. *"Luf-daungere."* In *Medieval Miscellany Presented to Eugène Vinaver by Pupils, Colleagues and Friends.* Ed. F. Whitehead, A.H. Diverres, and F.E. Sutcliffe. Manchester: Manchester UP, pp. 1–18.

BENNETT (1979), Michael J. *"Sir Gawain and the Green Knight* and the Literary Achievement of the North-West Midlands: The Historical Background." *JMH* 5, 63–88.

BENSON (1965), Larry D. "The Authorship of *St. Erkenwald." JEGP* 64, 393–405.

BISHOP (1957), Ian. "The Significance of the 'Garlande Gay' in the Allegory of *Pearl." RES, N.S.,* 8, 12–21.

BISHOP (1968), I. *Pearl in Its Setting: A Critical Study of the Structure and Meaning of the Middle English Poem.* Oxford: Blackwell; New York: Barnes & Noble.

BISHOP (1984), I. *"Solacia* in *Pearl* and in Letters of Edward III concerning the Death of His Daughter, Joan." *N&Q* 229, 454–56.

BISHOP (1987), I. "Relatives at the Court of Heaven: Contrasted Treatments of an Idea in *Piers Plowman* and *Pearl."* In *Medieval Literature and Antiquities: Studies in Honour of Basil Cottle.* Ed. Myra Stokes and T.L. Burton. Cambridge, England: Brewer, pp. 111–18.

BLANCH-B (1965), Robert J. "Precious Metal and Gem Symbolism in *Pearl." The Lock Haven Review,* No. 7. In *Blanch Collection,* pp. 86–97.

BLANCH (1966), R.J. Ed. *Sir Gawain and Pearl: Critical Essays.* Bloomington: Indiana UP. (*Blanch Collection.*)

BLANCH (1973), R.J. "Color Symbolism and Mystical Contemplation in *Pearl.*" *NMS* 17, 58–77.

BLANCH, MILLER, & WASSERMAN (1991), Robert J., Miriam Younger-man, & Julian N. *Text and Matter: New Critical Perspectives of the Pearl-Poet.* Troy, New York: Whitston. (*Blanch, Miller, & Wasserman Collection.*)

BLENKNER-C (1968), Louis, O.S.B. "The Theological Structure of *Pearl.*" *Traditio* 24. In *Conley Collection*, pp. 220–71.

BLENKNER (1971), L. "The Pattern of Traditional Images in *Pearl.*" *SP* 68, 26–49.

BLOOMFIELD (1969), Morton W. "Some Notes on *Sir Gawain and the Green Knight* (Lines 374, 546, 752, 1236) and *Pearl* (Lines 1–12, 61, 775–776, 968)." In *Studies in Honor of Rudolph Willard.* Ed. E. Bagby Atwood and Archibald A. Hill. Austin: Texas UP, pp. 300–302.

BOGDANOS (1983), Theodore. *Pearl: Image of the Ineffable. A Study in Medieval Poetic Symbolism.* University Park: Pennsylvania State UP.

BOITANI (1982), Piero. *English Medieval Narrative in the Thirteenth and Fourteenth Centuries.* Trans. Joan Krakover Hall. London: Cambridge UP. (Discusses *Pearl* on pp. 96–113 of Ch. 4, "Dream and Vision.")

BOND (1991), George. *The Pearl Poem: An Introduction and Interpretation.* Studies in Mediaeval Literature, Vol. 6. Lewiston, New York: Mellen.

BONE (1937), Gavin. "A Note on *Pearl* and *The Buke of the Howlat.*" *MÆ* 6, 169–70.

BORROFF (1962), Marie. *Sir Gawain and the Green Knight: A Stylistic and Metrical Study.* New Haven: Yale UP.

BORROFF (1967), M. *Sir Gawain and the Green Knight: A New Verse Translation.* New York: Norton.

BORROFF (1977), M. *Pearl: A New Verse Translation.* New York: Norton.

BORROFF (1982), M. "*Pearl*'s 'Maynful Mone': Crux, Simile, and Structure." In *Acts of Interpretation: The Text in Its Contexts, 700–1600: Essays on Medieval and Renaissance Literature in Honor of E. Talbot Donaldson.* Ed. Mary J. Carruthers and Elizabeth D. Kirk. Norman, Oklahoma: Pilgrim.

BRADLEY (1890), Henry. "An Obscure Passage in *The Pearl.*" *The Academy* 38, pp. 201–2 and 249. (On lines 689–92.)

BRASWELL (1983), Mary Flowers. *The Medieval Sinner: Characterization and Confession in the Literature of the Middle Ages.* Rutherford, New Jersey: Fairleigh Dickinson UP. (Discusses *Pearl* on pp. 92–95 of Ch. 3, "Confession as Characterization in the Literature of Fourteenth-Century England.")

BREWER (1966), Derek S. "Courtesy and the *Gawain*-Poet." In *Patterns of*

Love and Courtesy: Essays in Honor of C.S. Lewis. London: Arnold, pp. 54–85.

BREWER (1967), D.S. "The *Gawain*-Poet: A General Appreciation of Four Poems." *EIC* 17, 130–42.

BREWER (1983), D.A. *English Gothic Literature.* New York: Shocken. (Discusses *Pearl* on pp. 165–70 of Ch. 9, "The *Gawain*-Poet.")

BRIDGES (1984), Margaret. "The Sense of an Ending: The Case of the Dream-Vision." *DQR* 14, 81–96.

BRINK (1889), Bernhard ten. *Bis zu Wiclifs Auftreten. Geschichte der Englische Literatur,* I. Berlin: Oppenheim (1877). Trans. Horace M. Kennedy as *History of English Literature,* Vol. 1. New York: Holt (1889). (Discusses poet, pp. 336–51.)

BROOK (1967), Stella. "*Pearl.*" *JLDS* 16, 11–17.

BROWN (1916), Arthur C.L. "On the Origin of Stanza-Linking in English Alliterative Verse." *RR* 7, 271–83.

BROWN (1904), Carleton F. "The Author of *Pearl,* Considered in the Light of His Theological Opinions." *PMLA* 19, 115–53.

BROWN (1919), C.F. Review of Garrett (1918). *MLN* 34, 42–45.

BURKE (1980), Stephen M. "Temporal Metaphor in *Pearl*: 'In augoste in a hyȝ seysoun'." *FCS* 3, 41–54.

BURNLEY (1979), J.D. *Chaucer's Language and the Philosophers' Tradition.* Cambridge, England: Brewer.

BURROW (1971), John A. *Ricardian Poetry: Chaucer, Gower, Langland and the Gawain Poet.* New Haven: Yale UP.

BUSSE (1980), W.G. "*Pearl* 1104: An Unnecessary Emendation." *N&Q* 27, 3–4.

CARGILL & SCHLAUCH (1928), Oscar & Margaret. "*The Pearl* and Its Jeweler." *PMLA* 43, 105–23.

CARLSON (1987), David. "The *Pearl*-Poet's *Olympia.*" *Manuscripta* 31, 181–89.

CARLSON (1991), D. "*Pearl*'s Imperfections." *SN* 63, 57–67.

CARSON (1965), Mother Angela, O.S.U. "Aspects of Elegy in the Middle English *Pearl.*" *SP* 62, 17–27.

CASLING & SCATTERGOOD (1974), Dennis & V.J. "One Aspect of Stanza-Linking." *NM* 75, 79–91.

CAWLEY (1962), A.C. Ed. *Pearl and Sir Gawain and the Green Knight.* Everyman's Library. London: Dent; New York: Dutton.

CAWLEY & ANDERSON (1976), A.C. and J.J. Ed. *Pearl, Cleanness, Patience, Sir Gawain and the Green Knight.* Everyman's Library. London: Dent; New York: Dutton. Reissued as *Sir Gawain and the Green Knight, Pearl, Cleanness, Patience.* Everyman's Library. London: Dent; Rutland, Vermont: Tuttle (1991).

CHAMPION (1992), Margrét G. "Reception Theory and Medieval Narrative:

Reading *Pearl* as a Novel." *Neophil* 76, 629-37.

CHANCE-BMW (1991), Jane. "Allegory and Structure in *Pearl*: The Four Senses of the *Ars Praedicandi* and Fourteenth-Century Homiletic Poetry." In *Blanch, Miller, & Wasserman Collection*, pp. 31-59.

CHAPMAN (1931), Coolidge Otis. "The Musical Training of the *Pearl* Poet." *PMLA* 46, 177-81.

CHAPMAN (1932), C.O. "The Authorship of *The Pearl*." *PMLA* 47, 346-53.

CHAPMAN (1939), C.O. "Numerical Symbolism in Dante and *The Pearl*." *MLN* 54, 256-59.

CHAPMAN (1945), C.O. "Virgil and the *Gawain*-Poet." *PMLA* 60, 16-23.

CHASE (1932), Stanley P. Ed. *The Pearl: The Text of the Fourteenth-Century English Poem*. Boston: Humphries. (Modernized text edited by members of the Chaucer course at Bowdoin College.)

CHASE (1932), S.P. Trans. *The Pearl: The Fourteenth-Century English Poem Rendered in Modern Verse*. London: Oxford UP.

CHERNISS (1987), Michael D. *Boethian Apocalypse: Studies in Middle English Vision Poetry*. Norman, Oklahoma: Pilgrim. ("*Pearl*," Ch. 8, pp. 151-68.)

CLARK (1949), John W. "Observations on Certain Differences in Vocabulary between *Cleanness* and *Sir Gawain and the Green Knight*." *PQ* 28, 261-73.

CLARK (1950a), J.W. " 'The *Gawain*-Poet' and the Substantival Adjective." *JEGP* 49, 60-66.

CLARK (1950b), J.W. "Paraphrases for 'God' in the Poems Attributed to 'The *Gawain*-Poet'." *MLN* 65, 232-36.

CLARK (1951), J.W. "On Certain 'Alliterative' and 'Poetic' Words in the Poems Attributed to 'The *Gawain*-Poet'." *MLQ* 12, 387-98.

CLARK & WASSERMAN (1978), Susan L. & Julian N. "The *Pearl* Poet's City Imagery." *SoQ* 16, 297-309.

CLARK & WASSERMAN (1979), S.L. & J.N. "The Spatial Argument of *Pearl*: Perspectives on a Venerable Bead." *Interpretations: Studies in Language and Literature* 11, 1-12.

CLOPPER (1992), Lawrence M. "*Pearl* and the Consolation of Scripture." *Viator: Medieval and Renaissance Studies* 23, 231-45.

COHEN (1976), Sandy. "The Dynamics and Allegory of Music in the Concatenations of *Pearl*, a Poem in Two Movements." *LQ* 14, iii-iv, 47-52.

COLDSTREAM (1981), Nicola. "Art and Architecture in the Late Middle Ages." In *The Later Middle Ages*. Ed. Stephen Medcalf. London: Methuen, Ch. 4, pp. 172-224.

CONLEY-C (1955), John. "*Pearl* and a Lost Tradition." *JEGP* 54. In *Con-*

ley Collection, pp. 50–72.

CONLEY (1970), J. Ed. *The Middle English **Pearl**: Critical Essays*. Notre Dame: Notre Dame UP. (*Conley Collection*.)

COOK (1908), Albert S. "*Pearl*, 212 ff." *MP* 6, 197–200.

COOPER & PEARSALL (1988), R.A. & D.A. "The *Gawain* Poems: A Statistical Approach to the Question of Common Authorship." *RES, N.S.*, 39, 365–85.

COULTON (1906), G.G. "In Defense of *Pearl*." *MLR* 2, 39–43. (Opposes allegorical interpretation of Schofield [1904].)

COULTON (1906), G.G. Trans. *Pearl: A Fourteenth-Century Poem, Rendered into Modern English*. London: Nutt; 2nd ed. (1907); 3rd ed., Methuen's English Classic Series, London: Methuen (1921).

COWEN (1978), J.M. " 'In Krystes Dere Blessyng and Myn': *Pearl* 1208." *N&Q, N.S.*, 25, 203.

CRAWFORD (1967), John F. *The Pearl*. San Francisco: Robert Grabborn and Andrew Hoyem. (Unrhymed translation by Crawford with Andrew Hoyem—includes Middle English text printed interlinearly in red from the Cotton MS—only 225 copies printed.)

CURTIUS (1948), Ernst R. *Europäische Literatur und Lateinisches Mittelalter*. Bern: Francke. Trans. Willard R. Trask as *Literature and the Latin Middle Ages*. Princeton: Princeton UP (1953).

CUTLER (1952), John L. "The Versification of the '*Gawain* Epigone' in Humfrey Newton's Poems." *JEGP* 51, 562–70.

DAVENPORT (1974), W.A. "Desolation, Not Consolation: *Pearl* 19–22." *ES* 55, 421–23.

DAVENPORT (1978), W.A. *The Art of the Gawain-Poet*. London: Athlone.

DAVIS (1954), Norman. Review of Gordon's edition of *Pearl*. *MÆ* 23, 96–100.

DAVIS-C (1966), N. "A Note on *Pearl*." *RES, N.S.*, 17. In *Conley Collection*, pp. 325–29, with Appendix, pp. 329–34, based on Davis' "Correspondence" in *RES, N.S.*, 18 (1967) 294.

DAVIS (1967), N. Ed. *Sir Gawain and the Green Knight* (Second edition; revision of Tolkien & Gordon's *Gawain*). London: Oxford UP.

DAY (1919), Mabel. "The Weak Verb in the Works of the *Gawain*-Poet." *MLR* 14, 413–15.

DAY (1934), M. "Two Notes on *Pearl*." *MÆ* 3, 241–42.

DECKER (1916), Otto. Trans. *Die Perle: Das Mittelenglische Gedicht in Freier Metrischer Übertragung*. Beilage zum Jahresbericht des Grossherzoglichen Realgymnasiums zu Schwerin. Schwerin: Sengebusch.

DeFORD (1967), Sara. Ed. *The Pearl*. (Middle English text with verse translation on facing pages by DeFord and her former students: Dale Elliman Balfour, Donna Rosenbaum Blaustein, Myrna Davidov,

Clarinda Harriss Lott, and Evelyn Dyke Schroedl.) New York: Appleton.

DEROLEZ (1981), R. "Authorship and Statistics: The Case of the *Pearl*-Poet and the *Gawain*-Poet." In *Studies in English Language and Early Literature in Honour of Paul Christophersen*. Ed. P.M. Tilling. *OPLiLL* 8, 41–51. Coleraine: New University of Ulster.

DESPRES (1989), Denise. *Ghostly Sights: Visual Meditation in Late-Medieval Literature*. Norman, Oklahoma: Pilgrim. ("*Pearl*: Penance through the Dream Vision," Ch. 4, pp. 89–118.)

DONALDSON (1972), E. Talbot. "Oysters, Forsooth: Two Readings in *Pearl*." In *Studies Presented to Tauno F. Mustanoja on the Occasion of His Sixtieth Birthday*. *NM* 73, 75–82.

DONNER (1988), Morton. "A Grammatical Perspective on Word Play in *Pearl*." *ChauR* 22, 322–31.

DONNER (1989), M. "Word Play and Word Form in *Pearl*." *ChauR* 24, 166–82.

DOYLE (1982), A.I. "The Manuscripts." In *Middle English Alliterative Poetry and Its Literary Background*. Ed. David Lawton. Cambridge, England: Brewer, pp. 88–100.

DUNLAP (1977), Louise. "Vegetation Puns in *Pearl*." *Mediaevalia: A Journal of Mediaeval Studies* 3, 173–88.

EARL (1972), James W. "Saint Margaret and the Pearl Maiden." *MP* 70, 1–8.

EBBS (1958), John Dale. "Stylistic Mannerisms of the *Gawain*-Poet." *JEGP* 57, 522–25.

ECKHARDT (1980), Caroline D. "Woman as Mediator in the Middle English Romances." *JPC* 14, 94–107.

ELDREDGE (1975), Laurence. "The State of *Pearl* Studies since 1933." *Viator: Medieval and Renaissance Studies* 6, 171–94.

ELDREDGE (1978), L. "Imagery of Roundness in William Woodford's *De Sacramento Altaris* and Its Possible Relevance to the Middle English *Pearl*." *N&Q, N.S.*, 25, 3–5.

ELLER (1983), Vernard. Trans. *Pearl of Christian Counsel for the Broken-hearted*. Washington, D.C.: University Press of America.

ELLIOTT (1951), Ralph W.V. "*Pearl* and the Medieval Garden: Convention of Originality?" *LM* 45, 85–98.

ELLIOTT (1961), R.W.V. "Landscape and Rhetoric in Middle English Alliterative Poetry." *MCR* 4, 65–76.

ELLIOTT (1979), R.W.V. "Woods and Forests in the *Gawain* Country." *NM* 80, 48–64.

EMERSON (1921), Oliver F. "Imperfect Lines in *Pearl* and the Rimed Parts of *Sir Gawain and the Green Knight*." *MP* 19, 131–41.

EMERSON (1922), O.F. "Some Notes on *The Pearl*." *PMLA* 37, 52–93.

EMERSON (1927), O.F. "More Notes on *Pearl*." *PMLA* 42, 807–31.

EVANS (1967), W.O. " 'Cortaysye' in Middle English." *MS* 29, 143–57.

EVERETT (1932), Dorothy. "Middle English." *YWES* 13, 76–128.

EVERETT (1955), D. *Essays on Middle English Literature*. Ed. Patricia Kean. London: Oxford UP. (Discusses *Pearl* on pp. 85–96 of Ch. III, "The Alliterative Revival.")

EVERETT & HURNARD (1947), Dorothy & Naomi D. "Legal Phraseology in a Passage in *Pearl*." *MÆ* 16, 9–15.

FAIRCHILD (1931), Hoxie N. "*Of Vyrgyn Flour*." *TLS*, March 5, p. 178.

FARLEY-HILLS (1971), David. "The Authorship of *Pearl*: Two Notes." (Appears with Barbara Nolan's Presentation in *RES, N.S.*, 22, 295–302.)

FARLEY-HILLS (1975), D. "Correspondence." *RES, N.S.*, 26, 451. (Answer to Thorlac Turville-Petre's argument against the identification of John Massey as the author of *Pearl* in *RES, N.S.*, 26 [1975] 129–33.)

FAST (1992), Frances. "Poet and Dreamer in *Pearl*: 'Hys Ryche to Wynne'." *ESC* 18, 371–82.

FICK (1885), Wilhelm. *Zum Mittelenglischen Gedicht von der Perle: Eine Lautuntersuchung*. Kiel: Lipsius und Tischer.

FIELD (1986), Rosalind. "The Heavenly Jerusalem in *Pearl*." *MLR* 81, 7–17.

FINCH (1993), Casey. Trans. *The Complete Works of the Pearl Poet*. (Contains on facing pages Middle English texts of *Pearl, Cleanness, Patience, Sir Gawain and the Green Knight* from Andrew & Waldron [1978] and *Saint Erkenwald* from Peterson [1977b].) Berkeley: California UP.

FINKELSTEIN (1973), Dorothee Metlitzki. "The *Pearl*-Poet as Bezalel." *MS* 35, 413–32.

FINLAYSON (1974), John. "*Pearl*: Landscape and Vision." *SP* 71, 314–43.

FINLAYSON (1983), J. "*Pearl*, Petrarch's *Trionfo della Morte*, and Boccaccio's *Olympia*." *ESC* 9, 1–13.

FISHER (1961), John H. "Wyclif, Langland, Gower, and the *Pearl* Poet on the subject of Aristocracy." In *Studies in Medieval Literature in Honor of Professor Albert Croll Baugh*. Ed. MacEdward Leach. Philadelphia: Pennsylvania UP, pp. 139–57.

FLEMING (1981), John V. "The Centuple Structure of the *Pearl*." In *The Alliterative Tradition in the Fourteenth Century*. Ed. Bernard S. Levy and Paul E. Szarmach. Kent, Ohio: Kent State UP, pp. 81–98.

FLETCHER (1921), Jefferson B. "The Allegory of the *Pearl*." *JEGP* 20, 1–21.

FORD (1984), Boris. Ed. *The New Pelican Guide to English Literature*. Volume 1, Part One. *Medieval Literature: Chaucer and the Alliterative*

Tradition. Harmondsworth, England: Penguin. (Reprinted with revised and updated bibliographies in 1991.)

FOWLER (1959), David C. *"Pearl* 558: 'Waning'." *MLN* 74, 581–84.

FOWLER (1960), D.C. "On the Meaning of *Pearl,* 139–40." *MLQ* 21, 27–29.

FOWLER (1984), D.C. *The Bible in Middle English Literature.* Seattle: Washington UP. (Discusses *Pearl* on pp. 200–225 of Ch. 4, "The *Pearl* Poet.")

FRITZ (1980), Donald W. *"The Pearl*: The Sacredness of Numbers." *ABR* 31, 314–34.

FUHRMANN (1886), Johannes. *Die Alliterierenden Sprachformeln in Morris' Early English Alliterative Poems und in Sir Gawayne and the Green Knight.* Hamburg: Hintel.

GARBÁTY (1984), Thomas J. Ed. *Medieval English Literture.* Lexington, Massachusetts: Heath. (Contains the Middle English text of *Pearl.*)

GARDNER (1965), John. Trans. *The Complete Works of the Gawain-Poet.* Chicago: Chicago UP.

GARDNER (1977a), J. *The Poetry of Chaucer.* Carbondale: Southern Illinois UP.

GARDNER (1977b), J. *The Life and Times of Chaucer.* New York: Knopf.

GARRETT (1918), Robert M. *The Pearl: An Interpretation.* University of Washington Publications in English 4, pp. 1–45.

GATTA (1974), John, Jr. "Transformation Symbolism and the Liturgy of the Mass in *Pearl." MP* 71, 243–56.

GEROULD (1936), Gordon Hall. "The *Gawain*-Poet and Dante: A Conjecture." *PMLA* 51, 31–36.

GIACCHERINI (1989), Enrico. Ed. *Perla.* Parma: Pratiche Editrice. (Middle English text with Italian translation on facing pages.)

GILSON (1908), Julius P. "The Library of Henry Savile, of Banke." Transactions of the Bibliographical Society 9, pp. 127–210. London: Blades.

GINSBERG (1983), Warren. *The Cast of Character: The Representation of Personality in Ancient and Medieval Literature.* Toronto: Toronto UP.

GINSBERG (1988), W. "Place and Dialectic in *Pearl* and Dante's *Paradiso." ELH* 55, 731–53.

GOLLANCZ (1890), Sir Israel. "An Obscure Passage in *The Pearl." The Academy* 38, 223–24. (On lines 689–92.)

GOLLANCZ (1891a), I. "Notes on the Review of *Pearl." The Academy* 40, 36–37. (In answer to Morris' Review (in *The Academy* 39, 602–3) of Gollancz' 1891 edition of *Pearl.*)

GOLLANCZ (1891b), I. *"Pearl." The Academy* 40, 116–17. (In answer to Morris' observations in *The Academy* 40, 76.)

GOLLANCZ (1891c), I. Ed. *Pearl: An English Poem of the Fourteenth Century.* (With a Modern English translation.) London: Nutt.

(Revised and privately printed in 1897.)

GOLLANCZ (1898), I. "Strode, Ralph." In *The Dictionary of National Biography*. *Ed. Leslie Stephen and Sidney Lee*. Vol. 55, pp. 57–59. (Conjectures that Ralph Strode was the author of *Pearl, Cleanness, Patience*, and *Gawain*.)

GOLLANCZ (1901), I. Report of paper read to the Philological Society, "Recent Theories concerning Huchoun and Others." *The Athenæum*, November 23, p. 705.

GOLLANCZ (1907), I. "*Pearl, Cleanness, Patience*, and *Sir Gawain and the Green Knight*." In *CHEL*, Vol. 1. Ed. A.W. Ward and A.R. Waller. Cambridge: Cambridge UP. Ch. XV, pp. 357–73.

GOLLANCZ (1918), I. Trans. *Pearl: An English Poem of the Fourteenth Century, Re-Set in Modern English*. (British Red Cross Edition.) London: Jones.

GOLLANCZ (1921), I. Ed. *Pearl: An English Poem of the XIVth Century*. (With a Modern English translation, together with Boccaccio's *Olympia*.) London: Chatto and Windus. Rpt. New York: Cooper Square Publishers (1966).

GOLLANCZ (1923), I. Introduction to *Pearl, Cleanness, Patience, and Sir Gawain: Reproduced in Facsimile from the Unique MS. Cotton Nero A.x in the British Museum*. *EETS, OS*, 162. London: Oxford UP, pp. 7–44.

GOLLANCZ (1924), I. Ed. *Patience: An Alliterative Version of Jonah by the Poet of Pearl*. In *Select Early English Poems*, Vol. 1. London: Oxford UP. (Second edition of *Patience*, first edited in 1913.)

GORDON (1953), E.V. Ed. *Pearl*. London: Oxford UP. (Final revision by Ida L. Gordon.)

GORDON & ONIONS (1932), E.V. & C.T. "Notes on *Pearl*." *MÆ* 1, 126–36.

GORDON & ONIONS (1933), E.V. & C.T. "Notes on the Text and Interpretation of *Pearl*." *MÆ* 2, 165–88. (Continued from preceding article.)

GOSSE (1923), Edmund. "*Pearl*." In *More Books on the Table*. London: Heinemann, pp. 181–86.

GRADON (1971), Pamela. *Form and Style in Early English Literature*. London: Methuen. (Discusses *Pearl* on pp. 194–211.)

GRANT, PETERSON, & ROSS (1978), Judith, C., and Alan S.C. "Notes on the Rhymes of *Pearl*." *SN* 50, 175–78.

GREENE (1925), Walter Kirkland. "The *Pearl*—A New Interpretation." *PMLA* 40, 814–27.

GREENWOOD (1956), Ormerod. Trans. *Sir Gawain and the Green Knight: A Fourteenth-Century Alliterative Poem Now Attributed to Hugh Mascy*. (Translated in the original metre.) London: Lion and Unicorn Press.

GREG (1924), W.W. Review of Gollancz (1923) entry. *MLR* 19, 223–28.

GROSS-BMW (1991), Charlotte. "Courtly Language in *Pearl*." In *Blanch, Miller, & Wasserman Collection*, pp. 79–91.

GUEST (1838), Edwin. *A History of English Rhythms.* Two Volumes. London: Pickering. Revised edition in one volume, edited by Walter W. Skeat. London: Bell (1882).

HAMILTON (1943), Marie P. "The Orthodoxy of *Pearl* 603–4." *MLN* 58, 370–72.

HAMILTON (1955), M.P. Review of Gordon's edition of *Pearl*. *JEGP* 54, 123–26.

HAMILTON-B (1955), M.P. "The Meaning of the Middle English *Pearl*." *PMLA* 70. In *Blanch Collection*, pp. 37–59.

HAMILTON (1958), M.P. "Notes on *Pearl*." *JEGP* 57, 177–91.

HAMMERLE (1936), K. *The Castle of Perseverance* und *Pearl*." *Anglia* 60, 401–2.

HANNA (1974), Ralph, III. Ed. *The Awntyrs off Arthure at the Terne Wathelyn: An Edition Based on Bodleian Library MS. Douce 324.* Manchester: Manchester UP.

HART (1927), Elizabeth. "The Heaven of Virgins." *MLN* 42, 113–16.

HARWOOD-BMW (1991), Britton J. "*Pearl* as Diptych." In *Blanch, Miller, & Wasserman Collection*, pp. 61–78.

HEISERMAN (1965), A.R. "The Plot of *Pearl*." *PMLA* 80, 164–71.

HENDRIX (1985), Howard V. "Reasonable Failure: *Pearl* Considered as a Self-Consuming Artifact of 'Gostly Porpose'." *NM* 86, 458–66.

HIEATT (1976), A. Kent. "Symbolic and Narrative Patterns in *Pearl*, *Cleanness*, *Patience*, and *Gawain*." *ESC* 2, 125–43.

HIEATT (1965), Constance B. "*Pearl* and the Dream-Vision Tradition." *SN* 37, 139–45. Rpt. (revised) in *The Realism of Dream Visions: The Poetic Exploitation of the Dream Experience in Chaucer and His Contemporaries.* De Proprietatibus Litterarum, Series Practica 2. The Hague: Mouton (1967).

HIEATT (1974), C.B. "The Rhythm of the Alliterative Long Line." In *Chaucer and Middle English Studies in Honour of Rossell Hope Robbins.* Ed. Beryl Rowland. Kent, Ohio: Kent State UP, pp. 119–30.

HIGGS (1974), Elton D. "The Progress of the Dreamer in *Pearl*." *SMC* 4, 388–400.

HILL (1974), John M. "Middle English Poets and the Word: Notes toward an Appraisal of Linguistic Consciousness." *Criticism* 16, 153–69.

HILLMANN (1941), Sister Mary Vincent. "*Pearl*: 'Inlyche' and 'Rewarde'." *MLN* 56, 457–58.

HILLMANN (1943), M.V. "*The Pearl*: 'west ernays' 307; 'Fasor' 432." *MLN* 58, 42–44. ('Fasor', misnumbered, is in line 431.)

HILLMANN (1944), M.V. "*Pearl*: 'Lere Leke,' 210." *MLN* 59, 417–18.

HILLMANN-C (1945), M.V. "Some Debatable Words in *Pearl* and Its Theme." *MLN* 60. In *Conley Collection*, pp. 9–17.

HILLMANN (1953), M.V. "*Pearl*, 382: 'mare reʒ mysse?'." *MLN* 68, 528–31.

HILLMANN (1961), M.V. Ed. *The Pearl: Mediaeval Text with a Literal Translation and Interpretation.* Convent Station, New Jersey: College of Saint Elizabeth; 2nd ed. with Introduction and additional Bibliography by Edward Vasta. Notre Dame: Notre Dame UP (1967).

HOFFMAN-C (1960), Stanton. "The *Pearl*: Notes for an Interpretation." *MP* 68. In *Conley Collection*, pp. 86–102.

HOLMAN (1951), C. Hugh. " 'Marereʒ Mysse' in the *Pearl*." *MLN* 66, 33–36.

HOLTHAUSEN (1893), F. "Zur Textkritik me. Dichtungen—*Pearl*." *Archiv* 90, 144–48.

HORGAN (1981), A.D. "Justice in *The Pearl*." *RES, N.S.*, 32, 173–80.

HORRALL (1986), Sarah M. "Notes on British Library, MS Cotton Nero A x." *Manuscripta* 30, 191–98.

HORSTMANN (1881), Carl. Ed. *De Erkenwalde.* In *Altenglische Legenden: Neue Folge*, Heilbronn.

HOWARD & ZACHER (1968), Donald R. & Christian. *Critical Studies of Sir Gawain and the Green Knight.* Notre Dame: Notre Dame UP. (*Howard & Zacher Collection.*)

HULBERT (1921), James R. "The 'West Midland' of the Romances." *MP* 19, 1–16.

HULBERT (1927), J.R. Review of Gollancz' 1921 edition of *Pearl*. *MP* 25, 118–19.

JEWETT (1908), Sophie. Trans. *The Pearl: A Modern Version in the Metre of the Original.* New York: Crowell. Rpt. in *Medieval English Verse and Prose*. By Roger Sherman Loomis and Rudolph Willard. New York: Appleton (1948).

JOHNSON (1979), Lynn Staley. "The Motif of the *Noli Me Tangere* and Its Relation to *Pearl*." *ABR* 30, 93–106.

JOHNSON (1984), L.S. *The Voice of the Gawain-Poet.* Madison: Wisconsin UP.

JOHNSON-BMW (1991), L.S. "The *Pearl* Dreamer and the Eleventh Hour." In *Blanch, Miller, and Wasserman Collection*, pp. 3–15.

JOHNSON-C (1953), Wendell Stacy. "The Imagery and Diction of *The Pearl*: Toward an Interpretation." *ELH* 20. In *Conley Collection*, pp. 27–49.

JOHNSTON (1959), G.K.W. "Northern Idiom in *Pearl*." *N&Q, N.S.*, 6, 347–48.

JOYCE (1984), James. "Re-Weaving the Word-Web: Graph Theory and Rhymes." In *Computer Applications to Medieval Studies*. Ed. Anne

Gilmour-Bryson. *SMC* 17, 117–34.

KALMA (1938), D. Trans. *De Pearel: In Visioen ut it Middel-Ingelsk oer-brocht yn it Nij-Frysk.* Dokkum: Kamminga. (A Frisian version in original metre and rime, based on Gollancz' 1921 text.)

KASKE (1959), R.E. "Two Cruxes in *Pearl*: 596 and 609–10." *Traditio* 15, 418–28.

KEAN (1965), Patricia Margaret. "Numerical Composition in *Pearl*." *N&Q, N.S.*, 12, 49–51.

KEAN (1967), P.M. *The Pearl: An Interpretation.* London: Routledge.

KELLOGG-C (1956), Alfred L. "*Pearl* and the Augustinian Doctrine of Creation." *Traditio* 12. In *Conley Collection*, pp. 335–37.

KIRTLAN (1918), Ernest J.B. Trans. *Pearl: A Poem of Consolation.* London: Kelly.

KJELLMER (1975), Göran. *Did the "Pearl Poet" Write Pearl?* Gothenburg Studies in English 30. Göteborg: Acta Universitatis Gothoburgensis.

KNIGHTLEY (1961), William J. "*Pearl*: The 'hyʒ seysoun'." *MLN* 76, 97–102.

KOOPER (1982), Erik. "The Case of the Encoded Author: John Massey in *Sir Gawain and the Green Knight*." *NM* 83, 158–68.

KRIEG (1978), Laurence J. "Levels of Symbolic Meaning in *Pearl*." *Mythlore* 18, 21–23.

LASATER (1974), Alice E. *Spain to England: A Comparative Study of Arabic, European, and English Literature of the Middle Ages.* Jackson: Mississippi UP. (Discusses *Pearl*, pp. 69–95.)

LAWTON (1982), David. "Middle English Alliterative Poetry: An Introduction." In *Middle English Alliterative Poetry and Its Literary Background.* Ed. David Lawton. Cambridge, England: Brewer, pp. 1–19.

LEE (1977), Jennifer A. "The Illuminating Critic: The Illustrator of Cotton Nero A.X." *SIcon* 3, 17–46.

LEVINE (1977), Robert. "The Pearl-Child: Topos and Archetype in the Middle English *Pearl*." *M&H, N.S.*, 8, 243–51. (Review of Piehler [1971] entry.)

LOOMIS-HZ (1959), Laura Hibbard. "*Gawain and the Green Knight*." In *Arthurian Literature in the Middle Ages: A Collaborative History.* Ed. Roger Sherman Loomis. In *Howard & Zacher Collection*, pp. 3–23.

LUCAS (1977), Peter J. "Pearl's Free-Flowing Hair." *ELN* 15, 94–95.

LUCAS (1978), P.J. "Pearl's Head-Dress." *Archiv* 215, 82–83.

LUTTRELL (1955), C.A. "The *Gawain* Group: Cruxes, Etymologies, Interpretations." *Neophil* 39, 207–17.

LUTTRELL (1956), C.A. "The *Gawain* Group: Cruxes, Etymologies, Interpretations—II." *Neophil* 40, 290–301.

LUTTRELL (1962a), C.A. "A *Gawain* Group Miscellany." *N&Q, N.S.*, 9,

447-50.

LUTTRELL (1962b), C.A. "The Mediæval Tradition of the Pearl Virginity." *MÆ* 31, 194-200.

LUTTRELL-B (1965), C.A. *"Pearl:* Symbolism in a Garden Setting." *Neophil* 49. In *Blanch Collection*, pp. 60-85.

LUTTRELL (1978), C.A. "The Introduction to the Dream in *Pearl.*" *MÆ* 47, 274-91.

MacCRACKEN (1910), Henry Noble. "Concerning Huchown." *PMLA* 25, 507-34.

MACKENZIE (1933), Agnes Mure. *An Historical Survey of Scottish Literature to 1714.* London: MacLehose.

MACRAE-GIBSON-C (1968), O.D. *"Pearl*: The Link-Words and the Thematic Structure." *Neophil* 52. In *Conley Collection*, pp. 203-19.

MADDEN (1839), Sir Frederic. Ed. *Syr Gawayne and the Grene Knyȝt.* In *Syr Gawayne: A Collection of Ancient Romance-Poems by Scottish and English Authors, Relating to That Celebrated Knight of the Round Table.* The Bannatyne Club 61. London: Taylor. Rpt. New York: AMS Press (1971).

MADELEVA (1925), Sister Mary. *Pearl: A Study in Spiritual Dryness.* New York: Appleton. Rpt. New York: Phaeton Press (1968).

MAHL (1966), Mary R. "The Pearl as the Church." *EngR* 17, 27-29.

MANES (1986), Christopher. "A Plum for the *Pearl*-Poet." *ELN* 23, No. 4, pp. 4-6.

MANN (1983), Jill. "Satisfaction and Payment in Middle English Literature." *SAC* 5, 17-48.

MANZALAUOI (1965), Mahmoud. "English Analogues to the *Liber Scalæ.*" *MÆ* 34, 21-35.

MARTI (1991), Kevin. *Body, Heart, and Text in the Pearl-Poet.* Studies in Mediaeval Literature, Vol. 12. Lewiston, New York: Mellen.

MARTI (1993), Kevin. "Traditional Characteristics of the Resurrected Body in *Pearl.*" *Viator* 24, 311-35.

MATHEW (1948), Gervase. "Ideals of Knighthood in Late-Fourteenth-Century England." In *Studies in Mediaeval History Presented to F.M. Powicke.* Ed. R.W. Hunt, W.A. Pantin, and R.W. Southern. London: Oxford UP, pp. 354-62.

MATHEW (1968), G. *The Court of Richard II.* New York: Norton.

MATSUI (1971), Noriko. "Allegory of Courtesy in *Pearl* and *Sir Gawain and the Green Knight.*" *SELit* 47, 123-40. (English synopsis in English No. for 1971, pp. 165-67.)

MATTHEWS (1960), William. *The Tragedy of Arthur: A Study of the Alliterative Morte Arthure.* Berkeley: California UP.

McANDREW (1957), Bruno. *"The Pearl*: A Catholic Paradise Lost." *ABR* 8, 243-51.

McCOLLY & WEIER (1983), William & Dennis. "Literary Attribution and Likelihood-Ratio Tests: The Case of the Middle English *Pearl*-Poems." *CHum* 17, 65–75.

McGALLIARD (1969), John C. "Links, Language, and Style in *The Pearl*." In *Studies in Language, Literature, and Culture of the Middle Ages and Later: Studies in Honor of Rudolph Willard*. Ed. E. Bagby Atwood and Archibald A. Hill. Austin: Texas UP, pp. 279–99.

McINTOSH (1963), Angus. "A New Approach to Middle English Dialectology." *ES* 44, 1–11.

McLAUGHLIN (1963), John C. *A Graphemic-Phonemic Study of a Middle English Manuscript*. The Hague: Mouton.

McNEIL (1888), George P. "Huchown of the Awle Ryale." *Scottish Review* (April), pp. 266–88.

MEAD (1908), Marian. Trans. *The Pearl: An English Vision-Poem of the Fourteenth Century Done into Modern Verse*. Portland, Maine: Mosher.

MEANS (1972), Michael H. "*Pearl*." In *The Consolatio Genre in Medieval English Literature*. Gainesville: Florida UP. (Pages 49–59 of Ch. 4, "The 'Pure' Consolatio.")

MEDARY (1916), Margaret. "Stanza-Linking in Middle English Verse." *RR* 7, 243–70.

MEDCALF (1973), Stephen. "*Piers Plowman* and the Ricardian Age in Literature." In *Literature and Western Civilization*. Vol. 2, *The Mediaeval World*. Ed. David Daiches and Anthony Thorlby. London: Aldus, pp. 643–96.

MENNER (1920), Robert J. Ed. *Purity*. New Haven: Yale UP. Rpt. Hamden, Connecticut: Archon (1970).

MENNER (1922), R.J. "*Sir Gawain and the Green Knight* and the West Midland." *PMLA* 37, 503–26.

MENNER (1926), R.J. "Four Notes on the West Midland Dialect." *MLN* 41, 454–58.

METLITZKI (1988), Dorothee. Review of Vantuono (1987) entry. *SAC* 10, 197–201.

MIYATA (1954), Takeshi. Trans. *Shiratama: A Japanese Translation of Pearl*. Kobe: Konan University Bungakukai.

MILROY (1971), James. "*Pearl*: The Verbal Texture and the Linguistic Theme." *Neophil* 55, 195–208.

MITCHELL (1964), Bruce. "*Pearl*, Lines 609–10." *N&Q*, *N.S.*, 11, 47.

MOORMAN-C (1955), Charles. "The Role of the Narrator in *Pearl*." *MP* 53. In *Conley Collection*, pp. 103–21.

MOORMAN (1965), C. "Some Notes on *Patience* and *Pearl*." *SoQ* 4, 67–73.

MOORMAN (1968), C. *The Pearl-Poet*. New York: Twayne.

MOORMAN (1977), C. Ed. *The Works of the Gawain-Poet.* Jackson: Mississippi UP.

MORRIS (1864), Richard. Ed. *Early English Alliterative Poems in the West-Midland Dialect of the Fourteenth Century. (Pearl, Cleanness,* and *Patience.) EETS, OS,* 1; 2nd ed. (1869). Rpt. (1965). London: Oxford UP.

MORRIS (1891a), R. Review of Gollancz' 1891 edition of *Pearl. The Academy* 39, 602-3.

MORRIS (1891b), R. *"Pearl." The Academy* 40, 76.

MORSE (1975), Ruth. Ed. *St Erkenwald.* Cambridge, England: Brewer; Totowa, New Jersey: Rowman and Littlefield.

MURTAUGH (1971), Daniel M. *"Pearl* 462: 'Þe Mayster of Myste'." *Neophil* 55, 191-94.

MUSCATINE (1972), Charles. "The *Pearl* Poet: Style as Defense." In *Poetry and Crisis in the Age of Chaucer.* Notre Dame: Notre Dame UP, Ch. II, pp. 37-69.

MUSTANOJA (1960), Tauno F. *A Middle English Syntax.* (Part I: *Parts of Speech.)* Helsinki: Société Néophilologique.

NARUSE (1971), Masaiku. Ed. and Trans. *A Study of the Middle English Pearl.* (Part I: *A Text Newly Edited with Japanese Translation.) JCulS* 6, pp. 133-85, 221-88.

NEILSON (1900), George. "Huchown of the Awle Ryale." *TGAS* 4, 252-393.

NEILSON (1900-01), G. "Sir Hew of Eglintoun and Huchown off the Awle Ryale: A Biographical Calendar and Literary Estimate." *PRPSG* 32, 111-50.

NEILSON (1901), G. "Huchown of the Awle Reale." *Chamber's Cyclopaedia of English Literature.* Vol. I. London and Edinburgh: Chambers, pp. 171-75.

NEILSON (1902a), G. "Crosslinks between *Pearl* and *The Awntyrs of Arthure." The Scottish Antiquary* 16, 67-78.

NEILSON (1902b), G. *Huchown of the Awle Ryale, the Alliterative Poet: A Historical Criticism of Fourteenth Century Poems Ascribed to Sir Hew of Eglintoun.* Glasgow: MacLehose. (Revision of Neilson [1900] entry.)

NELSON (1973), Cary. *"Pearl:* The Circle as Figural Space." In *The Incarnate Word: Literature as Verbal Space.* Urbana: Illinois UP, pp. 25-49.

NEWSTEAD (1967), Helaine. "Arthurian Legends." In *A Manual of the Writings in Middle English: 1050-1500.* By Members of the Middle English Group of the Modern Language Association of America. General Editor, J. Burke Severs. Vol. 1. New Haven: The Connecticut Academy of Arts and Sciences, pp. 38-79.

NICHOLLS (1985), Jonathan. *The Matter of Courtesy: Medieval Courtesy Books and the Gawain-Poet*. Woodbridge, England: Brewer.

NIEMANN (1974), Thomas C. *"Pearl* and the Christian Other World." *Genre* 7, 213-32.

NOLAN (1977), Barbara. *"Pearl*: A Fourteenth-Century Vision in August." In *The Gothic Visionary Perspective*. Princeton: Princeton UP, pp. 156-204.

NOLAN & FARLEY-HILLS (1971), Barbara & David. "The Authorship of *Pearl*: Two Notes." *RES, N.S.*, 22, 295-302.

NORTHUP (1897), Clark S. "A Study of the Metrical Structure of the Middle English Poem *The Pearl*." *PMLA* 12, 326-40.

OAKDEN I (1930-35), James P. *Alliterative Poetry in Middle English: The Dialectal and Metrical Survey*. Manchester: Manchester UP. Rpt. Hamden, Connecticut: Archon (1968). (The reprints of this book and the next are in one volume.)

OAKDEN II (1930-35), J.P. (With assistance from Elizabeth R. Innes.) *Alliterative Poetry in Middle English: A Survey of the Traditions*. Manchester: Manchester UP. Rpt. Hamden, Connecticut: Archon (1968).

OAKDEN (1968), J.P. "The Liturgical Influence in *Pearl*." In *Chaucer und Seine Zeit: Symposium für Walter F. Schirmir*. Ed. Arno Esch. Buchreihe der Anglia, Zeitschrift für Englische Philologie 14. Tübingen: Niemeyer, pp. 337-53.

OIJI (1961), Takero. "The Middle English *Pearl* and Its Theology." *SELit*, English No. for 1961, pp. 39-57.

OLIVERO (1926), Federico. Trans. *La Perla, Poemetto Inglese del Secolo XIV: Traduzione, con Introduzione e Note*. Torino: Treves. (Italian verse translation from Osgood's [1906] text.)

OLIVERO (1936), F. *La Perla, Poemetto in Middle English: Introduzione, Testo, Traduzione, e Commento*. Bologna: Zanichelli. (Based on Osgood's [1906] text.)

OLMERT (1987), Michael. "Game-Playing, Moral Purpose, and the Structure of *Pearl*." *ChauR* 21, 383-403.

OLSON (1982), Glending. " 'Nawþer Reste ne Trauayle': The Psychology of *Pearl* 1087." *NM* 83, 422-25.

O'MARA (1992a), Philip F. "Robert Holcot's 'Ecumenism' and the Green Knight." (Part I.) *ChauR* 26, No. 4, pp. 329-42.

O'MARA (1992b), P.F. "Holcot and the *Pearl*-Poet." (Part II.) *ChauR* 27, No. 1, pp. 97-106.

OSGOOD (1906), Charles G. Ed. *The Pearl: A Middle English Poem*. Boston: Heath.

OSGOOD (1907), C.G. Trans. *The Pearl: An Anonymous English Poem of the Fourteenth Century, Rendered in Prose*. Princeton, New Jersey. (Privately printed.)

OTTEN (1971), Charlotte. "A Note on 'Gyltes Felle' in *Pearl*." *ES* 52, 209-11.

OVITT (1979), George. "Numerical Composition in the Middle English *Pearl*." *AN&Q* 18, 34–35.

OWST (1926), Gerald R. *Preaching in Medieval England*. Cambridge: Cambridge UP.

PARR (1970), Roger P. "Rhetoric and Symbol in *The Pearl*." *SMC* 3, 177–87.

PATCH (1950), Howard R. *The Other World: According to Descriptions in Medieval Literature*. Cambridge, Massachusetts: Harvard UP.

PATTISON (1978), Robert. *The Child Figure in English Literature*. Athens: Georgia UP.

PEARSALL (1981), Derek A. "The Origins of the Alliterative Revival." In *The Alliterative Tradition in the Fourteenth Century*. Ed. Bernard S. Levy and Paul E. Szarmach. Kent, Ohio: Kent State UP, Ch. 1, pp. 1–24.

PEARSALL (1982), D.A. "The Alliterative Revival: Origins and Social Backgrounds." In *Middle English Alliterative Poetry and Its Literary Background*. Ed. David Lawton. Cambridge, England: Brewer, Ch. III, pp. 34–53.

PEARSALL & SALTER (1973), Derek A. & Elizabeth. *Landscapes and Seasons of the Medieval World*. London: Elek; Toronto: Toronto UP. (Discusses *Pearl* on pp. 102–8 of Ch. 4, "The Enclosed Garden.")

PECK (1980), Russell A. "Number as Cosmic Language." In *Essays in Numerical Criticism of Medieval Literature*. Ed. Caroline D. Eckhardt. Lewisburg, Pennsylvania: Bucknell UP, pp. 15–64. (Discusses *Pearl* on pp. 44–51.)

PETERSON (1974a), Clifford J. "*Pearl* and *St. Erkenwald*: Some Evidence for Authorship." *RES, N.S.*, 25, 49–53.

PETERSON (1974b), C.J. "The *Pearl*-Poet and John Massey of Cotton, Cheshire." *RES, N.S.*, 25, 257–66.

PETERSON (1977a), C.J. "Hoccleve, the Old Hall Manuscript, Cotton Nero A.X., and the *Pearl*-Poet." *RES, N.S.*, 28, 49–55.

PETERSON (1977b), C.J. Ed. *Saint Erkenwald*. Philadelphia: Pennsylvania UP.

PETROFF (1981), Elizabeth. "Landscape in *Pearl*: The Transformation of Nature." *ChauR* 16, 181–93.

PHILLIPS (1984), Heather. "Mediaeval Glass-Making Techniques and the Imagery of Glass in *Pearl*." *Florilegium* 6, 195–215.

PHILLIPS (1985), H. "The Eucharistic Allusions of *Pearl*." *Mediaeval Studies* 47, 474–86.

PIEHLER (1971), Paul. "*Pearl*." In *The Visionary Landscape: A Study in Medieval Allegory*. Montreal: McGill-Queen's UP, Ch. 8, pp. 144–

62.

PILCH-C (1964), Herbert. "The Middle English *Pearl*: Its Relation to *The Roman de la Rose*.." *NM* 65, where it appeared on pp. 427–46 under the title "Das Mittelenglische *Perlengedicht*: Sein Verhältnis zum *Rosenroman*." Trans. Heide Hyprath in *Conley Collection*, pp. 163–84.

POPE (1966), John C. Ed. *Seven Old English Poems: Cædmon's Hymn, The Battle of Brunanburh, The Dream of the Rood, The Battle of Maldon, The Wanderer, The Seafarer, Deor.* Indianapolis: Bobbs-Merrill; 2nd ed., New York: Norton (1981).

RASTETTER (1989), Susan J. "The Liturgical Background to the Middle English *Pearl*." Doctoral Dissertation, University of Manchester.

RASTETTER (1992), S.J. " 'Bot Mylde as Maydenes Seme at Mas': The Feast of All Saints and *Pearl*." *BJRL* 74, 141–54.

RATHBORNE (1963), Isabel E. "New Light on *Pearl* 690." *Traditio* 19, 467–69.

REICHARDT-BMW (1991), Paul F. "Animal Similes in *Pearl*." In *Blanch, Miller, & Wasserman Collection*, pp. 17–29.

REISNER (1973), Thomas A. "*Pearl*, 44." *Explicator* 31, Item 55.

REISNER (1975), T.A. "The 'Cortaysye' Sequence in *Pearl*: A Legal Interpretation." *MP* 72, 400–3.

REVARD (1962), Carter. "A Note on 'stonden' [in] *Pearl* 113." *N&Q*, *N.S.*, 9, 9–10.

REVARD (1964), C. "A Note on 'at þe fyrst fyne' (*Pearl* 635)." *ELN* 1, 164–66.

RICHARDSON (1962), F.E. "*The Pearl*: A Poem and Its Audience." *Neophil* 46, 308–16.

ROBBINS (1943), Rossell Hope. "A *Gawain* Epigone." *MLN* 58, 361–66.

ROBBINS (1950), R.H. "The Poems of Humfrey Newton, Esquire, 1466–1536." *PMLA* 65, 249–81.

ROBERTSON-C (1950a), D.W., Jr. "The 'Heresy' of *The Pearl*." *MLN* 45. In *Conley Collection*, pp. 291–96.

ROBERTSON-C (1950b), D.W., Jr. "The Pearl as a Symbol." *MLN* 45. In *Conley Collection*, pp. 18–26.

ROBINSON (1977), Ian. "*Pearl* and Ontology." In *In Geardagum II: Essays on Old and Middle English Language and Literature.* Ed. Loren C. Gruber and Dean Loganbill. Denver: Society for New Language Study, pp. 1–8. (Corrected reprint, 1978.)

ROBINSON (1984), I. "*Pearl*: Poetry and Suffering." See Ford (1984) entry, pp. 224–34.

RØNBERG (1976), Gert. "A Note on 'Endorde' in *Pearl* (368)." *ES* 57, 198–99.

RØSTVIG (1967), Maren-Sofie. "Numerical Composition in *Pearl*: A

Theory." *ES* 48, 326-32.

RUPP (1955), Henry R. "Word-play in *Pearl*, 277-278." *MLN* 70, 558-59.

RUSSELL (1978), J. Stephen. "Meaningless Dreams and Meaningful Poems: The Form of the Medieval Dream Vision." *MSE* 7, 20-32.

RUSSELL (1983), J.S. "*Pearl*'s 'Courtesy': A Critique of Eschatology." *Renascence* 35, 183-95.

RUSSOM (1976), Geoffrey R. "A Syntactic Key to a Number of *Pearl*-Group Cruxes." *JEngL* 10, 21-29.

SALTER (1983), Elizabeth. *Fourteenth-Century English Poetry: Contexts and Readings*. London: Oxford UP.

SANDERLIN (1981), George. "The Negative Exemplum in the *Gawain*-Poet: A Most Ingenious Paradox." *StHum* 9, 52-55.

SANDERLIN (1985), G. "The *Gawain*-Poet's Heroes: Human or 'Something More than Man?'." *USFLQ* 23, Numbers 3-4, pp. 36-38.

SAVAGE (1926), Henry L. Ed. *St. Erkenwald*. New Haven: Yale UP. Rpt. Hamden, Connecticut: Archon (1972).

SAVAGE (1931), H.L. "A Note on *Sir Gawain and the Green Knight* 700-2." *MLN* 46, 455-57.

SAVAGE (1938), H.L. "*Sir Gawain* and the Order of the Garter." *ELH* 5, 146-49.

SAVAGE (1956a), H.L. *The Gawain-Poet: Studies in His Personality and Background*. Chapel Hill: North Carolina UP.

SAVAGE (1956b), H.L. Review of Gordon's edition of *Pearl*. *MLN* 71, 124-29.

SCHLESS (1989), Howard H. "*Pearl*'s 'Princes Paye' and the Law." *ChauR* 24, 183-85.

SCHMIDT (1984), A.V.C. " 'A Covenant More than Courtesy': A Langlandian Phrase in Its Context." *N&Q, N.S.*, 31, 153-56.

SCHOFIELD (1904), William Henry. "The Nature and Fabric of *The Pearl*." *PMLA* 19, 154-203. (On pp. 203-15 is an Appendix in which Schofield argues that Boccaccio's *Olympia* is the source of *Pearl*.)

SCHOFIELD (1909), W.H. "Symbolism, Allegory, and Autobiography in *The Pearl*." *PMLA* 24, 585-675.

SCHOTTER (1979), Anne Howland. "The Poetic Function of Alliterative Formulas of Clothing in the Portrait of the Pearl Maiden." *SN* 51, 189-95.

SCHOTTER (1981), A.H. "The Paradox of Equality and Hierarchy of Reward in *Pearl*." *Renascence* 33, 172-79.

SCHOTTER (1984), A.H. "Vernacular Style and the Word of God: The Incarnational Art of *Pearl*." In *Ineffability: Naming the Unnamable from Dante to Beckett*. Ed. Peter S. Hawkins and Anne Howland Schotter, with a Foreword by Allen Mandelbaum. New York: AMS, pp. 23-34.

SERJEANTSON (1927), Mary S. "The Dialects of the West Midlands in Middle English." (In Three Parts.) *RES* 3, pp. 54–67, 186–203, and 319–31.

SIEVERS (1885), Eduard. "Zur Rhythmik des Germanischen Alliterations-verses: Erster Abschnitt, Die Metrik des *Beowulf*." *Beiträge zur Geschichte der Deutschen Sprache und Literatur* 10, 209–314.

SIEVERS (1893), E. *Altgermanische Metrik*. Halle: Niemeyer.

SKLUTE (1973), Larry M. "Expectation and Fulfillment in *Pearl*." *PQ* 52, 663–79.

SLEDD (1940), James. "Three Textual Notes on Fourteenth-Century Poetry." *MLN* 55, 379–82.

SMITHERS (1948–49), G.V. "Four Cruces in Middle English Texts." *EGS* 2, 59–67.

SPEARING-B (1962), A.C. "Symbolic and Dramatic Development in *Pearl*." *MP* 60. In *Blanch Collection*, pp. 98–119.

SPEARING (1966), A.C. "*Patience* and the *Gawain*-Poet." *Anglia* 84, 305–29.

SPEARING (1970), A.C. *The Gawain-Poet: A Critical Study*. Cambridge: Cambridge UP.

SPEARING (1976), A.C. "*Pearl*." In *Medieval Dream-Poetry*. Pages 111–29 of Ch. 3, "The Alliterative Tradition." Cambridge: Cambridge UP.

SPEARING (1984), A.C. "Dream-Poems." See Ford (1984) entry, pp. 235–47.

STANBURY (1984), Sarah. "Visions of Space: Acts of Perception in *Pearl* and in Some Late Medieval Illustrated Apocalypses." *Mediaevalia* 10, 133–58.

STANBURY (1988), Sarah. "*Pearl* and the Idea of Jerusalem." *M&H* 16, 117–31.

STANBURY (1991), Sarah. *Seeing the Gawain-Poet: Description and the Act of Perception*. Philadelphia: Pennsylvania UP.

STANLEY (1990), E.G. "*Pearl*, 358, *And þy lurez of lyʒtly leme*: Metanalysed Tmesis for the Sake of Alliteration." *N&Q* 37, 158–60.

STERN-C (1955), Milton R. "An Approach to *The Pearl*." *JEGP* 54. In *Conley Collection*, pp. 73–85.

STILLER (1982), Nikki. "The Transformation of the Physical in the Middle English *Pearl*." *ES* 63, 402–409.

STONE (1964), Brian. Trans. *Pearl*. In *Medieval English Verse*. Baltimore: Penguin.

SUTTON (1970), Robert F. "Characterization and Structure as Adjuncts to Theme in *Pearl*." *MSE* 2, 88–94.

TAJIMA (1970), Matsuji. "On the Use of the Participle in the Works of the *Gawain*-Poet." *SHumF* 34, 49–70.

TAJIMA (1971), M. "On the Use of the Gerund in the Works of the *Gawain-*

Poet." *SHumF* 35, 1–24.

TAJIMA (1972), M. "On the Use of the Infinitive in the Works of the *Gawain*-Poet." *SHumF* 36, 1–56.

TAJIMA (1975), M. "The *Gawain*-Poet's Use of 'Con' as a Periphrastic Auxiliary." *NM* 76, 429–38.

TAJIMA (1976), M. "The Neuter Pronoun *Hit* in the Works of the *Gawain*-Poet." *LingS* 11–12, pp. 23–36. English Summary, pp. 89–90.

TAJIMA (1978), M. "Additional Syntactical Evidence against the Common Authorship of MS. Cotton Nero A.X." *ES* 59, 193–98.

TERASAWA (1960), Yoshio. Trans. *Shinju: A Japanese Translation of Pearl*. Ancient and Medieval. *Anthology of Great Poetry of the World*, I. Tokyo: Heibon-sha.

THOMAS (1938), Percy Goronwy. "Notes on *The Pearl*." In *London Medieval Studies*. Vol. I, Part 2. Ed. R.W. Chambers, F. Norman, and A.H. Smith, pp. 221–24.

THORPE (1991), Douglas. *A New Earth: The Labor of Language in Pearl, Herbert's Temple, and Blake's Jerusalem*. Washington, D.C.: Catholic UP. ("*Pearl*: Lessons in Interpretive Construction," Ch. 2, pp. 27–72.)

TOLKIEN (1975), J.R.R. Trans. *Sir Gawain and the Green Knight, Pearl, and Sir Orfeo*. London: Allen.

TOLKIEN & GORDON (1925), J.R.R. and E.V. Ed. *Sir Gawain and the Green Knight*. London: Oxford UP. (Reprinted with corrections, 1930.)

TOMASCH (1989), Sylvia. "A *Pearl* Punnology." *JEGP* 88, 1–20.

TORTI (1983), Anna. "Auenture, Cnawyng and Lote in *Pearl*." In *Literature in Fourteenth-Century England: The J.A.W. Bennett Memorial Lectures, Perugia, 1981–1982*. Ed. Piero Boitani and Anna Torti. Tübingen: Narr; Cambridge, England: Brewer.

TRISTMAN-C (1970), Richard. "Some Consolatory Strategies in *Pearl*." (Appears for the first time in *Conley Collection*, pp. 272–87.)

TRISTRAM (1976), Philippa. *Figures of Life and Death in Medieval English Literature*. New York: New York UP. (Discusses *Pearl* on pp. 205–12 of Ch. VI, "Christ and the Triumph of Eternal Life.")

TURVILLE-PETRE (1975), Thorlac. "Hoccleve, 'Maister Massy' and the *Pearl* Poet: Two Notes." (Appears with Edward Wilson's Presentation in *RES*, *N.S.*, 26, 129–43.)

TURVILLE-PETRE (1977), T. *The Alliterative Revival*. Cambridge, England: Brewer; Totowa, New Jersey: Rowman & Littlefield.

TURVILLE-PETRE (1984), T. Ed. *Pearl*. In Ford (1984) entry, pp. 473–523. (Includes a prose translation on the bottoms of the pages.)

TUTTLE (1920), Edwin H. "Notes on *The Pearl*." *MLR* 15, 298–300.

VANTUONO (1971), William. "*Patience, Cleanness, Pearl*, and *Gawain*:

The Case for Common Authorship." *AnM* 12, 37–69.

VANTUONO (1975), W. "A Name in the Cotton MS. Nero A.X. Article 3." *MS* 37, 537–42.

VANTUONO (1981), W. "John de Mascy of Sale and the *Pearl* Poems." *Manuscripta* 25, 77–88.

VANTUONO (1984), W. *The Pearl Poems: An Omnibus Edition.* Volume 1: *Pearl and Cleanness*; Volume 2: *Patience and Sir Gawain and the Green Knight.* New York: Garland.

VANTUONO (1984), W. "A Triple-Three Structure for *Cleanness*." *Manuscripta* 28, 26–32.

VANTUONO (1987), W. Ed. and Trans. *The Pearl Poem in Middle and Modern English.* Lanham, Maryland: University Press of America.

VASTA-C (1967), Edward. "*Pearl*: Immortal Flowers and the Pearl's Decay." *JEGP* 66. In *Conley Collection*, pp. 185–202.

VISSER-C (1958), F.T. "*Pearl* 609–611." *ES* 39. In *Conley Collection*, pp. 338–43.

WARTON (1774–1790), Thomas. *The History of English Poetry, from the Close of the Eleventh to the Commencement of the Eighteenth Century.* Four Volumes. Rpt. New York: Johnson (1968). (Citations from *Pearl* and *Cleanness* are in Volume 3, pp. 107–108.)

WATSON (1969), Andrew G. *The Manuscripts of Henry Savile of Banke.* London: Oxford UP.

WATTS (1984), Ann Chalmers. "*Pearl*, Inexpressibility, and Poems of Human Loss." *PMLA* 99, 26–40.

WATTS (1963), V.E. "*Pearl* as a *Consolatio*." *MÆ* 32, 34–36.

WELLEK-B (1933), René. "The *Pearl*: An Interpretation of the Middle English Poem." *Studies in English by Members of the English Seminar of Charles University,* IV. In *Blanch Collection*, pp. 3–36.

WESTON (1912), Jessie L. Trans. *Pearl.* In *Romance, Vision, and Satire: English Alliterative Poems of the Fourteenth Century.* Boston: Houghton Mifflin. Rpt. Gloucester, Massachusetts: Smith (1965).

WHITAKER (1981), Muriel A. "*Pearl* and Some Illustrated Apocalypse Manuscripts." *Viator* 12, 183–96.

WHITE (1987), Hugh. "Blood in *Pearl*." *RES, N.S.*, 38, 1–13.

WHITELEY (1931), M. "Of Vyrgyn Flour." *TLS*, January 15, p. 44.

WILLIAMS (1949), Margaret, R.S.C.J. Trans. "*Pearl*-Poetry." In *Glee-Wood: Passages from Middle English Literature from the Eleventh Century to the Fifteenth.* New York: Sheed and Ward.

WILLIAMS (1967), M. Trans. *The Pearl-Poet: His Complete Works.* New York: Random House.

WILLIAMS (1970), M. "Oriental Backgrounds & the *Pearl*-Poet." *Tamkang Review* 1, 93–107.

WILSON (1968), Edward. "The 'Gostly Drem' in *Pearl*." *NM* 69, 90–101.

WILSON (1971a), E. " 'Gromylyoun' (Gromwell) in *Pearl*." *N&Q, N.S.,* 18, 42–44.

WILSON (1971b), E. "Word Play and the Interpretation of *Pearl*." *MÆ* 40, 116–34.

WILSON (1975), E. "Hoccleve, 'Maister Massy' and the *Pearl* Poet: Two Notes." (Appears with Thorlac Turville-Petre's Presentation in *RES, N.S.,* 26, 129–43.)

WILSON (1976), E. *The Gawain-Poet*. Leiden: Brill

WILSON (1977), E. Note added to Peterson (1977a) article. RES, N.S., 28, 55–56.

WIMSATT (1970), James I. *Allegory and Mirror: Tradition and Structure in Middle English Literature*. New York: Pegasus. (Discusses *Pearl* in Ch. V, "The Allegory of Revelation," pp. 117–33.)

WINTERMUTE (1949), Edwin. "The *Pearl*'s Author as Herbalist." *MLN* 64, 83–84.

WOOD (1973), Ann Douglas. "The *Pearl*-Dreamer and the 'Hyne' in the Vineyard Parable." *PQ* 52, 9–19.

WRENN (1943), C.L. "On Re-Reading Spenser's *The Shepheardes Calender*." *E&S* 29, 30–49.

WRIGHT (1960), Cyril Ernest. *English Vernacular Hands from the Twelfth to the Fifteenth Centuries*. London: Oxford UP.

WRIGHT (1982), Dorena Allen. "The Meeting at the Brook-Side: Beatrice, the Pearl-Maiden, and Pearl Prynne." *ESQ: A Journal of the American Renaissance* 28, 112–20.

WRIGHT (1939), Elizabeth M. "Notes on *The Pearl*." (Wrongly entitled, "Additional Notes on *Sir Gawain and the Green Knight*.") JEGP 38, 1–22.

WRIGHT (1940), E.M. "Additional Notes on *The Pearl*." JEGP 39, 315–18.

WRIGHT (1977), M.J. "Comic Perspective in Two Middle English Poems." *Parergon* 18, 3–15. (On *Pearl* and Chaucer's *Knight's Tale*.)

BIBLIOGRAPHY II

Bibles

Biblia Sacra. Vulgatae Editionis. Editiones Paulinae. Rome, 1957.

The Holy Bible. Translated from the Latin Vulgate. Re-Edited by the Reverend James A. Carey. Turnhout, Belgium: Brepols, 1935. (The Old Testament was first published by the English College at Douay, 1609. The New Testament was first published by the English College at Rheims, 1582.)

The Holy Bible. Translated from the Latin Vulgate. Revised by Bishop Richard Challoner, 1749–1752. Baltimore, Maryland: John Murphy Company, 1899. Rpt. Rockford, Illinois: TAN Books and Publishers, 1971.

Saint Joseph Edition of the Holy Bible. New York: Catholic Book Publishing Company, 1963.

The Septuagint Bible. Trans. Charles Thomson. Ed. C.A. Muses. Indian Hills, Colorado: Falcon's Wing Press, 1954.

Wyclif Bible. Ed. J. Forshall and F. Madden. Four Volumes. London: Oxford UP, 1850.

Concordance, Dictionaries, Grammars, and Index of Names

An Anglo-Saxon Dictionary. Ed. J. Bosworth. Supplemented by T.N. Toller. London: Oxford UP, 1882–1920.

The Compact Edition of the Oxford English Dictionary. Two Volumes. London: Oxford UP, 1971. (Complete text reproduced micrographically from *A New English Dictionary on Historical Principles*. Ed. J. Murray, H. Bradley, W. Craigie, and C.T. Onions. Ten Volumes. London: Oxford UP, 1888–1928.)

Concise Dictionary of Old Icelandic. Ed. G.T. Zoëga. London: Oxford UP, 1910.

A Concordance to Five Middle English Poems: Cleanness, St. Erkenwald, Sir Gawain and the Green Knight, Patience, Pearl. Barnet Kottler and Alan M. Markman. Pittsburgh: Pittsburgh UP, 1966.

A Dictionary of the Old English Language: Compiled from Writings of the XIII, XIV, and XV Centuries. Ed. Francis H. Stratmann. Krefeld: Kramer and Baum, 1864–1867. Revised by Henry Bradley. London: Oxford UP, 1891. (Also known as *A Middle-English Dictionary.*)

Dictionnaire de l'Ancienne Langue Française et de Tous ses Dialectes du IXe au XVe Siècle. Ed. Frèdèric Godefroy. Ten Volumes. Paris: Vieweg, 1881–1902. Rpt. New York: Kraus, 1961.

An Elementary Middle English Grammar. Joseph Wright and Elizabeth Mary Wright. London: Oxford UP, 1923; 2nd ed., 1928.

The English Dialect Dictionary. Ed. Joseph Wright. Six Volumes. London: Oxford UP, 1898–1905.

Glossarium ad Scriptores Mediæ et Infimæ Latinitatis. Charles Dufresne Du Cange. Revised edition, G.A.L. Henschel. Ten Volumes. Graz, Austria: Akademische Druck-U. Verlagsanstalt, 1954.

An Index of Names in Pearl, Purity, Patience, and Gawain. Coolidge Otis Chapman. Ithaca, New York: Cornell UP, 1951.

Middle English Dictionary. Editor-in-Chief, Robert E. Lewis. Ann Arbor: Michigan UP, 1954–. (Completed through Part T.2.)

A Middle English Syntax. (Part 1: *Parts of Speech.*) Tauno F. Mustanoja. Helsinki: Sociètè Nèophilologique, 1960.

Promptorium Parvulorum. Galfridus Anglicus. (The first English-Latin Dictionary.) Ed. A.L. Mayhew. *EETS, ES,* 102. London: Trübner, 1908.

Webster's Third New International Dictionary of the English Language. Unabridged. Editor-in-Chief, Philip Babcock Gove. Springfield, Massachusetts: Merriam, 1966.

Facsimile of the Manuscript

Pearl, Cleanness, Patience, and Sir Gawain: Reproduced in Facsimile from the Unique MS. Cotton Nero A.x in the British Museum. With an Introduction by Sir Israel Gollancz. *EETS, OS,* 162. London: Oxford UP, 1923.

Texts and Translations

French

The Bodley Version of Mandeville's Travels. (From Bodleian MS. E Musaeo 116 with parallel extracts from the Latin text of British Museum MS. Royal 13 E. IX.) Ed. M.C. Seymour. *EETS, OS,* 253. London:

Oxford UP, 1963.

The Book of the Knight of La Tour-Landry. Ed. Thomas Wright. *EETS, OS,* 33. London: Trübner, 1868.

The Buke of John Maundeuill. Ed. Sir George F. Warner. (Printed for the Roxburghe Club.) Westminster: Nichols, 1889. (Contains Middle English version in unique Egerton MS. 1982 and a French text.)

Le Livre du Chevalier de la Tour Landry. Ed. Anatole de Montaiglon. Bibliothèque Elzévirienne. Paris: Jannet, 1854.

Mandeville's Travels. (Modernized English text.) Ed. M.C. Seymour. London: Oxford UP, 1968.

Mandeville's Travels: Texts and Translations. Ed. Malcolm Letts. London: The Hakluyt Society, 1953. (Vol. 1, 2nd series, No. 101, contains a modernized version of the Egerton text; Vol. 2, 2nd series, No. 102, contains the Paris text.)

Le Roman de la Rose. Par Guillaume de Lorris et Jean de Meun. Ed. Ernest Langlois. Five Volumes. Paris: Société des Anciens Textes Français, 1914–1924.

The Romance of the Rose. By Guillaume de Lorris and Jean de Meun. Trans. Harry W. Robbins. Edited, and with an Introduction, by Charles W. Dunn. New York: Dutton, 1962.

Romaunt of the Rose. In *The Complete Poetry and Prose of Geoffrey Chaucer.* Ed. John H. Fisher. New York: Holt, 1977.

Greek

Origen. "Commentary on Matthew." In *The Ante-Nicene Fathers.* Translation of *The Writings of the Fathers down to A.D. 325.* Ed. Allan Menzies. Vol. 9. New York: Scribner's, 1912.

Patrologia Graeca. In *Patrologiae Cursus Completus.* Ed. Jacques Paul Migne. 161 Volumes. Paris: Seu Petit-Montrouge, 1857–1866. (Contains Greek texts and Latin translations.)

Italian

The Divine Comedy. By Dante Alighieri. (Text with translation in the metre of the original.) By Geoffrey L. Bickersteth. Cambridge, Massachusetts: Harvard UP, 1965.

The Divine Comedy of Dante Alighieri. The Carlyle-Wicksteed Translation. Introduction by C.H. Grandgent; Bibliography by Ernest H. Wilkins. The Modern Library. New York: Random House, 1932.

Trionfo della Morte. In *Francesco Petrarca, Le Rime Sparse e i Trionfi.* Ed.

Ezio Chiorboli. Bari: G. Laterza e Figli, 1930.

The Triumphs of Petrarch. Trans. Ernest H. Wilkins. Chicago: Chicago UP, 1962.

Latin (Non-Religious)

(The works of Boccaccio, Boethius, and Marbodus, though they contain much Christian thought, are placed in this section rather than in the following one which lists literature that is primarily patristic in nature.)

Boccaccio, Giovanni. *Olympia*. (The Fourteenth Eclogue.) Ed. Sir Israel Gollancz. (Latin Text and English translation.) In the Appendix to his edition of *Pearl*. London: Chatto and Windus, 1921.

Boethius, Anicius Manlius Severinus. *De Consolatio Philosophiae*. With the English translation of "I. T." (1609). Revised by Hugh F. Stewart. (This book also contains *The Theological Tractates*, with an English translation by Hugh F. Stewart and Edward K. Rand.) The Loeb Classical Library. London: Heinemann, 1918.

Boece. In *The Complete Poetry and Prose of Geoffrey Chaucer*. Ed. John H. Fisher. New York: Holt, 1977.

Geoffrey of Vinsauf. *Documentum de Modo et Arte Dictandi et Versificandi, Poetria Nova,* and *Summa de Coloribus Rhetoricis*. In *Les Arts Poétiques du XIIe et du XIIIe Siècle*. Ed. Edmond Faral. Paris: Champion, 1924.

Marbodus, Bishop of Rennes. *De Gemmis*. In *Patrologia Latina* 171.1735-1780. (Trans. Charles W. King, *Antique Gems*. London: Murray, 1860; 2nd ed., 1866, pp. 391-417.)

Matthew of Vendôme. *Ars Versificatoria*. In *Les Arts Poétiques du XIIe et du XIIIe Siècle*. Ed. Edmond Faral. Paris: Champion, 1924.

Poetria Nova of Geoffrey of Vinsauf. Trans. Margaret F. Nims. Toronto: Pontifical Institute of Mediaeval Studies, 1967.

Latin (Religious)

Albertus Magnus. *De Laudibus Beatae Mariae Virginis*. In Volume 36 of his *Complete Works*. Ed. Augusti Borgnet. 38 Volumes. Paris: Lodovicum Vivès, 1890-1899. (From the earlier edition of Petri Iammi, 21 Volumes, 1651.)

The Apocrypha and Pseudepigrapha of the Old Testament in English. Ed. R.H. Charles. Two Volumes. London: Oxford UP, 1913.

Augustine. *De Civitate Dei*. Ed. Bernard Dombart and Alphonse Kalb. In

Corpus Christianorum (Series Latina). Volumes 47–48. Turnhout, Belgium: Brepols, 1955.

The City of God (De Civitate Dei). By Saint Augustine. Trans. John Healey. Ed. R.V.G. Tasker. Two Volumes. Everyman's Library. London: Dent; New York: Dutton, 1945.

Jacobus De Voragine. *Legenda Aurea Vulgo Historia Lombardica Dicta.* Ed. Johann Georg Theodor Grässe. Leipsig: Arnoldianae, 1850.

Patrologia Latina. In *Patrologiae Cursus Completus.* Ed. Jacques Paul Migne. 221 Volumes. Paris: Garnier, 1844–1905.

Sancti Aurelii Augustini. *Opera Omnia.* In Migne's *Patrologia Latina,* Volumes 32–44.

Old English and Middle English

The Awntyrs off Arthure at the Terne Wathelyn. Ed. Ralph Hanna, III. Manchester: Manchester UP, 1974.

The Complete Poetry and Prose of Geoffrey Chaucer. Ed. John H. Fisher. New York: Holt, 1977.

The Complete Works of John Gower. Ed. G.C. Macaulay. Four Volumes. London: Oxford UP, 1899–1902. (Besides the Middle English poem *Confessio Amantis*, Gower's principal works include French and Latin poetry: *Mirour de l'Omme* and *Vox Clamantis*.)

Cursor Mundi. Ed. Richard Morris. 6 Parts. *EETS, OS,* 57, 59, 62, 66, 68, 99. London: Trübner, 1874–1892. Part 7 by H. Hupe. *EETS, OS,* 101, 1893. (This series prints the four manuscripts of the poem in parallel texts: Cotton, Fairfax, Göttingen, Trinity.)

Death and Life. In *Bishop Percy's Folio Manuscript.* Ed. John W. Hales and Frederick J. Furnivall. Volume 3. London: Trübner, 1867-1868. (Edited also by Sir Israel Gollancz in *Select Early English Poems,* Volume 5, London: Oxford UP, 1930.)

An Early English Psalter. (Also known as *Northern Verse Psalter* and *Surtees Psalter.*) In *Yorkshire Writers: Richard Rolle of Hampole and His Followers.* Volume 2. Ed. Carl Horstmann. London: Swan, 1896, upper pp. 129–273.

English Mediaeval Lapidaries. Ed. Joan Evans and Mary S. Serjeantson. *EETS, OS,* 190. London: Oxford UP, 1932. Rpt. 1960.

The Fall and Passion. In *Early English Poems and Lives of Saints.* Ed. Frederick J. Furnivall. Berlin: Asher, 1862, pp. 12–15.

The Gest Hystoriale of the Destruction of Troy. (An alliterative romance translated from Guido de Colonna's *Hystoria Troiana*.) Ed. George A. Panton and David Donaldson. *EETS, OS,* 39 and 56. London: Trübner, 1869 and 1874. Rpt. New York: Greenwood, 1969.

The Grene Knight. In *Bishop Percy's Folio Manuscript.* Ed. John W. Hales and Frederick J. Furnivall. Volume 2. London: Trübner, 1867–1868.

The Harley Lyrics. Ed. G.L. Brook. Fourth Edition. Manchester: Manchester UP, 1968.

Hymns to the Virgin and Christ, The Parliament of Devils, and Other Religious Poems. Ed. Frederick J. Furnivall. EETS, OS, 24. London: Trübner, 1868. Rpt. New York: Greenwood, 1969.

Ipomedon. (Three Versions.) Ed. Eugen Kölbing. Breslau: Koebner, 1889.

Joseph of Arimathie. Ed. Walter W. Skeat. EETS, OS, 44. London: Trübner, 1871. Rpt. New York: Greenwood, 1969.

Morte Arthure. Ed. Erik Björkman. *Alt- und Mittelenglische Texte* 9. Heidelberg: Winter, 1915. (Edited also by Valerie S. Krishna as *The Alliterative Morte Arthure: A Critical Edition.* New York: Burt Franklin, 1976.)

The Pearl Poems: An Omnibus Edition. Volume 1: *Pearl and Cleanness*; Volume 2: *Patience and Sir Gawain and the Green Knight.* Ed. William Vantuono. New York: Garland, 1984.

Saint Erkenwald. Ed. Clifford J. Peterson. Philadelphia: Pennsylvania UP, 1977.

Seven Old English Poems: Cædmon's Hymn, The Battle of Brunanburh, The Dream of the Rood, The Battle of Maldon, The Wanderer, The Seafarer Deor. Ed. John C. Pope. Indianapolis: Bobbs-Merrill, 1966; 2nd ed., New York: Norton, 1981.

The Siege of Jerusalem. Ed. Eugen Kölbing and Mabel Day. EETS, OS, 188. London: Oxford UP, 1932. Rpt. New York: Kraus, 1971.

Sir Ferumbras. (From Ashmole MS. 33.) In *The Charlemagne Romances: 1.* Ed. S.J. Herrtage. EETS, ES, 34. London: Trübner, 1879.

St. Erkenwald. Ed. Henry L. Savage. New Haven: Yale UP, 1926. Rpt. Hamden, Connecticut: Archon, 1972.

St Erkenwald. Ed. Ruth Morse. Cambridge, England: Brewer; Totowa, New Jersey: Rowman and Littlefield, 1975.

*The Vision of William concerning **Piers the Plowman**, in Three Parallel Texts, Together with **Richard the Redeless**.* By William Langland. Ed. Walter W. Skeat. Two Volumes. London: Oxford UP, 1886. Rpt., with addition of Bibliography, 1954.

The Wars of Alexander. Ed. Walter W. Skeat. EETS, ES, 47. London: Trübner, 1886.

The Works of Geoffrey Chaucer. Ed. F.N. Robinson. Boston: Houghton Mifflin, 1933; 2nd ed., 1957.

Wynnere and Wastoure. Ed. Sir Israel Gollancz. (With Modern English rendering.) In *Select Early English Poems.* Volume 3. London: Oxford UP, 1920. Revised by Mabel Day, 1931. Rpt. Cambridge,

England: Brewer; Totowa, New Jersey: Rowman and Littlefield, 1974.

Yearly Bibliographies and Other Bibliographical Listings

Annual Bibliography of English Language and Literature. Modern Humanities Research Association of Great Britain, 1920–.

Bibliography of English Translations from Medieval Sources. Clarissa P. Farrar and Austin P. Evans. New York: Columbia UP, 1946.

The Gawain-Poet: An Annotated Bibliography, 1839–1977. Malcolm Andrew. New York: Garland, 1979.

"The *Gawain*-Poet: An Annotated Bibliography, 1978–1985." Michael Foley. *ChauR* 23 (1989), 251–82.

International Medieval Bibliography. Leeds, Great Britain, 1967–.

A Manual of the Writings in Middle English: 1050–1500. By Members of the Middle English Group of the Modern Language Association of America. General Editor, J. Burke Severs. Bibliography on *Gawain* in Volume 1, pp. 238–43. Bibliography on *Pearl, Patience,* and *Cleanness* in Volume 2, pp. 503–16. New Haven: The Connecticut Academy of Arts and Sciences, 1967 and 1970.

"A Middle English Bibliographical Guide." Compiled by Stanley B. Greenfield. In *Guide to English Literature from **Beowulf** through **Chaucer** and Medieval Drama.* David M. Zesmer. New York: Barnes and Noble, 1961. (Section X, "The Alliterative Revival," pp. 342–51, includes annotated references to *Pearl* and *Gawain.*)

MLA International Bibliography. Modern Language Association of America, 1921–.

The New Cambridge Bibliography of English Literature. Ed. George Watson. Volume 1, 600–1660. Cambridge: Cambridge UP, 1974. (Listings for *Gawain*, col. 401–6; for *Pearl, Cleanness,* and *Patience,* col. 547–54.)

"The *Pearl*-Poet (Fourteenth Century): *Patience, Pearl, Purity, St. Erkenwald, Sir Gawain and the Green Knight.*" Compiled by Walter H. Beale. In *Old and Middle English Poetry to 1500: A Guide to Information Sources.* Detroit: Gale, 1976.

"Supplement to the *Gawain*-Poet: An Annotated Bibliography, 1978–1985." Robert J. Blanch. *ChauR* 25 (1991), 363–86.

The Year's Work in English Studies. English Association. London: Oxford UP, 1919/1920–.

GLOSSARY

This Glossary lists the literal meanings of the Middle English vocabulary. Many of these meanings are also found in the notes placed beneath the Middle English text and Modern English verse translation. Information is provided for every form of every word. The words that appear frequently with the same spelling, meaning, and grammatical element usually have two entries followed by *etc.*

In the arrangement, ʒ follows *g*, þ follows *t*, and entries with the letters *u, v, w*, and *y* are alphabetized according to the Modern English system. The spelling does not always accord with Middle English pronunciation, but the pronunciation is often indicated by the etymon in brackets. Note, for example, *uoched* [OF *voch(i)er*], *vnder* [OE *under*], and *yuore* [OF *ivoire*]. A word like *vyf s.v. wyf* [OE *wīf*] is obviously a variant spelling. The graph þ is always sounded *th*, but ʒ has a variety of sounds depending on the word in which it appears and its position in that word. (For a fuller discussion of these two Middle English graphs and unusual forms concerned with spelling and phonology, see the section on Dialect and Language, pp. 174–76.)

Tables listing Abbreviations for Grammatical Terms and Other Terms, and for Languages and Dialects, are on pp. 181–82. An *n* after a line number, indicating a note in the Commentary, is to be distinguished from *n.* as the abbreviation for *noun*. The note in the Commentary may be in a cluster.For example, *s.v. mykeʒ* is 572n, and the note in the Commentary is in the 570–72 cluster. A *v.* may indicate *verb* or part of a *verbal*. For example, *s.v. say* a *v.* is used for the *verb* in the phrase *con say* (256) and for the second element of the infinitival verbal *to say* (258). The abbreviation *infin.* is used for the plain *infinitive*, as with *say* 'to say' (226), and when 'to' is understood, as with *dar say* 'dare (to) say' (1089).

The etymons of the headwords appear in brackets at the end of each entry. The symbol * before a word means it is theoretically reconstructed. The etymological information comes mainly from the *MED*, completed through fascicle T.3 at the time of this writing, and the OED for the remainder of the alphabet. Often the designation (*MED*) appears to credit that dictionary for the inclusion of significant information. The *MED* often lists Anglian, West Saxon, and Northumbrian forms of Old English, as well as Anglo-French and Central French forms of Old French. These are usually included in the Glossary.

Forms of the verb *to be*, of other common verbs, of personal pronouns, and of other common words are listed separately, except, of course, for variant spellings of a particular form. For example, *be, ben, bene*, and *betʒ* are together *s.v. be*, and the forms of *am, is, are, was* and *were* are separate. Forms of personal pronouns (1st, 2nd, and 3rd person singular and plural; masculine, feminine, and neuter; nominative, dative & accusative, possessive, and intensive & reflexive) are listed separately.

Gordon (1953) 105–6 argued for French linguistic influence on *Pearl* in the use of the 2nd person plural nominative ʒe as the polite form of the singular 'you' (usually indicated by þou). The other singular forms in *Pearl* are þe, þy (þyn), and þyself (þyseluen); plural forms are yow and yor (your). The plural forms were often used in Middle English to address one person considered a superior or to impart a tone of formality or humility, while the singular forms were colloquial, but, as Gordon himself noted, such distinctions were beginning to be blurred in this period. Though there seems to be validity, for the most part, to Gordon's argument that the poet employed the polite plural with distinctive criteria in mind, there are passages in *Pearl* where the forms are mixed. Note, for example, only in reference to the use of ʒe (to address one person) and þou, the following stanzas: 22, 31–32, 59, 77–78.

a (1) *indef. art.* a 19, 23, etc., an 446, (pleonastic in **vch a** every 78, 375, etc. and **vche a** every 117, 217, etc.); **an** an 640, a 869; **on** a 9, 1079. [OE ān]

a (2) 1058n. (shortened form of **as** in *correl. adv.* **so . . . a** as . . . as 1057–58)

a (3) 144n. (shortened form of **ay** used pleonastically in *correl. adv.* **euer . . . a** always)

a (4) *prep.* like 115n. (shortened form of **as**)

a (5) *prep.* in 1113. [Unstressed variant of OE on]

abate *infin.* to bow humbly 617; **abated** *pt. pl.* subdued 123. [OF abatre]

abiden. See **abyde.**

able *pr. pl. pass.* are able 599. [OF able]

abof *prep.* above 1017; *adv.* 1023. [OE abufan]

aboute *prep.* around 75, 1077, about 268, 513; *adv.* about 932; **abowte** *prep.* around 149. [OE onbūtan]

abroched *pp.* proclaimed 1123. [OF abrochier]

abyde *v.* endure 348; **abiden** *pp.* experienced 1090. [OE ābīden]

acheue *v.* achieve 475. [OF achever]

acorde *n.* harmony 371, agreement 509. [OF acorde]

acorded *pt. pl.* accorded 819. [OF acorder]

acroche *v.* gain 1069. [OF acrochier]

adaunt *v.* overwhelm 157. [OF adaunter]

adoun *adv.* down 988. [OE adūne]

adubbement *n.* adornment 84, 96, 108, 120; **adubbemente** *coll.* adornments 85; **adubmente** adornment 72. [OF adubement] Cf. **dubbement(e).**

adyte *pr. 2 sg. subj.* accuse 349. [OF aditer]

affray *n.* dismay 1174. [OF effrei]

after *prep.* along 125, after 998; **after þenne** *adv.* afterwards 256. [OE æfter]

agayn *prep.* against 28, 1199, 1200; *adv.* again 326; **agaynʒ** *prep.* against 79. [ON i gegn; OE ongegn]

age *n.* age 412. [OF aage, eage]

aglyʒte *pt. 2 sg.* slipped away 245. [*MED* indicates a blend of OE ālīhtan 'alight' and OI gljā 'glitter'.]

agrete *adv.* all told 560. [Modeled on OF en gros (*MED*)]

aʒt. See **owe.**

aʒtþe *n.* eighth 1011. [OE eahtoða]

al *adj.* all 16, 18, etc.; *pron.* all 360, 757, etc., everything 495, in phr. *of al and sum* 'in every respect' 584; *adv.* entirely 97, 258, etc., all 197, 386, etc., completely 204, 210, etc., very 1048; **alle** *adj.* all 73, 119, etc.; *pron.* all 404, 739, 1101, everybody 447; *adv.* all 467, 545, etc. [OE eal, ealle]

alas. See **allas.**

alder. See **olde.**

aldermen *n. pl.* ancients 887, 1119. [OE ealdorman]

aldest. See **olde.**

alegge *pr. 2 sg. subj.* declare 703. [OF alegier]

allas *interj.* alas 9; **alas** alas 1138. [OF a las]

alle. See **al.**

alle-kynneʒ *adj.* every kind of 1028. [OE ealra cynna]

Almyʒt *adj.* Almighty 498. [*MED* compares OE acc. sg. *drihten ælmihtne.*]

Almyʒty *adj. used as n.* Almighty 1063. [OE eal-mihtig]

alone *adv.* alone 933. [OE eal āna]

al-only *adv.* solely 779. [OE eal ānlīc]

alow *v.* recognize 634. [AF alouer]

aloyute *pp.* distant 893. [OF aloignier, alongier]

als *adv.* also 765. (reduced form of next entry)

also *adv.* also 685, 872, besides 1071. [OE eal swā, ealswā]

alþaʒ *conj.* although 759, 857, 878. [OE eal þēah]

alyue *adj.* living 445. [OE on līfe]

am *pr. 1 sg.* am 246, 335, etc. [OE eam, am]

amatyst *n.* amethyst 1016. [OF amatiste]

among *prep.* among 470, 848, 1145, 1150; *adv.* together 905. [OE onmang.]

an. See **a** (1).

and *conj.* and 16 (twice), 18, etc., and yet 153, while 247, if 378, 560, 598, 932, when 538; **and . . . and** *correl. conj.* both . . . and 342; **ande** and 35n. [OE and]

auende *prep.* concerning 697, near 1136; **anendeʒ** across from 975; **anvndeʒ** comparable to 1068n; **onende** concerning 186. [OE on efen, on-emn]

angel-hauyng *n.* angelic demeanor 754. [OF a(u)ngel + ME hauyng]

anger *n.* anguish 343. [ON angr]

ani. See **any.**

anjoynt *pp.* joined 895. [OF enjoindre]

anon *adv.* immediately 584, soon 629. [OE on ān]

218

anoþer *adj.* a second (thing) 297. [OE ān+ōþer]

answar *n.* answer 518. [OE andswaru]

anvndeʒ. See **anende.**

anvnder *prep.* below 166, beneath 1081, 1092, 1100; *adv.* beneath 991; **anvnnder** *prep.* beneath 775. [OE on under]

any *adj.* any 463, 617, 800, 1068; **ani**, any 1139. [OE ǣnig]

apassed *pp.* passed 540. [OF apasser]

apere *v.* appear 405. [OF *aper-*, tonic stem of *aparoir* (*MED*)]

apert *adv.* openly 589. [OF apert]

Apocalyppce *n.* Apocalypse 944, 1008; **Apokalyppeʒ**, 787, 996, 1020; **Apokalypce**, 983; **Apokalypeʒ**, 834; **Appocalyppece**, 866. [Latin, from Greek (*MED*)]

apostel *n.* apostle 790, 836, etc.; **appostel**, 1053. [OE apostol]

apparaylmente *n.* heavenly retinue 1052n. [OF appareillement]

apple *n.* apple 640. [OE æppel]

appose *pr. 1 sg. subj.* inquire 902. [OF aposer]

aproche *v.* approach 686; **aproched** *pt. 3 sg.* drew near 1119. [OF aprochier]

aquyle *v.* prevail 690; **aquylde** *pp.* prevailed 967. [OF acueillir]

ar *pr. pl.* are 923; **arn**, are 384, 402, etc., have 517; *pr. perf. pl.* have been 893, 895; **arne**, *pr. pl.* are 628; **art** *pr. 2 sg.* are 242, 276, etc.; *pr. perf. 2 sg.* have been 904; **arte** *pr. 2 sg.* are 707. [OE earon, eart]

aray *n.* position (rank) 491; **araye** array 5, 191. [OF arai]

arayde *pp.* resolved 1166; **arayed** prepared 719, arrayed 791. [AF *ar(r)ai-*, tonic stem of *ar(r)eer* (*MED*)]

areþede *n.* ancient folk 711. [OE ǣr, ON ār+OE þēod]

arme *n.* arm 459, 466. [OE earm]

arn(e). See **ar.**

aros *pt. 3 sg.* increased 181. [OE ārīsan]

art(e). See **ar.**

aryʒt *adv.* swiftly 112. [OE āriht]

aryue *v.* arrive 447. [OF ariver]

as *conj.* as 20, 96, etc., since, 915, 923, 997; just as 947, 1053, when 1193; *adv.* just as 836, as (three times) 1024; **as . . . as** *correl. adv.* as . . . as 76, 626, 822, 1085; *prep.* like 77, 88, etc.,

according to 595, 1041, as 723, 815 (twice), etc. [Reduced form of OE *ealswā* 'also']

asent *n.* harmony 94; **asente** intention 391. [OF as(s)ent]

ask *v.* ask 564; **aske** ask 316, 910; **to aske** *infin. tr. prog.* in seeking 580. [OE āscian]

assemblé *n.* union 760. [OF assemblée]

asspye *v.* observe 1035; **asspyed** *pp.* noted 704; *pt. 1 sg.* discovered 979. [AF & CF espi(i)er]

astate *n.* condition 393; **asstate** rank 490. [AF astat]

astraye *adv.* impetuously 1162. [OF *pp.* estraié]

as-tyt *adv.* quickly 645. [ME as+ON tītt]

asyse *n.* style 97. [OF assise]

at (1) *prep.* at 161, 198, etc., with 188, 287, etc., in 199, 321, etc., during 529, 647, to 1164, in phr. *at ene* 'simultaneously' 291, 'immediately' 953. [OE æt]

at (2) *rel. pron.* which 536n. [ON at]

atount *pp.* dazed 179. [Cf. ME astōned & F étonné (*MED*).]

atslykeʒ *pr. 3 sg. subj.* may slip away 575. [ME at+MLG slīken (*MED*)]

atteny *pr. 2 sg. subj.* reach 548. [OF *ateign-* stem of *ateindre* (*MED*)]

auenture *n.* adventure 64. [OF aventure]

Augoste *n.* August 39. [L Augustus]

aungeleʒ *n. pl.* angels 1121. [OF a(u)ngel]

aunte *n.* aunt 233. [AF aunte]

avysyoun *n.* vision 1184. [OF avisio(u)n]

away *adv.* away 488, 655, 823; **awaye** *adj.* absent 258. [OE on weg, aweg]

awayed *pp.* informed 710. [OF aveier]

awhyle *adv.* for a time 692. [OE āne hwīle]

ay *adv.* always 33, 44, etc., ever 101, still 156, forever 956, 1042; **aye** forever 1198. [ON ei]

ayþer *adj.* both 831. [OE ǣgþer]

babtem. See **baptem.**

bale *n.* anguish 18, grief 373, suffering 478, misery 1139; *coll.* torments 651; **baleʒ** *pl.* sorrows 123, sins 807. [OE bealo, bealu]

balke *n.* mound 62. [OE balca]

baly *n.* city 1083. [OF bai(l)le] Cf. **bayly.**

bantels *n. pl.* tiers 1017; **banteleʒ** 992n. [OF *bantel]

baptem *n.* baptism 653; **babtem** 627. [OF bapteme]

baptysed *pt. 3 sg.* baptized 818. [OF baptiser]

bare *adv.* plainly 836; *adj.* clear 1025. [OE bær]

Barne *n.* Child 426; **barneʒ** *pl.* children 712, 1040. [OE bearn]

basse *n.* foundation 1000. [OF base, basse]

basyng *ger.* base 992. [Prec.+-yng]

bayly *n.* domain 315, jurisdiction 442. [OF baillie] Cf. **baly.**

bayn *adj.* prepared 807. [ON beinn]

baysment *n.* bewilderment 174. [OF abaissement]

be *v.* be 29, 281, etc.; *pr. pl.* are 290, 958; *pr. sg. subj.* is 311, 794, be 352, 482, etc., may be 523, 911, are 694, 976; *pr. pl. subj.* be 379, are 470, 572, may be 1176; *imper. sg.* be 344, 406; *infin.* to be 480, 1155; **ben** *pp.* been 252, 373, 1194; *pr. pl.* are 572; **bene** *pr. pl.* are 785; **betʒ** *fut. 3 sg.* will be 611. [OE bēon]

be *prep.* 523. See **by.**

beau *adj.* excellent 197. [OF beau]

beauté *n.* beauty 749; **bewté** 765. [OF beauté]

bede *pt. pl.* ordered 715. [OE bēodan] Cf. **byddeʒ.**

bele *v.* burn 18. [OI bǣla]

bem *n.* beam (Christ's cross) 814. [OE bēam]

ben(e). See **be** *v.*

bene *adj.* fair 110; *adv.* beautifully 198. [? AF ben, CF bien 'good' (*MED*)]

bent *pp.* attached 664; *pt. 3 sg.* rose 1017; **bente** *pp.* aimed 1189. [OE bendan]

ber *pt. 3 sg.* bore 426; *pr. 2 sg. subj.* wear 466; **bere** *pt. 1 sg.* turned 67; *v.* suffer for 807, produce 1078; **bereʒ** *pr. 3 sg.* has 100, possesses 746, maintains 756, bears 1068; **beren** *pr. pl.* wear 854, 856, bloom 1079; **bore** *pp.* born 239; **borne** 626. [OE beran]

bereste. See **breste.**

beryl *n.* beryl 110, 1011. [OF beril]

best *adj. sup.* best 1131; **beste** 863; *as n.* most noble maiden 279. [OE betst]

besteʒ *n. pl.* beasts 886. [OF beste]

bete *pt. pl.* beat 93. [OE bēatan]

bete *v.* comfort 757. [OE bētan]

betʒ. See **be** *v.*

better *adv. comp.* rather 341. [OE betera, bet(t)ra *adj.*]

bewté. See **beauté.**

beyng *ger.* being 446. [From ME be *v.*]

bifore. See **byfore.**

bitalt *pp.* startled 1161. [Cf. OE *tealt(r)ian* 'waver' (*MED*).]

blaʒt *ppl. a.* white 212. [OE blǣcan, *ppl.* blǣced]

blake *adj.* black 945. [OE blæc]

blame *n.* reproof 715. [OF bla(s)me]

blame *pass. infin.* be blamed 303; **blameʒ** *pr. 2 sg.* censure 275. [OF bla(s)mer]

blayke *adj.* white 27. [ON bleik-r]

ble *n.* hue 76, complexion 212. [OE blēo]

bleaunt *n.* silk attire 163. [AF bliaunt & CF bliaut]

blent *pp.* engulfed 385; **blente** blended 1016. [OE blendan, corresp. to OI blanda]

blesse *infin.* to bless (make the sign of the Cross) 341; *pr. 3 sg. subj.* may bless 850. [OE ge)bletsian]

blessed *ppl. a.* blessed 436. [OE ge)bletsod]

blessyng *ger.* blessing 1208. [OE ge)bletsung]

blo *adj.* dark 83, leaden 875. [ON blā-r, OF blo]

blod *n.* blood 646, 650, etc.; **blode** 741. [OE blōd]

blody *adv.* bloodily 705. [OE blōdig]

blom *n.* supremacy 578; **blomeʒ** *pl.* blossoms 27. [ON blōm]

blose *n.* blast of wind 911n. [OE blæs]

blot *n.* stain 782. [Cf. OF blo(s)tre, var. of *blestre* 'a boil' (*MED*).]

blunt *adj.* senseless 176. [? Cf. OE *blinnan* 'stop, cease, come to an end' (*MED*).]

blusched *pt. 1 sg.* gazed 980, 1083. [OE blyscan & a)blysian]

blwe *adj.* blue 27, 76, 423. [OF bleu]

blynde *adj.* lusterless 83. [OE blind]

blynne *v.* cease 729. [OE blinnan]

blys *n.* happiness 123, joy 126, bliss 286, 729; Blys Glory (referring to the Lamb) 796; **blysse** bliss 372, 373, etc., happiness 478, 638, 658, blessing 611, renown 785, ecstasy 863. [OE blis]

blysfol *adj.* beautiful 279; **blysful** blissful 409, delightful 907, blessed 964, splendid 1104; *sb. adj.* blissful one 421, beautiful maiden 1100. [Prec.+ME ful]

blysnande *pr. p.* gleaming 163, shining 197; **blysned** *pt. 3 sg.* sparkled 1048. [OE *blysian*, with suffix as in *fæstnian, wæcnian* (*MED*)]

blyþe *n.* mercy 354. [Cf. *adj.* & OI blīða *n.*]

blyþe *adj.* glad 352, fair 738; **blyþest** *sup.*

most gracious 1131. [OE blīþe]

blyþely *adv.* eagerly 385. [OE blīþelīce]

bod. See **byde.**

body *n.* body 62, 460, 1070. [OE bodig]

bodyly *adj.* human 478, mortal 1090. [From prec.]

boffeteʒ *n. pl.* buffets 809. [OF buf(f)et]

boʒ *pr. 3 sg.* must 323; **byhod** *pt. 3 sg.* would oblige 928. [OE behōfian]

boʒe *v.* stroll 196; **bow** *imper. sg.* go 974; **bowed** *pt. 1 sg.* stepped 126. [OE būgan]

boʒt. See **bye.**

bok *n.* book 710; **boke** 837. [OE bōc]

bolde *adj.* bold 806. [A bald, WS beald]

bolleʒ *n. pl.* boles 76. [ON bol-r]

bolne *v.* swell 18. [ON bolgna]

bon *n.* in phr. *whalleʒ bon* 'ivory' 212n. [OE bān] See also **whalleʒ.**

bone *n.* plea 912, request 916, revelation 1090. [ON bōn]

bonerté *n.* goodness 762. [OF *bonerté*; ? also OF *boneurté* 'good luck' (*MED*)]

bonk *n.* hill 102; **bonke** slope 196; **bonc** shore 907, 1169; **bonkeʒ** *pl.* banks 110, shores 138, 931. [ON *bakki*, akin to OE *benc* 'bench' (*MED*)]

bor *n.* abode 964. [OE būr]

borde *pr. pl. emph.* do speak lightly 290. [OF border, bourder]

bore. See **ber.**

borʒ *n.* city 957, 989, 1048; **burghe** 980. [OE burg, burh, buruh]

borne. See **ber.**

borneʒ *n. gen.* stream's 974. [OE burna]

bornyst *pp.* burnished 77; **bornyste** *pp. tr. prog.* shining 220; **burnist** *pp.* burnished 990. [OF *burniss-*, extended stem of *burnir*]

boroʒt. See **bryng.**

bostwys *adj.* sturdy 814; **bustwys** boisterous 911. [OF *boisteus* 'rough']

bot *conj.* but 66, 143, etc., unless 308, 428, etc., if 331, than 952; *adv.* yet 17, 18, 613, but 83, 269, etc., moreover 91, 221, etc., only 551, 922, however 625, 695, etc., furthermore 849; *prep.* except 312, 658, etc., but 336, 337, etc. [OE būtan]

bote *n.* remedy 275, pardon 645. [OE bōt]

boþe *pron.* both 373, 950; *correl. conj.* **boþe . . . and** both . . . and 90, 329, 682, 731, 1056, 1203. [From OE *bā þā* 'both these'; cf. OFris. *bēthe*, OI *bāþir*.]

boun *adj.* arranged 534, built 992; *adv.* firmly 1103. [ON būin-n]

bounden *pp.* bound 198, fastened 1103. [OE bindan]

bourne. See **burne.**

bow(ed). See **boʒe.**

boyeʒ *n. pl.* ruffians 806. [OF *em)buié, em)boié* 'fettered, shackled', *ppl.* of *embuiier (MED)*]

brade. See **brode.**

brathe *n.* violent movement 1170; **braþeʒ** *pl.* agonies 346. [ON brāð]

braundysch *pr. 2 sg. subj.* (may) toss about 346. [OF *bra(u)ndiss-*, extended stem of *brandir*]

bray *pr. 2 sg. subj.* (may) vociferate 346. [OF brai-re]

brayde *pt. pl.* brought 712; *pt. 3 sg.* drew 1170. [OE bregdan]

brayneʒ *n. pl.* brains 126. [OE brægen]

bred *n.* bread 1209. [OE brēad]

brede *n.* breadth 1031. [OE brǣd(u)]

brede *v.* dwell 415. [OE brēdan]

brede *pass. infin.* (to be) stretched 814. [OE brǣdan]

bredful *adj.* brimful 126. [ON **bredd-* (corresp. to OE *brerd*) & **bradd-*; cf. Norw. *bredfuld*, Swed. *brädd-full.*]

bref *adj.* transient 268. [OF bref]

breme *adj.* fierce 346, wondrous 863. [OE brēme]

brende *pp.* pure (refined gold) 989; **brent** *pt. pl.* sparkled 106. [ON brenna, OE biernan]

breste *n.* breast 18, 222, 740, 1103, 1139; **bereste** 854. [OE brēost]

breue *imper. sg.* tell 755. [OE *gebrēfan* 'state briefly' & OI *brēfa* 'write down' (from ML *breviāre*)]

brode *adj.* gaping (wound) 650, broad 1022, wide 1024; **brade** broad 138. [OE brād]

broʒ, broʒte. See **bryng.**

brok *n.* brook 981; **broke** 141, 146; **brokeʒ** *gen.* of the brook 1074. [OE brōc]

broun *adj.* dark 537; *adv.* brightly 990. [OE *brūn* 'brown, dark; shining'; also OF *brun* (from Gmc.)]

brunt *n.* blow 174. [? ON; akin to OI *bruna* 'move speedily, rush' (*MED*)]

bryd *n.* bride 769. [OE brȳd]

bryddeʒ *n. pl.* birds 93. [OE brid]

bryʒt *adj.* bright 75, 110, glistening 989; *sb. adj.* bright maiden 755; *adv.* brightly 769, brilliantly 1048; **bryʒter** *adj. comp.*

brighter 1056. [OA breht, bryht; WS beorht(e)]

brym n. water 1074. [OE brim, ON brim]

brymme n. edge (of shore) 232. [Akin to MHG brem 'border, fringe']

bryng v. bring 853; imper. sg. bring 963; boroȝt pp. brought 628; broȝ 286n; broȝte pt. 3. sg. brought 527. [OE bringan, pt. brohte]

bukes n. pl. currents 106n. [Cf. OI bekkr]

bur n. grief 1158n; burre shock 176. [ON ᵇyr-r]

burde, ᵢ . subj. impers., þe burde 'you ought' 316. [OE ge)byrian; cf. OI byrja]

burghe. See borȝ.

burne n. man 1090; voc. sir 397; burneȝ pl. people 712; bourne man 617. [OE beorn]

burnist. See bornyst.

burre. See bur.

bustwys. See bostwys.

busyeȝ pr. 2 sg. refl. concern (yourself) 268. [OE bisgian]

by prep. by 107, 141, etc., alongside 140, along 152, 691, through 194, 480, etc., with 468, 1196, in 619, 751, 831, 921; be by 523. [OE bī, be]

bycalle pr. 1 sg. call upon 913; bycalt pp. called back 1163. [ME by+ON kalla; cf. late OE ceallian.]

bycawse conj. because 296. [ME by+OF cause]

bycom pt. 3 sg. became 537. [OE becuman]

byddeȝ pr. perf. 3 sg. has asked 520. [OE biddan] Cf. bede.

byde v. endure 664; infin. to linger 977; bydeȝ pr. pl. lie 75; pr. 2 sg. dwell 907; bod pt. 3 sg. remained 62. [OE bīdan]

bydene adv. forthwith 196. [? CF. dēn doen, Northumbrian ppl. of dōn 'do' (MED).]

bye v. buy 732; byye secure 478; boȝt pt. 3 sg. redeemed 651; pp. purchased 733, 893. [OE bycgan, bohte]

byfalle v. happen 186. [OE befallan]

byfore prep. before 294, 598, 885; adv. before 172, in front 1110; conj. before 530; bifore prep. before 49. [OE beforan]

byg adj. great 102; bygger comp. greater 374. [Origin obscure; ? cf. Norw. bugge 'strong man' (MED).]

bygly adj. stately 963. [ON byggiligr]

bygyn. imper. sg. begin 547; bygynne v. begin 581; bygynneȝ pr. 2 sg. emph. do

begin 561; bygonne pp. begun 33; pt. pl began 549. [OE beginnan]

bygyng ger. coll. buildings 932; bygyngeȝ pl. buildings 935n. [ON bygging]

Bygynner n. Beginner (Blessed Virgin) 436. [From prec.]

byȝe n. jewelry 466. [OE bēag, bēah, bēg]

byȝonde prep. beyond 141, 146, etc. [OE beȝeondan]

byhod. See boȝ.

byholde v. behold 810. [OE behealdan]

bylde n. edifice 727, city 963. [A blend of OE bold 'building' & byldan 'build' (MED)]

bylde pt. pl. produced 123. [OE byldan]

byrþ-whateȝ n. pl. dates of birth 1041. [OE ge)byrd or ON byrð+OE hwatu]

bysech v. urge 390. [OE besēcan]

byseme v. befit 310. [ME by+ON sœma]

byswykeȝ pr. 1 sg. deprive 568. [OE beswīcan]

bytaȝte pt. 1 sg. entrusted 1207. [OE betǣcan, -tǣhte]

byte v. arouse 355, bite 640. [OE bītan]

bytwene prep. between 140, 658; adv. in between 44. [OE betwēonum, -an]

bytwyste prep. among 464. [OE betwix, -tweox, -twux(t; cf. OFris. twiska]

bytyde v. befall 397. [ME by+OE tīdan]

byye. See bye.

caggen pr. pl. bind 512. [Prob. ON; ? cf. kǫgurr 'quilt', kǫgur-barn 'swaddled child' (MED)]

caȝt pt. 3 sg. came 50; caȝte took 237. [AF cach(i)er]

calder. See colde.

calle v. call 173, 721; infin. call 182; pr. pl. call 430; pp. called 572; called pp. called 273; pt 3 sg. called 542; calde pt. 3 sg. called 762. [ON kalla, OE ceallian]

calsydoyne n. chalcedony 1003. [OF calcedoine & L calchēdonius]

caumbe n. headdress 775. [OE camb]

can, line 499. See con (2).

care n. care 50, 371, 861; careȝ pl. sorrows 808. [OE caru, cearu]

carp v. speak 381; carpe pt. 3 sg. emph. did speak 752n; v. speak 949. [ON karpa]

carp n. hymn 883. [ON karp]

cas n. matter 673. [OF cas]

caste n. purpose 1163. [ON kast]

castel-walle n. coll. walls of the castle 917. [OE & AF castel+OE weall]

causeȝ *n. pl.* causes 702. [OF cause]
cayre *infin.* to extend 1031. [ON keyra]
ceté. See **cité.**
ceuer *v.* submit 319. [Combination of OE
    ācofrian & OF *covrer, reco(u)vrer*]
chace *v.* deprive 443. [OF chacier]
chambre *n.* bridal chamber 904. [OF
    chambre]
chapel *n.* chapel 1062. [OF chapel]
charde *pt. pl.* varied 608; **schereȝ** *pr. 3 sg.*
    flows 107n. [OE *cearrian & cierran]
charyté *n.* charity 470. [CF charité]
chayere *n.* throne 885. [OF chaiere]
chere *n.* behavior 407, mood 887, expres-
    sion 1109. [OF chiere, chere]
ches *pt. 3 sg.* chose 759; **chese** 954; **chos** *pt.
    1 sg.* found 187; **ichose** *pp.* chosen 904.
    [OE cēosan, *pt.* cēas]
Cheuentayn *n.* Chieftain (the Lord) 605.
    [OF chevetaine]
chos. See **ches.**
chyche *n.* miser 605. [OF chiche]
chyde *v.* dispute 403. [OE cīdan]
chylde *n.* child 723; **chylder** *pl.* children
    714, 718. [OE cild, *pl.* cildru]
cité *n.* city 1097; **ceté** 927; in phr. *Ceté of
    God* 'City of God' 952; **cyté** 792, 939,
    1023; **cyty** 986. [OF cité]
clad *pp.* covered 22. [From OE *clāþ* 'cloth'
    n; cf. Nhb. *geclāded*]
claube. See **clym.**
clanly *adj.* splendid 2n. [OE clænlīc]
clem *v.* claim 826n. [OF *clamer*, tonic stem
    claim- (MED)]
clene *adj.* elegant 227, pure 289, 737,
    innocent 682, splendid 969; *adv.* com-
    pletely 754, 972, splendidly 767, clearly
    949. [OE clǣne]
cleute *pp.* enclosed 259. [Cf. OE beclencan]
cler *n.* transparency 1050; *adj.* clear 74,
    207, 1011, 1111, bright 227; *adv.*
    clearly 274, 882, 913; **clere** *n.* bright-
    ness 620, 735; *adj.* bright 2, sparkling
    737. [OF cler]
clerkeȝ *n. pl.* clerks 1091. [OE clerc, clēric
    & OF clerc]
cleuen *pt. pl. pass.* were cleft 66. [OE
    clēofan]
clos *n.* setting 2n. [OF clos]
clos *ppl. a.* closed 183, secure 512; **close** *v.*
    enclose 271; **closed** *pt. 3 sg.* closed 803.
    [OF clos(e, *pp.* of clore]
clot *n.* clay 22, 320, knoll 789; **clotteȝ** *pl.*
    clods 857. [OE clot]

cloystor *n.* city 969n. [OF cloistre]
clyffe *n.* cliff 159; **klyfeȝ** *pl.* cliffs 66; **klyf-
    feȝ** 74. [OE clif; cf. OI klif.]
clym *v.* rise 1072; **clambe** *pt. 2 sg.* climbed
    773; **klymbe** *v.* climb 678. [OE climban;
    pt. clamb]
clynge *pr. pl. subj.* decay 857. [OE clingan]
clypper *n. coll.* shearers 802. [From ON
    klippa *v.*]
clyuen *pass. infin.* be allotted 1196. [OE
    cleofian, clifian, clīfan]
cnawyng *ger.* understanding 859. [From OE
    cnāwan *v.*]
cnoken *pr. pl.* knock 727. [OE cnocian; cf.
    ON knoka]
cofer *n.* coffer 259. [OF cofre]
colde *adj.* cold 50, grievous 808; **calder** *adv.
    comp.* more coldly 320. [OA cald & WS
    ceald]
color *n.* complexion 22; **colour** color 753.
    [OF colour]
colour *n.* collar 215n. [OF colier]
com *pt. 3 sg.* appeared 155, came 230, 645,
    originated 749; *pr. 3 sg. subj.* enter 262;
    pr. pl. subj. may come 574; *pr. 2 sg.
    subj.* come 598; *pt. 1 sg.* came 615; *v.*
    go 676, come 701; *pt. 3 sg. subj.* came
    723, could enter 724; **come** *pt. 1 sg.*
    came 582; **commeȝ** *pr. 3 sg.* comes 848;
    cum *imper. sg.* come 763. [OE cuman]
come *n.* approach 1117. [OE *cyme*, with
    early introduction of the vowel of ME
    cŏmen v. (MED)]
comfort *n.* solace 55; **comforte** 357; **coum-
    forde** *synthetic dat.* with (your) solace
    369. [OF co(u)nfort]
comly *sb. adj.* noble lady 775; *adv.* fittingly
    259; **cumly** *adj.* comely 929. [OE
    cӯmlic, cӯmlīce, with substitution of the
    vowel of ME *bicŏmelīch, bicŏmen*]
commeȝ. See **com.**
commune *adj.* common 739. [OF
    com(m)une]
compas *dat.* in phr. *compas clym* 'rise in
    an arc' 1072. [OF compas]
compayny *n.* company 851. [OF
    compa(i)gnie]
con (1) *pr. 2 sg.* can 381, 914; *pr. 3 sg.* can
    665, 709, 729, 827, 921; **conne** *pr. 2 pl.*
    can 521. [OE cunnan]
con (2) *auxil. v.*, *pr.* & *pt.*, do 78, 509, etc.,
    did 81, 88, etc., does 165, 271, etc.;
    coneȝ do 482, 925, does 909; **can** does
    499. [Variant of ME *gan, pt.* of *ginnen*

from OE *onginnan, pt. gan*]

concieus *n.* conviction 1089. [OF conscience]

contryssyoun *n.* contrition 669. [OF contricio(u)n]

corne *n.* corn 40. [OE corn]

coronde *pt. 3 sg.* crowned 767; *pp.* 1101; **corounde** *pt. 3 sg.* 415; *pp.* 480. [OF coroner, courouner]

coroun *n.* crown 237, 255; **coroune** 205; **coroune3** *pl.* crowns 451; **croun** crown 1100; **croune** 427. [OF corone, corune]

corse *n.* body 320; **corses** *pl.* corpses 857. [OF cors]

cortayse *adj.* courteous 433. [AF co(u)rteis]

cortaysé *n.* courtesy 469, 480, 481; **Cortaysye** Courtesy 432n, 444, 456; **cortaysye** courtesy 468; **courtaysye** 457. [AF curteisie, CF courtoisie]

cortaysly *adv.* courteously 381. [AF co(u)rteise + ME -ly]

corte. See **court.**

corte3 *pr. 3 sg.* accords 754n. [From OF *acorder*]

cortel *n.* kirtle 203. [OE cyrtel]

coruen *pp.* cut 40; **keruen** *pr. pl.* cut 512. [OE ceorfan]

couenaunde *n.* payment 563; **couenaunt** compact 562. [OF covenant]

coumforde. See **comfort.**

counsayl *n.* plan 319. [OF conseil]

counterfete *v.* be like 556. [From AF, CF *contrefait*, *pp.* of *contrefaire*]

countes *n.* countess 489. [AF, CF contesse]

countré *n.* region 297. [OF contrée]

court *n.* court 445; **corte** 701. [OF court]

courtaysye. See **cortaysé.**

couþe, *pt.* of *con* (1), *3 sg.* could 95; *3 pl.* 855; **cowþe** *1 sg.* 134; **cowþe3** *2 sg.* 484. [OE cūþe]

crafte3 *n. pl.* virtues 356, techniques 890. [WS, Nhb. cræft]

craue *v.* crave 663. [OE crafian]

Crede *n.* Creed (Apostles' Creed) 485. [OE crēda]

cresse *n.* in phr. *not a cresse* 'nothing at all' 343. [OE cressa]

creste *n.* diadem 856. [OF creste]

croke3 *n. pl.* sickles 40. [ON krōkr]

croun(e). See **coroun.**

crysolyt *n.* chrysolite 1009. [OF *crisolite* & ML *crīsolitus;* ult. Gr. (*MED*)]

crysopase *n.* chrysoprase 1013. [OF *crisopase;* cf. OE (11th-cent.)

crīsoprassus; ult. Gr. (*MED*).]

crystal *adj.* crystal 74, 159. [OF cristal, OE cristalla, L crystallus]

cum. See **com.**

cumly. See **comly.**

cure *n.* treatment 1091. [OF cure]

cyté, cyty. See **cité.**

dale3 *n. pl.* valleys 121. [OE dæl, ON dal-r]

dam *n.* stream 324. [ON *damm* 'dam', Dan. *dam* 'pond'; cf. OE *fordemman* 'block'.]

dampned *pp.* damned 641. [OF dam(p)ner]

damysel *n.* damsel 489; **damyselle** 361. [AF dameisele, OF damoisele]

dar *pr. 1 sg.* dare 1089; **dorst** *pt. 1 sg.* dared 143; **dorste** 182. [OE durran]

dard. See **dare.**

dare *v.* bow in awe 839; **dard** *pt. 3 sg.* stood in awe 609n. [OE darian]

dased *pp.* dazed 1085. [ON dasa-sk, dasað-r]

date *n.* beginning 492, end 493, 528, 540, season 504, 505, hour 516, dawning 517, time 529, 541; **date3** *pl.* dates 1040. [The *pp. dāte* (from L *datum*) used as a noun (*MED*)]

daunce *pr. 2 sg. subj.* may writhe 345. [OF da(u)ncer]

daunger *n.* frustration 250. [AF daunger]

dawe3. See **day.**

day *n.* day 486, 510, etc.; **daye** 517, 541, 1210; **daye3** *pl.* days 416; *gen.* of (this) day 533, day's 554; **dawe3** *pl.* in phr. *don out of dawe3* 'was deprived of life' 282. [OE dæg]

day-glem *n.* sun 1094. [OE dæg + OE glǣm]

dayly *v.* speak courteously 313. [OF dalier]

debate *n.* debate 390. [OF debat]

debonere *adj.* gentle 162. [CF debonaire]

debonerté *n.* meekness 798. [OF debonaireté]

declyne *infin. tr. prog.* in phr. *for to declyne* 'about falling from fortune' 333; *v.* submit 509. [OF decliner]

dede *adj.* dead 31. [OE dēad]

dede *n.* action 481, 524. [WS dǣd, A dēd]

degrés *n. pl.* steps 1022. [OF degré]

del(e) *n.* See **dol.**

dele *pr. 3 sg. subj.* act 606. [OE dǣlan]

delfully *adv.* painfully 706. [From OF *del n.*] Cf. **dol.**

delit *n.* delight 1129; **delyt** 642, 1104, etc. [OF delit]

delyuered *pt. 3 sg.* delivered 652. [OF delivrer]

dem *v.* judge 312; **deme** expect 336, ordain 348, 360, declare 1183; *imper. sg.* judge 313; *fut. 3 sg.* will direct 324; *pr. 2 sg. subj.* blame 349; **demed** *pt. 1 sg.* said 361; **demeȝ** *pr. 2 sg.* censure 325, describe 337. [OE dēman]

demme *v.* be frustrated 223. [Cf. OE *fordemman*]

dene *n.* valley 295. [OE denu, dænu]

denned *pt. 3 sg.* dwelled 51. [From OE *den(n, dæn(n, n.*]

dep *adv.* deeply 406; **depe** *adj.* deep 143, wide 215. [OE dēop *adj.*, dēope *adv.*]

departed *pt. pl. pass.* were parted 378. [OF departir]

depaynt *pp.* adorned 1102. [From OF *depeint, pp.* of *depeindre*]

depe *n. coll.* depths (of stream) 109. [OE dēop]

depres *v.* exclude 778. [OF depresser]

depryue *v.* deprive 449. [OF depriver]

dere *adj.* lovely 72, 108, delightful 85, royal 97, splendid 120, 121, precious 368, 758, 795, pleasing 400, glorious 492, 1208, excellent 504, noble 920, dear 1183; *sb. adj.* noble women 777; *adv.* dearly 733, highly 880. [OE dēore]

dere *v.* thwart 1157. [OE derian]

dereȝ *n. pl.* obstacles 102. [From prec.; cf. OE daru, *dearu (*MED*).]

derely *adv.* skillfully 995. [OE dēorlīce]

derk *n.* dusk 629. [OE deorc *adj.*]

derþe *n.* glory 99. [Cf. OS diuriða, OI dȳrþ]

derworth *adj.* splendid 109. [OE dēorwyrþe]

dese *n.* dais 766. [AF deis & CF dois]

desserte *n.* merit 595. [OF deserte]

dessypeleȝ *n. pl.* disciples 715. [OE discipul, L discipulus, OF desciple]

Destyné *n.* Destiny (referring to Christ) 758. [OF destinée]

determynable *adj.* definite 594. [OF determinable]

deth *n.* death 323, 630, 656; in phr. *deth secounde* 'second death' (doom at Last Judgment) 652n; **dethe** Christ's 'death' on the cross 860n. [OE dēaþ]

deuely *adj.* dismal 51. [From OE dēaf 'deaf, barren'; cf. OI daufligr 'dismal' (*MED*).]

deuise *infin. tr. prog.* in phr. *for to deuise* 'in observing' 1129; **deuyse** *infin. tr. prog.* in phr. *for to deuyse* 'of depicting' 99; **deuysed** *pt. 3 sg.* described 1021; **deuyseȝ** *pr. 3 sg.* portrays 984, 995. [OF deviser]

deuote *adj.* devout 406. [OF devo(u)t]

deuoyde *infin.* to dispel 15. [OF desvoid(i)er]

deuyse *n.* division 139, opinion 199. [OF devise]

deuyse *v.*, **deuysed, deuyseȝ**. See **deuise**.

deuysement *n.* description 1019. [OF devisement]

dewyne *pr. 1 sg.* lament 11; **dowyne** *pr. 1 sg. subj.* must languish 326. [OE dwīnan]

did. See **do** *v.*

do *n.* doe 345. [OE dā]

do *pr. 1 sg.* place 366; *v.* extend 424, do 496; *infin.* to do 520; *infin. tr. prog.* in phr. *to do* 'in doing' 566; *imper. pl.* in phr. *do way* 'step aside' 718; **did** *pt. 3 sg.* made 102, committed 1138; **don** *pp.* forced 250, affected 930, made 942; *pt. 3 sg. pass.* was deprived 282; *pr. pl.* exert 511; **done** *pp.* engraved 1042; **dotȝ** *pr. auxil.* does 17, 293, 630; *pr. 3 sg.* causes 330, takes 823; *pr. 2 sg.* do 338, consider 556; *imper. pl.* do 521, 536; **dyd** *pt. 3 sg.* condemned 306; **dyden** *pt. pl.* did 633; **dyt** *pt. 3 sg. emph.* did do 681. [OE dōn]

doc *n.* duke 211. [OF duc]

doel. See **dol**.

doel-doungoun *n.* miserable prison 1187. [OF doel+OF donjon]

doel-dystresse *n.* distress of sorrow 337. [OF doel+OF destrece, destresce]

dol *n.* sorrow 326; *del* sadness 250; **dele** grief 51; **doel** distress 336, 642, mourning 339. [OF dol, del, doel] Cf. **delfully.**

dole *n.* part 136. [OE dāl]

dom *n.* mind 157, 223, sentence 667; **dome** judgment 580, 699. [OE dōm]

don(e). See **do** *v.*

dorst(e). See **dar**.

dotȝ. See **do** *v.*

double *adj.* in phr. *double perle* 'paired pearls' 202. [OF double]

doun *n. coll.* hills 121; **downeȝ** *gen.* hills' 73; *pl.* hills 85. [OE dūn]

doun *adv.* down 30, 41, etc.; *prep.* down 196, 230. [OE dūne & ādūn(e]

dousour *n.* sweetness 429. [OF dousor]

doute *n.* doubt 928. [OF doute]

douth *n.* group 839. [OE duguþ]

downeȝ. See **doun** *n.*

dowyne. See **dewyne**.

draȝ *imper. sg.* bring 699; **drawen** *pr. p.* drawing 1193; **droȝ** *pt. pl.* went 1116.

[OE dragan; cf. OI draga]

drawen. See **draʒ.**

dred *pt. 1 sg.* feared 186. [From late OE *ādrǣdan*; cf. earlier *ondrǣdan*.]

drede *n.* uneasiness 181, doubt 1047. [From prec.]

drem *n.* dream 790, 1170. [Blend of OE *drēam* 'joy' & ON *draumr* 'dream'; cf. OS *drōm* 'jubilation, dream' *(MED)*.]

dresse *v.* ordain 495; **drest** *pp.* realized 860. [OF drecier]

dreue *v.* pass 323; **dreued** *pt. 1 sg.* strode 980. [OE drǣfan]

drof. See **dryf.**

droʒ. See **draʒ.**

drounde *pt. 3 sg.* drowned 656. [Cf. OI drukna, OE druncnian]

drwry *adj.* mournful 323. [OE drēorig]

dryf *v.* drive 777; **dryue** *pr. 3 sg. subj.* sinks 1094; **dryuen** *pp.* led 1194; **drof** *pt. 3 sg.* drove 30, entered 1153. [OE drīfan]

dryʒe *adj.* burdensome 823. [ON drjūg-r; cf. OE drēogan]

dryʒly *adv.* incessantly 125, 233. [From prec.]

Dryʒtyn *n.* God 324, 349. [OE Dryhten]

dryue(n). See **dryf.**

dubbed *pp.* adorned 73, 202; **dubbet** arrayed 97. [OE dubbian, OF aduber]

dubbement *n. coll.* adornments 121; **dubbemente** 109. [From OF adubement]

due *adj.* due 894. [OF dĕu, du]

dunne *adj.* dark 30. [OE dun]

durande *pr. p. as adj.* enduring 336. [OF durer]

dyche *n.* drain (watercourse) 607. [OE dīc]

dyd(en). See **do** *v.*

dyʒe *v.* die 306, 642; **dyʒed** *pt. 3 sg.* died 828; **dyed** 705. [ON deyja]

dyʒt *v.* determine 360; *pp.* established 920, embellished 987; **dyʒte** *pp.* set 202. [OE dihtan]

dylle *adj..* slow 680. [OE *dyl(le; cf. OE dol]

dym *adj.* dark 1076. [OE dim]

dyne *n. coll.* cries 339. [OE dyne]

dyscreuen *pass. infin.* be seen 68. [OF descrivre]

dyspleseʒ *imper. sg. pass.* be displeased 422; *pr. 3 sg.* displeases 455. [OF desplaisir]

dyssente *pr. pl.* descend 627. [OF descendre]

dysstresse *n.* in phr. *for no dysstresse* 'under any circumstance' 898; **dystresse** distress 280. [OF destresse]

dystryed *pt. pl.* dispelled 124. [OF destruire]

dyt. See **do** *v.*

efte *adv.* again 328, afterwards 332. [OE eft]

elleʒ *adv.* otherwise 32, instead 130, else 491, 567, 724. [[OE elles]

emerad *n.* emerald 118; **emerade** 1005. [OF emeraude]

Emperise *n.* Empress (Blessed Virgin) 441. [OF emper(e)ris, emperesse]

empyre *n.* empire 454. [OF empire]

enchace *v.* impel 173. [OF enchacier]

enclose *v.* reside 909. [OF *enclos, pp.* of *enclore*]

enclyin *adj.* humble 1206. [OF enclin]

enclyne *v.* yield 630; **enclynande** *pr. p.* bowing 236. [OF encliner]

encres *v.* increase 959. [AF *encress-*, stem of *encreistre*]

encroched *pt. 3 sg.* aroused 1117. [Cf. OF *acrochier* 'take hold, seize'.]

endeleʒ *adv.* perfectly 738. [OE endelēas]

endent *pp.* adorned 1012; **endente** 629. [OF endenter]

endorde *ppl. a. used as n.* golden maiden 368n. [OF endorer]

endure *v.* suffice 225; **endured** *pp.* endured 476; **endeure** *v.* endure 1082. [OF endurer]

endyte *pr. pl.* chant 1126. [AF enditer]

ene *adv.* in phr. *at ene* 'simultaneously' 291, immediately 953. [OE ǣne]

enlé *adj.* single 849. [OE ǣnlīc]

enleuenþe *n.* eleventh 1014. [OE endlefta]

enpresse *n.* glory 1097n. [OF enprise]

ensens *n.* incense 1122. [OF encens]

entent *n.* intent 1191. [OF entente]

enter *v.* enter 966; **entred** *pt. 1 sg.* entered 38; **entreʒ** *pr. 3 sg.* enters 1067. [OF entrer]

enurned *pp.* embellished 1027. [Cf. OF ao(u)rner]

er *adv.* before 188, 372, first 319; *prep.* before 517; *conj.* before 224, 324, 1030, 1140; **er euer** before 328; **er þenne** before 631, 1094; **ere** *adv.* before 164. [OE ǣr]

erber *n.* garden 38, 1171; **erbere** 9. [OF h)erbier]

erde *n.* land 248. [eard]

ere *n.* ear 1153. [OE ēare]

ere *adv.* See **er.**

226

erle *n.* earl 211. [OE eorl]

erly *adv.* early 506; *erly and late* 'all the time' 392. [OE ǣrlīce]

ernays *n.* pledge 307n. [OF erres]

errour *n. dat.* with ignorance 422. [OF errour]

erþe *n.* earth 840; vrþe 442, 893, 1125. [OE eorþe]

erytage. See herytage.

eschaped *pt. 3 sg. subj.* might escape 187. [CF eschaper]

eþe *adj.* easy 1202. [OE ēaþe, ēþe]

euel *adv.* ill 310, unfavorably 930. [OE yfele]

euen *adv.* exactly 740. [OE efen]

euen, *infin., to euen* 'compete' 1073n. [OE efnan]

euensonge *n.* evensong (about 5 P.M.) 529. [OE ǣfen-sang]

euentyde *n.* eventide (evening) 582. [OE ǣfen-tīd]

euer *adv.* always 153, 416, etc., ever 180, 200, etc., continually 349; euer . . . a *correl. adv.* always 144n. [OE ǣfre]

euermore *adv.* forever 591, always 666, 1066. [OE ǣfre mā]

excused *pp.* excused 281. [OF excuser]

expoun *pr. 1 sg.* describe 37. [AF espoundre]

expresse *adv.* directly 910. [L expressē; cf. OF expres *adj.*]

fable *n.* fable 592. [OF fable]

face *n.* face 67, 169, 434, 675, 809. [OF face]

Fader *n.* Father (the Lord Jesus) 736; Fa- dereʒ *gen.* Father's (God the Father) 872. [OE fæder]

faʒt *pt. pl.* conflicted 54. [OE feohtan]

faude. See fynde.

farande. See fare *v.*

fare *n. coll.* ways 832. [OE faru & fær]

fare *v.* wander 147; *pr. pl.* exist 467; fares *pr. 3 sg.* directs 129; farande *pr. p. used as adj.* splendid 865. [OE *faran*; cf. ON *farandi* 'fitting'.]

Fasor *n.* Creator 431. [OF faiseor]

fasoun *n.* appearance 983, fashion 1101. [OF faceon, fasson]

faste *adv.* severely 54, eagerly 150. [OE fæste]

fasure *n.* appearance 1084. [OF feisure]

fateʒ *pr. 3 sg.* fades 1038. [OF fader]

faunt *n.* child 161. [OF enfant]

fauor *n.* favor 968; fauour virtue 428. [OF favor, favour]

fax *n.* hair 213. [OE fæx, feax]

fay, *n., par ma fay* 'by my faith' 489; faye, *in faye* 'in truth' 263. [AF fei, fai]

fayle, *v., of graunt . . . fayle* 'fail to obtain consent' 317; fayled *pt. 3 sg.* faded 270; fayly *v.* fail to produce 34. [OF faillir]

fayn *adj.* happy 393, 450.[OE fægen]

fayr *adj.* pleasant 46, fair 147, 810, proper 490; fayre fair 169, 747, lovely 177, 946, splendid 1178; feier *comp.* fairer 103. [OE fæger, *comp.* fægerra]

fayr *adv.* courteously 714, fayre sweetly 88, skillfully 884, equally 1024. [OE fægre]

fech *v.* bring 1158; feche *pr. 3 sg. subj.* gathers 847. [OE *feccean,* var. of *fetian*]

fede *adj.* wasted 29n. [OF fade]

feier. See fayr *adj.*

fel *pt. 1 sg.* dropped down 1174; felle *pt. 1 sg.* fell 57; *pt. pl.* fell 1120. [OE feallan, *pt.* fēol]

felde *pt. 1 sg.* experienced 1087. [OE ge)fēlan, *pt.* ge)fēlde]

fele *n.* many 21, 439, 716; *adj.* 874, 927, 1114. [OE fela]

felle *n.* bitterness 655n. [OF fiel, L fel]

felle *adj.* austere 367. [OF fel]

felonye *n.* felony 800. [OF felonie]

Fenyx, *n., Fenyx of Arraby* 'Phoenix of Araby' 430. [OE, OF, & ML Fenix]

fer *adv.* far 334, 1076. [OE feor(r)]

fere *n. coll.* flocks 89; *n.* unison 884, company 1105. [OE gefēr 'company']

fereʒ *n. pl.* companions 1150. [OE gefēra]

fereʒ *pr. 3 sg.* carries 98; feryed *pp.* led 946. [OE ferian, *pp.* ferode]

ferly *adj.* marvelous 1084; *used as n.* wonder 1086. [OE fǣrlic, from fǣr 'danger, fear' *(MED)*]

feryed. See fereʒ *v.*

feste, *n., schal ma feste* 'shall rejoice' 283. [OF *feste* & L *festum* 'feast']

fete. See fote.

fewe *pron. pl.* few 572. [OE fēawe]

flaʒt *n.* turf 57. [OE **flæht, *fleaht,* akin to *flēan* 'flay'; cf. OScot. *flauchter spade* 'a turf spade' *(MED)*.]

flake *n.* blemish 947. [Cf. OE *flac-or* 'flying' & OI *flakna, flagna* 'flake, chip off' *(MED)*.]

flambe *v.* sparkle 769; flaumbande *pr. p.* glowing 90. [AF flaum(b)er, CF flam(b)er]

227

flauorez *n. pl.* fragrances 87. [OF flaur]
flayn. See flyze.
fle *v.* run 294. [OE flēon]
fleze *pt. 3 sg.* flew 431; flowen *pt. pl.* flew 89. [OE flēogan, *pt.* flugon]
fleme *pr. 3 sg. subj.* may banish 334; *pp., out fleme* 'driven out' 1177. [A ge)flēman, WS ge)flīeman]
flesch *n.* body 306. [OE flæsc]
fleschly *adj.* human 1082. [OE flæsclic]
flet *n.* source 1058. [OE flēot]
fleten *pt. pl.* floated 21. [OE flēotan] Cf. flot *v.*
flode *n.* water 736, stream 1058; flodez, *pl. gen.*, *flodez fele laden* 'voice of many waters' 874. [OE flōd]
flok *n.* flock 947. [OE floc(c)]
flonc *pt. 1 sg. subj.* would rush 1165. [Cf. OI flengja]
flor. See Flour.
flor-de-lys. See flour-de-lys.
flot *n. dat.* in company 786; flote *n.* company 946. [OF flote]
flot *pt. 3 sg.* wafted 46. [OE flotian, *pt.* flot] Cf. fleten.
floty *adj.* watery 127n. [Stem of OE *flotian*+adjectival *-ig*]
Flour *n.* Flower (referring to Jesus) 426; flor flower 29, flower (referring to pearl-maiden 962; flowrez *pl.* flowers 208. [OF flour, flor]
flour-de-lys *n.* fleur-de-lis 753; flor-de-lys 195. [AF flour de lis]
floury *adj.* blossoming 57. [From OF *flour*]
flowen. See fleze.
flowred *pt. 3 sg.* flowered 270. [OF florir]
flowrez. See Flour.
flurted *ppl. a.* ornamented (in the form of flowers) 208. [Cf. OF fleuretté *adj.*]
flyze *pass. infin.* to be whipped 813; flayn *pp.* bruised 809. [OE flēan]
flyte, *infin. tr. prog., to flyte* 'disputing' 353. [OE flītan]
fode *n.* food 88. [OE fōda]
folde *n.* land 334, 736. [OE folde]
folde *pp. tr. prog.* covering 434n; *pass. infin.* (to be) laid low 813. [OE fealdan]
folewande. See folzed.
folzed *pt. 1 sg.* followed 127; *3 sg.* resulted from 654; folewande *pr. p.* following 1040. [OE folgian]
fon. See fyne *v.*
fonde *v.* endeavor 150, seek 939. [OE fandian]

fonde, line 283. See fynde.
fonge *v.* obtain 479; *pt. pl.* followed 884; fongez *pr. pl.* receive 439. [OE fōn, *pt.* feng]
fonte. See fynde.
for *prep.* with 50, 858, 1139, from 154, for 211, 244, etc., because of 352, 429, etc., as 830, through 844, 1206, in spite of 890, under 898, due to 1086, 1152; *conj.* for 31, 71, etc., because 568, as 1032; fore *prep.* for 734; for to *prep.* of 99, about 333, to 403, 1118, in order to 613, in 1129. [OE for]
forbede *pr. 3 sg. subj.* forbid 379. [OE forbēodan]
forbrent *pp.* burned 1139. [OE forbeornan, ON brenna]
fordidden *pt. pl.* abolished 124. [OE fordōn, *pt.* fordyde]
fordolked *ppl. a.* grief-stricken 11. [Cf. late OE *dolg, dolh* 'wound' (*MED*).]
fore. See for.
foreste *n.* forest 67. [OF forest]
foreuer *adv.* forever 261. [OE for+ǣfre]
forfete *v.* forfeit 639; forfeted *pt. 3 sg. emph.* did forfeit 619. [OF *forfet, pp.* of *forfaire*]
forgarte *pp.* condemned 321. [Cf. OI *fyrirgøra* 'forfeit' & OI *göra*]
forgo *v.* surrender 328; forgos *pr. pl.* forsake 340. [OE forgān]
forzete *infin.* forget 86. [A forge(o)tan, WS forgitan]
forhedez *n. pl.* foreheads 871. [OE for-hēafod]
forlete *pa. perf. 1 sg.* had lost 327. [OE forlǣtan, forlētan]
forlonge *n. pl. gen.* furlongs' 1030. [OE furlang]
forloyne *pr. 1 sg. subj.* go astray 368. [OF forloignier]
forme *n.* form 1209. [OF fourme]
formed *pt. 3 sg.* formed 747. [OF fourmer]
forme-fader *n.* first father (Adam) 639. [OE forma+fæder]
forpayned *ppl. a.* tormented 246. [OE for+OF peiner]
forsake *infin.* to abandon 743. [OE forsacan]
forser *n.* coffer 263. [OF forcer]
forsoþe *adv.* truly 21, indeed 292. [OE forsōþ]
forth *adv.* forth 98, 510, 1116, onward 101, 980. [OE forþ]
fortune *n.* fortune 129, 306; fortwne 98.

228

[OF fortune]
forty *adj* forty 786, 870. [OE fēowertig]
forþe *n.* ford 150. [OE ford]
forþy *adv.* consequently 137, therefore 234, 701, 845. [OE for þy]
fote *n.* foot (lowest part of something) 161, foot (of measurement 350, 970; **fete** *pl.* feet 1120. [OE fōt, *pl.* fēt]
founce *n.* bottom 113. [AF founz, CF fonz]
foundementeȝ. See **fundament.**
founden. See *fynde.*
fowleȝ *n. pl.* fowls 89. [OE fugol]
fowre *adj.* four 870, 886. [OE fēower]
foysoun *n. used attrib.* blessed 1058. [OF foison, fuison]
fraunchyse *n.* privilege 609n. [OF fra(u)nchise]
frayneȝ *pr. 3 sg.* desires 129. [OE fregnan, gefrægnan; OI fregna]
frayste *pt. 1 sg.* scrutinized 169. [Cf. OI freista]
fre *adj.* splendid 299, liberal 481, noble 796. [OE frēo]
frech. See **fresch.**
freles *adj.* without fault 431n. [Cf. OF *frail, frele* (from L *fragilis*) & ON *fryjulaus*]
frely *sb. adj.* lovely maiden 1155. [OE frēolic]
frende *n.* friend 558, Friend (Christ) 1204. [OE frēond]
fresch *sb. adj. coll.* young bodies 958n; **frech** *sb. adj.* delightful damsel, fair maiden 195; *adj.* fresh 87; **freuch** *adj.* brilliant 1086n. [OE fersc, OF freis *(fem.* fresche)]
fro *prep.* from 10, 13, etc., after 803; *fro me warde* 'opposite me' 981; *adv.* fro 347; *conj.* since 251, after 375; **fro þat** *conj.* after 958. [ON frā]
frount *n.* face 177. [OF front]
frym *adv.* abundantly 1079. [Cf. OE *freme* 'excellent'.]
fryt *n. coll.* fruits 894; **fryte** *n.* fruit 29; **fryteȝ** *pl.* fruits 87, 1078. [OF fruit]
fryth *n.* forest 89, 98, 103. [Cf. OS *frīd-hof*, OHG *frīt-hof* 'enclosure' (*MED*).]
ful *adv.* very 28, 42, etc., full 50, 454, 1076, fully 159, 183, etc., quite 179, 879, indeed 307, 880, extremely 393, completely 1023; *adj.* full 1098. [OE full]
fundament *n.* foundation 1010; **foundementeȝ** *pl.* foundations 993. [OF fo(u)ndement]

furþe *n.* fourth 1005. [OE fēorþa]
fyf *n.* five 849; **fyue** 451. [OE fīf(e]
fyfþe *adj.* fifth 1006. [OE fīfta]
fygure *n.* form 170, figure 747, vision 1086. [OF figure]
fyin. See **fyn.**
fyldor *n.* gold filament 106. [OF fil d'or]
fylþe *n.* filth 1060. [OE fȳlþ]
fyn *adj.* fine 106, excellent 170; **fyin** excellent 1204. [OF fin]
fynde *v.* find 150; **fyndeȝ** *pr. 3 sg.* finds 508, 514; **fande** pt. 1 sg. found 871; **fonde** *pp.* found 283; **fonte** *pp.* perceived 170, found 327; **founden** *pp.* found 1203. [OE findan]
fyne *adv.* completely 635n. [OF fin]
fyne *pr. 1 sg.* die 328; *imper. sg.* stop 353; **fon** *pt. 3 sg.* ceased 1030. [OF finer]
fynger *n.* finger 466. [OE finger]
fyrre, *comp.* of **fer,** *adj.* more distant 148; *adv.* farther 103, 152, further 127, 347, furthermore 544, more 563. [OE firra]
fyrst *adj.* first 486, 999, 1000; *n.* first 549, 570, 571, first group 635n; *adv.* first 316, 583, 1042; **fyrste** *n.* first 548; *adv.* first 638. [OE fyrst]
fyrte *pp. tr. prog.* appalling 54n. [OE ge)fǣren]
fyue. See **fyf.**

galle (1) *n.* rancor 915; **gawle** envy 463. [OE; cf. A *galla,* WS *gealla* 'bile, gall' (*MED*).]
galle (2) *n.* blemish 189, scum 1060. [OE *gealla, galla* 'a galled place on the skin']
gardyn *n.* garden 260. [OF gardin]
gareȝ *pr. 3 sg. subj.* makes 331; **gart** *pt. 3 sg.* caused 1151; **garten** *pt. pl.* made 86. [ON göra]
garlande *n.* garland 1186n. [OF garlande]
gart, garten. See **gareȝ.**
gate *n.* kind 395, way 526, 619; **gateȝ** *pl.* roads 1106. [ON gata]
gaue. See **gyue.**
gawle. See **galle** (1).
gay *sb. adj.* bright maiden 189; *adj.* noble 1124, 1186; **gaye** *sb. adj.* fair maiden 433; *adj.* magnificent 7, bright 260. [OF gai]
gayn *prep.* beyond 138. [ON gegn]
gayneȝ *pr. 3 sg.* gains 343. [ON gegna]
gef. See **gyue.**
gele *v.* linger 931. [OE gǣlan]
gemme *n.* gem 118, 219, etc.; **gemmeȝ** *pl.*

229

gems 7, 253, stones 991. [OF gemme]

generacyoun *n.* generation 827. [OF generacio(u)n]

gent *adj.* splendid 1014, noble 1134; **gente** excellent 118, splendid 253, noble 265. [OF gent]

gentyl *sb. adj.* noble maiden 602; *adj.* noble 264, 605, 883, gentle 278, 895, precious 991; **gentyle** noble 632; **gentyleste** *sup.* gentlest 1015. [OF gentil]

gesse *v.* devise 499. [Cf. MDu. *gessen*, Swed. *gissa*, & Norw. dial. *gissa*]

geste *n.* child 277n. [ON gestr]

gete *v.* obtain 95; **ʒete** *infin.* to do 558n. [ON geta, WS gietan]

geuen. See **gyue.**

gilofre *n.* gillyflower 43. [OF gilofre]

glace *v.* glide 171. [OF glacier]

gladande. See **gladeʒ**

glade *adj.* rich 136, cheerful 1144; **gladder** *comp.* happier 231; **gladdest** *sup.* happiest 1109. [OE glæd]

gladeʒ *pr. 3 sg.* comforts 861; **gladande** *pr. p.* gladdening 171. [OE gladian]

gladneʒ *n. coll.* delights 136. [OE glædnes]

glas *n.* glass 114, 990, 1018; **glasse** 1025, 1106. [OE glæs]

glauereʒ *pr. pl.* deceive 688. [Prob. Celtic; cf. Gaelic *glafaire* & Welsh *glafru*.]

glayre *n.* glair 1026n. [OF glaire]

glayue *n.* spear 654. [OF glaive]

gle *n.* glee 95, bliss 1123. [OE glēo]

glem *n.* light 79; **glymme** spiritual light 1088n. [OE glæm]

glemande *pr. p.* gleaming 70, 990. [From prec.]

glene *v.* obtain 955. [OF glener]

glent *pt. 3 sg.* shone 70, glistened 1026; *pt. pl.* gleamed 1106; **glente** *pt. 3 sg.* deviated 671, glistened 1001. [Cf. Dan. *glente*, Norw. dial. *glanta*, & Swed. dial. *glänta* 'gleam, slide'.]

glente *n. coll.* flashes 114; **glenteʒ** *n. pl.* glances 1144. [From prec.]

glet *n.* slime 1060. [OF glete, glette]

glod. See **glydeʒ.**

glodeʒ *n. pl.* bright openings 79n. [? OE *glǣd, *glād 'bright place' (*MED*).]

glory *n.* glory 70, 171, 959, 1123, splendor 934. [OF glorie]

gloryous *adj.* glorious 799, 915, 1144. [OF glorïos]

glowed *pt. pl.* glowed 114. [OE glōwan]

glydeʒ *pr. 3 sg.* strikes 79; **glod** *pt. pl.*

proceeded 1105. [OE glīdan]

glyʒt *pt. pl.* glinted 114. [? ON gljā]

glymme. See **glem.**

glysnande *pr. p.* glistening 165; *used as adv.* glisteningly 1018. [OE glisnian]

go *imper. sg.* go 559; *pr. 3 sg. subj.* would go 530; **gon** *pp.* proceeded 63, gone 376; *v.* go 820; **gos** *imper. pl.* go 521; **gotʒ** *pr. 3 sg.* goes 365; *pr. pl.* go 510; *imper. pl.* go 535. [OE gān] Cf. **ʒede.**

God *n.* God 314, 342, etc.; **Goddeʒ** *gen.* God's 591, 1193; **Godeʒ** *gen.* God's 63, 601, 822, 885, 943; **Godeʒ self** 'God himself' 1054. [OE God]

god *n.* wealth 734; **goud** goodness 33, wealth 731; **goude** good thing 33. [OE gōd *n.*]

god *adj.* good 310, 1202; **goude** generous 568, good 818. [OE gōd *adj.*]

Godhede *n.* Godhead (divinity) 413. [OE God+hēafod; cf. OE godhād 'divine nature' (*MED*).]

godnesse *n.* goodness 493. [OE gōdnes]

golde *n.* gold 2, 165, etc. [OE gold]

golden *adj.* golden 1106. [From prec.; cf. OE *gylden, adj.*]

golf *n.* whirlpool 608n. [OF golf]

gome *n.* man 231, 697. [OE guma]

gon. See **go.**

gos. See **go.**

Gospel *n.* Gospel 498. [OE Godspel]

goste *n.* soul 63, 86. [OE gāst, gǣst]

gostly *adj.* spiritual 185, 790. [OE gāstlic]

gote *n.* stream 934; **goteʒ** *pl.* currents 608n. [OE *gota, akin to gēotan 'pour, flow'; cf. MDu. gōte & OF esgot (*MED*).]

gotʒ. See **go.**

goud(e). See **god** *n.* wealth.

goude. See **god** *adj.*

grace *n.* grace 63, 436, etc., good fortune 194, Grace (referring to Christ) 425. [OF grace]

gracios *adj.* beautiful 189; *adv.* beautifully 260; **gracos** gracious 95n; **gracous** delightful 934n. [OF gracïos]

grauayl *n. coll.* pebbles 81. [OF gravel(e)

graunt *n.* consent 317. [OF *grant*, var. of *crëant*.]

graye *adj.* gray 254n. [WS grǣg, A grēg]

grayneʒ *n. pl.* grains 31. [OF grain]

graybely *adv.* fittingly 499. [ON greiðliga]

greffe *n.* grief 86. [AF gref, CF grief]

greme *n.* anger 465. [ON gremi]

grene *adj.* green 38, 1005; *adv.* greenly

1001. [OE grēne]

gresse *n.* grass 10, 245, plant 31. [OE græs]

gret *adj.* severe 259, great 330, 511, etc., excellent 616, large 851, huge 926; *adv.* bountifully 648; **grete** *adj.* huge 90, great 237, 280, 470, proud 637. [OE grēat]

grete *infin.* lament 331. [OE grētan]

greue, *n.*, Paradys greue 'grove of Paradise' (Eden) 321. [OE græfa]

greue *pr. 3 sg. subj. emph.* does offend 471. [OF grever]

grewe. See grow.

gromylyoun *n.* gromwell 43n. [From OF gromil; cf. F (16th cent.) grumillon]

grouelyng *adv.* prostrate 1120. [From ON ā grūfu + ME adverbial -ling]

grounde, line 654. See grynde.

grounde *n.* earth 10, 1173, ground 81, 434, basis 372, 384, 396, 408, 420. [OE grund]

grow *v.* grow 31; **grewe** *pt. 3 sg.* came 425. [OE grōwan, *pt. sg.* grēow]

grym *adj.* dull 1070. [OE grim]

grymly *adv.* keenly (referring to sharpened spear) 654. [OE grimlīce]

grynde *v.* mingle 81n; **grounde** *pp.* sharpened 654. [OE grindan, *pp.* grunden]

gryste *n.* resentment 465. [From OE gristan]

gulte *n.* guilt 942; **gyltez** *gen.* of sin 655n. [OE gylt]

gyf. See gyue.

gyfte *n.* right to give 565; **gyftez** *pl.* gifts 607. [ON gift, OE gift]

gyle *n.* deceit 671, guile 688. [OF guile]

gyltez. See gulte.

gyltlez *adj. as n. coll.* guiltless (persons) 668; *adj as n.* guiltless One (Christ) 799. [OE gyltleas]

gyltyf *adj. as n. coll.* guilty (persons) 669. [OE gyltig]

gyng *n.* assemblage 455. [OE genge; cf. OI gengi]

gyngure *n.* ginger 43. [OF gingivre]

gyrle *n.* girl 205. [? OE *gyrela, akin to OE gierela 'a garment' (MED)]

gyse *n.* dress 1099. [OF guise]

gyternere *n.* gittern-player 91. [From OF guiterne *n.*; cf. OF guiternëor]

gyue *pr. 3 sg. subj.* may permit 707; **gaue** *pt. 3 sg.* imposed 667; **gef** *pt. 3 sg.* struck 174, directed 270, gave 734, 765; *pr. 3 sg. subj.* may allow 1211n; **geuen** *pp.* given 1190; **gyf** *imper. sg.* give

543, 546. [ON gefa]

ȝare *adv.* clearly 834. [OE gearwe]

ȝate *n.* gate 728, 1037; **ȝatez** *pl.* gates 1034, 1065. [WS geat; Nhb. gæt, geat]

ȝe, *pron. nom. pl.* form of þou, you 290 (twice), 515, 516, etc.; used as *sg.* in addressing one person, you 257, 307, 308, etc. [OE ȝē] Cf. þou. (See p. 217 on usage of ȝe and þou.)

ȝede, *pt.* of go, *pt. 3 sg.* went 526, passed 1049; *pt. pl.* flowed 713; **yot** *pt. 3 sg.* slipped 10n. [OE ēode] Cf. go.

ȝer *n. coll.* years 483; *sg.* year 1079; **ȝere** year 503, 505; *coll.* years 588n. [OE gēar]

ȝerned *pp.* desired 1190. [OE geornan]

ȝet *adv.* nevertheless 19, also 46, 205, 1009, 1021, yet, 145, 200, etc., moreover 215, even 825, still 1033; **ȝete** moreover 1061. [OE gīet]

ȝete, line 558. See gete.

ȝif *conj.* if 45, 662; **ȝyf** 482; **if** 147, 264, etc. [OE gif]

ȝon *adj.* that 693. [OE geon]

ȝong *adj.* young 412; **ȝonge** 474, 535. [OE geong]

ȝore *adv.* formerly 586. [OE gēara]

ȝorefader *n.* old father (Adam) 322. [OE gēara + fæder]

ȝyf. See ȝif.

ȝys *adv.* yes 635n. [OE gēse]

had, *pt.* & *pp* of haue, *pt.* had 170, 1034, etc.; *pp.* taken 1140; **hade** *pt.* had 134, 164, etc.; *pt. subj.* took 1091, would have 1194. [OE hæfde *pt.*, hæfd *pp.*]

haf. See haue.

hafyng *ger.* having 450. [From ME haue; cf. OE hæfen 'having, owning'.]

halde *pr. 1 sg.* consider 301; *v.* hold 490; **haldez** *pr. 3 sg.* holds 454; **halden** *pp.* maintained 1191; **helde** *pt. 3 sg.* occupied 1002, contained 1029. [OE haldan]

halez *pr. 3 sg.* flows 125. [OF haler]

half *n.* side 230. [A half, WS healf]

half *adv.* half 72. [A half, WS healf]

halle *n.* hall 184. [A hal(l, WS heal(l]

halte *infin.* to waver 1158n. [A haltian, WS healtian]

han. See haue.

happe *n.* joy 16, happiness 1195; *coll.* blessings 713. [ON happ]

231

harde adv. firmly 606. [OE hearde]

hardyly adv. certainly 3, 695. [OF hardi+ME -ly]

harme n. harm 681; **harmeʒ** pl. dat. by misfortunes 388. [OE hearm]

harmleʒ adj. innocent 676, 725. [From prec.]

harpe n. coll. harps 881. [OE hearpe]

harpen pr. pl. harp (play harps) 881. [OE hearpian]

harporeʒ n. pl. harpers 881. [OE hearpere]

hate adj. cruel 388. [OE hāt]

hate n. hate 463. [Prob. from OE v. hatian; cf. OI hatr.]

hated pp. despised 402. [OE hatian]

hatʒ. See **haue.**

haþel n. person 676. [Blend of OE hæleþ & æþel]

haue v. have 132, 661, 704; infin. to have 928; pr. 1 sg. have 967; **hauen** pr. pl. possess 859; **haf** pr. 1 sg. have 14, 242, etc.; pr. 3 sg. subj. have 194; pr. 2 sg. have 257 (after ʒe, used as sg.); pr. pl. have 519, 553, etc.; infin. to have 1139; **han** pr. 2 sg. have 373 (after ʒe, used as sg.); pr. pl. have 554; pr. 3 sg. has 776 (after mony a comly, a sg. subject); **hatʒ** pr. 3 sg. has 249, 274, etc.; pr. 2 sg. have 273, 291, etc.; pr. 3 sg. possesses 770. [OE ge)habban]

hawk n. hawk 184. [WS hafoc; Merc. heafuc]

haylsed pt. 3 sg. hailed 238. [ON heilsa]

he pron. nom. pl. they 332n. [OE hēo, hīe, hī]

he pron. masc. nom. sg. he 302, 348, etc.; (used as neut. subject) it 1001, 1140; (pleonastic) 414, 597, 619, 686, 710, 742, 748; **ho** he 479n. [OE hē]

hed n. head 209; **hede** 1172; **heued** 459, 465, 974. [OE heāfod]

hede v. see 1051. [OE hēdan]

heʒt. See **hyʒt** n.

helde adv. certainly 1193. [ON heldr]

helde v. See **halde.**

hele n. well-being 16; coll. healings 713. [OE hǣlu, hǣl]

helle n. hell 442, 651, 840, 1125; gen. hell's 643. [OE hel, helle]

hem 'to him' 1196n. See **hym** sg.

hem pron. pl. dat. & acc. them 69, 70, etc.; refl. themselves 551; dat. to them 717, for them 728; (used as subject) they 1044; **hym** acc. them 635n. [OE heom, him, hym]

hemme n. hem 217, fringe 1001. [OE hem]

hen. See **hyne.**

hende adj. reserved 184; **hynde** sb. adj. gracious damsel 909. [OE gehende]

hente pr. 1 sg. subj. pass. am caught 388; v. obtain 669; infin. to seize 1195. [OE hentan]

her (1), pron. sg., poss., dat., & acc., her 4, 6, etc.; **hir** her 22, 188, etc.; **hyr** her 8, 9, 163, 167, etc. [OE hire]

her (2), pron. pl., poss., their 92, 93, etc. [OE heora]

her (3) adv. here 263, 519; **here** here 262, 298, etc.; (used as n. dat.) for here 439. [OE hēr]

herde. See next entry.

here infin. to hear 96; **herde** pt. 1 sg. heard 873, 879, 1132. [A hēran, WS hīeran]

hereinne adv. herein 261, 577. [OE hēr+inne]

herneʒ n. pl. brains 58. [ON hjarni]

hert n. heart 17, 51, etc., mind 179; **herte** heart 128, 364, imagination 135, mind 176. [OE heorte]

herytage n. heritage 417n; **erytage** 443. [OF h)eritage]

heste n. bidding 633. [OE hǣs+t]

hete n. heat 554, 643. [OE hǣtu, hǣte]

hete pr. 1 sg. assure 402; **hyʒt** pp. called 950; pt. 3 sg. pass. was called 999; **hyʒte** pt. 3 sg. promised 305. [OE hātan, pt. hēht]

heterly adv. intensely 402. [? Blend of OE hetelīce & ON hatr-liga (MED)]

heþen adv. from here 231. [ON hēðan]

heue v. present (words) 314; pr. 2 sg. raise 473; **heuen** infin. increase 16. [OE hebban]

heued. See **hed.**

heuen infin. See **heue.**

heuen n. heaven 473, 490, 500, 873, 1126; coll. heavens 988; **heueneʒ** pl. heavens 423; gen. heaven's 620; **heuenesse** heaven's 735; **heuenʒ** pl. heavens 441. [OE heofon, heofen]

heuenryche n. kingdom of heaven 719. [OE heofon-rīce]

heuy adj. heavy (yearning) 1180. [OE hefig]

hider adv. here 517; **hyder** 249, 763. [OE hider]

hiʒe. See **hyʒ.**

hil n. hill 976; **huyle** mound 41n; **hyl** hill 789, 979; **hylle** hill 678, mound 1172;

hyul mound 1205. [OE hyl]
hir. See **her** (1).
his *pron. poss.* his 285, etc.; **hys** 307, etc.; **hysse** *pred. nom.* his 418. [OE his]
hit *pron. nom.* it 10, 13, etc., that 492; *coll.* they 88, 895, 1199; *dat. & acc.* it 46, 160, 308, etc.; *acc. coll.* them 512, 1007; *poss.* its 108, 120, 224, 740; (pleonastic) 41, 922, 1118; **hyt** *nom.* it 482; *dat. & acc.* it 270, 271, 284, etc.; *poss.* its 446. [OE hit]
ho 'he' 479n. See **he** *sg.*
ho *pron. nom.* she 129, 130, etc.; (pleonastic) 454. [OE hēo, hīe, hī]
hol *adj.* complete 406. [OE hāl]
holteʒ *n. pl.* woods 921. [OE holt]
holtewodeʒ *n. pl.* woods 75. [OE holtwudu]
holy *adj.* holy 618, 679. [OE hālig]
holy *adv.* entirely 418. [From OE hāl]
Holy Wryt *n.* Holy Writ 592. [OE hālig+OE writ] Cf. **Writ.**
homly *adj.* gracious 1211n. [OE hām+-lic]
honde *n. coll.* hands 49, 218; *sg.* in phr. *on honde* 'close by' 155; **houdeʒ** *pl.* hands 706. [OE hond, hand]
houdelyngeʒ *adv.* with his hands 681. [OE handlinga+-es]
hondred. See **hundreth.**
hone *pass. infin.* be situated 921. [Prob. Celtic; cf. OIr. *h)úan* 'a loan, lending' *n.* & Mn. Scot. *hūne* 'to loiter'. *(MED).]*
honour *n.* honor 424, 475, 852, 864. [OF h)onor, h)onur]
hope *n.* hope 860. [OE hopa]
hope *pt. 1 sg.* assumed 142n, imagined 185; *pr. 1 sg.* imagine 225; **hoped** *pt. 1 sg.* supposed 139. [OE hopian]
horneʒ *n. pl.* horns 1111n. [OE horn]
houreʒ *n. pl.* hours 555; **oure** *sg.* hour 530, 551. [OF h)oure]
how *adv.* how 334; *conj.* 690, 711, 1146. [OE hū]
hue *n.* voice 873. [OF hu, heu, hui(e)]
huee *n.* color 842; **hwe** appearance 896; **hweʒ** *pl.* colors 90. [Merc. hēow, hīow, hīo; WS, Nhb. hīw]
hwe(ʒ). See **huee.**
hundreth *n. coll.* hundreds 1107; **hundreþe** *n.* hundred 869; **hondred** hundred 786. [OE hundred, ON hundrað]
hurt *pp.* injured 1142. [OF hurter]
huyle. See **hil.**
hwe(ʒ). See **huee.**
hyde *n.* skin 1136. [OE hȳd]
hyder. See **hider.**

hyʒ *adj.* in phr. *hyʒ seysoun* 'holy occasion' 39n, high 678; *adv.* high 473, 773; **hyʒe** *adj.* special 395, arrogant 401, high 596, 1024, 1051, great 1054; *adv.* high 454; **hiʒe** *adv.* high 207. [OE hēh, hēah]
hyʒt *n.* in phr. *on hyʒt* 'on high' 501; **heʒt** height 1031. [OE hēhþu, hēahþu]
hyʒt(e) *v.* See **hete** *v.*
hyl, hylle. See **hil.**
hyl-coppe *n.* hilltop 791. [OE hyl+OE cop]
hym 'them' 635n. See **hem.**
hym *pron. sg. dat. & acc.* him 324, 349, 360, etc., to him 692, about him 836; *refl.* for himself 478, himself 691, 732, 813; *intens.* himself 711, 867, 1033; (used as subject in subjunctive construction) he 662; **hem** *dat.* to him 1196n. [OE him]
hymself *pron. sg. dat. & acc. refl.* himself 808, 811, 826, etc.; *intens.* himself 680, 812, 825, 1134. [OE him+OE self]
hynde. See **hende.**
hyne *n. coll.* households 505n, servants 1211; *dat.* as (his) servants 632; **hen** laborers 532n. [A hīgan, hīgna, hīna; Merc. hīona, *hēona *pl.*; WS hīwan]
hyr. See **her** (1) & (2).
hyre *n.* service 523n, hiring 534, payment 539, wage 543, reward 583, 587. [OE hȳr]
hyre *v.* hire 507; **hyred** *pt. 1 sg. subj.* hired 560. [OE hȳrian]
hys, hysse. See **his.**
hyt. See **hit.**
hytteʒ *pr. 3 sg.* happens 132. [Late OE hyttan, from ON hitta]
hyul. See **hil.**

I *pron. nom.* I 3, 4, etc. [OE ic]
ichose. See **ches.**
if. See **ʒif.**
ilk *adj.* same 995; **ilke** 704. [OE ilca]
ille *adv.* evilly 681, poorly 1177. [ON illa]
in *prep.* in 2, 5, etc., as 8, 742, 944, with 18, 22, etc., into 30, 61, etc., on 39, 116, etc., to 64, 267, 811, at 113, 366, etc., of 224, 785, according to 236, after 438, from 610, 1039, among 711, 875, inside 917, for 1091, 1152, through 1153, within 1186; **inne** *prep.* in 656, 940. [OE in, inne]
inlyche *adv.* fully 546n, 603. [OE inlīce]
in-melle *prep.* in the midst of 1127. [ON ī or ā millum; cf. OI ī or ā milli]

inmydde3 *prep.* amid 222, 740; inmyde3 835. [From OE on middan *prep.*]

inne. See in.

innocens *n.* innocence 708. [OF in(n)ocence]

innocent *n.* innocent child 625, 720; innosent innocent one 684, 696; innossent *coll.* (the) innocent 666; inoscente (the) innocent 672. [OF in(n)ocent]

innogh *adj.* enough 661; *adv.* 660; innoghe *n.* 625, 649; *adv.* 636, 648; inno3e 624; inoghe 612; ino3e well enough 637. [OE gēnog, gēnoh]

innome *pp.* trapped 703n. [OE geniman, *pp.* genumen]

insample *n.* parable 499. [AF ensample]

into *prep.* into 231, 245, etc., to 509. [OE intō]

inwyth *adv.* from within 970. [OE in+wiþ]

is *pr. 3 sg.* is 33, 40, etc., has 26, 63, 394; *pr. perf. 3 sg.* has been 860. [OE is]

iwyse *adv.* indeed 279; iwysse 151, 394, 1128. [OE gewis]

jacyngh *n.* jacinth 1014. [OF jacinte, jacincte, ML jacintus]

jasper *n.* jasper 999, 1026; jasporye 1018. [OF jaspre]

joly *adj.* elegant 929; jolyf beautiful 842. [OF joli, jolif]

joparde *n.* confusion 602. [From OF jeu parti]

joueler. See jueler.

joy *n.* joy 234, 266, 395, Joy (referring to Christ) 796; joye joy 128, 1126, 1197, glory 577. [OF joi]

joyfol *adj.* joyful 288, 300. [Prec.+OE -full]

joyle3 *adj.* joyless 252. [OF joi+OE -lēas]

joyned *pt. 3 sg.* enumerated 1009. [OF joindre]

juel *n.* jewel 249, 253, 277; juele 23; *coll.* jewels 929; juele3 *pl.* 278; Juelle Jewel (referring to Christ) 795, 1124. [OF jüel, jouel, jeuwiel]

jueler *n.* jeweler 264, 265, etc.; juelere 252; joueler 734. [OF jöelier]

jugged *pt. 1 sg.* judged 7; *pt. pl.* 804. [AF juger; cf. CF jugier]

justyfyet *pp.* justified 700. [OF justifier]

kaste *pt. 1 sg. pass.* was cast 1198; kest *pp.* cast away 861; keste *pp.* cast 66; kesten *pt. pl.* scattered 1122. [ON kasta]

kene *adj.* sharp 40. [OE cēne]

kenned *pt. perf. 3 sg. subj.* would have shown 55. [OE cennan; cf. ON kenna.]

keruen. See coruen.

kest(e), kesten. See kaste.

keue *v.* sink 320; keued *pp.* set down 981. [ON kefja]

klyfe3, klyffe3. See clyffe.

klymbe. See clym.

knaw *v.* know 410, 541, discover 1109; *pr. 1 sg.* know 673; *infin.* to know 794; knawe *pr. pl.* know 505; *pr. pl. emph.* do know 516; knawen *pp.* known 637; knew *pt. 1 sg.* discovered 66, knew 164, 168, 998, recognized 1019; knewe *pt. pl.* knew 890. [OE cnāwan]

knelande *pr. p.* kneeling 434. [OE cnēowlian]

knot *n.* throng 788. [OE cnotta]

Krysten *adj.* Christian 461; Krystyin *as n.* Christian 1202. [OE Cristen, OF Crestien, L Christiānus]

kynde *n.* character 55, 752, substance 74, nature 270, 271. [OE ge)cynd]

kynde *adj.* gracious 276. [OE gecynde]

kyndely *adv.* gently 369; kyntly *adj.* kindly 690n. [OE ge)cyndelic *adj.*, ge)cyndelīce *adv.*]

kyndom *n.* kingdom 445. [OE cynedōm]

kyng *n.* king 448, 480; *coll.* kings 468, King (God) 596. [OE cyning, cyng]

kyntly. See kyndely.

kyrk *n.* church 1061. [ON kirkja, from OE cir(i)ce]

kyste *n.* coffer 271. [ON kista]

kythe3 *n. pl.* lands 1198. [OE cȳþ, cȳþþu]

kyþe *v.* reveal 356. [OE cȳþan]

labor *v.* cultivate 504. [OF laborer]

labour *n.* labor 634. [OF labor]

lad. See lede *v.*

lade *pp.* charged 1146. [OE hladan]

laden. See ledden.

lady *n.* lady 491, Lady (Blessed Virgin) 453. [OE hlǣfdige]

ladyly *adj.* exalted 774. [From prec.]

ladyschyp *n.* ladyship 578. [OE hlǣfdige+OE -scipe]

laften *pt. pl.* abandoned 622. [OE lǣfan, *pt.* lǣfde]

la3t *pt. 1 sg.* experienced 1128; la3te 1205. [OE læccan, *pt.* læhte]

Lamb *n.* Lamb (Christ) 407; Lambe 757, 771; Lambes *gen.* Lamb's 785; Lombe Lamb 413, 741, etc., lamb 802; *gen.* Lamb's 1141; Lombe3 *gen.* Lamb's

234

872; **lomp** lamb 815n; **Lompe** Lamb 945; **Loumbe** 867. [OE lamb]

lambe-ly3t *n.* lamplight 1046n. [OF lamp + A lēht, WS lēoht]

lande *n. coll.* fields 802. [OF lande]

langour *n.* misery 357. [OF langour]

lantyrne *n.* lantern 1047. [OF lanterne]

lappe3 *n. pl.* loose sleeves 201. [OE læppa]

large *adj.* large 201, great 609. [OF large]

lasse *n.* in phr. *þe lasse in werke* 'those who work less' 599, less 600, 601, 853; *adj. comp.* lower 491; **les** *adj. comp.* less 864, 876, 901; *adv. comp.* less 888, 900; **lesse** *adj. comp.* insignificant 339, less 852. [OE lǣssa]

laste *adj. sup. as n.* last 547, 570, 571. [OE lætest]

laste *v.* last 956; **laste3** *pr. pl.* endure 1198. [OE lǣstan]

laste *pp.* filled 1146. [OE gehlæstan]

late *adj.* late 538; *adv.* in phr. *erly and late* 'all the time' 392, late 574, 615. [OE læt *adj.*, late *adv.*]

laue3 *pr. 3 sg.* pours forth 607. [OE lafian]

launce3 *n. pl.* branches 978. [OF lance]

lawe3 *n. pl.* laws 285. [OE lagu]

layd *pp.* laid away 958; **layde** laid 1172. [OE lecgan, *pp.* gelegd]

layned *pp.* concealed 244. [ON leyna]

ledden *n.* voice 878; **laden** 874. [OE lēden]

lede *n. voc.* man 542. [OE lēod(e), lēoda]

lede *pr. pl.* lead 392; *pr. 1 sg.* 409; *v.* 774; **lad** *pp.* led 801. [OE lǣdan]

lef *n. coll.* leaves (foliage) 77; **leue3** *n. pl.* pages (of book) 837. [OE lēaf]

lef *adj.* dear 266; *as n.* beloved (person) 418. [OE lēof]

legg *n.* leg 459. [ON leggr]

leghe. See **ly3.**

legyounes *n. pl.* legions 1121. [OF legion]

lelly *adv.* faithfully 305. [OF lëal, lëel *adj.* + OE -līce]

leme *v.* shine 358n; **lemed** *pt. 3 sg.* gleamed 119, shone 1043. [From OE lēoma *n.*]

lemman *n.* darling 763, Spouse (Christ) 796, Beloved (Christ) 805, 829. [OE lēof + OE man]

lenge *v.* linger 261; *pr. pl.* stay 933. [OE lengan]

lenger. See **long.**

lenghe *n.* length (of time) 167, 416. [OE lengu, lencge]

lenþe *n.* length (of measure) 1031. [OE lengþu, lengoþ]

lere (1) *n.* face 398. [OE hlēor; cf. ON hlŷr]

lere (2) *n.* abode 616n. [OE leger]

lere-leke *n.* face-cambric 210n. [OE hlēor + MDu., MLG laken]

les *adj.* false 865. [OE lēas]

lesande *pr. p.* opening 837. [OE lēsan]

les(se). See **lasse.**

lest *conj.* afraid that 187, lest 865. [OE þȳ (þē) lǣs þe; late (rare) þē lǣste (MED)]

leste *pt. 1 sg.* lost 9; **leste3** *pt. 2 sg.* lost 269. [Cf. OE forlēosan & belēosan.] Cf. **lose.**

lesyng *ger.* lying 897. [OE lēasung]

let *pt. 3 sg.* let 20; *infin.* to let 715; *imper. pl* let 718; *imper. sg.* let 901, 912, 964; **lette** *pt. 3 sg.* allowed 813. [A lētan, WS lǣten]

lette *pt. 3 sg.* obstructed 1050. [OE lettan, *pt.* lette]

lettrure *n.* writing 751. [OF letëure]

leþe3 *pr. 3 sg. pass.* is soothed 377. [A leoþian, WS liþian] Cf. **lyþe.**

leue *n.* permission 316. [OE lēaf]

leue *v.* believe 311; *pr. 1 sg.* believe 469, 876; *pr. 2 sg. subj.* should believe 865; **leue3** *pr. 3 sg.* believes 304; **leuen** *v.* believe 69; *pr. pl.* accept 425. [A lēfan, WS lŷfan, līfan]

leued *ppl. a.* in leaf 978. [From OE lēaf *n.*]

leue3 *n. pl.* See **lef** *n. coll.* leaves (foliage).

liuré3 *n. pl.* clothes 1108. [OF livree]

lo *interj.* behold 693, 740, 822. [OE lā]

lo3e *n.* water 119. [Nhb. *luh* (from Celt.); cf. OIr. *loch*, Gaelic *loch*, Welsh *llwch*.]

loke *imper. sg.* observe 463; *pr. 3 sg. subj.* may look 710; *v.* look 934; **loked** *pt. 1 sg.* looked 167, observed 1145. [OE lōcian]

loke3 *n. pl.* looks 1134. [From prec.]

lokyng *ger.* vision (sight) 1049. [Cf. OE þurhlōcung]

Lombe(3). See **Lamb.**

lomp, Lompe. See **Lamb.**

londe *n.* land 148, 937. [OE land, lond]

lone *n.* byway 1066. [OE lane, lone]

long, *n., for long* 'for (a) long while' 586; *adj.* long 597; **longe** long 1024; *adv., hys lyue3 longe* 'throughout the length of his life' 477, *þise daye3 longe* 'throughout the length of this day' 533; **lenger** *adv. comp.* longer 168, 180, 977; *euer þe lenger* 'increasingly' 600. [OE lang *adj.*, lange *adv.*, lengra *adj. comp.*]

longande *pr. p.* belonging 462. [From OE gelang *adj.*; cf. OE langian 'belong' *v.*]

235

longed, *pt. impers.*, *me longed* 'I yearned' 144. [OE langian, longian]

longeyng *ger.* longing 244, yearning 1180. [OE langung, longung]

Lorde *n.* Lord (exclamatory) 108, 1149, Lord (God) 285, 304, etc., lord (earthly) 502, 506, etc. [OE hlāford]

lore *n.* way (manner) 236. [OE lār]

lose *v.* lose 265, fade 908; **loste** *pp.* lost 1092. [OE losian; cf. OE forlēosan & belēosan.] Cf. **leste**.

lote (1) *n.* voice 238, sound 876, speech 896. [ON lāt]

lote (2) *n.* adventure 1205n. [OE hlot]

loþe *n.* sorrow 377. [OE lāþ]

loude *adj.* loud 878. [OE hlūd]

loue (1) *infin.* to love 342; **loueʒ** *pr. 3 sg. emph.* does like 403; *pr. 3 sg.* loves 407. [OE lufian]

loue (2) *v.* honor 285, 1124, praise 1127; **loueʒ** *pr. 3 sg.* honors 302n; *pr. pl.* honor 308. [OE lofian]

loueloker. See next entry.

louely *adj.* lovely 693; **loueloker** *comp.* fairer 148; **louyly** *adj.* proper 565; **lufly** pleasing 880, lovely 962; *adv.* beautifully 978. [OE luflic *adj.*, luflīce *adv.*]

Loumbe. See **Lamb**.

loute *pr. pl.* stroll 933. [OE lūtan]

louyly. See **louely**.

lowe *adv.* low 236, 547; **lowest** *adj. sup.* lowest 1001. [ON lāgr *adj.*, lægstr *sup.*]

luf *n.* love 467, 851. [OE lufu]

luf-daungere *n.* frustrated love 11n. [OE lufu+AF daunger]

luf-longyng *n.* loving desire 1152. [OE lufu+OE langung, longung]

lufly. See **louely**.

lufsoum *sb. adj.* lovely one 398. [OE lufsum]

lureʒ *n. pl.* losses 339, misfortunes 358. [OE lyre]

lurked *pt. 1 sg.* slipped (moved quietly) 978. [Cf. Norw. & Swed. dial. *lurka*.]

lyf *n.* life 247, spirit 305, 392, etc.; **lyueʒ** *gen.* of (his) life 477, life's 578, 908. [OE līf]

lyfed *pt. 2 sg.* lived 483; **lyued** *pp.* lived 477, 776; **lyuyande** *pr. p.* living 700. [OE lifian, lifiende]

lyfte *pp.* raised 567. [ON lypta]

lyʒ *v.* lie 930; **leghe** *pt. 3 sg.* lay 214; **lys** *pr. 3 sg.* lies 360, exists 602. [OE licgan]

lyʒe *n.* lie 304. [OE lyge]

lyʒt *n.* light 69, 119, 1043, 1050, 1073; *adj.* pure 682; **lyʒte** radiant 500, cheerful 238; *adv.* lightly 214. [A lēht, WS lēoht *n. & adj.*; lē(o)hte *adv.*]

lyʒt *pt. 3 sg.* descended 943; *pp.* come 988; **lyʒte** *pr. 2 sg. pass.* are settled 247. [OE līhtan]

lyʒtly *adv.* gently 358. [OE lēohtlīce]

lyk *adj.* similar 432, 501, 896. [OE gelīc; cf. ON līkr]

lyk *prep.* like 874; **lyke** 735. [From prec. & OE gelīce *adv.*]

lykeʒ *pr. 3 sg.* pleases 566. [OE līcian]

lykneʒ *pr. 3 sg.* compares 500. [From OE gelīc *adj.*; cf. ON līkr *adj.*]

lykyng *ger.* delight 247. [OE līcung]

lym *n.* member (Christian soul) 462; **lymmeʒ** *pl.* limbs 464. [OE lim]

lyne *n.* lineal descent 626. [OE līne, OF ligne]

lynne *adj.* linen 731. [OE līnen]

lys. See **lyʒ**.

lyste *n.* desire 173, happiness 467; *coll.* pleasures 908. [From OE lystan; cf. OI lyst]

lyste, *pt. impers.*, *me lyste* 'I wished' 146, 'I desired' 181; *pt. 3 sg. subj.* would wish 1141. [OE lystan, *pt.* lyste]

lysten *v.* listen to 880. [From OE hlystan; cf. Merc. hlysnan & Nhb. lysna]

lyth *n.* figure 398. [OE liþ]

lyttel *n.* little effort 574, little result 575; *adj.* little 387, 604, 1147; *adv.* shortly 172, little 301. [OE lȳtel]

lyþe *v.* soften 357; **lyþeʒ** *imper. sg.* soothe 369n. [OE līþian] Cf. **leþeʒ**.

lyþer *n.* malice 567. [From OE lȳþre *adj.*]

lyued. See **lyfed**.

lyueʒ. See **lyf**.

lyuyande. See **lyfed**.

ma (1), *pron. poss.*, *par ma fay* 'by my faith' 489. [OF par ma fei]

ma (2), line 323n. See **man** *indef. pron.*

ma (3), line 283. See **make** *v.*

mad *adj.* foolish 267, mad 1199; *adv.* madly 1166; **madde** *adj.* foolish 290. [OE gemǣdde *pp.*]

madde *pr. 2 sg. subj.* fume 359. [From prec.; cf. OE gemǣdan]

maddyng *ger.* madness 1154. [From prec.]

mad(e) *v.* See **make** *v.*

make *n.* spouse 759. [WS gemaca, Nhb. maca; cf. OI maki.]

236

make v. render 176, create 304, make 474; pr. 1 sg. render 281; **ma**, v., *ma feste* 'rejoice' 283; **mad** pp. made 274, 486, settled 953; pt. 3 sg. gave 539; **made** pp. created 140; pt. 2 sg. (with subject ȝe, addressing one person) established 371; pt. 3 sg. made 522, 1149; **man** pr. pl. make 512; **matȝ** pr. 3 sg. brings 610. [OE macian]

makeleȝ adj. matchless 435, 780, peerless 757, unequalled 784; **makelleȝ** peerless 733. [From ME make n.; see above.]

malte v. conceive 224; pt. 3 sg. pass. was reduced 1154. [A gemæltan, WS myltan]

man v., line 512. See make v.

man n. sg. man 386, 675, etc.; *in a coll. sense*, man (mankind) 1195; **maneȝ** gen. man's (mankind's) 940; *as adj.*, *maneȝ mynde* 'mortal mind' 1154; **manneȝ** gen. man's 223; **men** pl. men 290, 331, etc.; **mon** sg. man 310; coll. men 340, 799. [OE man(n), mon(n)]

man pron. indef. one 165, 314, man (a person) 334; **mon** man (person) 69, 95, etc., one 194; **ma** man 323n. [OE man]

manayre. See maner.

maneȝ. See man n.

maner n. coll. manors 918; **manayre** habitation (stronghold) 1029. [AF maner, CF manoir]

mankyn n. mankind 637. [OE mancynn]

manneȝ. See man n.

mare. See more.

marereȝ n. vitality 382n. [A merg, WS mearg]

margarys n. pl. pearls 199; **margyrye** sg. pearl 1037; **marjorys** pl. margarites 206n. [OF margarie, margerie]

marked n. market 513. [? Late OE market (from ON or ML); cf. ON markaðr; OF markié, marquiet; L mercātus (MED).]

marre pr. 2 sg. subj. fret 359; **marreȝ** pr. 2 sg. mar 23. [A merran, WS mierran]

maryag n. marriage 778; **maryage** 414. [OF marïage, marïaige]

mas n. mass 1115; **messe** 497. [WS mæsse, Merc. (or K) messe, OF messe]

mascelleȝ adj. spotless 732n; **maskeleȝ** 745, 900, 923; **maskelleȝ** 756, 768, 769, 780; **maskelles** 744, 781. [From next.]

mascle n. spot 726; **masklle** 843. [ML mascula, from Gmc.; cf. OE max, ON möskvi, & OF macle (MED).]

mate adj. subdued 386. [OF mat]

mate v. disconcert 613. [OF mater]

matȝ. See make v.

may n. maiden 780, 961, Virgin (Mother of Christ) 435. [OE mæg, ? mæg (MED)]

may v., pr. sg. & pl., may (do) 300, may 310, 355, etc., can 29, 296, etc., can (go) 347; **moun** pr. 2 pl. can 536. [OE magan, mæg; pl. magon]

mayden n. maiden 162; **maydeneȝ** pl. maidens 1115; **maydenneȝ** virgins 869n. [OE mægden, mæden]

maynful adj. great 1093. [OE mægen+ful]

Mayster n. Master (the Lord) 462, 900. [OF maistre]

maysterful adj. masterful 401. [From prec.]

me pron. dat. me 10, 13, etc.; acc. me 88, 98, etc.; dat. for me 102, 239, etc., from me 187, 245, to me 233, 267, etc., into me 1153, with me 1187; refl. myself 66, 366, 1191; (used as subject in impers. constructions) I 19, 144, 146, 181. [OE mē]

mede n. reward 620. [OE mēd]

meke adj. gentle 404, meek 815, 832, 961. [OI mjūkr, OSwed. miūker]

mekenesse n. meekness 406. [From prec.]

mele v. speak 925; **meled** pt. 1 sg. spoke 589; **meleȝ** pr. 3 sg. tells 497; **melle** v. speak 797, tell 1118. [OE mælan; cf. ON mæla]

membreȝ n. pl. members 458. [OF membre]

men n. See man n.

men pr. pl. appraise 802n. [OF aesmer]

mendeȝ n. coll. consolations 351. [Shortened form of OF amende(s]

mendyng ger. improvement 452. [Shortened form of OF amender]

mene v. mean 293, 951; **meneȝ** pr. 2 sg. mention 937. [OE mænan]

mensk n. honor 783; **menske** dignity 162. [ON mennska]

menteene v. maintain 783. [OF maintenir, meintenir]

mercy n. mercy 356, 623, 670; **merci** 576; **mersy** 383. [OF merci]

mere n. brook 158; **mereȝ** pl. streams 140n, 1166. [OE mere, mære; cf. OI marr]

merked pp. situated 142. [WS mearcian, ON marka & merkja]

mersy. See mercy.

meruayle n. coll. wonders 157; sg. amazement 1130; **meruayleȝ** pl. miracles 64; **merwayle** miracle 1081. [OF merveille]

meruelous adj. marvelous 1166. [OF merveillos]

merwayle. See meruayle.

mes *n.* festive gathering 862n. [OF mes]

meschef *n.* misfortune 275. [OF meschef]

messe. See mas.

mesure *n.* value 224. [OF mesure]

mete *n.* meal 641. [OE mete]

mete *adj.* suitable 833, proper 1063. [OE gemǣte]

mete *v.* find 329, meet 918; meten *pr. pl.* meet 380. [OE mētan]

meten *pp.* measured 1032. [OE metan; WS mǣton, *pp.* meten (*MED*)]

meued *pt. 3 sg.* stirred 156; meuen *pr. pl.* transpire 64. [OF movoir, meuvre]

meyny *n.* group 542, 892, assembly 899, 960, company 925, 1127, 1145. [AF meine, mesne; CF mainie, maisniee]

mirþe *n.* merriment 1149; myrþe melody 92; myrþeʒ delights 140. [OE myrgþ]

mo *n.* greater happiness 340, more 850, 1194; *adj.* more 151, 870. [OE mā, *n.* & *adj.*] Cf. more.

mod *n.* mood 401; mode appearance 738, mood 832. [OE mōd]

modeʒ *n. pl.* modes 884n. [OF mode]

Moder *n.* Mother (Blessed Virgin) 435. [OE mōdor, mōdur]

moʒt, moʒte, moʒten. See myʒt.

mokke *n.* dirt 905. [Perh. from OE -*moc*, akin to ON *myki* 'dung']

mol. See mul.

moldeʒ *n. pl.* molds 30. [OE molde]

mon *n. & pron.* See man *n. & pron.*

mon *n.* lamentation 374. [From OE *mānan v.*, an unumlauted by-form of *mǣnan* 'to lament' (*MED*)]

mone *n.* moon 923, 1044, etc. [OE mōna]

mony *n.* many 572; *adj.* many 160, 340; mony a many a 775. [OE manig]

moote. See mot.

more *adj. comp.* more 128, 157, etc.; *as n.* more 132 (twice), 133, etc.; *adv.* more 144 (twice), 145 (twice) etc.; mare *adv.* more 145. [OE *mǣre, neut.* of *māra, adj. comp.* used as *n.*; *māra, adj. & adv. comp.* of *micel & micle* 'much'] Cf. mo. (See similar usages of *more* as the linkword in Stanza-Group X, ll. 552ff.)

morne *pr. 2 sg. subj.* mourn 359. [OE murnan]

mornyf *adv.* mournfully 386. [From prec.]

mornyng *ger.* lamentation 262. [OE murnung]

moste *adj. sup.* greatest 1131. [OE *mǣst*; cf. Nhb. *māst, sup.* of *micel* 'much'.]

moste *v.* See next entry.

mot *pr. 3 sg.* must 25, 31, 320, 663; *pr. 3 sg. subj.* may 397; moste *pr. 2 sg.* must 319, 348; *pt. pl.* must 623. [OE *mōtan; 1 & 3 sg.* mōt; *2 sg.* mōst; *pt.* mōste]

mot *n.* stain 843; mote 726, 764, spot 924, 960, 972; moote 948. [OE mot]

mote (1) *n.* quarreling 855. [OE gemōt]

mote (2) *n.* castle 142, city 936, 937, 948, 973; moteʒ *pl.* cities 949. [OF mote]

moteʒ *pr. 2 sg.* claim 613. [OE mōtian]

moteleʒ *adj.* spotless 925, 961; moteles 899. [From OE mot]

moul. See mul.

moun. See may *v.*

mount *n.* mount 868. [OE munt, AF mount]

mounteʒ *pr. pl.* increase 351. [OF monter]

mouth *n.* mouth 183, 803. [OE mūþ, mūþa]

much *adv.* much 234, 303, etc.; *adj.* 244, 604, etc.; *as n.* 1149. [OE micel]

mul *n.* dust (mortal flesh) 905; mol 382; moul earth (burial ground) 23. [Cf. ML mollis, OE myl, MDu. mul.]

munt *n.* intention 1161. [From OE myntan]

my *pron. poss.*, my 15, 16 (twice), 17 etc.; myn my 128, 174, etc.; *dat. refl.* myself 243; *dat.* mine 566, 1208; myne *poss.* my 335. [OE mīn] Cf. myself.

myʒt *n.* power 765; myʒte 1069. [OE miht]

myʒt, *pt. sg. & pl.* of may *v.*, could 69, 135, etc., might 579; *pt. 2 sg.* might 317; moʒt *pt. sg. & pl.* could 34, 92, etc., might 223, 479, etc.; moʒte *pt. 3 sg.* might 475; moʒten *pt. pl.* could 1196n. [OE mihte; A mæhte; EWS meahte]

mykeʒ *n. pl.* chosen ones 572n. [L amīcus]

mylde *sb. adj.* humble disciples 721; *adj.* mild 961, 1115. [OE milde]

myn(e). See my.

mynde *n. coll.* thoughts 156; *sg.* reason 224, mind 1130, 1154. [OE gemynd]

mynge *v.* think 855. [OE myn(e)gian]

mynne *v.* think 583. [ON minna]

mynyster *n.* cathedral 1063n. [OE mynster]

myrþe(ʒ). See mirþe.

myrþeʒ *pr. 3 sg.* gladdens 862. [From OE myrgþ *n.*]

myry *adj.* beautiful 23, pleasant 158, fair 781, excellent 936; myryer *comp.* merrier 850; myryest *sup.* brightest 435; myryeste finest 199. [OE myrige]

mys (1) *n.* cloak 197n. [OF amit, amist]
mys (2) *n.* loss 262; mysse 364. [OE mis;
ON missir, missa]
myself *pron. acc.* me 414; *dat. refl.* myself
1175; myseluen *acc.* me 52. [From OE
mīn & self] Cf. my.
myserecorde *n.* mercy 366.[OF misericorde]
mysetente *pp.* misdirected 257. [OE mis-
+OF tendre]
mysse *n.* See mys (2).
mysse *v.* lose 329; *pr. 1 sg.* lack 382. [OE
missan, ON missa]
myssezeme *v.* forfeit 322. [WS misgȳman, A
*misgēman *(MED)*]
Myste *n. coll.* Spiritual Mysteries 462n. [Cf.
OE *mist* 'mist', L *mysticus*, & next
entry.]
mysterys *n. pl.* mysteries 1194. [L
mystērium, from Gr. & OF *mistere*
'secret' *(MED)*]
myte, *n.*, *not a myte* 'not a bit' 351. [MDu.,
MLG *mīte* 'coin (originally Flemish) of
very small denomination' *(MED)*]
myþe *pr. 2 sg. subj.* mutter 359n. [From OE
mūþ, *mūþa* 'mouth' *n.*]

nazt(e). See niyzt.
name *n. coll.* names 998; *sg.* name 1039;
nome 872. [OE nama]
nature *n.* nature 749. [OF nature]
naule *n.* navel 459n. [OE nafela]
nauþeles *adv.* nevertheless 877; nawþeles
950; nowþelese 889. [OE nā þē lǣs] Cf.
neuerþelese.
nauþer . . . ne *correl. conj.* neither . . . nor
465; (in triple neg. construction) either .
. . or 484; nawþer . . . ne neither . . .
nor 1044, 1087; (in quadruple neg.)
either . . . or 485; noþer . . . ne (in
triple neg.) either . . . or 848; nawþer
conj. (in double neg.) either 751. [OE
nāwþer, nā-hwæþer, nō-hwæþer & ne]
nawhere *adv.* nowhere 534; (in double neg.)
anywhere 932. [OE nā-hwǣ(ē)r, nō-]
nawþeles. See nauþeles.
nawþer, nawþer . . . ne. See nauþer . . .
ne.
ne *adv.* not 35, 65, etc.; *conj.* nor 334, 347,
etc.; (in double or multiple neg. con-
structions) or 764, 843, 897; (pleonastic)
4, 362, 403, 825, 898, 1071, 1082; nee
conj. nor 262. [OE ne]
nece *n.* niece 233. [OF niece, nece]
nedde, *pt. pl. impers.*, *hem nedde* 'they

needed' 1044. [From next entry & late
OE *ge)nēodian*]
nede *n.* need 1045. [A, K nēd; WS nēod]
nedez *adv.* necessarily 25, 344. [From OE
nēde, nēode *adv.*]
nee. See ne.
nemme *v.* designate 997. [OE ge)nemnan]
nente *n.* ninth 1012. [OE nigoþa, nigend]
ner *prep.* near 286; nere 404; nerre *adj.*
comp. nearer 233n. [A nēor, WS nēar]
nesch *adv.* gently 606. [OE hnesce]
neuer *adv.* never 4, 19, etc.; (in double or
multiple neg. constructions) ever 485,
864, 889, any 900; (in subj. construc-
tion) ever 571. [OE næfre]
neuermore *adv.* never again 724. [From OE
næfre & māra]
neuerþelese *adv.* nevertheless 912, 913.
[From OE nǣfre, þē, & lǣs] Cf.
nauþeles.
new *adv.* anew 662; newe, *adj.*, *newe fryt*,
'first fruits' 894; nw new 527; nwe new
155, 792, 879, 882, 987; *sb. adj.* New
Jerusalem 943; *adv.* again 1080, anew
1123. [OE nēowe, nīowe, nīwe]
niezbor *n.* neighbor 688. [A nēhgibūr,
nēhebūr; WS nēah-gebūr]
nis *pr. 3 sg.* is 100; nys 951 (=*ne*+*is* in
double neg. construction). [OE nis]
niyzt *n.* night 630n; nyzt 116, 1071; nyzte
243; nazt 523; nazte 1203. [A næht,
neht; WS neaht; late OE niht]
no *adj.*no 32, 69, etc.; (in double or multiple
neg. constructions) any 226, 898, 1050;
(pleonastic) 516; *adv.* no 347, 951, 977,
not 848. [OE nā & nō]
noble *adj.* splendid 922, noble 1097. [OF
noble]
nozt *pron.* nothing 274, 337, etc.; (in double
neg. construction) anything 520; *adv.*
not 563, 588. [OE nā(ō)wiht, nā(ō)ht]
nom *pt. perf. pl.* had received 587. [OE
niman]
nome. See name.
non *pron.* no one 443, 455, etc.; (in double
& triple neg. constructions) any 812,
825; *adj.* no 206, etc.; *adv.* not 215,
764, 1061; none *adj.* no 440. [OE nān].
not *adv.* not 29, 34, etc. [From OE
nā(ō)wiht, nā(ō)ht *adv.*]
note (1) *n.* marvel 155, city 922. [OE notu]
note (2) *n.* canticle 879; notez *pl.* notes 883.
[OF note]
noþer . . . ne. See nauþer . . . ne.

239

noþyng *pron.* nothing 1157; noþynk 308, 496, 587. [OE nā-þing]

now *adv.* now 271, 287, etc.; *conj.* since (now that) 283, 327, etc. [OE nū]

nowþelese. See nauþeles.

nw, nwe. See new.

nyȝt(e). See niyȝt.

nys. See nis.

o *interj.* o 23, 241, 745, 1182. [L & OF o]

o *prep.* of 309, 429, 792. (shortening of *of*)

obes *pr. pl.* obey 886. [OF obëir]

odour *n.* fragrance 58. [OF odor, odour]

of *adv.* of 925, about 1118; *prep.* by 11, for 12, 1206, with 25, 76, etc., from 31, 33, etc., of 55, 69, etc., in 74, 455, etc., to 84, 493, off 237, concerning 339, 601, 689, among 358, between 371, because of 450, due to 457, as 489, at 503, about 529, 793, associated with 800, through 860, 943, into 926, upon 967, on 1005; (pleonastic) 317. [OE of]

offys *n.* position 755n. [L officium & OF ofice]

ofte *adv.* often 14, 340, etc.; ofter *comp.* more often 621. [OE oft]

oȝe. See owe.

oȝt *pron.* something 274, anything 1200. [OE āwiht, ōwiht, āht, ōht]

oȝte. See owe.

olde *adj.* old 941, 942; alder *comp.* older 621; aldest *sb. adj. sup.* oldest 1042. [A ald, ældra, ældest; WS eald, ieldra (yldra), ieldest (yldest)]

on (1) *indef. art.*, lines 9 & 1079. See a (1).

on (2) *n.* one (the number) 293, 557; *pron.* one 450, 546, etc.; in phr. *at on* 'in harmony' 378; *adj.* only 425, one 530, 551, 860; one *adj.* alone 243, 312; oneȝ *pron. gen.* one's 863, 864, 1103. [OE ān, *gen.* ānes]

on (3) *adv.* upon 45, on 255; *prep.* on 41, 62, etc., above 60, upon 78, 808, etc., in 97, 874, 1095, at 167, 232, etc., against 466, to 826, over 1106; (pleonastic) 510. [OE on]

one, oneȝ. See on (2).

onende. See anende.

onslydeȝ *pr. pl.* hang 77. [OE on+slīdan]

onsware *v.* answer 680. [OE andswe(a)rian, onswarian]

onto. See vnto.

open *adj.* open 183; vpen 1066; vpon 198, spread 208n; *adv.* openly 824n. [OE open]

or *conj.* or 233. [From OE ōþer *conj.*]

orient *adj.* oriental 255. [From OF orient *n.*]

Oryent *n.* Orient 3; Oryente 82. [OF Orient]

oþer (1) *conj.* or 118, 130, etc. [OE ōþer, āhwæþer]

oþer (2) *adj.* other 206, 209, etc., another 319; *pron.* other 955; *coll.* others 449, 585, 773, 778; oþereȝ *gen.* others' 450. [OE ōþer]

ouer *prep.* over 318, 454, 773, 1166, across 324, upon 1205; *adv.* too 473. [OE ofer]

ouerte *adj.* simple 593. [OF overt]

ouerture *n. coll.* openings (of garment) 218. [OF overture]

our *pron. poss.* our 851; oure 304, 322, etc. [OE ūr, ūre]

oure 'hour', lines 530 & 551. See houreȝ.

oure *n.* mercy 690n. [OE ār]

out *adv.* out 365, 649, etc., away 642; out of *prep.* of 282, from 1058, 1163; oute of out of 3. [OE ūt(e) *adv.* & of *prep.*]

outryȝte *adv.* straight out 1055. [OE ūt+rihte]

owe *pr. 1 sg.* owe 543; oȝe, *pr. pl. impers.*, vus oȝe 'we ought' 552; aȝt *pt. 3 sg.* ought 1139; oȝte, *pt. 2 sg. impers.*, þe oȝte 'you ought' 341. [OE āgan, *pt.* āhte]

owne *adj.* own 559. [OE āgen]

pace *n.* passage (in Psalter) 677. [OF pas]

pakke *n.* group 929. [Cf. MDu., MLG pac & OI pakki]

pale *v.* glow dimly 1004. [OF palëir, palöir]

pane *n.* side 1034. [OF pan]

par, *prep.*, *par ma fay* 'by my faith' 489. [OF par ma fei]

Paradys *n. gen.* of Paradise (Heaven) 248, of Paradise (Garden of Eden) 321; Paradyse *n.* Paradise (Heaven) 137n. [OF Paradis]

parage *n.* lineage 419. [OF parage]

paraunter *adv.* perhaps 588. [OF par aventure]

parfyt. See perfet.

part *n.* share 573. [OF part]

partleȝ *adj.* deprived 335. [From prec.]

passe *v.* cross 299, pass 707, 1110; passed *pt. 3 sg. subj.* surpassed 428; *pp.* passed 528; passeȝ *pr. 3 sg.* surpasses 753. [OF passer]

Pater *n.* Pater (the Lord's Prayer) 485. [L *Pater*, shortening of *Pater Noster*] pay *n.* liking 1212; **paye** pleasure 1, liking 1164, 1176, 1188, 1189, 1200. [OF paie]

pay *imper. sg.* pay 542; *v.* recompense 635, pay 1201; **payed** *pp.* paid 584, compensated 603; *pt. 3 sg. impers.* pleased 1165; (with subject understood) *me payed* '(it) pleased me' 1177; **payeȝ** *pr. 3 sg.* rewards 632. [OF paiier]

payment *n.* compensation 598. [OF paiement]

payne *n.* penalty 664, pain 954; **payneȝ** *pl.* pains 124. [OF peine, paine]

paynted *pt. 3 sg.* delineated 750. [OF *peintier*; cf. *pa(e)int, pp.* of *peindre.*]

payred *pp.* afflicted 246. [Shortened form of CF *empeirier*, AF *ampeirier*]

pechche *n.* patch 841n. [AN peche]

penaunce *n.* penance 477. [AF pena(u)nce]

pené. See peny.

pensyf *adj.* pensive 246. [OF pensif]

peny *n.* penny (silver coin) 546, 560, 614; **pené** 510, 562. [OE pening, penig]

pere *n.* equal 4. [OF per, pier; AF peir]

pereȝ *n. pl.* pear trees 104. [OE peru, pere]

perfet *adv.* perfectly 208; **parfyt** *adj.* perfect 638, 1038. [OF perfet, parfit]

perle *n.* pearl 1, 12, 24, 36, etc.; *dat.* for (my) pearl 53; *coll.* pearls 202, 207, 216, 219, 229; **perleȝ** *pl.* pearls 82, 192, 193, 204, etc. [OF perle]

perré *n. coll.* stones (gems) 730; *sg.* jewelry 1028. [AF perree; cf. CF pierrerie.]

pertermynable *adj.* judging perfectly 596n. [OF per-+OF terminable]

peryle *n.* peril 695. [OF peril]

pes *n.* peace 742, 955, salvation 953n; *Syȝt of Pes* 'Vision of Peace' 952. [OF pais, peis, pes]

pitously *adv.* compassionately 798; **pytosly** 370. [From OF pitos, pitous *adj.*]

place *n.* place 175, 679, abode 405, 440, city 1034. [OF place]

planeteȝ *n. pl.* planets 1075. [OF planete]

plateȝ *n. pl.* plates (sheets of metal) 1036. [OF plate]

play *v.* exult 261. [WS plegan, A plagian]

playn *n. coll.* plains 104; **playneȝ** *pl.* plains 122. [OF plain *n.*]

playn *adj.* smooth 178; *adv.* clearly 689. [OF plain *adj.*]

playned *pt. 1 sg.* mourned 53; *pp.* lamented 242; **pleny** *v.* complain 549. [OF plaindre]

playnt *n.* lament 815. [OF plaint]

pleny. See playned.

plesaunte *adj.* pleasing 1. [OF plaisant]

plese *v.* please 484. [OF plaisir]

plete *pass. infin.* be claimed 563. [OF *plaitier*, var. of *plaidoüer*]

plontteȝ *n. pl.* saplings 104. [OE plante]

plye *v.* yield 1039. [Shortening of OF aplier]

plyȝt *n.* condition 1075; **plyt** undertaking (in reference to Christ's crucifixion) 647, setting 1015, arrangement 1114. [OE pliht & AF pleit; cf. CF ploit.]

plyt. See plyȝt.

pobbel *n.* pebble 117. [From OE papol-stān]

pole *n.* stream 117. [OE pōl]

porchace *infin.* (to) purchase 744; **porchaseȝ** *pr. pl.* strive 439. [OF porchacier]

pore. See pouer.

porfyl *n. coll.* borders 216. [OF porfil]

porpos *n.* purpose 508; **porpose** meaning 185, purpose 267. [OF porpos]

portaleȝ *n. pl.* gates 1036. [OF portal]

possyble *adj.* possible 452. [OF possible]

pouer *adj.* poor 1075; **pore** humble 573. [AF povers, pore; CF povre(s)]

poursent *n.* compass 1035n. [AF purceint, CF po(u)rceinte]

powdered *pp.* scattered 44. [OF poudrer]

poyned *n.* wristlet 217. [AF poinet; cf. CF poignet, puignet.]

poynt *n.* point 309, 594, note (of song) 891. [OF point]

pray *n.* reward 439. [OF praie, preie]

pray *v.* pray 484; *pr. 1 sg.* ask 524; **prayed** *pt. pl.* beseeched 714; *pt. 3 sg.* implored 1192. [OF preier, priier]

prayer *n.* prayer 355; **prayere** devotion 618. [OF praiere, preiere, priiere]

prayse *pass. infin.* be praised 301; **praysed** *pp.* prized 1112. [OF preisier]

precios *adj.* precious 4, 36, 204, 216, 228, 229, 230; **precious** 48, 82, 1212; **precos** 60n, 192. [OF precio(u)s]

pref, *n., put in pref* 'established with certainty' 272n. [CF prueve, preve]

pres, *adj.,* line 730. See prys sb. *adj.*

pres *n.* crowding 1114. [OF presse]

pres *pr. pl.* advance 957. [OF presser]

present *n.* presence 1193; **presente** 389. [OF present *adj. as n.*]

preste *n.* priest 1210. [OE prēost]

preued. See proued.

Prince *n.* Prince (the Lord) 1201; **Prynceȝ** *gen.* Prince's 1164, 1176, 1189; **prynces**

241

prince's 1n; **Prynseȝ** Prince's 1188. [OF prince]

priuy *adj.* special 24; **pryuy** 12. [OF privé]

profered *pt. 3 sg.* proffered 235; **proferen** *pr. pl.* present 1200. [AF profrer]

professye *n.* prophecy 821. [OF profecie]

profete *n.* prophet 797; **prophete** *coll.* prophets 831. [OF profete, prophete]

proper *adj.* perfect 686. [OF propre]

propertéȝ *n. pl. gen.* of (these) qualities 752; **property** attribute 446. [OF propriete]

prophete. See **profete.**

prosessyoun *n.* procession 1096. [OF procession]

proudly *adv.* proudly 1110. [OE prūd, prūt *adj.*; prūtlīce *adv.*]

proued *pt. 1 sg.* discovered 4n; **preued** *pp.* shown 983. [OF prover, preuver]

pryde *n.* pride 401. [Late OE prȳte, *infl.* prȳda]

Prynceȝ, prynces, Prynseȝ. See **Prince.**

prys *n.* value 193; *perle of prys* 'pearl of price' 272, 746. [OF pris, pres]

prys *sb. adj.* honored one 419; **pres** *adj.* precious 730. [From prec.]

pryse *v.* esteem 1131. [OF prisier]

pryuy. See **priuy.**

pure *adj.* pure 227, 745, 1088. [OF pur(e]

purly *adv.* truly 1004. [From prec.]

purpre *adj.* purple 1016. [AF purpre; OF porpre; OE purpure (from L)]

put, *pr. 2 sg. refl.*, *þe put* 'you apply (yourself)' 267; *pp.* established 272. [OE pytan (? pȳtan), akin to potian (MED)]

pyece *n.* damsel 192; **pyese** maiden 419n; **pyse** damsel 229n. [OF piece, pece]

pyȝt *pp.* placed 117, adorned 192, 217, 228, 229, 241, 991, decorated 205; *pt. 3 sg.* placed 742, adorned 768; **pyȝte** *pp.* adorned 193, 240, arrayed 216. [OE *piccan, pt. *piht(e); cf. OI pikka]

pyked *pt. pl. pass.* were adorned 1036; **pykeȝ** *pr. pl.* obtain 573. [Cf. OE picung *n.* & OI pikka] Cf. **pyȝt.**

pyle *n.* dwelling 686. [L pīla & OF pile]

pynakled *ppl. a.* pinnacled 207. [From OF pinacle, pinnacle, & L pinnāculum *n.*]

pyne *n.* anxiety 330, effort 511. [Prob. OE; cf. OE pīnian, pīnere, pīnung (MED).]

pyonys *n. pl.* peonies 44. [OE peonia (from L) & OF pïoine, pïonie, pïone]

pyse. See **pyece.**

pyté *n.* pity 355; **pyty** pity 1206. [OF pité, pitié]

pytosly. See **pitously.**

quat. See **what.**

quat-kyn. See **what-kyn.**

quatso *pron.* whatever 566. [Reduced form of OE swā-hwæt-swā] Cf. **what.**

quayle *n.* quail 1085. [OF quaille]

quelle *v.* slay 799. [OE cwellan]

queme *adj.* pleasing 1179. [OE ge)cwēme]

quen. See **when.**

Quen *n.* Queen (Blessed Virgin) 432, 433, 444, queen 448, 474, 486; **quene** queen 415, 423, 492, 781, 1147, Queen (Blessed Virgin) 456, 784; *coll.* queens 468. [OE cwēn]

quere. See **where.**

queresoeuer *conj.* wherever 7. [OE swā-hwǣr-swā + ǣfre] Cf. **where.**

query *n.* query 803. [From L quaerere & OF querre, querir 'to ask']

queþersoeuer *conj.* whether 606. [OE hwæþer + swā + ǣfre] Cf. **wheþer.**

quo, quom. See **who.**

quoþ *pt. 1 sg.* said 241, 279, 325, 421, 469, 746, 902, 1182; *pt. 3 sg.* said 569, 758, 781. [OE cweþan]

quoynt *adj.* clever 889. [OF cointe, quointe]

quy. See **why.**

quyke *adj.* vivid 1179. [OE cwic]

quyt(e). See **whyt.**

quyteȝ *pr. 2 sg.* reward 595. [OF quiter]

qwyte. See **whyt.**

raas *n.* racing 1167. [ON rās] Cf. **resse.**

ran *pt. 3 sg.* ran 646, 1055; **runne** *pp.* discharged 523; **runnen** *pp.* sunk 26n; *pr. p.* running 874. [OE rinnan & ON renna; cf. WS irnan & Merc. eornan.]

randeȝ *n. pl.* strands (land bordering water) 105. [OE rand]

rapely *adv.* hastily 363, immediately 1168. [ON hrapalliga]

rasch *adj.* swift 1167. [? OE *ræsc (cf. līg-ræsc 'lightning'); cf. MDu. rasch, OI röskr, & Dan. rask.]

raue (1) *pr. 1 sg.* rave 363. [OF rever, raver]

raue (2) *v.* err 665. [Cf. Icel. rāfa & OF raver, late 15th cent. var. of resver 'to stray' (MED).]

rauþe *n.* grief 858. [ON hrygð, OE hrēow]

rauyste *pp.* entranced 1088. [OF raviss-, extended stem of ravir]

rawe *n.* row 545; **raweȝ** *pl.* hedgerows 105.

242

[OE rǣw, rāw]

raxled *pt. 1 sg.* started up 1174. [From OE *raxan*, ME *rasken* 'to stretch', & *-el*-suf. (3) *(MED)*]

ray *n. coll.* rays 160. [OF rai]

raykande *pr. p.* flowing 112. [ON reika]

rayse *v.* raise 305. [ON reisa]

raysoun. See **resoun.**

rebuke *imper. sg.* rebuke 367. [AF rebuker]

recen *v.* recount 827. [OE gerecenian, LOE recenian]

rech *pr. 1 sg. subj.* could care 333. [OE rēcan, reccan; cf. ON rœkja.]

recorde *n.* account 831. [OF record(e]

red *adj.* red 1111; **rede** 27. [OE rēad]

rede *v.* read 709; *pr. 1 sg.* advise 743. [WS rǣdan, A rēdan]

redy *adj.* prompt 591. [OE ge)rǣde]

refete *v.* refresh 88. [AF *refeter*, CF *refaitier*; cf. OF *refait, pp.* of *refaire*.]

reflayr *n.* fragrance 46. [From OF flair *n.*]

reget, *pass. infin.,* to reget 'to be received again' 1064n. [L & OF pref. *re-*+ON geta, WS gietan]

regioun *n.* region 1178. [AF regioun]

regne *n.* realm 501; **rengne** kingdom 692. [OF regne, rengne]

regretted *pp. tr. prog.* grieving 243. [OF regreter]

reiateჳ *n. pl.* royal powers 770. [OF *realte, reaute, reyaute,* variants of *roiauté*]

reken *adj.* elegant 5, beautiful 92, 906. [OE recen]

reles, *n., wythouten reles* 'without cessation' 956. [OF reles]

relusaunt *adj.* radiant 159. [OF reluisant]

reme *n.* realm 448, 735. [OF rěaume]

remen *pr. pl. subj.* lament 858. [A hrēman, LWS hrȳman] Cf. **toreme.**

remnaunt *n.* remainder 1160. [AF remenaunt, CF remanant, remenant]

remorde *pp.* afflicted 364. [OF remordre]

remwe *v.* remove 427; *pass. infin.* be separated 899. [OF remuer, remuier]

rengne. See **regne.**

renoun *n.* renown 986, 1182. [AF renoun]

renowleჳ *pr. pl.* renew 1080. [OF renoveler]

rent *pp.* slit open 806. [OE rendan] Cf. **torente.**

reparde *pp.* withheld 611. [? From ME *parren* 'to confine' (OE *pearrian)]

repayre *pass. infin.* be gathered 1028. [OF repairier, repar(i)er]

repente, *pr. 3 sg. subj. impers., ჳif hym*

repente 'if he repent' 662. [OF repentir]

reprené *v.* censure 544. [OF *repreign-, repren-, pr.* stems of *reprendre*]

requeste *n.* entreaty 281. [OF requeste]

rere *v.* rise 160; **rert** *pp.* fixed (established) 591n. [OE rǣran]

rescoghe *n.* salvation 610.[From OF *rescou-,* stem of *resco(u)rre v.*]

reset *n.* refuge 1067. [AF reset, CF recet]

resonabele *adj.* reasonable 523. [OF reson(n)able, raison(n)able]

resoun *n.* reason 52, cause 665n; **resouneჳ** *pl.* statements 716; **raysoun** matter 268. [OF resoun, raison]

respecte *n.* comparison 84. [OF respect]

respyt *n.* respite 644. [OF respit]

resse *n.* rush 874. [OE rǣs] Cf. **raas.**

rest *v.* rest 679. [OE restan]

restay *v.* delay 437; **restayed** *pt. pl.* restrained 716; *pp.* restrained 1168. [OF *resteir,* var. of *rester*]

reste *n.* rest (repose) 858, 1087n. [OE rest]

restored *pp.* restored 659. [OF restorer]

retrete *v.* imitate 92. [OF retraitier, AF retreter]

reue *n.* reeve 542. [OE ge)rēfa]

reuer *n.* river 1055; **reuereჳ** *pl.* rivers 105n. [OF rivier(e), reviere; AF rivere, riveir]

rewarde *n.* reward 604. [AF reward]

rewfully *adv.* sorrowfully 1181. [From OE *hrēow* 'sorrow' *n.;* cf. OE *hrēowlīce adv.]* Cf. **ruful.**

riche *adj.* rich 993; **rych** rich 68, 1182, splendid 105, 1036; **ryche** rich 646, 770, noble 906, magnificent 1097. [OE rīce, OF riche; cf. ON rīkr.]

rode *n.* cross 646, 705, 806. [OE rōd, rōde]

roghe *adj.* rough 646. [OE rūh, rūg(e, rūwe]

rokkeჳ *n. pl.* rocks 68. [OF roque, roke; cf. OE stān-rocc.]

ronk *adj.* rich 844, strong 1167. [OE ranc]

ros. See **rys.**

rose *n.* rose 269, 906. [OE rōse, rose]

rot *n.* decay 26. [? From OE ge)rotian; cf. ON rot]

rote *v.* decay 958. [OE ge)rotian]

rote *n.* root 420. [ON rōt & LOE (from ON) rōt, ?rōte]

rounde *adj.* round 5, 657, 738. [OF rěonde, ronde; AF rǒunde]

rourde *n.* sound 112. [OE reord]

route *n.* crowd 926. [OF route]

rownande *pr. p.* whispering 112. [OE rūnian]

243

ruful *adj.* compassionate 916. [From OE hrēow *n.*; cf. OE hrēowlic *adj.*] Cf. **rewfully.**

runne, runnen. See **ran.**

ryal *adj.* royal 160, 193; **ryalle** 191, 919. [AF reial; CF rëal, rial]

ryally *adv.* royally 987. [From prec.]

rybé *n.* ruby 1007n. [OF rubi & rubïe]

rych(e) *adj.* See **riche.**

ryche *n.* kingdom 601, 722, realm 919. [OE rīce]

rychez *n.* wealth 26. [OF richece, richese]

ryf *adj.* abundant 770, 844. [OE hrīfe, rīfe; LOE (12th cent.) rȳfe *(MED)*]

ryzt *n.* right 496, 684, 720, justice 580, 591, 665, 1196, righteousness 622; **ryzte** right 696, justice 708. [WS, K riht; A reht, geriht] See Commentary (line 672) for connotations.

ryzt *adj.* just 703; **ryzte** justified 672n. [WS riht, A reht]

ryzt *adv.* right 298, just 461, 723, 1093, 1169, rightly 673, directly 885; *ryzt nozt* (after neg.) anything at all 520. [WS rihte, ryhte; A rehte]

ryztwys *adj.* righteous 675, 685, 697; *sb. adj.* righteous man 689; **ryztywys** righteous 739n. [WS, K riht-wīs; A reht-wīs]

ryztwysly *adv.* correctly 709. [OE rihtwīslīce]

ryztywys. See **ryztwys.**

rys *v.* rise 1093; **ryse** 103; **rysez** *pr. 3 sg.* rises 191; **ros** *pt. 3 sg.* rose 437, 506, 519. [OE ge)rīsan, *pt. sg.* rās]

sadde *adj.* dignified 887. [OE sæd]

sade *pt. 3 sg. pass.* was fit 211. [From prec. & OE sadian]

sade 'said'. See **say.**

saf *adj.* redeemed 672, 684, 720; **saue** 696. [OF sauf, saf, save, sauve]

saffer *n.* sapphire 118, 1002. [OF saf(f)ir]

saghe *n.* word 226; **sawez** *pl.* words 278. [OE *sagu* 'saying']

saz 'reveals' 689n. See **say.**

saz 'saw' *v.* See **se.**

sazt *ppl. a.* peaceful 52; **sazte** 1201. [From OE sehtan, LOE sæhtan; cf. ON sætta]

sake *n.* reason 800, sake 940. [OE sacu; cf. ON sök & AL saka *(MED)*.]

Sakerfyse *n.* Sacrifice (in reference to Christ) 1064. [OF sacrefise, sacrifice]

same *adj.* same 1099, 1101. [ON sami]

samen *adv.* together 518. [OE samen; cf. ON saman]

sange. See **songe.**

Sant. See **Saynt.**

sardonyse *n.* sardonyx 1006. [OE & OF sardonix; L sardonyx, sardonychis]

satz. See **say.**

saue *adj.* (line 696). See **saf.**

saue *v.* redeem 674; **sauez** *pr. 3 sg.* saves 666. [OF sauver, saver]

sauerly *adj.* enthusiastic 226. [From ME *saver, comp.* of *sauf adj.* (OF *sauf*)]

saule *n.* soul 845; **sawle** 461. [OE sāwol]

Sauter *n.* Psalter (Book of Psalms) 593, 677, 698. [OF Sautier, Sauter]

sawez. See **saghe.**

sawle. See **saule.**

say *infin.* to say 226, say 1089; *v.* say 256, 258, 1041, tell 391; **sayd** *pp.* spoken 593; *pt. 1 sg.* said 1175; **sayde** *pt. 3 sg.* said 289, 338, etc.; *pt. 1 sg.* said 589, 962; **sayden** *pt. pl.* said 534, 550; **saye** *pr. 1 sg.* say 3; *v.* say 482; **sayz** *pr. 2 sg.* say 615; **sade** *pt. 3 sg.* said 532; *pt. 1 sg.* said 784; **saz** *pr. 3 sg.* reveals 689n; **satz** *pr. 3 sg.* says 677; **says** *pr. 2 sg.* say 295, 297, 409; *pr. 3 sg. subj.* may say 693; *pr. 3 sg.* says 867; **saytz** *pr. 2 sg.* say 315; *pr. 3 sg.* says 457, 501, 697, tells 836; **syde** *pt. 3 sg.* said 433n. [OE secgan]

Saynt *n.* Saint (Paul) 457, Saint (John the Baptist) 818; **Saut** Saint (John the apostle) 788; **sayntez** *pl.* saints 835. [OF saint]

says(z), saytz. See **say.**

scale *n.* surface 1005. [ML scāla, OF escale]

schadowed *pt. pl.* provided shade 42. [OE sceadwian, scadwian]

schaftez *n. pl.* rays 982. [OE sceaft, scæft]

schal *v. pr. auxil.* (used for *sg. 1st, 2nd, & 3rd persons & pl.*) shall 265, 283, etc., must 328, 329, 332, 424; **schalte** *pr. 2 sg. auxil.* shall 564. [OE sc(e)al, sc(e)alt]

scharpe *adv.* sharply 877. [WS scearpe, A scerpe]

schede, *v., con schede 'slipped away' 411n; *pt. 3 sg.* shed 741. [OE scēadan]

schene *adj.* shiny 42, 80, gleaming 203, bright 1145; *sb. adj.* bright child 166, bright damsel 965. [OE scēne]

schente *pp.* punished 668. [OE scendan]

schep *n.* sheep 801. [OE scēap, scēp]

schere *v.* shear 165; **schorne** *pp.* shorn 213.

[OE sceran, scieran; *pp.* scoren]

schereʒ. See **charde.**

scheued. See next entry.

scheweʒ *pr. 3 sg.* shows 1210; **scheued** *pt. 3 sg.* appeared 692. [OE scēawian]

scho *pron. nom.* she 758. [Prob. from OE *hīo,* var. of *hēo,* with LOE stress shift in the diphthong *(MED)*] Cf. **ho** 'she'.

schon. See **schyneʒ.**

schore *n.* shore 107, 230, cliff 166n. [OE scora]

schorne. See **schere.**

schot *pt. 3 sg.* rose 58. [OE scēotan]

schowted *pt. 3 sg. subj.* sounded 877. [? From ON *skūta, skūti* 'a taunt' *(MED)*]

schrylle *adv.* clearly 80n. [? From ME *shille adj.* (OE *scill*) with intrusive *r* by analogy with verbs like ME *shrike (MED)*]

schulde, *pt.* of **schal,** should 153, 314, etc., would 186, 1159, was supposed (to) 1162. [OE sc(e)olde]

schylde *v.* prevent 965. [OE scildan]

schyldereʒ *n. pl.* shoulders 214. [OE sculdor; *pl.* sculdru, (Nhb.) scyldru]

schym *adj.* bright 1077. [Cf. OE scīma *n.*]

schymeryng *ger.* shimmering 80. [From OE scimerian]

schynde. See next entry.

schyneʒ *pr. pl.* shine 28; *pr. 3 sg.* shines 1074; **schon** *pt. 3 sg.* sparkled 166, 982, shone 213, 1018, 1057; **schynde** *pt. pl.* shone 80. [OE scīnan]

schyr *adj.* pure 213, bright 284; *adv.* brilliantly 28; **schyre** *adj.* bright 42; **schyrrer** *adj. comp.* more radiant 982. [OE scīr, scȳr; *adv.* scīre]

sclade. See **slade.**

Scrypture *n.* Scripture (the Bible) 1039. [L scriptūra; cf. OF e)scripture]

se *infin.* to see 96, see 964; *v.* see 146, 296, etc.; *pr. 1 sg.* see 377, 385; *pr. 1 sg. subj.* see 932; **saʒ** *pt. 1 sg.* saw 1021, 1147; **segh** *pt. 3 sg.* saw 790; **seghe** *pr. 1 sg.* saw 867; **seʒ** *pr. 1 & 3 sg.* saw 158, 175, 200, 531, 1155; *pt. pl. subj.* saw 698; *pr. 3 sg.* sees 302; **sen** *pp.* seen 164; **sene** *v.* look 45; *pp.* seen 194, 787, noticed 1143; **syʒ** *pt. 3 sg.* saw 788, 985, 1032; **syʒe** *pr. pl. subj.* see 308; *pt. 1 sg.* saw 986, 1033. [OE sēon]

sech *imper. sg.* seek 354; **soʒt** *pp.* given 518; **soʒte** *pt. 3 sg.* sought 730. [OE sēcan, *pt.* sōhte, *pp.* sōht; cf. ON soekja.]

secounde *adj.* second 652, 1002. [OF second(e, secund(e]

sede *n.* seed 34. [WS sǣd, A sēd]

segh(e). See **se.**

seʒ. See **se.**

selden *adv.* seldom 380. [OE seldan]

self *adj.* same 203, very 446, 1046, 1076; *n., Godeʒ self* 'God himself' 1054. [WS self, A seolf]

sely *adj* blessed 659. [WS ge)sǣlig; ? A gesēlig *(MED)*]

sembelaunt *n.* expression 1143; **semblaunt** appearance 211. [OF semblant]

seme *n.* border 838. [OE sēam]

seme *adv.* suitably 190; *adj.* sweet 1115. [ON sœmr]

semed *pr. perf. 3 sg. subj.* would have seemed 760. [ON sœma]

semly *adj.* excellent 34, beautiful 45, 789. [ON sœmiligr]

sen(e). See **se.**

sende *pr. 3 sg. subj.* send 130. [OE sendan]

sengeley *adv.* apart 8. [From OF sengle *adj.*]

serlypeʒ *adj.* separate 994. [From ON *sēr* & OE *-lēpes* in word like *sunderlēpes adv.* 'separately')]

sermoun *n.* speech 1185. [AF sermoun]

sertayn *adv.* certainly 685. [OF certain]

seruaunt *n.* servant 699. [AF servaunt]

serued *pp.* deserved 553. [Shortened form of OF *deservir*; cf. OF *servir* 'to merit'.]

serueʒ *pr. 3 sg. emph.* does avail 331. [OF servir, AF serveier]

sesed *pp.* endowed 417. [OF seisir, saisir]

set (1) *pt. 3 sg.* sat 1054; **sete** *pt. 3 sg.* sat 161; *pt. pl.* sat 835. [OE sittan, *pt.* sæt]

set (2) *pt. 3 sg.* put 255, submitted 811; *imper. sg.* set 545; *pp.* built 1062; **sete,** *pass. infin., sete saʒte* 'to be made peaceful' 1201; **sette** *pt. 1 sg.* set 8; *pr. perf. 3 sg. subj., sette myseluen saʒt* 'would have made me peaceful' 52; *pp.* set 222, 838; **setten** *pr. pl.* make 307. [OE settan]

seuen *adj.* seven 838, 1111. [OE seofon]

seuenþe *adj.* seventh 1010. [From prec.; cf. WS seofoþa, LWS seofende *(MED)*.]

sexte *n.* sixth 1007. [OE sixta, siexta, sexta]

seysoun *n.* occasion 39n. [OF seison]

sir *n.* sir 257, 439. [OF sire]

skyfte *v.* arrange 569. [ON skifta; cf. OE ge)sciftan.]

skyl *n.* reason 312; **skylle** agreement 674; **skylleʒ** *pl.* assertions 54. [ON skil]

slade *n.* valley 141; sclade 1148. [OE slæd]
slaȝt *n.* slaughter 801. [OE sleht, slæht; cf. ON slātr]
slake *v.* abate 942. [OE slacian]
slayn *pp.* slain 805. [OE slēan; *pp.* slægen]
slente *n.* hillside 141. [Prob. from ME *slenten v.* (Dan. *slente* 'to slide'); cf. Swed. *slänt* 'slope' *(MED).*]
slepe *pr. pl.* sleep 115. [WS slǣpan, A slēpan]
slepyng-slaȝte *n.* deep slumber 59n. [From prec.+OE *slǣht]* Cf. slaȝt.
slode *pt. 1 sg.* slid (into sleep) 59. [OE slīdan; cf. OE āslīdan, *pt.* āslād]
slyȝt *adj.* slender 190. [Cf. ON *slēttr* (from **sleht)*]
smal *adj.* small 6, 190; smale 90. [OE smæl]
smelle *n.* (sweet) smell 1122. [LOE (12th cent. *dat. sg.*) smelle *(MED)*]
smoþe *adj.* smooth 6, 190. [LOE smōþ]
so *adv.* so 2, 5, etc., thus 97, 467, etc., then 1187; so . . . a *correl. adv.* as . . . as 1057–58. [OE swā]
soberly *adv.* seriously 256. [From next entry; cf. MDu. *soberlike (MED).*]
sobre *adj.* serious 391, 532. [OF sobre]
sodanly *adv.* suddenly 1095, 1098; sodenly 1178. [From OF sodain *adj.]*
soffer. See suffer.
soȝt(e). See sech.
solace *n.* solace 130. [OF solace, solas]
solde *pt. 3 sg.* sold 731. [OE sellan]
sommoun. See sumoun.
sonde *n.* dispensation 943. [OE sand, sond]
sone *adv.* soon 537, 626, 1197, quickly 1078. [OE sōna]
songe *n.* song 882, 888, 891; sange melody 19. [OE sang, song]
songe(n) *v.* See synge.
sonne. See sunne.
sor *n.* sorrow 940; sore 130. [OE sār]
sore *adv.* strenuously 550. [OE sāre]
sorȝ *n.* regret 663; sorȝe grief 352. [OE sorg]
sorquydryȝe *n.* pride 309. [OF sorquiderie, sorcuiderie; AF/ONF surquiderie]
soth *adj.* true 482, 1185; soþe *n.* truth 653. [OE sōþ] Cf. forsoþe.
sothfol *adj.* truthful 498. [From prec.]
sotyle *adj.* tenuous 1050. [OF sotil]
soþe. See soth.
soun *n.* voice 532. [AF *soun;* cf. OE sōn 'sound' (from L *sonus).*]
sounande *pr. p.* melodious 883. [OF soner;

AF suner, sonir; L sonāre]
space *n.* space 61n, 1030, interval 438. [AF space, OF espace]
spakk. See speke.
sparred *pt. 1 sg.* sprang 1169. [Origin unknown; ? cf. F (17th cent.) *esparer* 'to kick' & OE *sperran* 'to strike' *(MED).*]
spech *n.* statement 704; speche speech 37, 235, etc., conversation 471. [OE spǣc, spēc, variants of sprǣc]
special *adj.* special 235; specyal 938. [AF speciel; OF especial]
spede *pr. 3 sg. subj* may bless 487. [OE spēdan]
speke *pr. 1 sg. subj.* speak 422; *pt. 3 sg.* spoke 438; spekeȝ *pr. 3 sg.* relates 594; spakk *pt. 3 sg.* said 938; spoken *pp.* uttered 291. [OE specan, sprecan]
spelle *n.* speech 363. [OE spell]
spelle *fut. 1 sg.* shall tell 793. [OE spellian]
spenned *pp.* enclosed 53; spenud *pt. 1 sg.* clasped 49n. [ON spenna]
spent *pp.* described 1132. [OE spendan]
spoken. See speke.
sponne *pt. pl. subj.* would spring 35. [OE spinnan, *pt. pl.* spunnon]
spornande *pr. p.* stumbling 363. [OE spornan]
spot *n.* spot (blemish) 12, 48, 60, 764, 1068, spot (place) 25, 37, 49, 61; spote spot (place) 13; spotte spot (blemish) 24, 36; spotteȝ *pl.* spots (blemishes) 945. [OE spot; cf. MDu. spotte & ON spotti]
spotleȝ *adj* spotless 856. [From prec.]
spotty *adj.* spotty 1070. [From spot]
sprang(e). See spryng.
sprede *pass. infin.* be spread 25. [OE sprǣdan]
sprent *pt. 3 sg.* spurted 1137. [From OE *gesprintan* & ON **sprent-;* cf. OI *spretta* 'to spring up' *(MED).*]
spryg *n. coll.* shrubs 35n. [From ME *spring* 'twig' (OE *spring);* cf. MLG *spricken* 'twigs' & OE *sprǣc* 'a shoot' *(MED).*]
spryng *v.* spring 453; sprang *pt. 3 sg.* sprang 61; sprange 13. [OE springan]
spyce *n.* damsel 235n, 938; spyceȝ *pl.* spices (on plants) 35; spyse *coll.* spices (on plants) 104; spyseȝ *pl.* 25. [OF espice, AF spece (from L speciēs)]
spyryt *n.* spirit 61. [AF spirit, OF espirit]
spyse, spyseȝ. See spyce.
spyt *n.* outrage 1138. [Shortened form of OF *despit]*

246

stable *adj.* stable 597. [AF stable, OF estable]

stable *v.* settle 683. [OF establir, establer]

stage *n.* stage 410n. [OF estage]

stale *n.* position 1002. [Cf. OE *steall* & *stæl* 'place, position' & AF *e)stale*.]

stalked *pt. 1 sg.* stepped (cautiously) 152. [From OE *-stealcian* (as in *bestealcian*)]

stalle *v.* delay 188. [Cf. OF estaler & OE forð-steallian]

stande *infin. tr. prog.* standing 514, 867; *pr. pl. emph.* do stand 515; **standeʒ** *pr. pl.* stand 547; **standen** *pp.* stood 519, 1148; **stod** *pt. 1 sg.* stood 182, 1085, remained 184; *pt. 3 sg.* remained 597, stood 1023; **stonde** *pr. pl. emph.* do stand 533; **stonden** *pt. pl.* shone 113n. [OE standan, stondan]

stare *v.* stare 149; **staren** *pr. p.* gleaming 116n. [OE starian]

start, *infin. tr. prog., to start* 'from starting' 1159; *infin.* to spring 1162. [OE *styrtan; cf. Nhb. sturtende, MDu. storten, & OFris. sterta *(MED)*.]

stayre *adj.* steep 1022. [OE *stæger* (as in *wiðer-stæger* 'steep') *(MED)*]

stele *infin.* slip (come softly) 20. [OE stelan]

step *n. coll.* footsteps 683. [OE stepe]

stepe *adj.* bright 113. [OE stēap]

stere *v.* guide 623, restrain 1159. [OE stēoran, stēran; WS stīeran, stȳran]

sterneʒ *n. pl.* stars 115. [ON stjarna]

steuen *n.* speech 188n, sound 1125. [OE *stefn, stæfn* 'voice, sound']

stod. See **stande**.

stode *n.* position 740n. [OE stede, steode]

stok *n.* stock 380. [OE stoc(c); cf. OI stokkr]

stoken *pp.* locked 1065. [OE *stecan; cf. OFris. *steka* & MDu. *stēken*]

ston *n.* gem 206, stone 380, 822, (precious) stone 994, 1006; **stoneʒ** *pl.* (precious) stones 113, 997. [OE stān]

stonde, stonden. See **stande**.

stonge *pt. 3 sg.* stung 179. [OE stingan]

store *n.* group 847. [AF stor(e), OF estor]

stote *v.* stop 149. [Prob. from MDu., MLG *stōten (MED)*]

stound *n.* hour 20, 659. [OE stund]

stout *adj.* proud 779; **stoute** stately 935. [OF estout, stout]

strange *adj.* strange 175. [OF estrange, AF stra(u)nge]

strateʒ. See **strete**.

stray *adv.* uncontrollably 179. [Shortened form of OF *pp. estraié*] Cf. **astraye**.

strayd *pa. perf. 3 sg.* had strayed 1173. [From OF *estraier*]

strayn *v.* direct 691; **strayneʒ** *pr. 3 sg.* stirs 128; **streny** *v.* strain 551. [From OF *estrei(g)n-, pr.* stem of *estreindre*]

strech *v.* stride 971; **streche** spread 843. [OE streccan]

streʒt *adj.* straight 691. [From ME *streight, pp.* of prec. (OE *pp. streaht*)]

strem *n.* stream 125, 1159, 1162. [OE strēam]

stremande *pr. p.* streaming (stars) 115. [From prec.]

strenghþe *n.* ardor 128. [OE strengðu, strengð]

streny. See **strayn**.

stresse *n.* distress 124. [Shortened form of OF *destresse*] Cf. **dysstresse**.

strete *n.* street 971, 1059; **streteʒ** *pl.* streets 1025; **strateʒ** 1043. [WS stræt, A strēt]

strok. See **stryke**.

stronde *n.* shore 152. [OE strand]

stronge *adj.* strong 531; *adv.* steadfastly 476. [OE strang, strong]

strot *n.* strife 353, contention 848. [OE *strūt; cf. strūtian 'to struggle' *(MED)*.]

stroþe-men *n. pl.* woodsmen 115n. [OE strōd, strōð + OE men]

stryf *n.* strife 248, hardship 776, discord 848. [AF strif, OF estrif]

stryke *v.* strike (passage of sound) 1125; **strykeʒ** *pr. 3 sg.* enters 570; **strok** *pt. 3 sg.* sent 1180. [OE strīcan, *pt. *strāc]

stryuen *pr. pl.* strive 1199. [OF estriver]

styf *adj.* firm 779. [OE stīf]

stykeʒ *pr. 2 sg. pass.* are set 1186n. [OE stician]

stylle *adj.* silent 20; *adv.* still 182, 1085, permanently 683. [OE stille]

stynst *imper. sg.* cease 353n. [OE styntan]

such *adj.* such 26, 176, etc.; *pron.* such 727; **suche** *adj.* 58, 171; *pron.* 719. [OE swilc, swylc, swelc]

suffer *v.* suffer 954; **suffred** *pp.* endured 554; **soffer** *v.* suffer 940. [AF suf(f)rir, OF sof(f)rir]

suffyse *v.* suffice 135. [AF suffiser]

sulpande *pr. p.* polluting 726. [Origin unknown; cf. G dial. *sölpern* 'to soil' & Norw. dial. **sulpa** 'to plunge or wade'.]

sum *adj.* some 428; *pron., of al and sum* 'in every respect' 584; **summe** *pron.* some 508. [OE sum] sumkyn *adj.* some kind of 619. [OE sum+OE cynna]

sumoun *n.* summons 539; sommoun 1098. [From OF *somonre* v. or back formation from OF *somonse n.*]

sumtyme *adv.* at some time 620, formerly 760. [OE sum+OE tīma]

sunne *n.* sun 28, 519, etc.; sonne 530. [OE sunne]

sunnebemeʒ *n. pl.* sunbeams 83. [OE sunne-bēam]

supplantoreʒ *n. pl.* supplanters 440n. [From L supplantāre v. & OF supplanter v.; cf. AF supplantour n.]

sure *adv.* securely 222; *adj.* positive 1089. [OF sëur(e, sŏur]

sute, *n.*, *self sute schene* 'same gleaming pattern' 203; *in sute* 'alike' 1108. [AF sute]

sve *v.* follow 976; swe *pr. pl.* follow 892. [OF sivre, seure, suir, suiwir]

swalt *pt. 3 sg.* died 816; swalte *pt. 1 sg. subj.* would perish 1160. [OE sweltan]

swange (1) *pt. 3 sg.* sped 1059. [OE swingan, *pt.* swang]

swange (2) *pa. perf. pl.* had labored 586. [OE swincan, swingan; *pt.* swanc]

swangeande *pr. p.* swirling 111. [Cf. OE *swangettung* 'movement', OE *swengan* 'to rush', & swang (1) above.]

sware *n.* square 1029. [OF esquar(r)e]

sware *adj.* square 837, 1023. [AF squarr(e]

sware *v.* answer 240.[ON *svara*; cf. also OE *-swarian* (in *andswarian*).] Cf. onsware.

swat *pa. perf. pl.* (had) sweat 586; swatte *pt. 3 sg.* suffered 829n. [OE swǣtan]

swe. See sve.

swefte. See swyft.

sweng *n.* labor 575. [OE *sweng*; cf. OE *swenc* 'toil' & *swinc* 'toil'.]

swepe *v.* sweep 111. [From OE *swipian* or *swēop, pt.* of *swāpan;* cf. OS *swēpan.*]

swete *adj.* lovely 19, sweet 94, 763, 1122; *sb. adj.* sweet girl 240, sweet maiden 325; *adv.* pleasantly 111, 1057. [OE swēte]

swetely *adv.* graciously 717. [OE swētlīce]

sweuen *n.* sleep 62. [OE swefen]

swone *n.* swoon 1180. [From ME *aswone* (OE *pp.* geswōgen 'fainted')]

swyft *adj* swift 571; swefte *adv.* swiftly 354. [OE swift]

swymme *v.* swim 1160. [OE swimman]

swyþe *adv.* sincerely 354, swiftly 1059. [OE swīðe, swȳðe]

syde 'said' 433n. See say.

syde *n.* side 975, 1137; sydeʒ *pl.* sides 6, 73, 198, 218. [OE sīde]

syʒ(e). See se.

syʒt *n.* sight 226, 839, 968, vision 985, 1151; *Syʒt of Pes* 'Vision of Peace' 952; syʒteʒ *pl.* sights 1179. [OE ge)siht]

sykyng *pr. p.* sighing 1175. [OE sīcan]

syluer *n.* silver 77. [OE sylfor]

sympelnesse *n.* simplicity 909. [From OF simple *adj.*]

symple *adj.* humble 1134. [OF simple]

syn. See syþen.

synge *v.* sing 891; songe *pt. pl.* sang 1124; songen *pt. pl.* sang 94, 882, 888. [OE singan, *pt. pl.* sungon]

synglerty *n.* singularity 429. [OF senglerté]

synglure *n.* in phr. *in synglure* 'as unique' 8n. [From OF sengler *adj.*]

syngnetteʒ *n. pl.* seals 838. [OF signet]

synne *n.* sin 610, 726, 811; synneʒ *pl.* sins 823. [OE syn(n]

synneʒ *pr. 3 sg.* sins 662. [OE syngian, syn(n)igan, synnian]

syt *n.* grief 663. [Cf. ON *sȳta* 'to lament' & *sūt* 'grief'.]

sytole-stryng *n.* citole-string 91. [OF citole+OE streng]

syþeʒ *n. pl.* times 1079. [OE sīþ, sȳþ]

syþen *conj.* since 13, 245; *adv.* then 643, 1207; syn (shortened form) *conj.* since 519. [OE siððan]

tabelment *n.* tier 994. [AF tablement]

table *n.* tier 1004. [OF table, OE tabele (from L)]

tached *pp.* rooted 464. [AF tacher]

take *pr. pl.* pay 387; *v.* receive 539, 552, 599, 1067, take 944, cause 1158; *imper. sg.* take 559; takeʒ *pr. pl.* spend 687; taken *pp.* revealed 830; tan *pp.* obtained 614; toke *pt. 3 sg.* accepted 414, took 808; *pt. pl.* spent 585; totʒ *pr. 3 sg.* goes 513. [LOE tacan (from ON taka)]

tale *n.* speech 257, story 311, 590, tale 897, account 998; talle story 865n. [OE talu]

talle. See tale

tan. See take.

tech *imper sg.* lead 936. [OE tǣcan]

teche *n.* guilt 845. [OF teche]

telle *v.* tell 134, 653; telleʒ *pr. 2 sg.* tell 919; tolde *pt. 3 sg.* sounded 815. [OE tellan]

temen *pr. pl.* belong 460. [OE tēman]

temple *n.* temple 1062. [OF temple, OE

248

tempel (from L)]

tempte v. try 903. [OF tempter, L temptāre]

tender adj. tender 412. [AF tender, OF tendre]

teneʒ n. pl. sufferings 332. [OE tēona]

tenoun n. coll. jointings 993. [AF tenoun, OF tenon]

tente n. attention 387. [From OF entente]

tenþe adj. tenth 136; n. tenth 1013. [From OE tēoða, tēða, assimilated to OE tēn]

terme n. period 503; termeʒ pl. words 1053. [OF terme]

that adj. See þat adj.

the def. art. See þe def. art.

theme n. theme 944. [OF teme, theme; L thema]

then, thenne adv. See þen adv.

this adj. See þis adj.

thow. See þou.

throne n. throne 1113; trone 835, 920, 1051, 1055. [OF trone, L thrōnus]

thys adj. See þis adj.

to prep. for 1, 2, etc., into 10, 26, etc., to 20, 21, etc., at 37, 167, 1120, upon 50, 131, on 209, as 272, 468, 759, in 326, 566, etc., toward 567, 671, 1193, of 610, before 700, with 819, from 1159, in order to 954; to hym warde 'toward him' 820; (pleonastic) 1073n. [OE tō] See also for to s.v. for.

to, adv., to ne fro 'to nor fro' 347; too 481, 492, 615, 1070 (twice), 1075, 1076, 1118. [OE tō]

todone pp. revealed 914. [OE tōdōn]

todraweʒ pr. 2 sg. dispel 280. [OE tō-+OE dragan]

togeder adv. together 1121. [OE tōgædere]

toʒt adj. binding 522. [Perhaps from OE tēon 'to settle'; cf. OE teohhian 'to determine']

toke. See take.

token n. token 742. [OE tācen]

tolde. See telle.

tom n. time 134, 585. [ON tōm]

tong n. tongue 225; tonge 100, 898. [OE tunge]

topasye n. topaz 1012. [OF topase]

tor n. kingdom 966. [OF tor, tur; Cf. OE torr 'tower'] Cf. torreʒ.

tor adj. difficult 1109. [ON tor- in compounds like tor-næmr 'hard to learn'; cf. OE tor-cyrre 'hard to convert']

toreme v. lament 1181. [OE tō-+OE hrēmen] Cf. remen.

torente pp. torn 1136. [OE tōrendan] Cf. rent.

toriuen pp. shattered 1197. [OE tō-+ON rīfa]

torreʒ n. pl. peaks 875. [OE torr 'rock, crag', from Gaelic tòrr] Cf. tor n.

totʒ. See take.

touch v. touch 714; towched pt. pl. touched 898. [OF tochier, tuchier]

toun n. town 995. [OE tūn]

towarde prep. toward 67, 974, 1113, to 438. [OE tōweard]

towen pp. pulled 251. [OE tēon, pp. togen]

tras, n., trone a tras 'stepped in line' 1113. [OF trace]

trauayle n. anxiety 1087. [OF travail]

trauayled pp. labored 550. [OF travailler]

traw v. believe 487; trawed pt. 1 sg. believed 282; traweʒ pr. 2 sg. believe 295; trowe pr. 1 sg. subj. would imagine 933. [OE trūwian, trēowian]

trawþe n. truth 495. [OE trēowþ]

trendeled pt. 3 sg. rolled 41. [From OE ātrendlian 'to roll']

tres n. pl. trees 1077. [OE trēo]

tresor n. treasure 331; tresore value 237. [OF tresor]

trone n. See throne.

trone pt. pl. stepped 1113. [Cf. OSwed. trina 'go, step, march' & ODan. trene.]

trowe. See traw.

true adj. trustworthy 311; trw true 831; trwe true 421, 822, 1191, secure 460, honest 725. [OE trēowe]

tryed pp. tried 702, 707; tryʒe pass. infin. be considered 311. [OF trier]

trylle v. trail 78n. [Cf. Swed. & Norw. trilla, Dan. trille, & EFris. trullen.]

twayned pp. separated 251. [From OE twēgen 'two']

twelfþe n. twelfth 1015. [OE twelfta]

twelue adj. twelve 992, 993, 1022, 1030, 1078, 1079; n. 1035. [OE twelf]

two adj. two 483, 555, 674, 949. [OE twā]

twyeʒ adv. twice 830. [LOE twiges]

twynne, n., in twynne 'apart' 251. [OE twinn adj., getwinn n. & adj.]

twynne-how adj. double-colored 1012. [OE twinn+OE hēow] Cf. huee.

tyʒed pp. fastened 464; tyʒt 1013. [OE tīgan]

tyʒt (1) infin. come 718. [OE tyhtan]

tyʒt (2) pp. appointed 503; tyʒte pt. 3 sg. set down (in writing) 1053. [Perhaps from

prec. infl. by OE *dihtan* 'to appoint']
ty3t (3), line 1013. See **ty3ed**.
tyl *conj.* until 976; **tyl . . . þat** *correl. conj.*
until 548, 979; **tylle** *prep.* to. [ON
til; OE (Nhb.) til]
tyme *n.* time 503, 833. [OE tīma]
tynde *n.* branch 78. [OE tind]
tyne *v.* surrender 332. [ON tȳna]
tyste *ppl. a.* joined 460n. [OF tistre]
tyt *adv.* quickly 728. [ON tītt] Cf. **as-tyt**.

þa *rel. pron.* who 856n. [OE þā] Cf. **þat** *rel.
pron.*
þa3 *conj.* though 52, 55, etc., if 352, even if
1160; **þo3** though 345. [OE *þēah*; ON
þō (from **þauh*)]
þare. See **þer**.
þat *rel. pron.* that 15, 50, etc., which 37,
78, etc., who 100, 286, etc., (you) who
372, (he) who 408, 812, (she) who
1150; *acc.* whom 187, 799, 1209; *dat.*
for whom 242, to whom 424, whom
425, which 656, 957, in whom 909;
demons. or *anaphoric pron.* (used as
neut. subject) that 179, 309, etc., it 17,
982; *nom.* those who 631, 687, he who
681, 748, 828, you 904; *acc.* that 300,
536, etc.; *dat.* to it 880; (pleonastic)
939, 951, 1026. [OE þæt, þat]
þat *adj.* that 12, 13, etc.; **that** 253, 481,
937. [OE þæt, þat]
þat *conj.* so that 35, 119, etc., that 137, 142,
etc., what 269, 302, etc., that which
(what) 312, since 471, 1188, as 1100,
when 1126; (pleonastic) 65, 548, 958,
979. [OE þæt]
þay *pron. nom. pl.* they 80, 94, etc.;
(pleonastic) 587. [ON þeir]
þe *def. art.* the 28, 69, etc.; (used as *poss.*)
my 67, its 983; **the** the 85, 109, 121,
445, 541, 685, 1069, 1141. [OE þe]
þe *adv.* (with *comp.*) the 152, 234, etc.; *cor-
rel. adv.*, **þe . . . þe** 'the . . . the' 127–
28, 180, etc.; **the** the 169. [OE þȳ, þē]
þe *pron. dat. sg.* you 244, 263, etc., to you
266, 973, 1200, for you 274, 747, 967;
acc. sg. you 385, 397, etc.; *acc. sg.
refl.* yourself 268, 474, 703; (used as
subject) you 267, 316, 341. [OE þē]
þede *n.* land (country) 483. [OE þēod]
þef *n.* thief 273. [OE þēof]
þen *adv.* then 277, 398, etc.; *conj.* than
134, 181, etc.; **þenn** *conj.* than 555;
þenne *adv.* then 155, 177, etc.;

(pleonastic) *after þenne* 'afterwards' 256,
er þenne 'before' 631, 1094; **then** then
589; **thenne** then 361. [OE þænne,
þenne, þanne, þonne, þon(e)
þenk *v.* intend 1151; **þenkande** *pr. p.* being
mindful (thinking) 370; **þenke** *v.* remind
22; **þo3t**, *pt. 1 sg. impers.*, *þo3t me
neuer* 'I never was aware of' 19; *pt. 1
sg.* thought 137, 1138, 1157. [OE
þenc(e)an, *pt.* ge)þōht]
þenn, þenne. See **þen**.
þer *adv.* there 21, 28, etc., then 61, in that
way 1191; *conj.* where 26, 30, etc.;
þere *adv.* there 167, 194, 942, 1155;
conj. where 838; **þare** *adv.* there 830,
1021; **þore** *adv.* then 562. [OE þær, þār,
þēr; ON þar]
þeras *conj.* wherever 129, where 818, 1173.
[OE þær+OE ealswā]
þerate *adv.* in that place 514. [OE þǣræt]
þerfore *adv.* therefore 1197. [OE þær+OE
for]
þerinne *adv.* in that place 447, therein 644,
1061, into that place 724, in that matter
1168; **þereine** therein 633. [OE þærin,
þærinne]
þerof *adv.* of it 99, 968, thereof 161, 410, in
that place 1069, of that place 1084. [OE
þǣrof]
þeron *adv.* to it 387, after that 645, thereon
1042. [OE þǣron]
þeroute *adv.* in the open 930. [OE þǣrūt]
þerto *adv.* also 172, to it 664, for this pur-
pose 833, in that 1140. [OE þǣrtō]
þese. See **þis**.
þike *adv.* thickly 78. [OE þicce]
þis *adj.* these 42, this 65, 260, etc.; **þise**
adj. these 287, 997, 1022, 1119; *pron.*
these 384; *adj.* this 533; **þese** *pron.* these
551; *adj.* these 752; **þys** *adj.* this 250,
277, etc.; *pron.* this 421; *adj.* these
505; **þyse** *pron.* these 555; *adj.* these
921, 931; **þysse** *pron.* this 370; **this** *adj.*
this 733; **thys** *adj.* this 841. [OE þis,
þēs, þisse]
þo *adv.* then 451; **þoo** 873. [OE þā, ON þā]
þo *adj.* those 73, 85, etc.; *pron.* them 557.
[OE þā] Cf. **þos(e)**.
þo3. See **þa3**.
þo3t, lines 19, 137, 1138, 1157. See **þenk**.
þo3t, line 153. See **þynk**.
þo3te *n.* intention 524. [OE ge)þōht]
þole *v.* suffer 344. [OE þolian]
þonc *n. coll.* thanks 901. [OE þanc, þonc]

þoo. See þo adv.
þore. See þer.
þos pron. them 515; þose adj. those 93, 127. [OE þās] Cf. þo adj. & pron.
þou pron. nom. sg. you 23, 242, 245, 247, 264, 265, 269, 273, 275, 276, 280, etc.; þow 411; thow 337. [OE þū] Cf. ȝe.
þousandeȝ n. pl. thousands 926; þowsande sg. thousand 786, 869, 870; þowsandeȝ pl. dat. of thousands 1107. [OE þūsend]
þrange adv. grievously 17. [ON þröngr]
þre adj. three 291, 292, 1034. [OE þrēo]
þrete v. wrangle 561. [ON þrǣta]
þro adj. perverse 344; in phr. þryuen and þro 'noble and steadfast' 868. [ON þrár 'stubborn, persistent, eager, keen']
þroweȝ pr. 3 sg. peals 875. [OE þrāwan]
þrych v. oppress 17; þryȝt pp. thrust 670, pierced 706, gathered 926. [OE þryccan]
þryd adj. third 1004; þrydde n. third 299; þryde adj. third 833. [OE þridda]
þryf v. flourish 851; þryuen ppl. a. noble 868, beautiful 1192. [ON þrīfask, þrīfa; pp. þrifinn]
þryȝt. See þrych.
þryuen. See þryf.
þunder n. thunder 875. [OE þunor]
þurȝ prep. through 10, 114, etc., because of 1048. [OE þurh]
þurȝoutly adv. completely 859. [OE þurhūt+-līce]
þus adv. thus 526, 569, etc., so 673, therefore 673. [OE þus]
þy pron. poss. sg. your 266, 273, etc.; þyn 559, 567, 754. [OE þīn]
þyder adv. there 723, to that place 946. [OE þider]
þyn. See þy.
Pyng n. Being (Christ the Lamb) 771; þynge thing 910. [OE þing]
þynk, pr. impers., me þynk '(it) seems to me' 267, 316, 'seems to me' 590; vus þynk '(it) seems to us' 552, 553; þoȝt, pt. impers., me þoȝt '(it) seemed to me' 153. [OE þync(e)an, pt. ge)þūht]
þys(e). See þis.
þyself pron. sg. intens. (used as subject) (you) yourself 298, 313; acc. refl. yourself 473; dat. intens. by yourself 779; þyseluen acc. refl. yourself 341. [OE þīn+OE self]
þysse. See þis.

ueray. See veray.

uesture n. vesture 220. [OF vesture]
uoched pp. called 1121. [OF voch(i)er]
uyne. See vyne.
valeȝ n. pl. vales 127. [OF val]
vayl infin. avail 912. [OF valoir.]
vayn, n., set hymself in vayn 'submitted himself to contempt' 811n; vayne vanity 687. [OF vain, vein]
vayned. See wayneȝ.
vch adj. each, every 31, 323, etc.; vche 5, 33, 310, etc.; vch a every 78, 375, 436, 461, 862, 1015, 1059, 1210; vche a 117, 217, 1066, 1080. [OE ælc]
veray adj. truthful 1184; ueray reliable 1185. [AF veray]
verce n. verse 593. [OF vers (L versus); cf. OE fers & ON vers (from L versus)]
vered pt. 3 sg. lifted 254; vereȝ pr. 3 sg. lifts 177. [Cf. OF virer 'to turn'.]
vergyneȝ n. pl. virgins 1099; Vyrgyn gen. sg. Virgin (Mary) 426. [OF virgine]
vergynté n. virginity 767. [OF virginité]
Vertues n. pl. Virtues 1126n. [OF vertu]
veued. See weue.
vmbegon pp. tr. prog. encompassing 210. [OE ymb-gān]
vmbepyȝte pt. 3 sg. pass. was surrounded 204; pp. arrayed round about 1052. [OE ymbe+ME pyȝte] Cf. pyȝt.
vnavysed adj. unwise 292. [OE un-+OF avisé]
vnblemyst pp. unblemished 782. [OE un-+OF ble(s)mir]
vncortoyse adj. discourteous 303. [OE un-+AF co(u)rteis] Cf. cortayse.
vndefylde pp. undefiled 725. [OE un-+a blend of OE fylan & OF defo(u)ler]
vnder n. the third hour (about 9 A. M.) 513. [OE undern]
vnder prep. beneath 923. [OE under]
vnderstonde pass. infin. be understood 941. [OE understondan, understandan]
vnhyde v. reveal 973. [OE un-+OE hȳdan]
vnlapped pp. unclasped 214. [OE un-+OE -læppede]
vnmete adj. unsuitable 759. [OE unmæte] Cf. mete.
vnpynne v. open 728. [From OE un-+OE pinn 'pin' n.; cf. OE gepyndan 'to enclose'.]
vnresounable adj. unreasonable 590. [OE un-+OF resonable] Cf. resonabele.
vnstrayned pp. freed 248. [OE un-+pp. of

251

ME strain] Cf. **strayn.**

vnto *prep.* against 362, to 712, 718, 1169, 1212, as 772; **onto** to 810. [Cf. OS untō.]

vntrwe *adj.* untrue 897. [OE untrēowe] Cf. **true.**

vp *adv.* up 35, 177, etc. [OE up]

vpen. See **open.**

vpon, lines 198, 208, 824. See **open.**

vpon *prep.* upon 57, 814, etc., into 59, of 370, in 545, to 1196; *adv.* upon 640; **vpone** *prep.* upon 1054. [From OE *up* & *on*; cf. LOE *uppon* 'upon'.]

vrþe. See **erþe.**

vrþely *adj.* mortal 135. [OE eorþlic]

vtwyth *adv.* from without 969. [OE ūt+OE wiþ]

vus *pron. dat.* us 454, 658, etc., to us 552 (first one in line), 553, 853, 1210; *acc.* us 520, 556, etc.; (used as subject) we 552 (second one in line). [OE ūs]

vyde. See **wade.**

vyf. See **wyf.**

vygour *n.* strength 971. [AF vigour]

vyne *n.* vineyard 504, 507, 521, 525, 527, 535, 582, 628; **uyne** 502. [OF vine]

Vyrgyn. See **vergyneȝ.**

vys *n.* visage 750; **vyse** face 254. [OF vis]

vysayge *n.* visage 178. [OF visage]

vyueȝ. See **wyf.**

wace. See **watȝ.**

wade *infin.* wade 143; *v.* wade 1151; **vyde** *v.* wade 399n. [OE *ge)wadan;* ON *vaða;* Scottish *wide*]

wage *v.* endure 416. [ONF wagier]

wakned *pt. 1 sg.* awoke 1171. [OE wæcnan]

wal *n.* wall 1017, 1026. [OE wall]

wale *v.* perceive 1000, 1007. [From ON val *n.;* cf. ON velja *v.*]

walk *v.* walk 399; **welke** *pt. 1 sg.* wandered 101; *pt. 3 sg.* walked 711. [OE wealcan]

wallande *pr. p.* pouring 365. [OE weallan]

walte *pp.* upset 1156. [OE ge)wæltan]

wan. See **wynne** *v.*

waning *ger.* harm 558n. [OE wanung]

war *adj.* aware 1096. [OE wær]

warde (part of *prep.*) in phr. *to hym warde* 'toward him' 820; *fro me warde* 'opposite me' 981. [Cf. OE tōweard & fromweard.]

ware. See **were.**

warpe *infin.* sing 879. [OE weorpan]

wascheȝ *pr. 3 sg.* washes 655; **wesch** *pt. 3*

sg. cleansed 766. [OE wascan]

wasse. See **watȝ.**

wate. See **wot.**

water *n.* stream 107, 299, 318, water 111, 122, etc.; *gen.* of the stream 230. [OE wæter]

watȝ *pt. 1 & 3 sg.* was 15, 45, etc.; *pt. 2 pl.* were 372; *pa. perf. 2 sg.* had been 375, 474; *pt. 3 sg.* had 376, 528, 540, 988; *pa. perf. 3 sg.* had been 534; *pt. 3 pl.* were 1065, 1123; **wace** *pt. 3 sg.* was 65; **wasse** *pt. 3 pl.* were 1108, 1112. [OE wæs] Cf. **were.**

waweȝ *n. pl.* waves 287. [From OE *wagian* 'to move, shake, totter'; cf. ON *vaga.*]

wax *pt. 3 sg.* streamed 649; **wex** *pa. perf. 3 sg.* had grown 538, *pt. 3 sg.* flowed 648. [OE ge)weaxan, *pt.* wēox]

way *n.* path 350; *coll.* means 580; **wayeȝ** *pl.* paths 691. [OE weg]

way *adv.* aside 718. [Shortened form of OE *on weg, aweg*] Cf. **away.**

wayneȝ *pr. 3 sg.* urges 131; **vayned** *pp.* sent 249. [Cf. OE *wægen* 'carriage' & OE *bewægnan* 'to offer'.]

wayted *pt. 1 sg.* pondered 14. [ONF waitier]

we *pron. nom. pl.* we 251, 378, etc. [OE wē]

webbeȝ *n. pl.* tapestries 71. [OE web(b)]

wedde *v.* wed 772. [OE geweddian]

weddyng *ger.* wedding 791. [OE weddung]

wede *n.* vesture 748, garment 766; **wedeȝ** *pl.* robes 1102, garments 1112, 1133. [OE wæd, wæde, gewæde]

weete *adj.* wet (with blood) 1135. [OE wæt]

wel *adj.* well 239, 1187; *adv.* much 145, 148, well 164, 411, etc., fully 302, very 537. [OE wel]

welcum *adj.* welcome 399. [OE wilcuma *n.;* cf. ON velkominn.]

wele *n.* splendid pearl 14n, splendor 133, well-being 394; *dat., and wele and wo* 'both in prosperity and in misfortune' 342; **weleȝ** *pl.* riches 154. [OE wela]

welke. See **walk.**

welkyn *n.* sky 116. [OE wolcen]

welle *n.* well 365, source 649. [OE wella]

welneȝ *adv.* almost 528; **welnygh** 581. [OE wel-nēh]

wely *adj.* joyful 101. [OE welig]

wemleȝ *adj.* spotless 737. [From next entry; cf. Icel. *vammlauss* 'faultless'.]

wemme *n.* flaw 221, stain 1003. [OE wam(m, wom(m, infl. by OE *wemman v.*]

wende, line 1148. See **wene.**

252

wende *infin.* to go 643; **went** *pt. 3 sg.* passed 1130; **wente** *pt. pl.* went 525, departed 631; *pt. 1 sg.* went 761. [OE wendan]

wene, *pr. 1 sg., wot and wene* 'realize indeed' 47, 'know indeed' 201; *v.* doubt 1141; **wende** *pt. 1 sg.* believed 1148. [OE wēnan]

went(e). See **wende.**

wer (variant of *were*). See **were.**

wer *pt. 3 sg.* wore 205. [OE werian]

were *pt. pl.* were 6, 87, etc.; *pt. 2 sg.* were 264; *pt. pl. subj.* would be 739; *pt. 1 sg. subj.* were 287, would be 288, 1167; *pt. 3 sg. subj.* were 139, 452, 849, 878, 1142, would be 32, 263, 1118, 1156; **wer** *pt. pl.* were 68, 641; *pt. 3 sg. subj.* would be 490, 930, 1092; *pt. 2 sg. subj.* were 972; **wern** *pt. pl.* were 71, 73, etc., revealed 110; **werne** *pt. pl.* were 585; **ware** *pt. pl.* were 151, 1027; **wore** *pt. pl.* were 154; *pt. 3 sg. subj.* would be 142; *pt. 3 sg. subj.* was 232. [OE wǣron, wǣre, wǣren] Cf. **watȝ.**

werke, *n., þe lasse in werke* 'those who work less' 599. [OE weorc]

werkmen *n.* workmen 507. [OE weorcmann]

werle *n.* circlet 209n. [Cf. ON *hvirfill* 'circle, crown of the head'; MLG, MDu. *wervel*; OE *hwyrfel.*]

wern(e). See **were.**

wesch. See **wascheȝ.**

west *adj.* idle 307n. [OE wēste]

wete *ppl. a.* maddened 761n. [OE ge)wēdan]

weþer. See **wheþer.**

weue *v.* cross 318; **veued** *pp.* directed 976. [Cf. ON veifa & MDu. weiven.]

weuen *pt. pl.* wove 71. [OE wefan]

wex. See **wax.**

whalleȝ, *n. gen. sg., whalleȝ bon* 'ivory' (whale's bone) 212n. [OE hwæl] See also **bon.**

wham. See **who.**

what *adj.* what 249, 392, etc.; *conj.* what 463; *pron.* what 331, 336; *adv.* why 1072; **quat** *pron.* what 186; *conj.* what 293. [OE hwæt] Cf. **quatso.**

what-kyn *adj. as n.* what kind 794; **quat-kyn** *adj.* what kind of 755, 771. [OE hwæt+OE cynna]

when *conj.* when 332, 335, etc.; **quen** *conj.* when 40, 79, etc., after 170. [OE hwænne]

where *conj.* where 68, 617; **quere** *conj.* where 376; *quere þat* 'where' 65. [OE

hwǣr] Cf. **queresoeuer.**

whete *n.* wheat 32. [OE hwǣte]

wheþer *conj.* whether 130, 604, even if 581; *adv.* nevertheless 826; **weþer** *adv.* and yet 565. [OE hwæþer, *adv.* hwæþere] Cf. **queþersoeuer.**

who *pron.* who 344, 1138; **wham** *dat.* whom 131; **quo** who 427, 678, 827, one (who) 693, whoever 709, 747; **quom** *dat.* whom 453. [OE hwā, *dat.* hwǣm]

why *adv.* why 329, 338, 515, 634; *interj.* why 769; **wy** *adv.* why 290, 533, 564; **quy** *adv.* why 561. [OE hwȳ]

whyle *adv.* previously 15. [OE hwīle]

whyt *adj.* white 163, 178, 197, 1133; **whyte** 219; **quyt** *n.* white 842; *adj.* white 207, 1011, 1150; **quyte** 220, 844, 1137; **qwyte** 1102. [OE hwīt]

with. See **wyth.**

wlonc *adj.* superb 903; **wlonk** beautiful 122, 1171. [OE wlanc, wlonc]

wo *n.* misery 56, adversity 154; *dat.* in misfortune 342. [OE wā]

wod *n.* wood 122. [OE wudu]

wode *adj.* mad 743. [OE wōd]

wodschaweȝ *n. pl.* groves 284. [OE wudu+OE sceaga, scaga]

woghe *n.* wrong 622. [OE wōh]

woȝe *n.* wall 1049. [OE wāg, wāh]

wolde *v.* subdue 812. [WS wealdan, A waldan]

wolde, *pt.* of **wyl,** *pl.* would 304, 391, would wish 849; *sg.* would 390, 488, 772, 910, would wish 451, 1195, wished 977, desired 1155; **woldeȝ** 2 *sg.* would 410. [OE wolde]

wolen *adj.* woolen 731. [LOE wullen]

wolle *n.* wool 844. [OE wull]

wommon *n. gen. sg.* woman's 236. [OE wīfmann, wīfmonn]

won *n.* city 1049; **woneȝ** *pl.* barns 32, houses 917, abodes 924, 1027. [ON vān; cf. OE ge)wuna.]

won *v.* dwell 298, 315, remain 644, linger 918; **woneȝ** *pr. pl.* dwell 404; **wony** *v.* dwell 284; **wonys** *pr. 3 sg.* lies 47. [OE wunian]

wonde *v.* shrink (from adversity) 153. [OE wandian, wondian]

wonder *adj.* marvelous 221, wonderful 1095. [From OE *wundor n.*, used in compounds]

woneȝ. See **won** *n. & v.*

wonne. See **wynne** *v.*

wont *ppl. a.* accustomed 15; wonte 172. [OE *gewunod, pp.* of *gewunian*]

wonted *pt. 3 sg.* was void 215. [ON vanta]

wony, wonys. See won *v.*

worchen *pr. pl.* toil 511; wraȝte *pt. 3 sg.* moved 56; wroȝt *pt. pl.* toiled 555, did 631; *pp.* created 638, committed 824; *pt. 3 sg.* designed 748, committed 825; wroȝte *pt. pl.* worked 525; wroȝten *pt. pl.* did 622; wyrkeȝ *imper. pl.* work 536. [OE wyrcan, *pt.* worhte, *pp.* geworht]

worde *n.* speech 294; wordeȝ *pl.* statements 291, words 307, 314, 367, 819. [OE word]

wore (variant of *were*). See were.

wore *pr. pl. subj.* (may) expend 574n. [ON *verja*; cf. OE *werian, wærian* 'to wear, to use'.]

worlde *n.* world 65n, 293, etc., earth 537. [OE weorold, worold, world]

worschyp *n.* honor 394, 479. [OE weorþscipe, worþscipe]

worteȝ *n. pl.* plants 42. [OE wyrt]

worthyly *adj.* worthy 846; worþyly *sb. adj.* worthy gem 47; worþly *adj.* glorious 1073; *adv.* becomingly 1133. [OE weorþlic *adj.*; weorþlīce *adv.*]

worþe *adj.* worth 451. [OE weorþ]

worþe *pr. 3 sg. subj.* let be 362; worþen *pp.* come 394. [OE weorþan]

worþé *adj.* capable 100; worþy worthy 494, worthy of 616. [OE *weorþ+y*; cf. OE *wyrþig* 'fitting, deserved'.]

wost(e). See next entry.

wot *pr. 1 sg.* know 1107; *wot and wene* 'realize indeed' 47n, 'know indeed' 201; wate *pr. 1 sg.* know 502; wost *pr. 2 sg.* know 411; woste *pr. 2 sg.* know 293; wyste *pt. 1 sg.* knew 65, 376; wysteȝ *pt. 2 sg. emph.* did know 617. [OE witan; *pr. 1 sg.* wāt; *pr. 2 sg.* wāst; *pt.* wiste]

woþe *n.* tribulation 375n; woþeȝ *pl.* perils 151n. [ON vāði]

wounde *n.* wound 650, 1135, 1142. [OE wund]

wraȝte. See worchen.

wrang *n.* wrong 631; *adv.* wrongly 614; wrange *n.* distress 15; *adv.* wrongly 488. [LOE *wrang n*; cf. ON **wrangr, rangr* 'awry, unjust'.]

wrathþe *n.* offense 362. [wræþþu]

wreched *adj.* wretched 56. [From OE wrecca, wræcca *n.*]

Writ *n.* Scripture 997; Wryt, *Holy Wryt* 'Holy Writ' 592. [OE writ]

wro *n.* passage (in the Apocalypse) 866. [ON **wrā, rā*]

wroȝt, wroȝte, wroȝten. See worchen.

wroken *pp.* delivered 375. [OE wrecan]

wroþe *adj.* angry 379. [OE wrāþ]

wryteȝ *pr. 3 sg.* writes 1033; wryten *pp.* written 834, 866, 871. [OE wrītan]

wryþe *v.* turn 350, 488; wryþen *pr. pl.* twist about 511. [OE wrīþan]

wy. See why.

wyde *adj.* wide 1135. [OE wīd]

wyf *n.* wife 846; vyf wife 772; vyueȝ *pl.* wives 785. [OE wīf]

wyȝ *n.* man 100, 131, 722; wyȝeȝ *pl.* men 71, people 579. [OE wiga]

wyȝt *n.* damsel 338; wyȝte maiden 494. [OE wiht]

wyȝte *adj.* courageous 694. [ON vīgt, *neut.* of vīgr 'skilled in arms']

wyl *conj.* until 528. [Abbr. of OE þā hwīle þe]

wyl *fut. 3 sg. auxil.* will 350, 443, 965; *pr. 1 sg.* intend 558; *pr. 2 sg. subj.* wish 794. [OE willan, wile, wille]

wylle *n.* will 56, 131. [OE willa]

wylneȝ *pr. 2 sg.* desire 318. [OE wilnian]

wyn *n.* wine 1209. [OE wīn (from L vīnum)]

wyngeȝ *n. pl.* wings 93. [ON vængir, *pl.* of vængr; Swed. & Dan. vinge]

wynne *adj.* precious 154, fine 647. [OE *wyn(n n.,* used in compounds; cf. *wynbēam* 'tree of gladness'.]

wynne *v.* gain 579, reach 694, attain 722; wan *pt. 1 sg.* strolled 107; wonne *pp.* taken 32, come 517. [OE ge)winnan, *pt.* wann, *pp.* wunnen]

wynter *n. gen. sg.* winter's 116. [OE winter]

wyrde *n.* fate 249, 273. [OE wyrd]

wyrkeȝ. See worchen.

wys *adj.* wise 748. [OE wīs]

wyschande *pr. p.* desiring 14. [OE wӯscan]

wyse *n.* fashion (wise, way) 101, array 133, way 1095. [OE wīse]

wyse *v.* show 1135. [OE ge)wīsian]

wyste, wysteȝ. See wot.

wyt *n.* intelligence 903; wytte reason 294. [OE ge)witt]

wyth *prep.* with 40, 54, etc., in 94, 467, etc., through 478, 688, by 629, 806, 809, 1088; with with 200, 202, 837. [OE wiþ, ON við]

wythdroȝ *pt. 3 sg.* rescinded 658. [OE

wiþ+OE dragan]

wythinne *prep.* within 440, 679, 966; *adv.* within 1027. [LOE wiþinnan]

wythnay *pr. 2 sg. subj.* would refuse 916. [OE wiþ+OF neier; cf. ON nei *interj.*]

wythoute *prep.* without 644, 695; **wythouten** without 12, 24, etc., beyond 1104n. [LOE wiþūtan]

wytte. See **wyt.**

wyþer *adj.* opposite 230. [OE wiþer]

ydel *adj.* idle 514, 515, 531, 533. [OE īdel]

yȝe *n.* eye 302, 567, 1153; **yȝen** *pl.* eyes 183, 200, 254, 296. [OE ēage, *pl.*

ēagan; A ēge]

yle *n.* isle 693. [OF isle, ille]

ynde *n.* indigo (color of indigo blue) 76, 1016. [OF inde]

yot. See **ȝede.**

yor *pron. poss.* (used as *sg.* in reference to one person) your 761; **your** *pl.* your 924; (used as *sg.* in reference to one person) your 257, 258, etc. [OE ēower]

yow, *pron. acc. & dat., pl.* you 470, 928, of you 524; (used as *sg.* in reference to one person) you 287, 471, 951, on you 913. [OE ēow]

yuore *n.* ivory 178. [OF ivoire]

AN INDEX OF NAMES

Adam Adam 656.

Arraby, *Fenyx of Arraby* 'Phoenix of Araby' 430n. [OF *adj.* ar(r)abi; ult. Arabic] (See also **Fenyx** in Glossary.)

Arystotel Aristotle 751.

Crystes *gen.* Christ's 383; **Kryst** Christ 55, 776; *Jhesu Kryst* 'Jesus Christ' 458; **Kryste** Christ 569; **Krysteȝ** *gen.* Christ's 904, 1208. [OE Crīst; ult. Gr.]

Dauid David 698, 920.

Galalye Galilee 817.

Grece Greece 231. [L Græcia]

Ihecu. See **Jesu.**

Israel *gen.* Israel's 1040.

Jerusalem Jerusalem (Heavenly City) 792, 793, 987; 950 (refers to both heavenly and earthly); Jerusalem (city on earth) 805, 816, 817, 828, 829, 919; *dat.* in Jerusalem (Heaven) 840, as (the old) Jerusalem (on earth) 941; *gen.* of Jerusalem (Heaven) 841; **Jherusalem** Jerusalem (on earth) 804.

Jesu Jesus 453; **Jhecu** 711, 717, 820; **Jhesu**

in *Jhesu Kryst* 'Jesus Christ' 458; **Ihecu** 721. [L Jēsus; ult. Gr.]

Johan John (the apostle) 788, 836, 867, 985, 996, 997, 1008, 1009, 1021, 1032, 1033, 1053; **Jon** John (the apostle) 383, John (the Baptist) 818n; **Jhan** John (the apostle) 1020; **Jhoan** John (the apostle) 984. (See also **Saynt** in Glossary.)

Jordan Jordan 817.

Judee Judea 922; **Judy,** *gen., Judy londe* 'land of Judea' 937. [L Jūdaea]

Jueȝ Jews 804. [OF Gïu, AF Geu]

Kryst, Kryste, Krysteȝ. See **Crystes.**

Mary Mary (Blessed Virgin) 383; **Marye** 425. [OE & L Marīa, OF Marie]

Mathew Matthew 497.

Poule Paul 457. (See also **Saynt** in Glossary.)

Pymalyon Pygmalion 750.

Salamon Solomon 689.

Syon Sion (hilltop in Heaven) 789, 868. [L Siōn]

Ysaye Isaias 797, 819.

CPSIA information can be obtained
at www.ICGtesting.com
Printed in the USA
LVHW05s0110020918
588894LV00019B/385/P